LEGAL TRANSCRIPTION

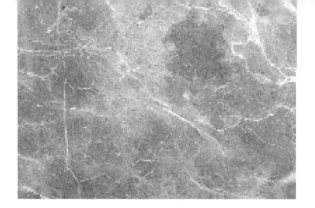

LEGAL TRANSCRIPTION

BY

LINDA R. LYLE, B.S., M.A.
NASHVILLE STATE TECHNICAL INSTITUTE

NASHVILLE, TENNESSEE

G. HOWARD DOTY, B.S., J.D.
NASHVILLE STATE TECHNICAL INSTITUTE

NASHVILLE, TENNESSEE

PARADIGM

Linda R. Lyle, B.S., M.A., is an Associate Professor of legal topics in the Business Technologies Department of Nashville State Technical Institute. Through her career, she has taught courses in office procedures, secretarial accounting, word processing, legal office procedures, legal transcription, and legal research.

G. Howard Doty, B.S., J.D., is an Instructor in the Business Technologies Department at Nashville State Technical Institute. He teaches courses in law, ethics, business, human development, banking, finance, and accounting, with the main emphasis on law and law-related subjects.

Developmental Editor: Cynthia Miller
Manuscript Editor: Carol Kennedy
Cover Design: Joan Silver
Production and Design: Electronic Publishing Services, Inc.

ACKNOWLEDGEMENTS
We wish to thank the following experts who contributed to this book:

Denise Goss, Instructor
Worldwide Educational Services
Soquel, California

Karen Mira Resnick, Instructor
F.E.G.S. Trade and Business School
New York, New York

We also wish to thank the legal secretaries and attorney who reviewed the material and provided documents for the projects.

Library of Congress Cataloging-in-Publication Data
Lyle, Linda R.
     Legal transcription / by Linda R. Lyle and G. Howard Doty.
          p.   cm.
     Includes index.
     ISBN 1-56118-671-6
     1. Legal transcription—United States. 2. Legal secretaries--United States—Handbooks, manuals, etc. I. Doty, G. Howard.
II. Title.
KF320.S4L95   1995
653—dc20   94-21342
                                                                         CIP
© 1995 by Paradigm Publishing Inc.
          Published by **EMC**Paradigm
          875 Montreal Way
          St. Paul, MN 55102
          (800) 535-6865
          E-mail educate@emcp.com
          Web site: www.emcp.com

Printed in the United States of America.

10   9   8   7   6   5

To my husband, Harold, and to my two daughters,
Beverly Lyle and Lisa Shiao.

Linda R. Lyle

To my three sons, Christopher, Timothy, and Andrew.

G. Howard Doty

TABLE OF CONTENTS

INTRODUCTION: WORKING IN THE LEGAL OFFICE OF THE 90s

UNIT I   LITIGATION

CHAPTER 1   INITIATING A LAWSUIT

CHAPTER 2   ANSWERING A LAWSUIT

CHAPTER 3   DISCOVERY/JUDGMENT

UNIT IV   LEGAL INSTRUMENTS

UNIT V   BANKRUPTCY

UNIT VI   APPELLATE PRACTICE
CHAPTER 14   TYPING CITATIONS

CHAPTER 15   PREPARING AN APPELLATE BRIEF

LIST OF FIGURES

PREFACE

Legal Transcription is designed to help students learn the activities performed by a transcriptionist in a law firm or other legal setting where documents are to be converted from the spoken word to printed form. While the text specifically prepares students to transcribe the most common legal documents, it also equips them with the perspective and capacity for decision making they will need later to adapt their knowledge and skills to any situation they encounter in a law office.

The material in this book has been organized in a logical way to provide students with the knowledge, terminology, and background needed to prepare legal documents. The textbook is simple and concise and is organized into six units of study, each centered around a type of law practice.

The textbook begins with an introduction that gives background on the law office and those persons involved in its operation. Students will learn that the legal secretary is a vital position in a law firm because of the increasing demands on lawyers' time. Unit I teaches preparation of documents related to litigation using easy-to-comprehend instructions and examples; Unit II highlights probate practice and includes formatting and transcription instructions for wills and other probate procedures; Unit III, Family Law, deals with divorce, adoptions, and paternity; Unit IV, Legal Documents, teaches formatting and transcription of contracts, corporate documents, and real estate deeds. Unit V details documents involved in bankruptcy; and Unit VI teaches students to prepare appellate briefs.

Each chapter includes information about the content of legal documents, correspondence, forms, or instruments; formatting guidelines to follow in preparing the various documents; and procedures to be followed in executing, filing, recording, or serving the documents. The content of each document is analyzed so students will understand the purpose and function of each segment of the document. Since each chapter covers a unique area of law, new terminology is presented in each chapter. Marginal definitions are provided for each new term as it is presented.

The figures in each chapter serve as a style manual for students to follow when transcribing projects. In most cases, a complete or partial sample document is shown in the figures and can be followed when transcribing the projects. Even though each state has its own style for formatting court documents, a consistent style for each document has been maintained throughout the text.

Upon completion of this textbook, students will have a greater knowledge of the terminology, guidelines, and formatting skills needed to prepare authentic, accurate legal documents.

INTRODUCTION: WORKING IN THE LEGAL OFFICE OF THE 90's

THE LEGAL SECRETARY'S RESPONSIBILITIES

Can you look into the future and visualize the day you will be looking for your first job in a legal office? To be ready for that day, you should prepare now by learning what a legal secretary does so you can determine whether you want to be one. Your first thought might be, "Where do I want to work?" Law firms come in all sizes, from small, one-attorney firms to large firms that have a complete staff of attorneys, law clerks, paralegals, legal secretaries, law library clerks, receptionists, file clerks, bookkeepers, and even a runner to deliver documents to be filed. A secretary in a small firm works with many types of documents and cases; in a large firm, a secretary's responsibilities focus on specific areas of law and specific responsibilities.

Working in a legal office can be both interesting and exciting. You have an opportunity to learn many things about the law by working under the supervision of an attorney. Every client of the office is different, and every case or situation is different. You, as secretary, prepare documents, but you may also have an opportunity to observe a happy couple as they adopt a much-wanted child, a young couple as they purchase a house for the first time, or a couple dissolving a marriage. The assignment may be to sit in on a meeting where a will or a partnership agreement is being signed, or it may be to prepare a charter to organize a new corporation. Some secretaries go to court with their attorneys to provide secretarial support, including such things as locating and organizing items in a trial notebook.

One of the first things you, as a legal secretary, must be aware of is that everything that occurs in the office must stay in the office. Nothing should be repeated or discussed with anyone outside the firm, including family and close friends.

You at all times work under the direction of the attorney, and the end product represents the attorney and the law firm. You must be able to do the following:

- Transcribe legal documents for the area of law in which the attorney practices, which may include litigation, probate, divorce, adoption, bankruptcy, corporate organization, and real estate.

- Have an understanding of legal terminology, legal procedures, grammar, punctuation, number expression, word division, word choice, and spelling so that documents can be prepared accurately and efficiently.

- Keyboard quickly and accurately, using the firm's word processing software program.

- Serve as a public relations representative for the law firm. As clients, attorneys, and others make contact with the firm in person or by phone, greet them and handle any requests appropriately.

- Operate the copy machine, and know the number of copies of each document to prepare.

- Set up a calendaring or reminder system to aid the attorney in keeping up with filing deadlines, court dates, and appointments. (Many offices use a computer software package for recording this information.)

- Use legal billing packages to record and bill clients for services performed by the attorney.

- Be resourceful in obtaining information by calling other offices, such as the offices of the secretary of state, Internal Revenue Service, clerk of the court, newspaper, and registrar.

This list is by no means all-inclusive; however, it draws a partial picture of the responsibilities a secretary will face in the law office.

ADVANCES IN COMPUTER TECHNOLOGY

TODAY

New technology is affecting the way work in a legal office is performed. The reduced cost of computers and the availability of software specially designed for legal firms have replaced much of the manual work with computerized operations. Nearly all firms now use word processors for producing legal documents.

Software programs are available for entering due dates for documents and dates and times of appointments. The secretary or attorney can retrieve the calendar, enter the due date or appointment, and print a daily or monthly calendar.

Through the use of billing software programs, any charges to the client can be entered into the computer. Some examples of charges are the time an attorney spends on a case, filing fees paid by the attorney for the client, and costs of copies or long distance phone calls. When it is time to bill a client, the secretary accesses the client's file and prints a statement.

West Publishing Company is currently selling CD-ROM diskettes that contain court opinions written by judges. Attorneys can use the material for legal research. Rather than purchase a whole set of law books or go to the library, attorneys can stay in their offices and use a computer.

Specialized programs for generating the documents for bankruptcy and real estate matters are also on the market.

TRENDS FOR TOMORROW

In the future, we are likely to see courtrooms where all testimony is videotaped. A number of experimental courtrooms are set up at this time to determine the cost-effectiveness and efficiency of such a project. Voice-activated microphones are installed where the judge, attorney, and witness speak. Once the individual begins speaking, the cameras are activated and the activities are videotaped. To replay testimony, the attorney or judge needs to access the information on the videotape. The secretary could certainly play an important role in this setting.

Another expected trend for the future is that documents will be sent by fax (short for facsimile) to the clerks of the courts and to the registrar's office. With a fax machine, documents can be sent directly from printed copy by placing the original in a copyholder, dialing a number, and pressing the "send" button. This eliminates the need for personal delivery of the document to the courthouse and allows for immediate filing or recording of the documents.

There is a continued demand for qualified legal secretaries. The job is likely to become more technical, requiring the secretary to be computer literate. The need to continue training, to learn new software packages, and to learn to operate new equipment will be a part of the growing profession. It remains important that documents be produced in an efficient manner with correct grammar, punctuation, and spelling.

THE IMPORTANCE OF TRANSCRIPTION

One of the most popular methods of preparing legal documents and correspondence is for the attorney to dictate into a recording device and have the secretary transcribe that dictation. Figure I-1 (page 4) shows an office worker transcribing a cassette-tape system at a workstation with a computer. This method is obviously much faster than drafting handwritten documents. It is also more efficient than having the secretary record the dictation by shorthand and then transcribe, thus taking more of the secretary's time, which could be used to transcribe directly from a machine.

The training in this course focuses on preparing you for the transcription segment of a job in a law office. You will be responsible for formatting documents, transcribing accurately and completely, and using correct word choices.

Formatting Think about some questions you must answer when you sit down to a transcription unit and are ready to transfer the spoken word to written form. For example, What are the margins? Do I double- or single-space? How do I set up the heading on the document? Do I number pages? If so, where? In addition, you must make other decisions related to grammar, punctuation, and capitalization. You may even need to get out the operator's manual to learn how to use the equipment in your office.

Transcribing accurately and completely What are some of the types of errors that could occur while you are transcribing, and what are the results of those errors? Let's suppose that you have a cassette tape in the transcription unit,

FIGURE I-1. Office Worker Transcribing at a Workstation

have the earphones set to listen, and have learned the necessary skills for preparing a correctly transcribed document. As you are transcribing, the phone rings and you are interrupted. You return to your word processor and transcribe the name Robert Johnson as Robert Jones; when you deliver the document to your attorney, the error goes undetected. The document is signed and taken to the clerk's office, where it is filed. The error is later discovered. To correct the error, the attorney must draft an amended document, will be embarrassed over the situation, and will have to pay an additional fee to have the document filed. "Not so bad!" you might say.

Let's consider another situation for a moment. What if you skipped a line in a client's will that read, "I leave my silver flatware to my only daughter"? The attorney, who is ultimately responsible, failed to read every word you transcribed, assuming that you would carefully check your work, and he or she allowed the will to be signed. The client later died, and the daughter claimed that she was to get the silver flatware. The person handling the estate of the deceased insisted that nothing was mentioned in the will about the silver, and it would have to be divided equally among the eight children. The result would likely be that the silver did not go where it was intended. As you can see, documents must be transcribed not only accurately but also completely.

Making correct word choices You, as a transcriptionist, should also know the difference in word meanings. You should be able to correctly use such words as approximate, meaning almost or near, and proximate, meaning nearest or direct. The proximate cause of an accident is the direct cause, but the filing fee is approximately, or almost, $15. Depository should be correctly transcribed to mean a place money is deposited; depositary means a person receiving funds.

HISTORY OF MACHINE TRANSCRIPTION

YESTERDAY

About a hundred years ago, Alexander Bell invented a wax cylinder, which was used as a medium for recording voice dictation. The voice was etched into the wax as it was being recorded. The cylinder was then taken to a transcriber. After the material recorded on the cylinder was transcribed, the secretary then took the cylinder to a third device and shaved off the outer surface of the wax cylinder, and it was ready for recording another document. The beeswax cylinder was used from the late 1800s through the 1940s.

In the 1950s recording was done on a thin vinyl belt. The new device was coined as the "sound you can see" because as dictation was recorded on the belt, small visible lines were etched into its surface. During that same time period, other devices emerged, such as a circular disk similar to the diskettes we use on computers.

TODAY

In the 1970s cassette tapes became the popular medium for recording dictation. Cassette tapes are still widely used today. They range in size from the standard cassette to the minicassette to the microcassette. The standard cassette records from 30 to 60 minutes of dictation on each side of the tape. A minicassette is about half the size of a standard cassette and has about 15 minutes of recording time on each side. The microcassette is slightly shorter than the mini and will record 30 minutes of dictation at regular speed and a full hour at half speed.

Digital technology is the newest innovation in designing dictation equipment. The voice is recorded on digital recorders and stored on a hard disk within the dictation unit. There is no need for a cassette of any type. The advantages of this new technology are:

- It provides excellent sound quality.

- It gives instant access to documents.

- The speed can be increased or decreased without distortion.

- A digital display shows a summary of the workload.

- Dictation and transcription can be done simultaneously.

- Additional material can be inserted within the dictation.

The clarity and quality of sound is one of the advantages of a digital system. The sound quality of cassette tapes decreases with use over a period of time. With digital recorders, the quality of the sound today is the same as it will be a year from today.

Instant access means the secretary can immediately go to a document that needs to be transcribed first. Priority items are automatically moved to the front. If the attorney dictates five items and marks the third one as priority, the first document the secretary hears is the priority item.

Generally, with a cassette system, increases in speed create a "Mickey Mouse" sound and decreases in speed create a slow, dragging sound. With digital systems, change in the speed does not affect the quality of the sound.

The digital display allows the secretary to see the day's workload at a glance. Some models show how many priority items are recorded, who the author is, when each item was dictated, and what the length of the items to be transcribed is. Digital technology allows the secretary to transcribe shortly after the attorney begins dictating.

If the attorney dictates two paragraphs of a document and then decides to insert a paragraph between the first two, he or she can move to the place where the first paragraph ends, then dictate the material to be inserted. The paragraphs will be played back in the desired order. The technology can be compared to that used in word processing, where paragraphs can be inserted between existing paragraphs.

TOMORROW

Voice recognition is a machine's capacity to receive spoken words and print them on a screen. This technology is the direction of the future in dictation equipment. Even though it is being used in some environments today, it is not yet widely used. The problems are that the user must go through a setup process, speaking slowly and clearly into the system, and that dictation must be done in that same slow, clear manner. With improved technology in this area, the secretary's role may change from keying a completely dictated document to formatting and editing the voice-dictated draft.

TYPES OF DICTATION UNITS AND TRANSCRIBERS

Those who compose the dictation are known as originators. They can record their dictation by using a small handheld recording unit, by using a standard telephone to dial into a recording unit in the office, or by using a desktop dictation unit with a handheld microphone.

Transcriptions generally work from either a desktop unit or a centralized system. Desktop units are usually cassette-tape machines. Centralized systems may use cassette tapes to record the spoken word or hard disks to record digital images of the spoken word.

Some of the features available on today's transcribers are:

- Document queuing to mark instructions and ends of documents

- Recall to automatically replay a few words each time the dictation unit starts, which eliminates skipped words in the transcript

- Electronic display to indicate the length of documents and number of documents on a tape

- Telephone recording for recording dictation from an outside phone

- Conference recording for recording voices of several individuals in a meeting

TECHNIQUES FOR TRANSCRIBING

Transcription is an intermittent listening, continuous keying exercise. To transcribe, you should place the headset comfortably in place and adjust the volume, speed, and tone controls. Place your right foot on the foot control. When the center portion of the foot control is depressed, the playback of the recording begins. The left and right sides are used for forwarding or rewinding the tape. The three-step process is:

- Listen

- Stop the tape

- Transcribe

As you become more efficient, you should be able to listen to an earful (as much material as you can remember) and transcribe continuously.

TO THE STUDENT

Legal Transcription was designed to provide you with a knowledge of legal terminology and to help you develop skills necessary to accurately transcribe and format documents routinely prepared in a law office. You will need to have basic keyboarding and formatting skills before starting a transcription course of this type.

FORMAT OF THE TEXT

The text is divided into the following six units of study:

- Litigation

- Probate practice

- Family law

- Legal instruments

- Bankruptcy

- Appellate practice

Performance Objectives. Each chapter of the text provides performance-based objectives. Read them carefully before studying the chapter as these are the activities you will be asked to perform when completing end-of-chapter projects. The level at which you will fulfill these objectives will vary depending on your beginning skill.

Chapter Content. The content of each chapter focuses on the types of documents to be prepared for the area of law being studied. Each document is analyzed for purpose, content, and format. Proper court procedures for executing, recording, serving, or filing documents are also presented. Definitions of legal terms are provided in the text of the chapters when legal terms are encountered. In addition, marginal definitions are included to aid you in reviewing and finding those terms.

Chapter Summaries. Each chapter includes a chapter summary. These reinforce the key concepts presented in the chapter.

True/False Questions. True/False questions give you an opportunity to check your understanding of the material presented in the chapter.

Transcription Rules. Punctuation, number style, and capitalization rules are presented in each chapter. Not only basic grammar rules but also those unique to legal typing are included. Legal material is used in the examples.

Written Transcription Exercises. These exercises are designed to provide practice in transcribing, applying punctuation, number style, and capitalization rules presented in the chapter as well as practice in formatting portions of documents.

Research Activities. Suggestions for researching practices in your state or local area are listed. These types of activities will provide you with the opportunity to search for and find rules of court, laws, and forms to use in your county and state.

Projects. The types of projects you will be transcribing, a discussion of the type of case, and information about the parties and attorneys is provided in the text. The material to be transcribed has been recorded on cassette tapes and is similar to the documents discussed in the text. Use the figures in the text as a forms manual.

Performance Assessment. A performance assessment is provided at the end of each unit. Each of the assessments has three parts. Part A is a printed document in the text with errors to be corrected, keyed, and printed. Part B is a document on tape to be transcribed in its entirety. Part C instructs you to retrieve previously transcribed documents and to revise them according to the taped instructions.

In-Basket Exercises.   At the end of the text is an in-basket exercise that provides an opportunity for you to incorporate what you have learned while completing this course into an office-type situation. On arriving at work, you check your in-basket. You review its contents and set priorities on the work to be completed. You then apply your decision-making skills and determine the most efficient method of drafting the documents the lawyer needs upon his or her return to the office. During the time allotted, you complete as many exercises as possible.

Appendices. Appendix A summarizes the punctuation and number style rules presented in the chapters. Appendix B provides various arrangements of information in court captions. Appendix C lists state abbreviations.

Glossary. An alphabetical glossary of terms presented throughout the text is included at the back of the text for your convenience in locating terms and definitions.

IMPORTANCE OF STUDYING THE CHAPTER MATERIAL

The more a legal secretary is familiar with the content and format of legal documents and forms, the more he or she can do to aid the attorney. It is important to read the chapter materials thoroughly and to study the figures for content, language, and format. The content of a document provides an insight into its purpose. The language used in the figures will familiarize you with the sometimes unusual terminology and phraseology used by attorneys. You should be familiar with the format of the documents to the extent that you recall them without repeated reference to a previous model. Only if you understand the purpose of the material being transcribed and are familiar with the terminology used can you produce accurate documents.

Always remember that terminology and customs vary from state to state and from office to office. If your state or your law office has different requirements from those outlined in this book, follow the local or office practice.

STUDY PLAN FOR STUDENTS

The following plan for studying each chapter is recommended:

1. Read the chapter.

2. Carefully review the figures.

3. Answer the true/false review exercises.

4. Transcribe the projects and present them for grading or class discussion.

BEFORE BEGINNING EACH PROJECT, ANALYZE THE JOB TO BE PERFORMED.

What materials do I need to have at hand to complete this project?

What word processing features do I need to know to complete this project?

What sources of information are available if I do not know how to use a software feature?

What can I do to simplify it?

BEFORE SUBMITTING EACH PROJECT, ASK YOURSELF THE FOLLOWING QUESTIONS:

Did I include all parts of the document?

Did I look in a dictionary for the definition of all terms I did not understand?

Did I add the new terms to my electronic legal dictionary?

Did I spell-check?

Did I hyphenate?

Did I proofread the document for understanding of content?

Did I proofread the document for keystroking errors?

Can I give a reason for each punctuation mark I supplied?

Did I check and compare dates, names, etc.

If I revised the document, did I check all references to him/her, names of parties, names of the document, etc.?

Did I arrange the pages in the correct order?

How many copies of the document should I prepare?

If I were in an office, what will be my responsibility for further handling the document?

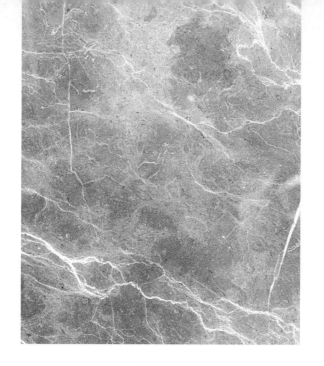

UNIT I
LITIGATION

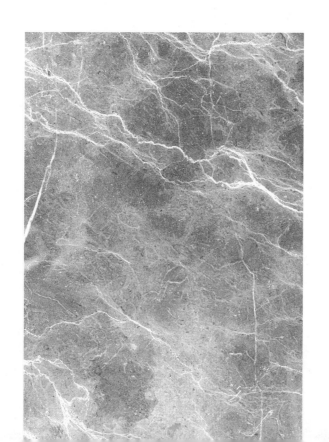

JOB DESCRIPTION

TRANSCRIPTION RESPONSIBILITIES

JOB TITLE: Legal Secretary

AREA OF PRACTICE: Litigation

TRANSCRIPTION DUTIES:

1. Is responsible for the accurate transcription, preparation of the required number of copies, and mailing of litigation correspondence and documents.

2. Prepares summonses to accompany complaints to be mailed out of the office.

3. Drafts litigation documents from previously transcribed documents for attorney's approval or editing.

4. Assists the attorney in calculating and docketing due dates for filing and answering litigation documents.

5. Is responsible for checking completed documents to determine if the correct court caption, signature lines, verifications, cost bonds, approved-for-entry lines, certificates of service, or acknowledgments have been included on legal documents.

6. Is responsible for efficiently using a word processing software program or electronic typewriter to create and edit documents.

INITIATING A LAWSUIT

INTRODUCTION

A legal secretary who works as a litigation secretary will be closely involved in preparing court documents. **Litigation**, or the legal process followed when one party sues another party in a court of law, can be either criminal or civil. Criminal cases occur when someone has broken the law, such as committing a robbery or murder. Civil cases occur when someone has been injured or wronged, and the parties cannot agree on a solution to the matter. To sue a party, one must have what is referred to as a cause of action. A **cause of action** is the wrong or injury. A cause of action might be an injury as a result of a defective lawn mower, an injury in an automobile accident, or an injury from slipping and falling on someone else's property.

We will examine a civil case where William F. Oldham is suing James A. Pizzini and Express Delivery Services, Inc. William was injured when his automobile was struck by a truck owned by Express Delivery Services, Inc., and driven by James A. Pizzini.

Each litigation case will have at least one plaintiff and at least one defendant. The **plaintiff** is the party who is suing and the **defendant** is the party who is being sued. In our case, William F. Oldham is the plaintiff because he is the person who was injured and who is suing. James A. Pizzini and Express Delivery Services, Inc., are the defendants. They are being sued, one as the driver and one as the owner of the truck, and may both be liable for the losses caused by the injury.

The plaintiff in this case contacted his attorney, Robert Mitchell, who prepared documents to begin the lawsuit. For this case you will become familiar with the following documents prepared on behalf of the plaintiff:

LITIGATION

The process of carrying on a lawsuit when one party sues another party in a court.

CAUSE OF ACTION

The wrong or injury that occurred to cause a party to sue another.

PLAINTIFF

The party who is suing.

DEFENDANT

The party who is being sued.

> **SUMMONS**
>
> **COMPLAINT**
>
> **MOTION FOR A DEFAULT JUDGMENT**

SUMMONS

PURPOSE AND FORMAT

SUMMONS

A document notifying the defendant that a lawsuit is being filed against him or her.

CLERK OF THE COURT

An official of the court whose job includes filing of documents, officially issuing summonses, and keeping records of court proceedings.

FILE WITH THE CLERK

To be signed, stamped, and dated by the clerk of the court.

A **summons** is a document used to notify the defendant that a lawsuit has been filed against him or her and states that the defendant is to appear and defend the charges. To appear, in this context, means the defendant should seek the advice of an attorney and file the appropriate documents. Most courts provide forms to use for the summons. They can be obtained from the **clerk of the court**. It is also acceptable to key the entire text of the summons. The type of information placed on a summons is essentially the same from one court to another, but the form and arrangement varies.

In this case, we have two defendants, James A. Pizzini and Express Delivery Services, Inc. Some courts prefer that a separate summons be prepared for each defendant with only one defendant's name appearing on each summons; others want names of all defendants on the summons, with enough copies to deliver to (serve on) each defendant. It is the legal secretary's responsibility to prepare the summons and make copies as follows: one for the clerk of the court, one to be served on each defendant, and one for the office files. The summons, along with the complaint discussed in the next section, is taken to the clerk's office to be signed, stamped, and dated. This procedure is known as **filing** the summons and complaint. The summons and complaint are then served on each defendant. The summons:

- Includes the name of the court, names of the parties, and file number (which is assigned by the clerk of the court when the summons is taken to the clerk's office)

- Is addressed to the defendant

- Informs the defendant of the time within which to appear

- Notifies the defendant that failure to defend against the cause of action will result in judgment by default, thus losing the lawsuit

- Is dated and signed by the clerk

- Includes the name and address of the plaintiff's attorney or of the plaintiff, if the plaintiff chooses to represent himself or herself

Refer to the Circuit Court Summons to be served on James A. Pizzini shown in Figures 1-1 and 1-2 on pages 18 and 19. Information is provided in the blanks as follows.

File No.: The clerk of the court assigns this number when the summons is filed. Since the number is unknown when the form is being completed, the secretary leaves it blank. Once assigned, the number is retained throughout the entire case and is placed on all further documents.

Plaintiff: The full name of the plaintiff is keyed in full caps.

Defendant: The full name of the defendant is entered in full caps. A complete address where the summons can be served follows the defendant's name. A post office box number without a street name and number does not provide enough information to personally serve a defendant.

If the first summons is not served because the defendant cannot be located, a second, third, or fourth summons may need to be prepared. The subsequent summonses would each need to have a new, different address. The second summons is known as an **alias** summons; the third and following, as **pluries** summonses. The word ALIAS should be inserted above the word SUMMONS on the form for the second summons, and the word PLURIES, on the third and following summonses. When it is likely that a defendant will be difficult to locate, additional information can be provided on the summons, such as a photograph of the defendant, information about where the defendant works or eats breakfast regularly, or a description of the type and color of car.

ALIAS SUMMONS

The second summons delivered to a defendant.

PLURIES SUMMONS

The third and subsequent summonses delivered to a defendant.

To the Above-Named Defendant: The instructions on the summons to the defendant are that a lawsuit has been filed and that failure to appear and defend those charges within 30 days, 20 days in federal court, will result in a judgment by default. The requirement to appear and defend can be accomplished by seeing an attorney, who usually files a document called an **answer** responding to the charges made by the plaintiff. The defendant is further instructed to file the defense with the clerk of the court and send a copy to the plaintiff's attorney.

ANSWER

A document in which the defendant responds to the allegations in the complaint and defends against those charges.

Issued: An employee of the court clerk's office enters the date when the summons is filed. A summons is officially issued by the court clerk.

By Deputy Clerk: The deputy clerk enters the date and signature when the summons is filed. A deputy clerk has authority to sign and act on behalf of the court clerk.

Attorney for Plaintiff or Plaintiff's Address: Enter the attorney's name and address.

To the Sheriff: Space is provided for the sheriff to enter the date and sign the document when the summons is received for service.

Return on Personal Service of Summons: This section of the summons is completed when the summons and complaint are personally served on the defendant and should be left blank when it is initially prepared. After serving the document, the one who serves the summons — sheriff, deputy sheriff, individual of legal age, or company hired to serve the summons — enters the date of service and an explanation of where and how served, and signs the "Return on Personal Service" section on the form.

CIRCUIT COURT SUMMONS   **NASHVILLE, TENNESSEE**

STATE OF TENNESSEE
20th JUDICIAL DISTRICT   **FILE NO.**_____

WILLIAM F. OLDHAM _____

_____

_____

                                         Plaintiff

VS.

JAMES A. PIZZINI _____

Serve at: 2407 Old Lebanon Road _____

             Nashville, TN 37200 _____

_____

_____

                                         Defendant

To the above named Defendant:

You are summoned to appear and defend a civil action filed against you in Circuit Court, Davidson County, Tennessee, and your defense must be made within thirty (30) days from the date this summons is served upon you. You are further directed to file your defense with the Clerk of the Court and send a copy to the Plaintiff's attorney at the address listed below.

In case of your failure to defend this action by the above date, judgement by default will be rendered against you for the relief demanded in the complaint.

ISSUED:_____, 19_____.   **GEORGE L. ROOKER**
                                           Circuit Court Clerk
                                     Davidson County, Tennessee

                                   By_____
                                             Deputy Clerk

ATTORNEY FOR PLAINTIFF   ROBERT W. MITCHELL _____

            or   804 Stahlman Building _____
                             Address

PLAINTIFF'S ADDRESS   Nashville, TN 37201 _____

TO THE SHERIFF:
Please execute this summons and make your return hereon as provided by law.

                                       GEORGE L. ROOKER
                                       Circuit Court Clerk

Received this summons for service this _____ **day of** _____, 19_____

                                       _____
                                         SHERIFF

FIGURE 1-1. Summons, Page 1

RETURN ON PERSONAL SERVICE OF SUMMONS

I hereby certify and return, that on the _____ day of _____, 19____ I served this summons together with the complaint herein as follows:

_____

_____

_____

_____

                                              SHERIFF
                                              BY:_____

RETURN ON SERVICE OF SUMMONS BY MAIL

I hereby certify and return, that on the _____ day of _____, 19____ I sent, postage prepaid, by registered return receipt mail or certified return receipt mail, a certified copy of the summons and a copy of the complaint in Case No. _____ to the defendant, _____. On the _____ day of _____, 19____ I received the return receipt for said registered or certified mail, which had been signed by _____ on the _____ day of _____, 19____. Said return receipt is attached to this original summons and both documents are being sent herewith to the Circuit Court Clerk for filing.

SWORN TO AND SUBSCRIBED BEFORE ME ON   PLAINTIFF PLAINTIFF'S ATTORNEY OR
THIS _____ DAY OF _____, 19____   OTHER PERSON AUTHORIZED BY
                                              STATUTE TO SERVE PROCESS

_____
_____ NOTARY PUBLIC or _____ DEPUTY CLERK
MY COMMISSION EXPIRES: _____
_____ NOTICE _____

TO THE DEFENDANT(S):

Tennessee law provides a four thousand dollar ($4,000.00) debtor's equity interest personal property exemption from execution or seizure to satisfy a judgement. If a judgement should be entered against you in this action and you wish to claim property as exempt, you must file a written list, under oath, of the items you wish to claim as exempt with the clerk of the court. This list may be filed at any time and may be changed by you thereafter as necessary; however, unless it is filed before the judgement becomes final, it will not be effective as to any execution or garnishment issued prior to the filing of the list. Certain items are automatically exempt by law and do not need to be listed; these include items of necessary wearing apparel (clothing) for yourself and your family and trunks or other receptacles necessary to contain such apparel, family portraits, the family Bible, and school books. Should any of these items be seized you would have the right to recover them. If you do not understand your exemption right or how to exercise it, you may wish to seek the counsel of a lawyer.

ATTACH
RETURN
RECEIPT
HERE
(IF APPLICABLE)

STATE OF TENNESSEE   I, George L. Rooker, Clerk of the Circuit Court in the State and
                          County aforesaid, do hereby certify this to be a true and
COUNTY OF DAVIDSON   correct copy of the original summons issued on this case.
                                    GEORGE L. ROOKER, CLERK
(To be completed only if
copy certification required).   By: _____ D.C.

FIGURE 1-2. Summons, Page 2

Return on Service of Summons by Mail: Rules in many states now provide for service by registered or certified mail with a return receipt. Service by mail is accomplished by taking the original and the defendant's copy of the summons to the clerk's office to have them **certified** by stamping or embossing the clerk's seal on the copy. The clerk also assigns a file number at this time. After certifying the copies, the clerk returns the original and the defendant's copy of the summons to the plaintiff's attorney or legal secretary. The defendant's copy of the summons and complaint (discussed in the next section of this chapter) is mailed registered or certified with a return receipt. Return receipt and certified or registered forms can be obtained from the U.S. Postal Service. When the documents are mailed, the "Return on Service of Summons by Mail" portion of the original summons should be completed by inserting the date the documents were mailed and the number assigned to the case. The original copy of the summons is held until the completed return receipt, signed by the defendant when the documents are delivered, and is returned to the attorney by the postal service. The remaining portion of the "Return on Service of Summons by Mail" section of the summons is completed by entering the name of the person who signed the receipt and the date it was signed. The return receipt is attached to the original summons and then delivered to the clerk's office.

METHODS OF SERVICE

Service of the summons and complaint (discussed later) can usually be done in one of three ways:

- Service by certified or registered mail with return receipt, as described above

- Personal service

- Service by publication

Personal service is a process in which the sheriff, a company in the business of serving papers, or an individual of legal age personally delivers the summons and complaint to the defendant. Service by individuals, attorneys, and service companies has grown rapidly in the last few years. Most states provide for service by publication when the defendant cannot be located. It is accomplished by running a notice in a newspaper of general circulation for a period of time specified by law. Since the purpose of service is to give the defendant notice of the lawsuit, this type of service is least desirable and used only as the last option.

To determine the procedure in your state, check with your attorney. You can also consult the rules of court for your state or state laws.

CAPTION — A PART OF EVERY COURT DOCUMENT

PURPOSE AND FORMAT

A **caption** is the introductory part or heading of a court document. It appears at the top of each document filed in a lawsuit. The arrangement of the data in the

---

CERTIFIED COPY

A copy of a document upon which the clerk of the court has stamped or embossed the clerk's seal.

CAPTION

The introductory part of a court document. It includes the name and location of the court, style of the case, docket number, and title of the document.

caption varies from one jurisdiction to another. Refer to Appendix B for information and format for your state. It is also suggested that you contact a legal secretary in your area to get a copy of a court caption. Court captions generally provide the following information:

- Name of the court and **venue** (geographic location)

- Names of the plaintiff(s) and defendant(s), also referred to as the style of the case

- File or docket number

- Title of the document

The court name and venue is the first line of the caption. In a state court the venue is the county, parish, or judicial district, and in federal court the venue is the district, such as Middle District of Tennessee or Northern District of Ohio. Shown below are venues for three state courts and a federal court. Notice that each court is fully identified by name and location.

VENUE FOR A STATE CIRCUIT COURT

IN THE FIRST CIRCUIT COURT FOR DAVIDSON COUNTY, TENNESSEE

VENUE FOR A STATE CHANCERY COURT

IN THE CHANCERY COURT FOR DAVIDSON COUNTY, TENNESSEE

PART III

VENUE FOR A STATE DISTRICT COURT

STATE OF OHIO	)	In the District Court
	) ss.	First Judicial District
COUNTY OF ADAMS	)	Civil Action No. _____

VENUE FOR A FEDERAL DISTRICT COURT

IN THE UNITED STATES DISTRICT COURT
FOR THE MIDDLE DISTRICT OF TENNESSEE
NASHVILLE DIVISION

STYLE OF THE CASE

The names of the plaintiffs and defendants in a case. For example, Cynthia Whitson, Plaintiff vs. George Kelly, Defendant.

The **style** of the case on the complaint consists of the full names of all plaintiffs and defendants; however, on subsequent documents, it is sufficient to state the name of the first party on each side with an appropriate designation of other parties. In Figure 1-3, the defendants are identified as JAMES A. PIZZINI and EXPRESS DELIVERY SERVICES, INC. In subsequent documents, defendants can be identified as JAMES A. PIZZINI et al. "Et al." is an abbreviation meaning "and others."

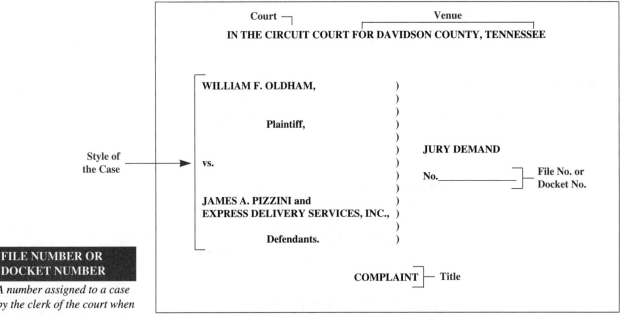

FIGURE 1-3. Caption

FILE NUMBER OR DOCKET NUMBER

A number assigned to a case by the clerk of the court when the completed summons and complaint are filed.

The **file number** or **docket number** is the number assigned by the clerk of the court when the summons and complaint are filed; the clerk inserts it at the time of filing. Some courts may specify that if in the last clause of the complaint, known as the **prayer** clause, a jury trial is demanded, the words JURY DEMAND are typed above the file or docket number. The demand for a jury may be prepared as a separate court document.

PRAYER CLAUSE

The last paragraph of each count or the last paragraph of the complaint or petition, in which the plaintiff demands judgment against the defendants. Often referred to as the "WHEREFORE" clause.

The **title** should indicate the type of document, such as complaint, complaint for damages, or motion to dismiss.

In cases where there is a lawsuit as the result of an injury to a minor child, a parent must join in the suit as a "next friend." A caption is shown in Figure 1-4 for a case filed in the United States District Court in Cleveland, Ohio, where the plaintiff John J. McGowan, a minor, joined by Mark A. McGowan, his father and next friend, are suing Sleepwear Manufacturing, Inc., for an injury believed to have been caused by pajamas made of flammable cotton fabric.

TITLE OF THE DOCUMENT

A name given to a document, indicating its purpose, such as a complaint, complaint for damages, or motion to dismiss.

See Appendix B or your instructor for instructions for formatting captions for your state or use the following guidelines.

IN THE UNITED STATES DISTRICT COURT
FOR THE NORTHERN DISTRICT OF OHIO
CLEVELAND DIVISION

JOHN J. McGOWAN, a Minor,   )
by MARK McGOWAN, his Father and   )
Next Friend,   )
)
          Plaintiffs,   )
)
)   **Civil No. _____**
vs.   )
)
SLEEPWEAR MANUFACTURING, INC.,   )
)
          Defendant.   )

COMPLAINT

FIGURE 1-4. Caption Where Father Joins as Next Friend

Formatting Instructions for Captions

- Begin the caption 1½ inches from the top of the page.

- Center the court name and venue in full caps.

- Triple space after the court name and venue.

- Type the parties' names in full caps.

- If multiple lines are needed for the name of defendants or plaintiffs, single space the lines; otherwise, double space the style of the case.

- Indent the words "Plaintiff" and "Defendant" one inch.

- Key the right parentheses at the center point on the page, separating the style of the case from the file number.

- Place a comma after the name of the plaintiff, the word "Plaintiff," and the name of the defendant, and a period after the word "Defendant." Use "Plaintiffs" or "Defendants" if there are multiple parties.

- Key the document title in full caps, centered. Triple space before and after the title.

COMPLAINT

PURPOSE AND FORMAT

PETITION

Also known as a complaint or declaration. A method of legally asking for something.

JURY

A group of citizens selected to hear a case who are sworn to arrive at the truth of a matter and make a decision for or against the defendants.

COMPLAINT

The first document filed in a lawsuit.

JURISDICTION

The authority of a court to hear a case.

COUNT

Each separate cause of action.

ALLEGATIONS

Statements the accusing party expects to prove.

A complaint, also known as a **petition or declaration**, is the initial document that starts a lawsuit. It is prepared by the attorney who represents the plaintiff, and it gives the facts and circumstances surrounding the case and requests a decision from the judge or **jury** in favor of the plaintiff. Refer to Figures 1-5 through 1-7 as you examine the complaint filed on behalf of William F. Oldham.

Caption — This case is to be heard in the Circuit Court of Davidson County, Tennessee. The caption identifies William F. Oldham as the plaintiff and James A. Pizzini and Express Delivery Services, Inc., as the defendants. JURY DEMAND is placed above the case number to indicate that the plaintiff demands that this case be heard by a jury. The title of the document is "Complaint."

Body— In order for a court to decide on a matter, the matter must be filed in the court that has authority to hear the case. That authority is known as **jurisdiction**. The opening paragraph of the body of the complaint gives the residences of the plaintiff(s) and defendant(s) to establish that the court has jurisdiction over the parties.

Beginning with the paragraph numbered 1, the facts and circumstances that are the basis for the action are stated. There may be one or more causes of action. Causes of action are also known as counts. A **count** is composed of one or more **allegations**, which are statements the plaintiff expects to prove. In our case, there are two counts. Count I charges that the defendants were negligent and that negligence was the direct cause of the injuries to the plaintiff. Count II charges that the vehicle was driven in violation of Tennessee laws and that violation is the direct cause of the damages and injuries to the plaintiff. Each allegation is numbered, beginning with the arabic numeral 1; each group of allegations making up a count are identified with a centered heading and a roman numeral — COUNT I, COUNT II.

Prayer Clause — The prayer, or WHEREFORE, clause is the last paragraph of each count or the last paragraph of the complaint, in which the plaintiff demands judgment against the defendant for a sum of money or equitable settlement and prays for anything else the judge determines is just and proper. In the complaint by William Oldham, he is specifically asking for $100,000 in damages and a jury to try the case.

Signature Block — Signature block refers to the place on the document where the attorney signs. The arrangement of information presented in Figure 1-7 is a suggestion. In most states it is placed at the end of the document with the signature line, but in some states it may be placed in the upper left-hand corner of the first page of the document.

Some attorneys conclude their documents with "Respectfully submitted"; others choose to eliminate the complimentary closing. In any case, complaints should provide a line for the attorney's signature, with the attorney's name keyed below the line. In about half of the states, the courts require that the attorney place an assigned number in the closing lines of documents filed in state courts.

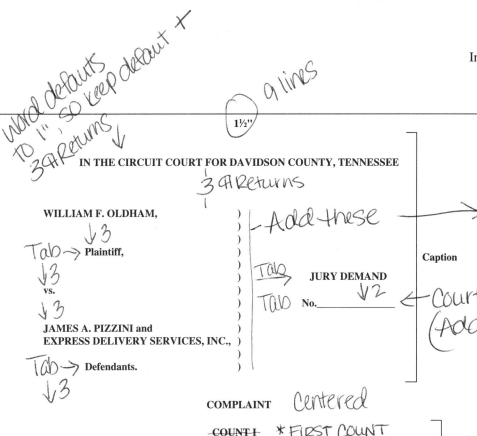

Handwritten annotations: Word defaults to 1", so keep default ✗ / 3¾ Returns ↓ / 1½" / ⊙ 9 lines / 3¾ Returns / ← Add these → Center 50 spaces / Caption / Tab → JURY DEMAND ↓2 / Tab No.____ ↓2 ← Court case # (Add # if assigned) / Tab ↓3 / ↓3 / ↓3 / Tab → ↓3 / Centered / ✳ FIRST COUNT / Body is Double Spaced / Additional children not caps

IN THE CIRCUIT COURT FOR DAVIDSON COUNTY, TENNESSEE

WILLIAM F. OLDHAM,

Plaintiff,

vs.

JAMES A. PIZZINI and
EXPRESS DELIVERY SERVICES, INC.,

Defendants.

JURY DEMAND

No._____

COMPLAINT

~~COUNT I~~

Plaintiff WILLIAM F. OLDHAM a resident of Davidson County, Nashville, Tennessee, sues the Defendants, JAMES A PIZZINI, a resident of Davidson County, Tennessee, who lives at 2407 Old Lebanon Road, and EXPRESS DELIVERY SERVICES, INC., a corporation organized under the laws of the State of Tennessee and having its principal place of business at 2800 Wallace Road, Nashville, Tennessee, both jointly and severally, in a cause of action for damages in the sum of One Hundred Thousand Dollars ($100,000) and for cause of action would show:

1. That on June 27, (~~current year~~ 2010), the Defendant EXPRESS DELIVERY SERVICES, INC., was the registered owner of a Ford truck bearing Tennessee License No. CEW-549 which was being operated by one of its employees, the Defendant JAMES A. PIZZINI. The Defendant EXPRESS DELIVERY SERVICES, INC., had placed this vehicle under the control and in the custody of the Defendant JAMES A. PIZZINI, who was on this occasion the agent, servant, and employee of EXPRESS DELIVERY SERVICES, INC., and who, at the time of the collision, was operating the said vehicle within the course of his employment, within the scope of his authority, and in the furtherance of the business of Defendant EXPRESS DELIVERY SERVICES, INC.

2. That on June 27, (~~current year~~ 2010), the Plaintiff, WILLIAM F. OLDHAM, was driving his Dodge automobile in a northwardly direction on Lebanon Road in a careful, cautious, and prudent manner. While the Plaintiff was driving his automobile, the Defendant JAMES A. PIZZINI carelessly and negligently drove his vehicle in a southwardly direction at a high rate of speed, in excess of a reasonable or safe speed under the road conditions, without keeping a proper lookout ahead, without having his

FIGURE 1-5. Complaint, Page 1

vehicle under control, and crossed the center line dividing traffic traveling in opposite directions and struck the Plaintiff's vehicle along the length of the left side of Plaintiff's automobile.

3. That Defendant PIZZINI struck the Plaintiff's vehicle with such great force as to cause the Plaintiff to lose control of his vehicle and go off the shoulder of the road on his right side, whereupon the Plaintiff struck a utility pole and came to rest. Through both the impact with the Defendant's vehicle and the subsequent impact with the utility pole, the Plaintiff was suddenly and abruptly jerked and thrown in and about his automobile; and in so doing, it caused serious injuries to the body of the Plaintiff.

4. That the negligence of the Defendant PIZZINI, who was at the aforedescribed time and place acting as the agent, servant, and employee of the Defendant EXPRESS DELIVERY SERVICES, INC., within the scope of his employment, within the scope of his authority, and in the furtherance of the business of the Defendant EXPRESS DELIVERY SERVICES, INC., was gross and wanton and showed an indifference to rights of other persons, including the Plaintiff; and further, the Plaintiff would show that he is entitled to punitive damages in addition to compensatory damages.

5. That the Plaintiff sustained serious and permanent injuries, was hospitalized and under continual medical care, and will require additional medical treatment and care into the foreseeable future. The Plaintiff incurred extensive medical and hospital bills, along with physical therapy costs which he still is incurring.

6. That the acts of negligence by the Defendant PIZZINI as stated herein were the direct and proximate cause of the injuries and damages that he has sustained and that under the facts herein set out, the Defendant EXPRESS DELIVERY SERVICES, INC., is jointly and severally liable to the Plaintiff for all injuries and damages, both compensatory and punitive.

Body

WHEREFORE, the Plaintiff, WILLIAM F. OLDHAM, demands judgment against the Defendants, JAMES A. PIZZINI and EXPRESS DELIVERY SERVICES, INC., jointly and severally, for damages in the sum of One Hundred Thousand Dollars ($100,000) and further demands a jury to try this cause of action.

Prayer

COUNT II

Plaintiff WILLIAM F. OLDHAM sues the Defendants, JAMES A. PIZZINI and EXPRESS DELIVERY SERVICES, INC., jointly and severally, for damages of One Hundred Thousand Dollars ($100,000); and for an additional cause of action, Plaintiff would show:

- 2 -

FIGURE 1-6. Complaint, Page 2

WHEREFORE
        AS
   ∧
Always
ALL CAPS

1. That Plaintiff adopts by reference each and every allegation in COUNT I and, for an additional cause of action against both of the above-named Defendants, would show that the Defendant JAMES A PIZZINI, at the aforesaid time and place, operated his vehicle in violation of the following numbered statutes of the State of Tennessee (more commonly known as The Rules of the Road for Operation of Vehicles) covering the operation of motor vehicles on the streets and roads of the State of Tennessee. Said statutes are set out in <u>Tennessee Code Annotated</u>, which are incorporated fully herein by reference and will be read in their entirety at the trial of this cause of action, said code sections being:

Tenn. Code Ann. § 55-8-193, "Required Obedience to Traffic Laws";

Tenn. Code Ann § 55-8-115, "Driving on the Right Side of Roadway";

Tenn. Code Ann. § 55-8-120, "Limitation on Driving to Left of Center";

Tenn. Code Ann. § 55-8-152, "Speed Limit"; and

Tenn. Code Ann. § 55-10-205, "Reckless Driving."

2. That the acts of negligence by the Defendant JAMES A. PIZZINI herein stated were negligent per se in violation of the Tennessee statutes and laws governing the operation of a motor vehicle. Further, Plaintiff would show that they were the direct and proximate cause of the damages and injuries to the Plaintiff and that both Defendants, JAMES A. PIZZINI and EXPRESS DELIVERY SERVICES, INC., are jointly and severally liable to the Plaintiff for both compensatory and punitive damages.

WHEREFORE, Plaintiff WILLIAM F. OLDHAM demands judgment against the Defendants, both jointly and severally, for the sum of One Hundred Thousand Dollars ($100,000) and further demands a jury to try this cause.

Prayer

4 ↓

Signature Block

ROBERT W. MITCHELL (No. 32112)
Attorney for the Plaintiff
804 Stahlman Building
Nashville, TN 37201
(615) 555-5555

At Center
| ⟶

- 3 -

FIGURE 1-7. Complaint, Page 3

Generally, the number is not used on documents filed in federal courts, as federal rules do not require the number at this time. In Figure 1-7, Robert Mitchell's number is 32112 and is placed in parentheses after his name. Below his name is "Attorney for Plaintiff," along with his complete address and phone number.

Cost Bond — A few courts require a bond making the plaintiff and attorney liable for costs of the lawsuit, not to exceed a stated amount. The bond is known as a cost bond and the form can be obtained from the clerk of the court.

COST BOND

A statement signed by the plaintiff and attorney that they will guarantee the payment of court costs not to exceed a stated amount.

Formatting Instructions for a Complaint

- Prepare an original for the court, a copy for each defendant, and a copy for the office files.

- Use paper of the type and size required by the court. Federal courts and most state courts require 8½ by 11-inch paper; a few state courts still use 8½ by 14-inch paper. Some courts require that paper with numbered lines be used for court documents.

- Set 1-inch left, right, top, and bottom margins on all pages except page 1, on which the top margin should be 1½ inches. If the documents are to be bound at the top, all top margins should be at least 1½ inches.

- Arrange the lines of the caption as shown in the illustration of the complaint.

- Triple-space before and after the title of the document.

- Double-space the document.

- Number all pages except page 1 at the bottom center of the page; do not place a number on page 1. The number may be preceded by a hyphen and space and followed by a space and hyphen (- 2 -) or printed at center position without the hyphens.

- Number all allegations. Here are some suggested formats:
  Use arabic numerals (1, 2, 3) from the beginning of the document to the prayer clause. If there are subdivisions, use lowercase letters (a, b, c). For example,

---

1. The Defendant is a physician duly licensed to practice medicine within the state.

2. On April 1, 1992, Defendant held himself to be a skilled orthopedic surgeon in:

a. Postoperative treatment and care of patients who had undergone surgery for the removal of tissue from the ligaments of the right knee;

b. Postoperative treatment of patients who had surgery and had not experienced relief of the pain; and

- Use roman numerals (I., II., III.) centered on a line preceding each allegation.

or

- If the allegations are grouped into counts, number the counts with a centered title and roman numerals (COUNT I, COUNT II) and number the allegations with arabic numerals.

or

- If the allegations are grouped into counts, label the counts as FIRST COUNT, SECOND COUNT and use centered roman numerals for the allegations. For example,

---

FIRST COUNT

COMES the Plaintiff, DALE M. ROEHNIG, a minor, and for cause of action would show:

I.

That both the Plaintiffs and the Defendant were residents of Davidson County, Tennessee.

- Begin the prayer clause with WHEREFORE typed in full caps followed by a comma. If the prayer consists of several items, number the paragraphs following the WHEREFORE paragraph with arabic numerals, beginning with 1.

- Begin signature lines at the horizontal center point on the page. Three blank lines should precede the signature line to allow adequate space for the written name. The signature line should extend from the center of the page to the right margin, usually three inches in length.

- Do not leave orphan or widow lines (one line of a paragraph at the bottom or top of a page). If the document is printed on paper with numbered lines, each blank line may be filled with four diagonals.

- Place a signature line on a page with at least two lines of text.

MOTION FOR DEFAULT JUDGMENT AND DEFAULT JUDGMENT

If there is no response to the summons and complaint by the defendant within the time stated on the summons, the plaintiff can request a default judgment. A default judgment means that the defendant will have no further opportunity to defend the charges brought against him or her. The procedure for obtaining a default judgment is to (1) file a motion for a default judgment and (2) prepare a default judgment. A **motion** is a method of asking a judge to approve or disapprove a matter related to the case. Motions are often used before the actual trial, as in the case of a motion for default. Figure 1-8, a motion for default judgment filed on behalf of William Oldham, the plaintiff, requests that the judge grant a default judgment because the defendant did not answer the complaint within the time allowed by law. The procedure is to set a hearing, which is a short court proceeding where the judge will rule on the motion. At that hearing the motion will either be granted or denied.

An application to the court, based on a specific ground or reason, requesting that the court make an order (rule) in favor of the applicant.

A written motion has a caption, body, and signature block followed by a certificate of mailing, including a statement indicating the time when the motion is expected to be heard. The caption, body, and signature block are prepared as in the complaint. The certificate is placed at the end of the motion.

In Figure 1-8, the certificate states that a copy of the motion is being mailed to the defendants, who have not contacted an attorney. In cases where the defendants have contacted an attorney to represent them, the motion is mailed to the attorney.

A certificate stating that the document has been mailed to the opposing attorney or opposing party if there is no attorney.

In the case of <u>Oldham v. Pizzini et al.</u>, the judge denied the motion for a default judgment and the case proceeded. Had the judge granted the motion, a judgment by default, a document signed by the judge ordering that the defendant lose by default, would have been prepared.

IN THE CIRCUIT COURT FOR DAVIDSON COUNTY, TENNESSEE

WILLIAM F. OLDHAM,   )
)
)
        Plaintiff,   )
)
)
)   No. C-20886   **Caption**
vs.   )
)
)
JAMES A. PIZZINI et al.,   )
)
        Defendants.   )

MOTION FOR A JUDGMENT BY DEFAULT

COMES the Plaintiff, WILLIAM F. OLDHAM, and respectfully moves the
Court for a Judgment by Default, the Defendants, JAMES A. PIZZINI and EXPRESS   **Body**
DELIVERY SERVICES, INC., having failed to answer or plea within the time allowed
by law.

Signature Block

ROBERT W. MITCHELL (No. 32112)
Attorney for the Plaintiff
804 Stahlman Building
Nashville, TN 37201
(615) 555-5555

CERTIFICATE

I, ROBERT W. MITCHELL, Attorney for the Plaintiff, do hereby certify
that a true and exact copy of the foregoing Motion for a Judgment by Default has been
mailed to the Defendant JAMES A. PIZZINI and Defendant EXPRESS DELIVERY
SERVICES, INC., by placing the same in properly addressed, stamped envelopes and   ◄— **Certificate of Mailing**
depositing them for delivery with the United States Postal Service. I further give notice
that I expect this motion to be heard on the _____ day of January, (current year), at
9 a.m. in the Circuit Court for Davidson County, Tennessee.

        This the _____ day of January, (current year).

Date and Time Motion Is to Be Heard

_____
ROBERT W. MITCHELL

FIGURE 1-8. Motion for a Judgment by Default

SUMMARY

- A plaintiff is the party who sues; a defendant is the party being sued.

- A summons and complaint are the first documents prepared to begin a legal action.

- The summons notifies the defendant that an action has been brought against him or her and that the defendant should appear and defend within a stated period of time — usually 30 days in state court and 20 days in federal court.

- Failure to respond to a summons and complaint can result in a judgment by default against the defendant.

- A summons that has been properly served by mail should be stamped by the clerk of the court, have the "Return on Service by Mail" section completed, and have an attached return receipt.

- Summonses can be served personally, by registered or certified mail with a return receipt, or by publication.

- Every court document has a caption. The caption consists of the name of the court and venue, style of the case, file or docket number, and title of the document.

- The complaint has allegations in numbered paragraphs and a prayer clause demanding judgment.

REVIEW EXERCISES

T F   1. The first step in a civil action is to prepare a summons and complaint to be served on the plaintiff.

T F   2. If there is no response to the summons and complaint within 30 days, a motion for a default judgment can be filed.

T F   3. Before a summons can be served, it must be dated and signed by the clerk of the court.

T F   4. You can list multiple defendants on a summons by typing the first defendant's name followed by "et al."

T F   5. A second summons is called a pluries summons.

T F   6. A summons and complaint can be served by first-class mail.

T F   7. A caption must appear on every court document.

T   F   8.   A caption includes the court name and venue, style of the case, verification, and file number.

T   F   9.   If a plaintiff wishes to request a jury, the words JURY REQUESTED are typed above the docket numbers in the caption.

T   F   10.   A cause of action may be composed of one or more allegations.

T   F   11.   The prayer clause usually begins with THEREFORE typed in full caps.

T   F   12.   A certificate of service is included on all documents after the complaint to indicate that a copy has been served on the attorney for the opposing party.

T   F   13.   In many states, the attorney's number should be included in the signature block on documents filed in state courts.

T   F   14.   A certificate is typed on every complaint.

T   F   15.   Prepare all court documents on 8½- by 14-inch paper.

T   F   16.   Number all pages of a complaint.

T   F   17.   All margins for litigation documents are 2 inches except for page 1, which has a 1½-inch top margin.

T   F   18.   A signature line is usually 3½ inches in length.

> The rules presented here are to provide some guidance in transcribing legal documents. They apply to the transcription of legal documents. It should be noted here that capitalization patterns vary from firm to firm and the secretary should follow the pattern preferred by the attorney.

TRANSCRIPTION RULES

CAPITALIZATION

Attorney

Capitalize "Attorney for Plaintiff" and "Attorney for Defendant" when it is part of an address. The term *attorney* is not capitalized if used alone as a common noun.

I have sent a copy of the documents to Mr. ROBERT W. MITCHELL, ***Attorney for the Plaintiff,*** 804 Stahlman Building, Nashville, TN 37201.

COMES NOW the Plaintiff, JOHN J. McGOWAN, through his ***attorney*** and presents the following allegations:

Document Titles

When a document title is used within the body of a legal document, capitalize the first letter of each word that has four or more letters except short prepositions, conjunctions, or articles (a, an, the). Some firms choose to use lowercase letters. Consistently use one method or the other.

The Plaintiff's attorney filed a ***Complaint for Damages*** on January 1, 19—.

or

The Plaintiff's attorney filed a ***complaint for damages*** on January 1, 19—.

Geographic Terms

Capitalize the words "City," "County," "State," and similar terms when they appear before the name of the geographic location. In routine correspondence, these terms are not capitalized. Capitalize City, County when they appear after the geographic name of the location. Always capitalize the name of the county and state.

He is a resident of the ***City of Nashville, County of Davidson, State of Tennessee.*** (legal document)

He is a resident of the ***city of Nashville, county of Davidson, state of Tennessee.*** (routine correspondence)

He is a resident of ***Davidson County, Tennessee.***

Names of Parties

Many legal firms use full caps on names of parties, attorneys, and judges in legal documents; others use initial caps. Always check the preference of your firm by looking at documents in the files. Consistently use one method or the other.

The Plaintiff, *WILLIAM F. OLDHAM*, is a resident of the County of Davidson, State of Tennessee.

or

The Plaintiff, *William F. Oldham*, is a resident of the county of Davidson, State of Tennessee.

Party Designation

Capitalize the first letter of the party designation (Plaintiff or Defendant) in legal documents. Some firms choose to use lowercase letters. Within a document, consistently use one method or the other

On June 27, (current year), the *Defendant* EXPRESS DELIVERY SERVICES, INC., was the registered owner of a Ford truck.

or

On June 27, (current year), the *defendant* EXPRESS DELIVERY SERVICES, INC., was the registered owner of a Ford truck.

Phrases in Full Caps

Capitalize WHEREFORE at the beginning of the prayer clause and place a comma after the expression.

WHEREFORE, the Plaintiff demands judgment against the Defendants.

Some attorneys wish to capitalize COME(S) and COME(S) NOW when they are the first words in the introductory paragraph of a document.

COME the Plaintiffs, by and through their attorneys. . .

COMES NOW your Plaintiff and pursuant to Rule 36 of . . .

NUMBER EXPRESSION

Dollar Amounts

In legal documents, dollar amounts are written in words and figures. The first letter of each word is capitalized. The second term in a hyphenated number is keyed in lowercase letters. Place parentheses around the numeric figures that express exactly what is written in words. Note the use of "and" between dollars and cents.

One Hundred Thousand Dollars ($100,000)—do not include .00 because cents is not referred to in the spelled-out version.

One Hundred Thousand and no/100 Dollars ($100,000.00)

(All numbers)

Twenty-one Thousand and 00/100 (21,000.00) Dollars—do not include the $ in parentheses because the words before the parentheses do not refer to dollars.

Twenty-five and 25/100 Dollars ($25.25)

Twenty-five Dollars and Twenty-five Cents ($25.25)

Numbers in Legal Documents

In legal documents, numbers other than dollar amounts are written in words and figures. The written amount is keyed in lowercase letters.

Plaintiff requests that the facts be admitted within *thirty (30)* days.

PERIODS

Enumerated Paragraphs Beginning with "That"

Use a period after paragraphs beginning with the word "That" when they occur after an introductory statement that serves as the subject. If the last paragraph is preceded by the word "and," a semicolon is used after each one except the last paragraph, which ends with a period (see semicolon rule and example below).

The Plaintiff would show:

1. That on June 17, (current year), the Defendant was the registered owner of a Ford truck bearing Tennessee License No. CEW-549.

2. That on June 17, (current year), the Plaintiff, WILLIAM F. OLDHAM, was driving his Dodge automobile in a northwardly direction.

3. That Defendant PIZZINI struck the Plaintiff's vehicle.

SEMICOLONS

Enumerated Lists

In legal writing, semicolons are often used after consecutive paragraphs or items in a list. Place a semicolon after each item in the list except the last item, which ends with a period. If the word "and" appears before the last item in the list, it is a signal to use semicolons rather than periods. Place a semicolon before the word "and."

The following statutes will be read at the trial in their entirety:

Tenn. Code Ann. § 55-8-103, "Required Obedience to Traffic Laws";
Tenn. Code Ann. § 55-8-115, "Driving on the Right Side of Roadway"; and
Tenn. Code Ann. § 55-8-120, "Limitations on Driving to Left of Center."

Transcription Hints:

When using a word processing program with justification turned on, leave required spaces, sometimes called fixed spaces, after numbered paragraphs. Tab in one inch from the left margin, key the number and period, then insert required spaces. Some programs use code space to create a fixed space. This keeps an equal amount of space locked in following each number.

When section numbers are cited, such as Tenn. Code Ann. § 2-35-7889, the section symbol can be created in most software programs by holding down the Alt key and entering 21 from the ten key pad. Space once before and after the symbol.

TRANSCRIPTION EXERCISES

1. Prepare a caption for the complaint in the case of James J. Roehnig as father and next friend; Linda F. Roehnig as mother and next friend; and Dale Roehnig, a minor, plaintiffs, vs. Herman A. Shulman, defendant. It is to be heard in the Circuit Court for Davidson County, Tennessee. A jury is requested. Name this caption "Cap" and save it. You will be asked to retrieve it at the beginning of Project 1-1.

2. Prepare a signature block for Robert W. Mitchell (No. 32112), Attorney for the Plaintiffs, 804 Stahlman Building, Nashville, TN 37201. His phone number is (615) 555-5555. Name this address block "Add" and save it. You will be asked to retrieve it at the end of Project 1-1.

Use a secretarial reference manual and the rules presented in this chapter to aid you in correctly transcribing the following material. The sentences are presented in lowercase letters without punctuation, as you would hear them on a transcriber.

3. wherefore the plaintiffs sue the defendant and demand a jury to try this cause

4. the plaintiff should be awarded $22,000

5. both the plaintiffs and defendant were residents of davidson county tennessee on june 29 1993

6. comes the plaintiff and sues the defendant in the amount of $25000

7. the plaintiff was only 1½ years old on the date of the injury

8. dale m roehnig a minor plaintiff sues herman a shulman the defendant

9. plaintiffs would show 1 that both parties were residents of davidson county and live next door to each other at 2413 valley crest drive nashville tn 37201 2 that on june 29 1993 the plaintiff was attracted to a riding lawn mower being driven by the defendant. the child approached the mower from the rear of the defendant and the blade struck his toes 3 that as a direct and proximate result of the negligence of the defendant the plaintiff was injured

10. (Transcribe No. 9 above. Insert the word *and* before the third paragraph.)

11. come the plaintiffs dale m roehning at al and move for a judgment by default

12. comes the plaintiff through his attorney and moves for a judgment by default

13. my address is robert w mitchell attorney for the plaintiffs 804 stahlman building nashville tn 37201

RESEARCH ACTIVITIES

1. Contact the clerk of a court in your county to learn the size of paper to use for filing documents.

2. Request a summons form from your local court clerk's office. Also request a cost bond if used in your state.

PROJECTS

Insert the cassette tape for Chapter 1 and transcribe the following projects.

Project 1-1   This case is a personal injury lawsuit where a minor child was injured by a lawn mower through the negligence of a next-door neighbor. The attorney for the plaintiff is Robert W. Mitchell (No. 32112), 804 Stahlman Building, Nashville, Tennessee 37201. Phone (615) 555-5555. The attorney for the defendant is Warner C. Watkins (No. 87045), 1612 14th Avenue North, Nashville, Tennessee 37201 (615) 555-6666.

Use the caption you named "Cap" in Transcription Exercise 1. Then transcribe the complaint for the case of Dale M. Roehnig, a Minor, by James J. Roehnig, Father and Next Friend; Linda F. Roehnig, Mother and Next Friend, Plaintiffs vs. Herman A. Shulman, Defendant. The case is to be filed in the Circuit Court of Davidson County, Tennessee. Use the address block you named "Add" in Transcription Exercise 2. After the complaint is transcribed, label the parts of the complaint in the right margin.

Project 1-2   Prepare a summons for the case in Project 1-1, using the form provided at the back of this text or a form from your local court. Obtain the defendant's address from the complaint.

Project 1-3   Transcribe the motion for judgment by default in the <u>Roehnig v. Shulman</u> case.

CHAPTER 2

ANSWERING A LAWSUIT

OBJECTIVES

After successfully completing this chapter, you will be able to:

➤ Transcribe an answer

➤ Calculate time within which to file or answer

➤ Identify parts of an answer

➤ Transcribe a motion to dismiss an affidavit in support of the motion

➤ Transcribe an answer, counterclaim, and cross-complaint

INTRODUCTION

This chapter is a continuation of the <u>Oldham</u> case from Chapter 1 and focuses on the documents prepared on behalf of the defendants. Once the summons and complaint were served on the defendants, each defendant contacted an attorney. Express Delivery Services, Inc., contacted Marilyn C. Finch to represent the corporation, and James A. Pizzini contacted Mario Vassalo to represent him.

The first thing each attorney did was to check the **time** within which to file the documents in response to the complaint, known as **responsive pleadings;** then each began drafting the appropriate documents listed below.

CALCULATING TIME

Using the rules of court to determine when a document should be filed or served.

RESPONSIVE PLEADINGS

The documents filed in response to a complaint, counterclaim, or cross-claim.

MOTION TO DISMISS

AFFIDAVIT IN SUPPORT OF MOTION TO DISMISS

ANSWER AND COUNTERCLAIM

ANSWER AND CROSS-COMPLAINT

THIRD-PARTY COMPLAINT

CALCULATING TIME

All documents are to be served upon the opposing party (in this case, the plaintiff's attorney) within a period of time required by the rules of the courts. Those rules also specify a method of calculating time.

In federal cases, the answer to a complaint must be sent to the plaintiff's attorney within 20 days after service of the summons on the defendant; in state cases, the courts usually allow 30 days for a response. The time period will always be stated on the summons, so there is no question as to the length of time within which one should respond to a complaint.

Even though it is the attorney's responsibility to respond to the complaint within the allotted time, the secretary often supports the attorney by calculating the time within which that response must be served. This is extremely important since it is the secretary who will actually produce the finished document that is filed to meet the deadline. The secretary should set up a tickler, or reminder, system indicating the last date to serve the document.

FEDERAL RULES OF CIVIL PROCEDURE

The procedural rules for federal civil cases.

The guidelines for calculating time as stated in Rules 6 and 12 of the *Federal Rules of Civil Procedure* are (1) do not include the first day, (2) include the last day unless it is Saturday, Sunday, or a legal holiday; if it is a Saturday, Sunday, or a legal holiday, count the next work day, and (3) exclude Saturday, Sunday, or a holiday if the total time being calculated is less than 11 days (usually 7 days in state court). Add 3 days if the document is to be mailed.

As an example of calculating time, assume that a summons and complaint were served on the defendant on Thursday, August 25, 19—. The summons stated that an answer was to be filed within 30 days after service upon the defendant. The 6 days left in August and 24 days in September would total 30 days; however, September 24 is a Saturday, so the last day to serve the answer would be Monday, September 26.

KEEPING A TICKLER SYSTEM

The legal secretary should support the attorney by keeping a tickler file of dates litigation documents are mailed out of the office, as well as due dates for responses due from the opposing party or due to be sent out to the opposing party.

CERTIFICATE OF SERVICE

PURPOSE AND FORMAT

Litigation documents prepared after the summons and complaint are served by first-class mail or hand-delivered to the opposing attorney. On each document so served, a certificate of service is placed at the end of the document, stating the name and address of the party to whom it is mailed and the date of mailing. The

---

CERTIFICATE OF SERVICE

     I hereby certify that a true and exact copy of the foregoing (enter name of document here) has been mailed first-class, postage prepaid to (enter name, position, such as Attorney for Defendant or Attorney for Plaintiff, and address of the opposing attorney), this the _____ day of _____, (current year).

                        _____
                        ROBERT W. MITCHELL

FIGURE 2-1. Certificate of Service

certificate is signed by the attorney (legal secretary in some jurisdictions). See Figure 2-1.

Formatting Instructions for the Certificate of Service

- The certificate may be double-spaced or single-spaced. It is single-spaced when there is limited room at the bottom of a page. It is acceptable to put the certificate on a page by itself.

- Begin the title a triple-space below the last line of the document. Key the title, "Certificate of Service," in full caps followed by a triple space.

- When entering the name of the document being mailed, use the exact title shown on the first page of the document. Use the same capitalization style for the name of the document (initial caps or all lowercase letters) as was used within the text of the document.

- The attorney's name can be preceded by a title (such as Mr. or Ms.) and followed by "Attorney for Plaintiff" or "Attorney for Defendant." If the attorney's name is followed by Esq., omit the designation "Attorney for ____" because "Esquire" means "attorney" when used in the United States.

- Insert the day and month the document is to be mailed. If there is any question as to the day it will be mailed, type a line for writing in the day and month the document is mailed, and handwrite or key in the day and month when the document is mailed.

- Provide a three-inch line for the signature beginning at the center of the page four lines below the body of the certificate. Key the attorney's (or in states where the secretary signs, the legal secretary's) name in full caps below the signature line.

MOTION TO DISMISS

PURPOSE AND FORMAT

MOTION TO DISMISS

A request to the judge to dismiss a case.

AFFIDAVIT

A statement under oath by the person who signed it.

HEARING ON A MOTION

An appearance before a judge at which the motion is either granted or denied.

If there are grounds to dismiss a lawsuit at its beginning, **a motion to dismiss** can be filed before any other document is submitted. A motion to dismiss is a request to the judge to dismiss the case. Some courts require that a supporting statement under oath, an **affidavit**, be attached to the motion. Such an affidavit lends support for the motion. At the time the motion is filed, a time and date for the judge to hear the case is determined. At the **hearing** the judge either grants or denies the motion. In figuring time as discussed earlier in this chapter, a motion to dismiss stops the time from running. In such a case, time would be calculated 30 days (20 days in federal court) from the court hearing on the motion. On certain occasions, a motion to dismiss may be filed well into the lawsuit and its form would be the same as shown in Figure 2-2, page 44.

The Federal Rules of Civil Procedure provide for dismissal of lawsuits based on Rule 12(b) motions as outlined below. Many of the state courts have adopted similar grounds for dismissal.

- Lack of jurisdiction over the subject matter — This ground can be used if the case is filed in the wrong court. A domestic relations (family) court may be the only court that can hear divorces. If a case for a divorce is filed in another court that has no authority to hear it, the case could be dismissed for lack of jurisdiction over the subject matter (the divorce).

- Lack of jurisdiction over the person — A court has jurisdiction over the person if that person has significant contacts with the state. Generally speaking, if a person lives in a state, that state has personal jurisdiction. If "significant contacts" do not exist, then the court cannot make a judgment that is binding against that individual. This most often occurs when bringing a suit against a corporation where the question is whether or not it is doing "sufficient business" in this state to establish personal jurisdiction. A question may arise as to whether a mail-order business has enough sales in a state to call them significant.

- Improper venue — Venue is the geographical location of a court. At the state level that means filing the lawsuit in the correct county, parish, or judicial district; at the federal level, it means filing in the correct district. Failure to file in the proper venue can be grounds for filing a motion to dismiss; however, if there is no objection, venue is waived and the case continues in the court where it was filed. If a wreck occurred in one county of a state but the lawsuit was filed in another county, venue would be improper.

- Insufficiency of process — Process refers to the material typed on the summons itself. Refer to Chapter 1 for the contents of the summons.

Failure to prepare the form completely and accurately may result in the defendant's filing a motion for dismissal.

- Insufficiency of service of process — Service of process is delivering the summons and complaint. As discussed in Chapter 1, court rules allow for personal service, service by mail, and service by publication. If the method of service does not follow the rules, it may be grounds for dismissal of the suit.

- Failure to state a claim on which relief can be granted — For a lawsuit to be valid, a person must have grounds for filing the suit. This ground for dismissal can be made for a variety of reasons. Often the basis is that the wording in the complaint does not state a legal grounds for the lawsuit. For example, laws require that certain types of lawsuits be filed within a stated period of time after the event occurred. Failure to do so bars the right to file the case and would be grounds to dismiss the lawsuit.

If any of the grounds for dismissal exist, the attorney may draft a motion to dismiss. Refer to Figure 2-2 as you examine the motion to dismiss for failure to state a claim and for lack of service of process. This motion is filed by the attorney for Express Delivery Services, Inc.

Caption — The caption is the same as the one on the complaint except the title is "Motion to _____." or "Motion for_____."

Body — Even though court rules usually do not require specific wording, many motions begin with the phrase "COMES NOW the Plaintiff" or "COMES NOW the Defendant." The motion must state the grounds for the motion and request that the judge dismiss the case.

The motion for Express Delivery Services, Inc., claims that the case should be dismissed because the corporation is a Delaware corporation and not subject to the Tennessee courts, and therefore has not been properly served.

Signature Block — The signature block for Marilyn C. Finch, the attorney for the defendant, with her name, office address, attorney's number, and telephone number is shown below the body.

Certificate of Service — The certificate (also called a proof of service) indicates that a copy has been sent to Robert Mitchell, the attorney for the plaintiff, and Mario Vassalo, the attorney for James A. Pizzini. It gives a date and time when the motion is expected to be heard. The certificate was single-spaced to make the document fit on one page.

Date to be Heard — There are several ways to indicate when a motion is to be heard: One way is to incorporate it into the certificate as in Figure 2-2. Another method is to type a sentence at the bottom of the last page of the motion stating: "This motion is expected to be heard on _____(day), _____(date) at 9 a.m." In some jurisdictions, the date and time are placed on the first page below the case number and title of the motion.

IN THE CIRCUIT COURT FOR DAVIDSON COUNTY, TENNESSEE

WILLIAM F. OLDHAM,	)	
	)	
Plaintiff,	)	
	)	
vs.	)	No. C-20886
	)	
JAMES A. PIZZINI and EXPRESS	)	
DELIVERY SERVICES, INC.,	)	
	)	
Defendants.	)	

MOTION TO DISMISS FOR FAILURE TO STATE A CLAIM
AND FOR LACK OF SERVICE OF PROCESS

COMES NOW the Defendant EXPRESS DELIVERY SERVICES, INC. and respectfully moves the Court as follows:

1. To dismiss the Plaintiff's cause of action because the Complaint fails to state a cause of action against the Defendant upon which relief can be granted.

2. To dismiss the action or in lieu thereof to quash the return of service of the summons on the grounds (a) that the Defendant EXPRESS DELIVERY SERVICES, INC., is a corporation organized under the laws of Delaware and was not and is not subject to service of process within the State of Tennessee and (b) that the Defendant EXPRESS DELIVERY SERVICES, INC., has not been properly served with process in this action, all of which more clearly appears in the affidavits of ALVIN M. MILLER, president of EXPRESS DELIVERY SERVICES, INC., annexed hereto as Exhibit A.

_____
MARILYN C. FINCH (No. 44386)
Attorney for the Defendant
EXPRESS DELIVERY SERVICES, INC.
338 Fentrice Building
Nashville, TN 37201
(615) 555-6600

CERTIFICATE

I, MARILYN C. FINCH, Attorney for Defendant EXPRESS DELIVERY SERVICES, INC., do hereby certify that a true and exact copy of the foregoing Motion to Dismiss for Failure to State a Claim and for Lack of Service of Process has been mailed to Mr. ROBERT W. MITCHELL, Attorney for the Plaintiff, 804 Stahlman Building, Nashville, TN 37201, and to Mr. MARIO VASSALO, Attorney for Defendant PIZZINI, 1209 West 22d Street, Nashville, TN 37221, on this the ___ day of January, (current year), and that this Motion to Dismiss is expected to be heard on the _____ day of February, (current year), at 9 a.m.

_____
MARILYN C. FINCH

FIGURE 2-2. Motion to Dismiss

AFFIDAVIT IN SUPPORT OF MOTION TO DISMISS

An affidavit in support of a motion to dismiss is often included when the attorney for the defendant cannot (because of distance) or does not want to produce a witness for the hearing of a motion. Refer to Figure 2-3. Express Delivery is located in Delaware. The president of the company signed the affidavit to attach to the motion, thus eliminating the need to appear in court. The affidavit has the following elements:

- Caption
- Venue
- Body
- Signature line
- Jurat

An affidavit to be used in court has a caption as any other court document. The venue on the affidavit is the geographical location where the sworn statement is made; in this case, the statement was made by the president of Express Delivery who lives in the State of Florida, County of Dade. The fact that the corporation was organized under the laws of Delaware does not mean its president is at that location. The body states that James Pizzini was not an employee of Express Delivery; therefore, Express Delivery is not liable for his actions.

One who signs an affidavit is known as an **affiant.** In Figure 2-3, Alvin C. Miller is the affiant. The officer before whom the affidavit is signed and sworn to is a **notary public.** The statement, "Sworn to and subscribed before me this the _____ day of _____, 19–" is known as a **jurat.** After the affiant signs the affidavit, the notary public signs the jurat and enters the date when the notary's commission expires.

AFFIANT

The person who signs an affidavit.

NOTARY PUBLIC

A public officer who administers oaths and takes acknowledgments.

JURAT

The following statement: "Sworn to and subscribed before me this the _____ day of ____, 19–."

Secretaries are often notaries. To become a notary public, one submits an application to the county or state. In some states, the applicant is tested over the rules and regulations. Once elected, the notary takes an oath to faithfully perform the duties of the office and may be required to purchase an insurance policy (a bond) to cover misuse of the notary's seal. The notary is commissioned to serve for a period of time, which varies from state to state. After the oath and bonding, the notary purchases a seal, which the notary is required to place on all documents that are notarized. Some of the seals are "raised-letter" seals and others are rubber stamps.

IN THE CIRCUIT COURT FOR DAVIDSON COUNTY, TENNESSEE

WILLIAM F. OLDHAM,	)	
	)	
Plaintiff,	)	Caption
	)	
vs.	)	No. C-20886
	)	
JAMES A. PIZZINI and EXPRESS	)	
DELIVERY SERVICES, INC.,	)	
	)	
Defendants.	)	

AFFIDAVIT IN SUPPORT OF MOTION TO DISMISS

STATE OF FLORIDA)

COUNTY OF DADE   )   Venue of State where Document is to be Notorized

Sworn Statement →

COMES ALVIN M. MILLER, a citizen and resident of Dade County, Florida, who having been duly sworn according to law, states as follows:

That I, ALVIN M. MILLER, am the president of EXPRESS DELIVERY SERVICES, INC., which was incorporated under the laws of the State of Delaware.

That EXPRESS DELIVERY SERVICES, INC., does not maintain, nor did it have sufficient contacts with the State of Tennessee on the date of the wreck on June 27, (last year), to give the courts of the State of Tennessee jurisdiction over the Defendant EXPRESS DELIVERY SERVICES, INC.

That even though EXPRESS DELIVERY SERVICES, INC., lists an address in the Nashville telephone directory of 2800 Wallace Road, Nashville, Tennessee, it maintains no employees at that location, has no equipment there, and only receives mail at that address.

That on the date of the wreck, June 27, (last year), the Defendant EXPRESS DELIVERY SERVICES, INC., had a written contract with the Defendant JAMES A. PIZZINI whereupon Mr. PIZZINI was an independent contractor and not an employee of EXPRESS DELIVERY SERVICES, INC.

Affiant's Signature   ALVIN M. MILLER
                        _____

Sworn to and subscribed before me
this the ___ day of January, (current year).   Jurat

_____

NOTARY PUBLIC

My Commission Expires: _____

FIGURE 2-3. Affidavit in Support of Motion to Dismiss

ANSWER

Purpose and Format

Unless there are grounds for dismissal of a case, the answer is the defendant's first pleading. The **answer** is a document in which the defendant responds to the allegations. The defendant also has an option to counterclaim (claim the plaintiff is responsible) or cross-claim (claim a codefendant is responsible).

An answer has the following elements:

- Caption

- Introductory paragraph

- Denials or admissions

- Prayer clause

- Signature block

- Certificate of service

In addition, an answer may have:

- Affirmative defenses

- A counterclaim

- A cross-complaint

Admissions or Denials. The answer should address each and every allegation in the complaint. The defendant may deny some, or all, of the allegations; may deny some of the allegations and admit that others are true; or may state that he or she is without knowledge or information sufficient to form a belief as to the truth of an allegation, which has the same effect as denying it. This may be done in various ways — the defendant might admit allegations (sometimes called **averments**) in certain paragraphs of the complaint and deny each allegation not admitted, or each one might be admitted or denied separately.

Affirmative Defenses. The defendant may include a section in the answer titled affirmative defenses. An **affirmative defense** is a legal defense even if the allegations in the complaint are true. In other words, "I did it, but I had a legal right to do it." Some affirmative defenses follow.

Statute of Limitations — There is a certain amount of time within which a lawsuit may be filed, and failure to file within that time period results in the plaintiff's never being legally able to bring the lawsuit. State and federal statutes specify periods of time for various types of claims. For example, a plaintiff may have to file a personal injury lawsuit or a contract case within two years.

AVERMENTS

Allegations.

AFFIRMATIVE DEFENSE

A legal defense when the defendant has allegations made against the plaintiff.

Statute of Frauds — Certain types of contracts must be in writing to be enforceable. Most often this involves contracts for the sale of real estate or the sale of goods worth $500 or more.

Discharge in Bankruptcy — If a creditor sues a defendant for nonpayment of an amount owed and the defendant's debts had been dismissed in a bankruptcy proceeding, no further lawsuit for that indebtedness can be filed against the debtor.

Assumption of the Risk — If a plaintiff sued a company for a $200 silk dress that was ruined by touching a painted wall, the defense might be that "Wet Paint" signs were posted near the wall and the plaintiff assumed the risk of ruining the dress by walking too closely to the wall.

Contributory or Comparative Negligence — The defendant was negligent, but the plaintiff was also negligent; therefore, either no recovery or partial recovery for a loss could be possible. In states that have adopted contributory negligence laws, the defendant is not liable if negligence on the part of the plaintiff can be proven. In the 46 states that have adopted comparative negligence, the plaintiff would be awarded a percentage of the claim based on the proportion of negligence contributed by the defendant.

COUNTERCLAIM

An allegation made by the defendant against the plaintiff in the same action.

Counterclaim. A **counterclaim** is an allegation made by the defendant against the plaintiff in the same lawsuit. If in the complaint the charge is that the defendant was negligent in operating a motor vehicle and as a result of the negligence caused an automobile accident, a counterclaim might be that the plaintiff was also partially or solely negligent in crossing over into the defendant's lane of traffic without turning on a signal. It is required by court rules that the counterclaim be made at the same time as the answer.

CROSS-COMPLAINT

Allegations made by one defendant against a person or business not in the original lawsuit.

Cross-Complaint. A **cross-complaint** is a charge made by one defendant against another codefendant or codefendants. For example, if plaintiff A sues defendants B and C, and defendant B feels that defendant C is liable for any damages caused to A, then B can file a cross-claim against C. The word **cross** describes a claim between parties on the same side of a case; **counter** describes an action by a defendant against a plaintiff. The arrows in the illustration below indicate the direction of the claims:

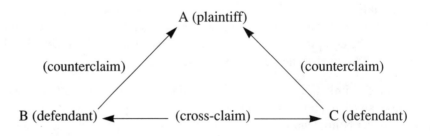

ANSWER AND COUNTERCLAIM

Refer to Figures 2-4 and 2-5, an answer and counterclaim on behalf of the defendant, James A. Pizzini, in the personal injury case we have been following. This document has an answer to the original allegations and then charges or counterclaims that the plaintiff actually caused the accident.

Caption — The caption may be identical to that on the complaint; however, when there are multiple parties, the names may be shortened by adding et al. (and others), et ux. (and wife), or et vir (and husband). In the illustration, names of both parties were retained.

Introduction — The introductory paragraph begins with the standard COMES NOW statement. Notice that it is keyed in full caps. Some attorneys use opening phrases such as "The Defendants _____ and _____ for their Answer to the Complaint state" or "COMES Defendant _____ and for his Answer to the Complaint filed against him says."

Denials or Admissions — The reference to paragraph numbers in the answer must match the numbered paragraphs in the complaint. For example, the statement that "Defendant denies the allegations in paragraph 1" refers to paragraph 1 in the complaint. If the allegations are numbered with roman numerals, the statement should read, "Defendant denies the allegations in paragraph I."

Defenses or Affirmative Defenses — There are no affirmative defenses in the Pizzini answer and counterclaim. If defenses had been included, they would be inserted with a centered heading, AFFIRMATIVE DEFENSES, immediately after the numbered paragraphs in the answer and before the prayer clause.

Counterclaim — After responding to allegations made by the plaintiff, the defendant James Pizzini counterclaims that William Oldham was guilty of negligence because he crossed into the oncoming lane and caused the accident. See Figure 2-5. This part of the document also has numbered paragraphs and a prayer clause.

Prayer Clause — After answering the allegations, James Pizzini's attorney demands that the case be dismissed and that the plaintiff pay costs. The prayer clause for the counterclaim states that Pizzini sues Oldham for $200,000 and demands a jury to try the case.

Signature Block — The signature block is prepared for Mario Vassalo, attorney for defendant James A. Pizzini.

Certificate of Service — The certificate indicates the document is mailed to Robert Mitchell, the plaintiff's attorney, and to Marilyn Finch, attorney for Express Delivery Services, Inc.

Double spaced

IN THE CIRCUIT COURT FOR DAVIDSON COUNTY, TENNESSEE

WILLIAM F. OLDHAM,	)	
	)	
Plaintiff,	)	**Jury**
	)	**JURY DEMAND** — **Demanded**
vs.	)	**in Prayer**
	)	**No. C-20886** **for**
JAMES A. PIZZINI and EXPRESS	)	**Counterclaim**
DELIVERY SERVICES, INC.,	)	
	)	
Defendants.	)	

ANSWER AND COUNTERCLAIM OF JAMES A. PIZZINI

ANSWER

COMES NOW the Defendant JAMES A. PIZZINI and for answer to the Complaint filed against him would say the following:

Defendant PIZZINI admits the allegation as to his residence but denies that EXPRESS DELIVERY SERVICES, INC., is a corporation organized under the laws of the State of Tennessee. Defendant further denies that he is jointly or severally liable to the Plaintiff.

Answer to Allegation 1 of the Complaint ←

1. Defendant denies all of the allegations of paragraph 1 of the Complaint but would affirmatively plead that he was an independent contractor and not an employee of Defendant EXPRESS DELIVERY SERVICES, INC.

Answer to Allegation 2 ←

2. Defendant denies all of the allegations in paragraph 2 of the Complaint but would admit that the Plaintiff was driving on the same roadway as he was on June 27 (last year).

3. Defendant denies each and every allegation of paragraph 3 and demands strictest proof thereof.

8. Defendant furthermore denies generally all allegations that have not been heretofore admitted, denied, or explained as fully as though they had been separately denied.

Prayer for Answer ←

WHEREFORE, the Defendant JAMES A. PIZZINI, having answered each and every allegation in the Complaint, demands that it be dismissed with costs adjudged against the Plaintiff.

FIGURE 2-4. Answer and Counterclaim, Page 1

COUNTERCLAIM

COMES NOW JAMES A. PIZZINI and takes the role of a Counterplaintiff and sues the Counterdefendant, WILLIAM F. OLDHAM, in the amount of Two Hundred Thousand Dollars ($200,000) and for cause of action would show the following:

1. Defendant PIZZINI repeats and affirms all allegations in the Complaint concerning Plaintiff WILLIAM F. OLDHAM's residence and domicile.

2. Defendant PIZZINI would show that the Counterdefendant, OLDHAM, was guilty of negligence in the operation of his automobile on June 27, (last year); that through the Counterdefendant's negligence, he crossed into the oncoming path of the Counterplaintiff, PIZZINI; and that such negligence was the direct and proximate cause of the wreck.

WHEREFORE, the Counterplaintiff, PIZZINI, sues the Counterdefendant, OLDHAM, for Two Hundred Thousand Dollars ($200,000) and further demands a jury to try this cause.

Prayer for Counterclaim

↓4

MARIO VASSALO (No. 98777)
Attorney for Defendant PIZZINI
1209 West 22d Street
Nashville, TN 37221
(615) 555-1111

Single spaced

CERTIFICATE

I, MARIO VASSALO, Attorney for the Defendant JAMES A. PIZZINI, do hereby certify that I have mailed a true and exact copy of this Answer and Counterclaim of JAMES A. PIZZINI to Mr. ROBERT W. MITCHELL, Attorney for the Plaintiff, 804 Stahlman Building, Nashville, TN 37201, and to Ms. MARILYN C. FINCH, Attorney for the Defendant, EXPRESS DELIVERY SERVICES, INC., 338 Fentrice Building, Nashville, TN 37201, on this the 8th day of March, (current year).

Single spaced

Put line in! (underscore)

MARIO VASSALO

- 2 -

FIGURE 2-5. Answer and Counterclaim, Page 2

ANSWER AND CROSS-COMPLAINT

In Figures 2-6 and 2-7, the defendant, Express Delivery, after responding to allegations made by the plaintiff, cross-claims against Pizzini, a codefendant in the original complaint. The first page of the document is the answer to the original complaint with a caption, denials, and prayer clause asking that the complaint be dismissed. Page 2 is the cross-complaint alleging that Pizzini was in no way under the control of Express Delivery, that Express Delivery is not responsible for Pizzini's negligent acts, and that if the Court finds Express Delivery guilty of negligence, the company be awarded damages from Pizzini.

The answer and cross-complaint is prepared in the same format as an answer and counterclaim; however, in addition to identifying the parties as plaintiff and defendant, they may be further identified as cross-complainant and cross-defendant. See the caption in Figure 2-6. A copy of the answer and cross-complaint would be mailed to the attorney for the plaintiff and to the attorney for the codefendant. No summons would be prepared as both defendants are already under the jurisdiction of the court.

THIRD-PARTY COMPLAINT

A complaint filed by the defendant against a person or business not in the original lawsuit.

THIRD-PARTY DEFENDANT

A party being brought into a lawsuit who was not in the original action.

THIRD-PARTY PLAINTIFF

The defendant in the original action who filed a third-party complaint.

THIRD-PARTY COMPLAINT

A defendant may serve a summons and complaint on a person not a party to the action who may be liable to the defendant for all or part of the plaintiff's claim. The party being brought in is known as a **third-party defendant.** The defendant in the original action becomes the **third-party plaintiff.**

If the third party is brought in within a stipulated number of days after service of the answer, usually ten days, it can be done without Court approval. If not, the procedure to bring in the third party is to file a motion with the Court, requesting permission to bring in a third party and to mail a notice to all other parties. With Court approval, the third party can be made part of the lawsuit.

It might be noted that a third-party complaint is different from an answer and counterclaim or answer and cross-complaint in that it is a separate document filed for the purpose of bringing in a new party.

The documents that should be served are:

- A copy of the original complaint on the third party

- A third-party summons and third-party complaint on the third party

- Third-party summons and third-party complaint (by a certificate of service on the attorneys or parties already involved in the action)

Refer to Figure 2-8 for an example of a caption for a third-party complaint. This is a caption that would be used in the Oldham case if James Pizzini had reason to believe that International Motor Company had manufactured a

IN THE CIRCUIT COURT FOR DAVIDSON COUNTY, TENNESSEE

WILLIAM F. OLDHAM,   )
)
     Plaintiff,   )
)
vs.   )
)
JAMES A. PIZZINI and EXPRESS)
DELIVERY SERVICES, INC.,   )
)   JURY DEMAND
     Defendants.   )
_____)   No. C-20886
)
EXPRESS DELIVERY SERVICES, INC.,)
)
     Cross-Complainant,)
)
vs.   )
)
JAMES A. PIZZINI,   )
)
     Cross-Defendant.)

ANSWER AND CROSS-COMPLAINT OF EXPRESS DELIVERY SERVICES, INC.

ANSWER

COMES NOW the Defendant EXPRESS DELIVERY SERVICES, INC., and for Answer to the Complaint filed against it would plead:

Defendant EXPRESS DELIVERY SERVICES, INC., denies it is a corporation organized under the laws of the State of Tennessee. Defendant further denies that it is jointly or severally liable to the Plaintiff.

1. Defendant denies all allegations in paragraph 1 of the Complaint and would specifically plead that Codefendant JAMES A. PIZZINI was an independent contractor and not an employee of Defendant EXPRESS DELIVERY SERVICES, INC.

2. Defendant would plead that it does not have sufficient knowledge of the allegations in paragraph 2 of the Complaint to either deny or admit.

8. Furthermore, Defendant EXPRESS DELIVERY SERVICES, INC., denies generally all allegations that have not been heretofore admitted, denied, or explained as fully as though they had been separately denied.

WHEREFORE, Defendant EXPRESS DELIVERY SERVICES, INC., having answered each and every allegation in the Complaint, demands that the Complaint be dismissed with costs adjudged against the Plaintiff.

FIGURE 2-6. Answer and Cross-Complaint, Page 1

CROSS-COMPLAINT

COMES NOW EXPRESS DELIVERY SERVICES, INC., and cross sues the Codefendant JAMES A. PIZZINI in the amount of Two Hundred Thousand Dollars ($200,000) and for cause of action would show:

1. Cross-Defendant PIZZINI was an independent contractor at the time and place of the wreck that gave cause to this suit; and at this time and place, the Cross-Complainant, EXPRESS DELIVERY SERVICES, INC., had no control, dominance, or supervision over the Cross-Defendant, PIZZINI, or any of his negligent acts.

2. Any negligent acts of Cross-Defendant PIZZINI should not be imputed on Cross-Complainant EXPRESS DELIVERY SERVICES, INC.

3. If the Court or jury finds Cross-Complainant EXPRESS DELIVERY SERVICES, INC., guilty of negligence, then EXPRESS DELIVERY SERVICES, INC., be granted a Cross-Judgment against PIZZINI for all amounts assessed.

WHEREFORE, the Cross-Complainant EXPRESS DELIVERY SERVICES, INC., sues the Cross-Defendant PIZZINI for Two Hundred Thousand Dollars ($200,000) and further demands a jury to try this cause.

MARILYN C. FINCH (NO. 44386)
Attorney for Cross-Complainant
338 Fentrice Building
Nashville, TN 37201
(615) 555-6600

CERTIFICATE

I, MARILYN C. FINCH, Attorney for Defendant and Cross-Claimant EXPRESS DELIVERY SERVICES, INC., do hereby certify that I have mailed a true and exact copy of this Answer and Cross-Complaint of EXPRESS DELIVERY SERVICES, INC., to Mr. ROBERT W. MITCHELL, Attorney for the Plaintiff, 804 Stahlman Building, Nashville, TN 37201, and to Mr. MARIO VASSALO, Attorney for Codefendant and Cross-Defendant PIZZINI, 1209 West 22d Street, Nashville, TN 37221, on this the _____ day of February, (current year).

MARILYN C. FINCH

- 2 -

FIGURE 2-7. Answer and Cross-Complaint, Page 2

defective part on his truck, thus causing the accident. Note that James Pizzini is not only the defendant but is also the third-party plaintiff, and the new party brought into the case, International Motor Company, is a third-party defendant.

A third-party complaint would have a caption, allegations against the third party, prayer clause, and signature block. On the summons, the words "Third-party" would be inserted before the word "summons." Court clerks provide forms to use for third-party summonses.

IN THE CIRCUIT COURT FOR DAVIDSON COUNTY, TENNESSEE

WILLIAM F. OLDHAM ,	)	
	)	
Plaintiff,	)	
	)	
vs.	)	
	)	
JAMES A. PIZZINI,	)	
	)	No. _____
Defendant and	)	
Third-Party Plaintiff,	)	
	)	
vs.	)	
	)	
INTERNATIONAL MOTOR COMPANY,	)	
	)	
Third-Party Defendant.	)	

THIRD-PARTY COMPLAINT

FIGURE 2-8. Third Party Caption

SUMMARY

- To calculate time for serving documents, do not include the first day but include the last day unless it is a Saturday, Sunday, or a holiday. If fewer than 11 days (usually 7 days in state cases), exclude the weekends and holidays. Add 3 days if served by mail.

- All documents served after the summons and complaint should have a certificate of service addressed to the opposing attorney.

- A motion to dismiss can be filed before an answer. Some of the reasons for dismissal are lack of jurisdiction over the subject matter, lack of jurisdiction over the person, improper venue, insufficiency of process, insufficiency of service of process, or failure to state a claim on which relief can be granted.

- Many courts require that a supporting affidavit accompany a motion to dismiss, especially on complicated matters.

- For each allegation in the complaint, the answering party must admit the allegations, deny the allegations, or state that he or she is without knowledge or information sufficient to form a belief as to the truth of the allegations.

- An answer to a complaint may include counterclaims alleging that the plaintiff, not the defendant, is responsible for the cause of action.

- An answer to a complaint may have affirmative defenses, which serve as defenses even if the allegations in the complaint are true.

- A cross-claim is between parties on the same side of a case; a counterclaim is between parties on opposing sides.

- A third-party defendant who may be liable for damages can be brought into a case by a defendant. This is accomplished by filing a third-party complaint.

REVIEW EXERCISES

T   F   1. Calculating time is of little importance to the legal secretary as his or her responsibility is only to prepare documents.

T   F   2. A certificate of service is included on all litigation documents prepared after the summons and complaint.

T   F   3. A certificate of service may be double- or single-spaced.

T   F   4. If a complaint was served improperly, it is grounds for filing a motion to dismiss.

T F   5. Lack of jurisdiction over the subject matter means that a case was filed after the deadline.

T F   6. A motion should indicate the date a motion is expected to be heard.

T F   7. In an answer to a complaint, all allegations should be denied.

T F   8. An error on the face of the summons is always unimportant.

T F   9. The attorney signs the affidavit for his or her client.

T F   10. Counterclaims are actions between parties on the same side of a case.

T F   11. An answer to a complaint does not need a caption.

T F   12. Assumption of the risk can be used as an affirmative defense.

T F   13. Affirmative defenses are made in the answer to a complaint before allegations are admitted or denied.

T F   14. The prayer clause is usually not a part of the answer to a complaint.

T F   15. In a third-party complaint, the defendant is also known as the third-party plaintiff.

T F   16. A third-party complaint always requires the judge's approval.

T F   17. A third party being brought into a case is served with a copy of the original complaint, a third-party summons, and third-party complaint.

T F   18. An affidavit is sworn to and signed before a notary public.

TRANSCRIPTION RULES

CAPITALIZATION

Word/Number Sequences

Capitalize word/number sequences, except numbers used with the terms *page* and *paragraph*.

> Book 3368 (refers to the book number where deeds are recorded)
>
> Interrogatory No. 5
>
> Interrogatory 7
>
> Allegation IV
>
> Allegation 4
>
> Room 24
>
> Question 6
>
> page 504
>
> paragraph I
>
> paragraph 1

COMMA

Apposition

An appositive explains the noun or pronoun that precedes it. Use commas to set off (place a comma before and after) a word or words in apposition that are nonessential; do not place commas around the word or words that are essential. In legal documents, a name often appears after the designation "Plaintiff" or "Defendant." If there is only one plaintiff or one defendant in a case, the name is nonessential because the party is fully identified by the word "plaintiff" or "defendant"; however, if there are multiple defendants or plaintiffs, the name is essential to identify which plaintiff or defendant. If the word "the" does not precede the word "Plaintiff" or "Defendant," treat it as a title and do not set it off with commas. In some cases, the writer may be the only one to know whether an appositive is essential.

In a case where William F. Oldham is the plaintiff and James A. Pizzini and Express Delivery Services, Inc., are the defendants, reference to the parties would be as follows:

The Plaintiff, ***WILLIAM F. OLDHAM***, sustained serious and permanent injuries. (Nonessential — there is only one plaintiff.)

Plaintiff WILLIAM F. OLDHAM sustained serious and permanent injuries. (Plaintiff is used as a title.)

Plaintiff OLDHAM sustained serious and permanent injuries. (Plaintiff is used as a title.)

The Defendant *JAMES A. PIZZINI* carelessly and negligently drove his vehicle at a high rate of speed. (Essential — there are two defendants, so the name is necessary to identify which one.)

The Plaintiff, WILLIAM F. OLDHAM, demands judgment against the Defendants, *JAMES A. PIZZINI and EXPRESS DELIVERY SERVICES, INC.* (Nonessential — there are only two defendants, so the names are not necessary to identify the defendants.)

Dependent Clauses — Introductory

A dependent clause has a subject and verb but cannot stand alone as a sentence because it does not express a complete thought. Dependent clauses often begin with words such as the following: if, when, after, as, although, before, since, and unless. Place a comma after an introductory dependent clause.

Although EXPRESS DELIVERY SERVICES, INC., lists an address in the Nashville telephone directory, it maintains no employees or equipment in Tennessee. (Dependent clause beginning with "although.")

Since the Cross-Defendant was an independent contractor at the time and place of the accident, the Cross-Complainant had no control over any of his negligent acts. (Dependent clause beginning with "since.")

Phrases — Introductory

A phrase is a group of two or more words with no subject. Place a comma after an introductory phrase if it has five or more words, if it contains a verb, or if it is an independent comment. If the phrase is short and does not contain a verb form and is not an independent comment, the comma may be omitted. Some writers prefer to place commas after all introductory phrases.

After hearing the decision of the Court, the Plaintiff was devastated. (Contains a verb form.)

For an answer to paragraph I of the Complaint, Defendant admits that the accident occurred on May 21, (current year), about 5 p.m. (Long phrase.)

Of course, the Defendant would show to the Court that the Plaintiff was a licensee. (Short phrase but used as an independent comment; comma not omitted.)

In 19— the Defendant purchased a riding lawn mower. (Short phrase; comma omitted.)

Two Independent Clauses Joined by a Conjunction — No Other Commas

An independent clause has a subject and verb and expresses a complete thought. Place a comma between two independent clauses joined by a conjunction such as *and, but, or,* or *nor.* If the clauses are short and closely related, no comma is needed. If commas appear within either independent clause, a semicolon is placed between the two clauses (see semicolon rule on page 60).

TWO INDEPENDENT CLAUSES JOINED BY A CONJUNCTION — NO OTHER COMMAS

An independent clause has a subject and verb and expresses a complete thought. Place a comma between two independent clauses joined by a conjunction such as *and, but, or,* or *nor.* If both clauses are short and closely related, no comma is needed. If commas appear within either independent clause, a semicolon is placed between the two clauses. (See the semicolon rule below.)

The mower is not an attractive nuisance, and the Defendant did not breach any duty of care owed to the Plaintiff. (Two independent clauses joined by a conjunction)

The Defendant had written a contract and it is sufficient proof. (Short, closely related clauses)

SEMICOLON

Independent Clauses with Commas Joined by a Conjunction

Place a semicolon between two independent clauses joined by a conjunction if either clause contains commas.

Defendant HERMAN SHULMAN denies the allegations in paragraphs 1, 2, 3, and 4; and he demands that the Complaint be dismissed with costs adjudged against the Plaintiff.

WORD DIVISION

Keep the following elements together at the end of a line:

June 29

DALE M. or D. M. (first and middle name or initial; two initials)

7 p.m.

paragraph III

Book 3368

page 504

22d Floor

201 Finch (street number and name)

AL 55201 (Two-letter state code and ZIP code)

Question 15

Interrogatory 12

TRANSCRIPTION EXERCISES

Use a secretarial reference manual and the rules presented in this and the previous chapter to aid you in correctly transcribing the following material. The sentences are presented in lowercase letters without punctuation, as you would hear them on a transcriber.

1. to the best of the defendants knowledge information and belief the deed is recorded in book 1404 page 332 in the registers office for baldwin county alabama

2. his predecessors in title constructed a sewer line through the property and he acquired all rights as an appurtenance to the property owned by him

3. plaintiff avers that on april 4 (current year) defendant emily cunningham did willfully maliciously negligently and recklessly shoot the plaintiff rodney albert and he suffered extensive and severe injuries.

4. after traveling on the pathway for some distance defendant began moving over to the sidewalk because the path was too steep and rough

5. when the court found the cross complainant guilty of negligence the defendant was granted a cross judgment against the cross defendant

6. if the plaintiff was injured as a result of a breach of duty then the breach should be attributed to others who were present and responsible for the child

7. for answer to the complaint filed against him and others the defendant respectfully states to the court as follows

8. on june 29 the mower would not start because the battery was down

9. in my opinion the plaintiff was negligent

10. in preparing for trial the plaintiffs assembled a list of medical bills

11. Insert a diagonal where each of the following expressions can be divided.

   April 14, (current year)

   Dr. Christine Dunbar

   Book 3784, page 14

   605 Peachtree Street

   Atlanta, GA 37892

For exercises 12 through 15, there are three plaintiffs: Dale M. Roehnig, a minor plaintiff, James J. Roehnig, and Linda F. Roehnig; there is one defendant, Herman A. Shulman.

12. the plaintiff james j roehnig helped the defendant start the mower

13. the minor plaintiff dale m roehnig was injured by the blade of the mower

14. this defendant denies that he is responsible for damages to the plaintiffs james j roehnig or linda f roehnig

15. the defendant herman a shulman respectfully demands that this action be dismissed and that costs be adjudged against the plaintiffs dale m roehnig james a roehnig and linda f roehnig

RESEARCH ACTIVITIES

1. Check your state rules to determine the time period within which an answer must be filed.

2. Do your state codes specify exact wording for a certificate of service?

PROJECTS

Insert the cassette tape for Chapter 2 and transcribe the following projects.

Project 2-1   This is the defendant's answer to the personal injury complaint found in Project 1-1, where a child who is a next-door neighbor is injured. The defendant here uses affirmative defenses of contributory negligence on the part of the child's parents. Warner C. Watkins is the attorney for the defendant. The Roehnig case has been assigned the number 93-4281.

Transcribe the answer to complaint for <u>Roehnig v. Shulman</u>.

Identify the parts of the answer to complaint by labeling them in the right margin.

February 1994

S	M	T	W	Th	F	S
		1	2	3	4	5
6	7	8	9	10	11	12
13	14	15	16	17	18	19
20	21	22	23	24	25	26
27	28					

March 1994

S	M	T	W	Th	F	S
		1	2	3	4	5
6	7	8	9	10	11	12
13	14	15	16	17	18	19
20	21	22	23	24	25	26
27	28	29	30	31		

Assume that service was completed on February 2, 1994. What is the last date the answer can be filed if the time expires in 30 days?

Project 2-2   Transcribe the motion to dismiss on behalf of the defendant in <u>Roehnig v. Shulman</u>.

Project 2-3   Transcribe the affidavit to support motion to dismiss on behalf of the defendant in <u>Roehnig v. Shulman</u>.

Project 2-4   This is a case where a sewer line of adjoining businesses is
backing up and causing damage. Guy Dowling (the defendant
herein) owns a restaurant (Steaks and Grits) that is dumping a lot
of grease into the lines. He answers, cross-sues, and countersues.

The attorney for the plaintiffs and other defendants will be dictated
in the certificate of service. The attorney for the defendant Guy
Dowling is David J. Crockett (32251), Crockett, Mathis & Edison,
508 Gulf Shores Trust Building, 2000 Westgate Drive, Gulf
Shores, AL 35721. Phone: (205) 555-6433.

Transcribe the answer, counterclaim, and cross-complaint for
defendant Guy Dowling. The parties are Harry T. Bradley and
Emory Bradley, plaintiffs; and Honey Lou Cartwright, Frank
Bradley, Guy Dowling, Gulf Shores Gas Company, and William O.
Sims, defendants. Mr. J. B. Merry, Jr., represents Gulf Shores Gas
Company and William O. Sims. The case is Civil Action No.
G3233P.

CHAPTER 3

DISCOVERY/JUDGMENT

OBJECTIVES

When you successfully complete this chapter, you will be able to:

➤ Transcribe interrogatories and answers to interrogatories

➤ Transcribe a request for admissions

➤ Transcribe a request for production

➤ Prepare a subpoena for taking a deposition

➤ Transcribe a notice of taking deposition

➤ Transcribe a final judgment

As we continue our discussion of litigation, this chapter focuses on the methods used by the plaintiff's attorney and the defendant's attorney to gather information about a case. This process is referred to as **discovery.** Documents for four methods of discovery (interrogatories, request for admissions, depositions, and request for production) and the final judgment will be presented in this chapter.

You will learn to prepare the documents shown in the box on page 66 as we follow the case of <u>McGowan vs. Sleepwear Manufacturing, Inc.</u> where John McGowan, a minor, was injured when wearing pajamas that did not meet federal flammability standards. The case is filed for John McGowan by Mark McGowan, his father and next friend, against Sleepwear Manufacturing, Inc. This case is filed in the United States District Court, Cleveland Division, for the Northern District of Ohio.

INTERROGATORIES

ANSWERS TO INTERROGATORIES

REQUEST FOR ADMISSIONS

ANSWERS TO REQUEST FOR ADMISSIONS

SUBPOENA FOR DEPOSITION

NOTICE OF TAKING DEPOSITION

REQUEST FOR PRODUCTION

ANSWERS TO REQUEST FOR PRODUCTION

FINAL JUDGMENT

INTERROGATORIES

INTERROGATORIES

Written questions about a case submitted by one side of the lawsuit to the other.

Interrogatories are written questions about a case submitted by one side of the lawsuit to the other. All discovery documents, including interrogatories, can be served on the plaintiff by the defendant or on the defendant by the plaintiff.

Refer to Figures 3-1 and 3-2 as you examine the interrogatories issued on behalf of the McGowans, the plaintiffs, to Sleepwear Manufacturing, Inc., the defendant.

Caption — The caption on the interrogatories indicates that the lawsuit is filed on behalf of John McGowan, the minor child, by his father and next friend, Mark McGowan.

TO or Address Line — An optional line that some attorneys include is the name and identification of the party to whom the interrogatories are being addressed and/or the name and address of the attorney. Examples are:

TO: SLEEPWEAR MANUFACTURING, INC., Defendant
     ROY A. CHAFFIN, Defendant's Attorney

                              or

TO: Mr. ROY A. CHAFFIN
     Attorney for Defendant
     1824 Cypress Street
     Cleveland, OH 84212

                              or

TO: JOHN J. McGOWAN, Plaintiff, through his attorney, JANICE MOSS

**IN THE UNITED STATES DISTRICT COURT
FOR THE NORTHERN DISTRICT OF OHIO
CLEVELAND DIVISION**

JOHN J. McGOWAN, a Minor,   )
by MARK McGOWAN, his Father)
and Next Friend,   )
)
      Plaintiffs,   )
vs.   )   Civil No. 92 C 288
)
SLEEPWEAR MANUFACTURING, INC.,)
)
      Defendant.   )

FIRST SET OF INTERROGATORIES

TO: Mr. ROY A. CHAFFIN
      Attorney for Defendant
      1824 Cypress Street
      Cleveland, OH 84212

COMES NOW the Plaintiff JOHN J. McGOWAN through his attorney and propounds the following interrogatories to the Defendant, SLEEPWEAR MANUFACTURING, INC., pursuant to Rule 33 of the Federal Rules of Civil Procedure:

1. Please state your name, address, and the position you hold with SLEEPWEAR MANUFACTURING, INC.

    ANSWER:

2. Did your company manufacture and sell sleepwear designed for children on or before January 1, (four years ago)?

    ANSWER:

3. Did your company manufacture and sell sleepwear bearing the name/code designation "140 Series" on or before January 1, (four years ago)?

    ANSWER:

FIGURE 3-1. Interrogatories, Page 1

18. Did your company have any express warranties that were given to the general public concerning the products manufactured by your company?

ANSWER:

19. If your answer to Interrogatory 18 is yes, state the express warranties.

ANSWER:

Answers to the above questions should be mailed to the Plaintiffs' attorney at the following address:

_____

JANICE MOSS
Attorney for Plaintiffs
2400 Broadway
Cleveland, OH 84210
(712) 555-4729

CERTIFICATE

I hereby certify that a true and exact copy of the foregoing First Set of Interrogatories has been forwarded by first-class, U.S. mail to Mr. ROY A. CHAFFIN, Attorney for Defendant, 1824 Cypress Street, Cleveland, OH 84212, this the ___ day of _____, (current year).

_____

JANICE MOSS

- 4 -

FIGURE 3-2. Interrogatories, Last Page

Opening Paragraph — For cases filed in the federal court, as in the McGowan case, the opening paragraph often states that "Pursuant to Rules 33 and 34 of the *Federal Rules of Civil Procedure*, the questions are being propounded (set forth)." For state courts, reference would be made to the state rules.

Questions — Each question is numbered and questions are spaced so as to allow room for answers. Court rules often limit the number of questions so the answering party does not have an excessive number of questions to answer.

The questions in the McGowan interrogatories are centered around the company's knowledge of manufacturing and selling sleepwear that did not meet flammability standards.

Signature Block — For these interrogatories, a signature block is prepared for the attorney who represents the plaintiff. The attorney's number does not appear on the interrogatories because this document is filed in a federal court.

Certificate of Service — The certificate states that the interrogatories have been mailed to the attorney for the defendant. The legal secretary should note in the tickler file the date the response is due, usually 30 days after service of the interrogatories.

ANSWERS TO INTERROGATORIES

Interrogatories are to be answered by the party who receives them, usually within 30 days after service or 45 days if served with the summons and complaint. Each and every question is to be addressed — with an answer or an objection. If the attorney objects to any question, a reason for the objection is given as an answer. The questions may by answered on the original set of interrogatories, or the questions and the answers may be rekeyed.

Federal court rules and many state rules require that the answering party answer the question under oath. An oath stating that the answers are true, also called a **verification**, is included for the answering party to sign. It is placed after the signature block for the attorney and before the certificate of service. Some states do not require the notary public's seal and signature and may call the statement a **declaration** rather than a verification. To convert the verification shown in Figure 3-3 to a declaration, (1) change the wording in the first paragraph to "I declare under penalty of perjury" and (2) delete the jurat.

The attorney signs the answers to interrogatories and any objections, and the client signs the verification or declaration.

Answers to interrogatories have a caption, "To" or address line, questions with answers, signature block for the answering party's attorney, verification for the answering party, and certificate of service to the opposing attorney.

VERIFICATION

A statement under oath as to the correctness and truthfulness of a matter. The statement is made before a notary public.

DECLARATION

A statement similar to a verification. The statement is not made before a notary public. Some states call complaints declarations.

REQUEST FOR ADMISSIONS

When there are certain facts about a case the attorney does not want to waste court time proving, he or she can request that the opposing party admit to those

STATE OF _____)

COUNTY OF _____)

        I, (answering party's name), after being duly sworn state as follows:

        I have read the response made to (Plaintiff's or Defendant's) First Set of Interrogatories, and the responses thereto are true to the best of my knowledge, information, and belief.

_____

(Name of Authorized Individual)

Sworn to and subscribed before me
this the _____ day of _____, (current year).

_____

NOTARY PUBLIC

My commission expires: _____

FIGURE 3-3. Verification for Answers to Interrogatories

REQUEST FOR ADMISSIONS

A document requesting the party on the opposing side of a case to admit or deny certain listed statements.

facts before the trial. The document, **request for admissions**, is used to list those facts. The opposing party is then requested to admit the facts. As the case goes to trial, all statements admitted will be assumed to be fact.

Refer to Figures 3-4 and 3-5, as you examine the request for admissions served on Sleepwear Manufacturing, Inc., the defendant, by John J. McGowan, the plaintiff. Sleepwear Manufacturing is asked to admit statements about the dates certain pajamas were manufactured, flammability tests that were conducted, its knowledge of flammability problems, and the dates any warnings were given to customers.

As you review the request for admissions, observe the format. The document has a caption, "To" or address line, facts to be admitted, prompts where responses can be inserted, a signature block for the attorney requesting the admissions, and a certificate of service to the opposing attorney.

ANSWERS TO REQUEST FOR ADMISSIONS

Responses to request for admissions are to be made within a stipulated period of time, usually 30 days after service or 45 days if served with the summons and complaint.

Each statement can be addressed in one of three ways: with an admission, a denial, or an objection with reasons. The answering party may not give lack of information or knowledge as a reason for not answering unless it is stated that reasonable inquiry was made and that there is insufficient information with which

IN THE UNITED STATES DISTRICT COURT
FOR THE NORTHERN DISTRICT OF OHIO
CLEVELAND DIVISION

JOHN J. McGOWAN, a Minor,)	
by MARK McGOWAN, his Father)	
and Next Friend,)	
)	
Plaintiffs,)	
)	Civil No. 92 C 288
vs.)	
)	
SLEEPWEAR MANUFACTURING, INC.,)	
)	
Defendant.)	

REQUEST FOR ADMISSIONS

TO: Mr. ROY A. CHAFFIN
Attorney for Defendant
1824 Cypress Street
Cleveland, OH 84212

Set Tab ↗ ← Single Spaced

Plaintiff JOHN J. McGOWAN requests through his attorney, JANICE MOSS, that the Defendant, SLEEPWEAR MANUFACTURING, INC., admit the truth of the following facts pursuant to the Federal Rules of Civil Procedure. Plaintiff requests that all of the following facts be admitted within thirty (30) days after service of this Request for Admissions for the purpose of being introduced into the trial of this matter.

1. The Defendant, SLEEPWEAR MANUFACTURING, INC., on or before January 6, (four years ago), manufactured cotton sleepwear for children, more commonly known as pajamas.

RESPONSE:

2. The Defendant before and after January 6, (four years ago), manufactured a particular brand commercially known as "Jammies" marked with "140 Series."

RESPONSE:

3. Before January 6, (four years ago), the Defendant filed with the Federal Trade Commission under the Federal Flammable Fabrics Act, a Continuing Guaranty No. 38776 for "140 Series" fabric.

RESPONSE:

4. On and after January 6, (four years ago), the Defendant conducted a series of tests to determine the flammability of "140 Series," and those tests were made in conformity with the Department of Commerce Commercial Standard 884-29.

RESPONSE:

5. After testing as stated in Request No. 4 above, the Defendant began treating their cotton sleepwear pajama "140 Series" with flame retardant chemicals.

RESPONSE:

Double spaced
1. a. b. c. } indent 5

FIGURE 3-4. Request for Admissions, Page 1

6. Before January 6, (four years ago), the Defendant had performed no tests or studies to determine the characteristic or ease of ignition of "140 series."

RESPONSE:

7. Before January 6, (four years ago), the Defendant had performed no tests or studies as to how quickly heat transfers from "140 Series" to the human skin.

RESPONSE:

8. It was technologically feasible for the Defendant to produce a flame retardant cotton material before January 6, (four years ago).

RESPONSE:

9. Before January 6, (four years ago). Defendant knew that a flammable cotton product manufactured to be worn by children was a particular problem.

RESPONSE:

10. Before January 6, (four years ago), Defendant never warned the general public nor any of its consumers who had purchased "140 Series" of the dangers inherent in its product.

RESPONSE:

11. After January 6, (four years ago), the Defendant began warning consumers of the flammability and combustibility hazard in "140 Series."

RESPONSE:

12. The "140 Series" sleepwear manufactured after January 6, (four years ago), had the same appearance, texture, and finish as that manufactured before January 6, (four years ago), except that the fabric "140 Series" manufactured before January 6, (four years ago), had not been treated with the flame retardant THPC.

RESPONSE:

_____
JANICE MOSS
Attorney for Plaintiffs
2400 Broadway
Cleveland, OH 84210
(712) 555-4729

CERTIFICATE

I hereby certify that a true and exact copy of the foregoing Request for Admissions has been forwarded by first-class, U.S. mail to Mr. ROY A. CHAFFIN, Attorney for Defendant, 1824 Cypress Street, Cleveland, OH 84212, this the _____ day of _____, (current year).

 2010

_____
JANICE MOSS

- 2 -

FIGURE 3-5. Request for Admissions, Page 2

to answer. If there is no response to a statement, the courts interpret that lack of response as an admission.

Answers to a request for admissions are usually signed by the attorney and verified by the client.

The answers to the request for admissions for <u>McGowan v. Sleepwear Manufacturing, Inc.</u>, are shown in Figures 3-6 and 3-7. Compare this document with Figures 3-4 and 3-5. Look at each statement in the request and note the answer to that request. A verification for the answering party has been added and names in the signature blocks and certificates of service have been reversed.

SUBPOENA FOR DEPOSITION

A **subpoena** is a document that commands a witness to appear and give sworn testimony at a given time and place. The out-of-court testimony is taken in question-and-answer format and is known as a **deposition**. Attorneys for both sides, the person being questioned, and a court reporter (who records the testimony word for word) are present at the deposition. Depositions can be taken of parties to the lawsuit or of witnesses.

A subpoena form is available from the clerk of the court. Each one provides essentially the same information, but arrangement of the data varies from one court to another.

Refer to Figure 3-8, a subpoena in the <u>McGowan</u> case commanding Barbara Ann York to appear and testify on behalf of the plaintiff. The subpoena is on a preprinted form for the United States District Courts. As you read the form, note that it can be used to subpoena a witness to appear and testify in court or appear for the taking of a deposition, as well as command that the witness produce and permit inspection and copying of documents or objects listed on the form.

Three copies of the subpoena should be prepared — one to be served on the witness, one to be filed with the clerk, and one for the office files. Blanks are provided for entering the venue of the court, case number, the style of the case, the name and address of the witness, and the place, date, and time for taking the testimony. If the witness is to produce documents, the items should be listed on the subpoena. Once the copies have been prepared, they are taken to the clerk of the court to be officially issued, after which a copy is personally served on the witness.

NOTICE OF TAKING DEPOSITION

The purpose of a notice of taking deposition is to notify parties to a lawsuit that a deposition has been scheduled. It states the name of the person who is to be deposed, where and when the deposition will take place, items to be brought to the deposition, and other relevant details.

SUBPOENA

A command to appear at a certain time and a certain place to give testimony.

DEPOSITION

Question and answer testimony taken under oath out of court and usually recorded by a court reporter.

NOTICE OF TAKING A DEPOSITION

A document notifying parties of the time, date, and place of taking a deposition.

**IN THE UNITED STATES DISTRICT COURT
FOR THE NORTHERN DISTRICT OF OHIO
CLEVELAND DIVISION**

JOHN J. McGOWAN, a Minor,	)	
by MARK McGOWAN, his Father	)	
and Next Friend,	)	
	)	
Plaintiffs,	)	
	)	Civil No. 92 C 288
vs.	)	
	)	
SLEEPWEAR MANUFACTURING, INC.,	)	
	)	
Defendant.	)	

ANSWERS TO REQUEST FOR ADMISSIONS

TO: Ms. JANICE MOSS
      Attorney for Plaintiffs
      2400 Broadway
      Cleveland, OH 84210

        In answer to your Request for Admissions to the genuineness of certain documents in the above-styled litigation and pursuant to Rules 26 and 36 of the <u>Federal Rules of Civil Procedure</u>, the Defendant, SLEEPWEAR MANUFACTURING, INC., answers as follows:

        1. Defendant admits.

        2. Defendant admits.

        3. Defendant admits.

        4. Defendant admits.

        5. Defendant admits.

        6. Defendant denies and demands strictest proof thereof.

        7. Defendant denies and demands strictest proof thereof.

        8. Reasonable inquiry was made and there is not sufficient knowledge to admit nor deny.

        9. Defendant denies.

FIGURE 3-6. Answers to Request for Admissions, Page 1

10. Defendant denies and would show that the general public was warned through disclaimers in advertisements.

11. Defendant admits.

12. Defendant admits.

ROY A. CHAFFIN
Attorney for Defendant
1824 Cypress Street
Cleveland, OH 84212
(712) 555-9277

STATE OF OHIO   )

COUNTY OF COOPER)

    I, HARRY A. DAVENPORT, being first duly sworn, make oath that the foregoing answers are true to the best of my knowledge, information, and belief. Signed this the 12th day of July, (current year).   ←———— Verification

Representative for Sleepwear
           Manufacturing, Inc.   HARRY A. DAVENPORT

Sworn to and subscribed before me,
this the _____ day of July, (current year).

_____
NOTARY PUBLIC

My Commission Expires: _____

CERTIFICATE

    I hereby certify that a copy of the foregoing Answers to Request for Admissions was mailed or hand delivered to Ms. JANICE MOSS, Attorney for Plaintiffs, 2400 Broadway, Cleveland, OH 84210, on this the _____ day of July, (current year).

ROY A. CHAFFIN

- 2 -

FIGURE 3-7. Answers to Request for Admissions, Page 2

AO 88 (Rev. 11/91) Subpoena in a Civil Case

United States District Court

NORTHERN _____ DISTRICT OF _____ OHIO

JOHN J. McGOWEN, a Minor,
by MARK McGOWAN, his Father
and Next Friend,
      Plaintiffs,
        v.
SLEEPWEAR MANUFACTURING, INC.,
      Defendant

SUPOENA IN A CIVIL CASE

CASE NUMBER:

TO: Ms. BARBARA ANN YORK
905 Wood Crest Circle
Cleveland, OH 84209

☐ **YOU ARE COMMANDED** to appear in the United States District Court at the place, date, and time specified below to testify in the above case.

PLACE OF TESTIMONY	COURTROOM
	DATE AND TIME

☒ **YOU ARE COMMANDED** to appear at the place, date, and time specified below to testify at the taking of a deposition in the above case.

PLACE OF DEPOSITION	DATE AND TIME
The office of Janice Moss 2400 Broadway Cleveland, OH 84210	October 24, (current year) 4 p.m.

☐ **YOU ARE COMMANDED** to produce and permit inspection and copying the following documents or objects at the place, date, and time specified below (list documents or objects):

PLACE	DATE AND TIME

☐ **YOU ARE COMMANDED** to permit inspection of the following premises at the date and time specified below.

PREMISES	DATE AND TIME

       Any organization not a party to this suit that is subpoenaed for the taking of a deposition shall designate one or more officers, directors, or managing agents, or other persons who consent to testify on its behalf, and may set forth, for each person designated, the matters on which the person will testify. Federal Rules of Civil Procedure, 30(b)(6).

ISSUING OFFICER SIGNATURE AND TITLE (INDICATE IF ATTORNEY FOR PLAINTIFF OR DEFENDANT)	DATE
Attorney for Plaintiffs	October 14, (current year)

ISSUING OFFICER'S NAME, ADDRESS AND PHONE NUMBER
JANICE MOSS, Esq.
2400 Broadway, Cleveland, OH 84210   (712) 555-4729

(See Rule 45, Federal Rules of Civil Procedure, Parts C & D on Reverse)

FIGURE 3-8. U.S. Subpoena in a Civil Case

Refer to Figure 3-9 as you examine the notice of deposition in the McGowan case. It has a caption, "To" or address line, body, signature block and certificate of service. The attorney for the opposing side is notified when the deposition of Barbara Ann York is to be taken at the law office of the attorney for the plaintiff and will continue from day to day until completed. The attorney who scheduled the deposition, Janice Moss, signed the notice.

REQUEST FOR PRODUCTION

A party can make a request to inspect any item related and relevant to the case, to make copies of documents, to test samples, and to inspect, measure, or survey land. The document to make that request is a **request for production**.

In the body of the document, the request must describe each item desired to be inspected, copied, or tested and request a reasonable time, place, and method for doing so.

Examine the content and format of Figure 3-10, a request for production, in the case of Rodriquez v. Dow Corning, Inc. The plaintiff is requesting that the defendant produce examples of the implant device.

REQUEST FOR PRODUCTION

A document requesting the opposing side of the case to produce documents or things relevant to the case for inspection, copying, etc.

ANSWERS TO REQUEST FOR PRODUCTION OF DOCUMENTS

After a request for production of documents or things is received, either the items are produced to be copied or inspected as requested then or a response objecting to the production is drawn up and served on the attorney making the request. If the latter, the attorney who initiated the request files a motion to compel the party to produce the item. A judge denies or grants the motion.

FINAL JUDGMENT

A **final judgment** is the official final decision of a jury or judge in a case brought before it. The judge generally asks the successful or prevailing attorney to prepare the final judgment; otherwise, it is prepared and entered by the clerk of the court or the judge's secretary.

Examine the final judgment in the case of Oldham v. Pizzini, shown in Figures 3-11 and 3-12. The judgment has the standard caption plus the following elements.

Body — The body of the judgment usually consists of two paragraphs, with the first telling what the jury or judge decided and the second stating the order of the court. The words ORDERED, ADJUDGED, AND DECREED; IT IS

IN THE UNITED STATES DISTRICT COURT
FOR THE NORTHERN DISTRICT OF OHIO
CLEVELAND DIVISION

JOHN J. McGOWAN, a Minor,   )
by MARK McGOWAN, his Father)
and Next Friend,   )
)
      Plaintiffs,   )
)   Civil No. 92 C 288
vs.   )
)
SLEEPWEAR MANUFACTURING, INC.,)
)
      Defendant.   )

NOTICE OF TAKING DEPOSITION

TO: Mr. ROY A. CHAFFIN
      Attorney for Defendant
      1824 Cypress Street
      Cleveland, OH 84212

      Please take notice that at 4 p.m. on Thursday, October 24, (current year), at the law office of Ms. JANICE MOSS, 2400 Broadway, Cleveland, OH 84210, the Plaintiff in the above-captioned case, by and through his attorney, will take the deposition by oral examination of Ms. BARBARA ANN YORK pursuant to Rule 30 et seq. of the Federal Rules of Civil Procedure before a Notary Public for the State of Ohio, who is duly authorized by law to administer oaths.

      The deposition examination will continue from day to day until completed, and you are invited to attend and cross-examine.

                                          _____

                                        JANICE MOSS
                                        Attorney for Plaintiffs
                                        2400 Broadway
                                        Cleveland, OH 84210
                                        (712) 555-4729

CERTIFICATE

      I hereby certify that a true and exact copy of the foregoing Notice of Taking Deposition has been forwarded by first-class, U.S. mail to Mr. ROY A CHAFFIN, Attorney for Defendant, 1824 Cypress Street, Cleveland, OH 84212, this the _____ day of _____, (current year).

                                        _____

                                        JANICE MOSS

FIGURE 3-9. Notice of Taking Deposition

IN THE UNITED STATES DISTRICT COURT
FOR THE NORTHERN DISTRICT OF OHIO
CLEVELAND DIVISION

JOHN J. McGOWAN, a Minor,
by MARK McGOWAN, his Father
and Next Friend,
 	
       Plaintiffs,
 	
vs.
 	
SLEEPWEAR MANUFACTURING, INC.,
 	
       Defendant.
	)
	)
	)
	)
	)
	) Civil No. 92 C 288
	)
	)
	)
	)
	)

REQUEST FOR PRODUCTION

TO: JANICE E. MOSS
     Attorney for Plaintiffs
     2400 Broadway
     Cleveland, OH 44121

       Pursuant to Rule 34 of the <u>Federal Rules of Civil Procedure</u>, the Defendants request that the Plaintiffs produce the following within thirty (30) days of the date of this Request for Production: the pajamas that JOHN McGOWAN, the minor, was wearing at the time of the injury in question for the purpose of conducting a chemical analysis and testing, which might result in the destruction of a small portion thereof.

       Said pajamas shall be delivered to the office of the attorney for the Defendant, ROY A. CHAFFIN, 1824 Cypress Street, Cleveland, OH 84212.

                           _____
                           ROY A. CHAFFIN
                           Attorney for Defendant
                           1824 Cypress Street
                           Cleveland, OH 84212
                           (712) 555-1277

CERTIFICATE

       I hereby certify that a true and exact copy of the foregoing Request for Production has been forwarded by first-class, U.S. mail to Ms. JANICE MOSS, 2400 Broadway, Cleveland, OH 44121, this the _____ day of _____, (current year).

                           _____
                           ROY A. CHAFFIN

FIGURE 3-10. Request for Production

**IN THE UNITED STATES DISTRICT COURT
FOR THE NORTHERN DISTRICT OF OHIO
CLEVELAND DIVISION**

JOHN J. McGOWAN, a Minor, by MARK McGOWAN, his Father and Next Friend,) Plaintiffs,) vs.) SLEEPWEAR MANUFACTURING, INC.) Defendant.)	No. C-20886

Caption

FINAL JUDGMENT

This cause came on to be heard on the 14th day of December, 1994, before the Honorable BEVERLY K. LATHAM, Judge of the United States District Court for the Northern District of Ohio; and in attendance were the Plaintiffs and the Defendant, their attorneys, and a jury of good and lawful citizens who, being duly elected, impaneled, and sworn to well and truly try the issues joined between the Plaintiffs and the Defendant, heard the evidence and arguments of counsel, were duly charged and instructed by the Court, retired to consider their verdict, and after due deliberation, returned a verdict in favor of the Plaintiff, JOHN J. McGOWAN, a minor, compensatory damages in the amount of Seventy-five Thousand Dollars ($75,000) and punitive damages in the amount of Twenty-five Thousand Dollars ($25,000) and Plaintiff MARK McGOWAN, as Father and Next Friend, compensatory damages in the amount of Nine Thousand Seven Hundred Forty-eight Dollars ($9,748) for a total of One Hundred Nine Thousand Seven Hundred Forty-eight Dollars ($109,748).

Order of the Court

IT IS THEREFORE ORDERED, ADJUDGED, AND DECREED by the Court that the Plaintiff JOHN J. McGOWAN, a minor, have and recover of the Defendant, SLEEPWEAR MANUFACTURING, INC., compensatory damages in the amount of Seventy-five Thousand Dollars ($75,000) and punitive damages in the amount of Twenty-five thousand Dollars ($25,000) and Plaintiff MARK McGOWAN have and recover compensatory damages in the amount of Nine Thousand Seven Hundred Forty-eight Dollars ($9,748) and the costs of this cause, all of which execution issue if need be.

Date of Entry of Judgment

ENTERED this the ____ day of December, (current year).

Signature Line for the Judge

BEVERLY K. LATHAM, JUDGE

FIGURE 3-11. Final Judgment, Page 1

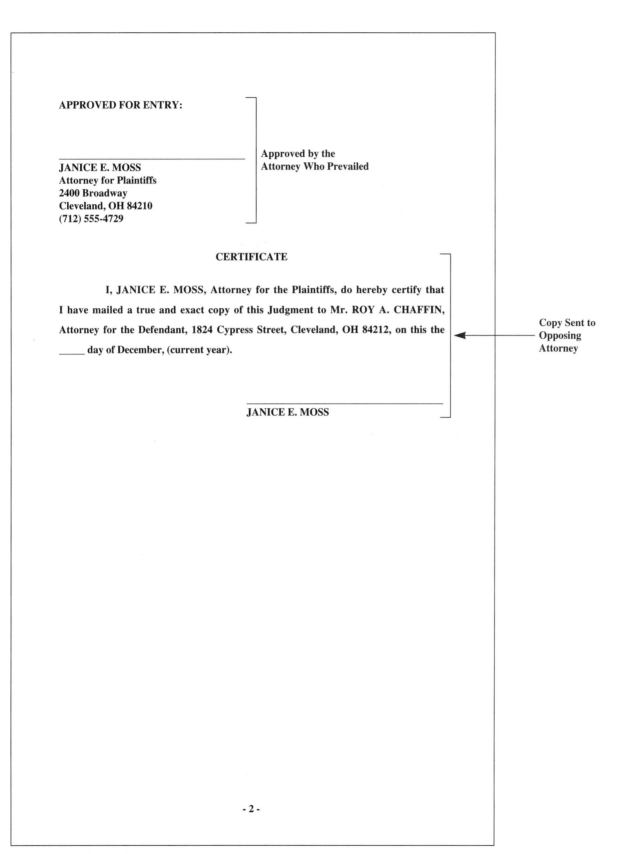

APPROVED FOR ENTRY:

—————————————————————
JANICE E. MOSS
Attorney for Plaintiffs
2400 Broadway
Cleveland, OH 84210
(712) 555-4729

Approved by the
Attorney Who Prevailed

CERTIFICATE

I, JANICE E. MOSS, Attorney for the Plaintiffs, do hereby certify that I have mailed a true and exact copy of this Judgment to Mr. ROY A. CHAFFIN, Attorney for the Defendant, 1824 Cypress Street, Cleveland, OH 84212, on this the _____ day of December, (current year).

Copy Sent to
Opposing
Attorney

—————————————————————
JANICE E. MOSS

- 2 -

FIGURE 3-12. Final Judgment, Page 2

FURTHER ORDERED, ADJUDGED AND DECREED; IT APPEARING TO THE COURT, and similar phrases at the beginnings of paragraphs are typed in full capitals. The last paragraph of the body is "Entered this the _____ day of _____, (current year)."

In the <u>McGowan</u> case, the judge ruled in favor of the minor plaintiff, John J. McGowan, in the total amount of $100,000 and Mark McGowan, as father and next friend, in the amount of $9,748. Some of the damages are compensatory, which means they are actual losses; others are punitive, which means they are awarded for punishment to the defendant for negligent actions.

Signature — A signature line beginning at center point is included with the judge's name and the word JUDGE typed below it. It is a good practice to include the judge's name, if known, in full caps. After service of a copy of the judgment on the attorney for the defendant, and provided there is no objection within the required number of days, the judge before whom the case was heard signs the judgment.

Approved for Entry — The APPROVED FOR ENTRY: section is placed after the judge's signature on the judgment and provides a place for Janice Moss, the attorney for the plaintiff, to sign to indicate that she is satisfied with the contents of the judgment and is ready for it to be entered into the record.

Certificate of Service — Since Janice Moss, the attorney for the plaintiff, won the case, she prepared the final judgment and mailed a copy to Roy A. Chaffin, the opposing attorney. If Mr. Chaffin had objections to the wording or content of the final judgment, he would have filed a document specifying his reasons for objecting.

SUMMARY

- Interrogatories, requests for admissions, depositions, and requests for production are discovery devices used to gather information about a case prior to the trial.

- Discovery documents can be served by the plaintiff on the defendant or by the defendant on the plaintiff.

- Interrogatories are written questions about a case submitted by one side of the lawsuit to the other.

- Each interrogatory is numbered, with space provided for an answer.

- A "To" or address line can be inserted after the document title on discovery documents.

- A request for admissions contains written statements about a case, which can be admitted or denied by the opposing party.

- A deposition is sworn testimony of a party or witness, in the presence of counsel for both sides, taken by a court reporter.

- A subpoena is a document commanding a person to appear and give testimony at the stated time and place.

- A notice of taking deposition notifies parties to a lawsuit that a deposition has been scheduled.

- A deposition is sworn question-and-answer testimony taken out of court and recorded word for word.

- The party who answers interrogatories or a request for admissions signs a verification or declaration.

- A final judgment is an official decision of a court in a case heard before it. The prevailing attorney usually prepares the judgment.

REVIEW EXERCISES

T   F   1.   Interrogatories are always to be answered within 20 days after service of the summons and complaint.

T   F   2.   Answers to interrogatories are under oath.

T   F   3.   A verification is also called an oath.

T   F   4.   The answering party signs answers to the request for admissions and the attorney signs the verification.

T F   5. Only the defendant's attorney can serve interrogatories.

T F   6. The "To" or address line is always required on discovery documents.

T F   7. Requests for admissions are written questions about a case submitted by one side of a lawsuit to the other.

T F   8. Attorneys can take depositions of either the plaintiff or the defendant.

T F   9. Attorneys for both sides, the witness, and a court reporter should attend a deposition.

T F   10. A subpoena is used to command attendance of a witness at a deposition.

T F   11. If a subpoena lists items to bring to the deposition, those items would not be identified in the notice.

T F   12. A notice is addressed to the attorney for the opposing party.

T F   13. The secretary should prepare at least two copies of a subpoena.

T F   14. The judge before whom a case is heard signs the judgment.

TRANSCRIPTION RULES

CAPITALIZATION

Court

Capitalize the word "Court" when it refers to the Judge. Also capitalize Court when used with the official name of a tribunal.

It is ordered by the *Court* that the Plaintiff recover compensatory damages.

The Honorable BETTY C. TRAUBER is Judge of the *Circuit Court* of Davidson County.

Phrases in Full Caps

Use full caps on the following expressions, which introduce paragraphs:

ENTERED

IT IS THEREFORE ORDERED, ADJUDGED, AND DECREED

COMMA

Addresses

Set off the elements of an address with commas if used within a sentence. The two-letter state code may be used if a ZIP code is included.

The law firm is located at *2800 Wallace Road, Nashville, Tennessee.*

The law firm is located at *2800 Wallace Road, Nashville, TN 37000.*

Dates

Set off the year with commas when used with a month and day. If the day precedes the month, add *d*, *th*, or *st* to the day. No commas are needed when referring to a month and year with no day.

On *June 27, 19 –,* the Defendant was the registered owner of a Ford truck.

On the *27th day of June, 19 –,* the Defendant was the registered owner of a Ford truck.

It was *June 19 –* when the accident occurred.

Elliptical Expressions

Elliptical expressions have key words (usually subject and verb) omitted. The expression "If possible," is interpreted to mean "if it is possible"; and the expression "If so," is interpreted to mean "if it is so." If the elliptical expression precedes an independent clause, place a comma after the elliptical expressions, treating it as an introductory dependent clause.

If so, what is the nature of his physical condition?

State whether a prognosis has been made by anyone; and **if so,** state the prognosis, when made, and by whom made. (The elliptical expression precedes the second independent clause.)

Geographic Locations

Separate geographic locations with commas. Set off the name of the state when used with the city.

He is a resident of the *City of Nashville, County of Davidson, State of Tennessee.*

The principal places of business are Nashville, *Tennessee,* and Paducah, *Kentucky.*

Jr. and Sr.

If a person prefers a comma before Jr. or Sr. in his name, also place a comma after Jr. unless it is the end of a sentence. If a person does not use a comma before Jr. or Sr., the comma after Jr. or Sr. is omitted.

Send the Answers to Interrogatories to J. B. Merry, *Jr.* (Individual writes his name with a comma before Jr.)

Send the Answers to Interrogatories to J. B. Merry *Jr.* (Individual writes his name without a comma before Jr.)

Ask J. B. Merry, *Jr.,* to review the documents before they are placed in the mail. (Individual writes his name with a comma — the sentence continues, so a comma is placed after Jr.)

Phrases within a Sentence — Interrupting

Set off phrases that interrupt the flow of a sentence.

He still has some thickening, *some residual thickening,* of the tissue on the great toe. (nonessential)

Would you please tell, *for the jury,* the purpose of the operation? (interrupting)

Series

Set off three or more items in a series with commas.

In attendance were *the Plaintiffs, the Defendant, their attorneys,* and *a jury of good and lawful citizens.* (four items in a series)

TRANSCRIPTION EXERCISES

Use a secretarial reference manual and the rules presented in this and the previous chapters to aid you in correctly transcribing the following material. The sentences are presented in lowercase letters without punctuation, as you would hear them on a transcriber.

1. this cause came on to be heard on the 23d day of november (current year) before the honorable betty c trauber judge of the circuit court of davidson county tennessee

2. i have sent a copy of the documents to mr warner c watkins, 1612 14th avenue north nashville tn 37201

3. i have sent a copy of the documents to mr warner c watkins, 1612 14th avenue north nashville tennessee

4. the interrogatories are being mailed on this the 25th day of june (current year)

5. the interrogatories were mailed on june 25 (current year)

6. state whether the ill effects from the accident have been diagnosed by a physician and if so state the diagnosis and the doctor who made the diagnosis

7. if so provide the name and address of the doctor who gave the advice

8. state your criminal record if any and the nature date and place of the arrest

9. state your gross income for (4 years ago) (3 years ago) (2 years ago) and (1 year ago)

10. state whether you will authorize a member of our law firm to obtain at our expense copies of your tax returns

11. to the best of this defendants knowledge information and belief the rights to the sewer line were acquired around 1970

12. (Mr. Mills writes his name without a comma) the sewer line was constructed by a plumber under contract with william n mills jr whose deed of record is in book 1404 page 332

RESEARCH ACTIVITIES

1. Obtain a copy of the subpoena form used by your local state and federal courts.

2. What is the time period for answering interrogatories, request for admissions, and request for production of documents and things in your local courts?

3. Does your state use a verification or declaration on answers to interrogatories?

PROJECTS

Insert the cassette tape for Chapter 3 and transcribe the following projects.

Project 3-1   This case is a personal injury case where the defendant as well as the plaintiff was injured in an automobile accident. In this set of interrogatories, the plaintiff's attorney is asking questions about the medical condition of the defendant to determine loss of earnings for being out of work.

The attorney for the plaintiff is F. Bryant Silver (No. 84882), Silver and Associates, West 23d Street, New York, NY 10020. Phone: (212) 555-8673. The attorney for the defendant is Emily P. Hill-North, 1492 Avenue of the Americas, New York, NY 10020. Phone: (212) 555-6222. The case number is 93C-2550.

Transcribe the interrogatories for the case of Lewis A. Metterick, Plaintiff, vs. Libby R. Leverette, Defendant. The case is filed in the Supreme Court of the State of New York, County of New York.

Project 3-2   Transcribe the answers to interrogatories in Bradley v. Cartwright et al. This is the same case as Project 2-4. Guy Dowling is answering interrogatories sent to him by other defendants in the case.

Include the following parts in the answers to interrogatories: caption, body, attorney's signature block, verification by Guy Dowling, jurat, certificate of service.

Project 3-3   This case is a medical malpractice case where a doctor who operated on the plaintiff prescribed codeine without inquiring whether the plaintiff was allergic to it.

The attorney for the plaintiff is Hardy W. Dearborn (No. 33266). 342 Wallace Boulevard, Suite 401, New Orleans, LA 70119. Phone: (504) 555-3911. The attorney for the defendant is Mr. Marice F. LaQuay, Saint Stephens Memorial Hospital, 632 Third Street, New Orleans, Louisiana 70124. Phone: (504) 555-1288.

Transcribe the request for admissions for the case of Leon D. Picknard, Plaintiff, v. Saint Stephens Memorial Hospital, Allen E. Finch, et al., Defendants. The case is filed in the Fifth District Court of Orleans Parish, Louisiana. The case Number is 92-401.

Project 3-4   Transcribe the request for production in the <u>Picknard v. Saint Stephens Memorial Hospital</u> case.

Project 3-5   Prepare a subpoena for Dr. Ben Hunt in the case styled <u>Roehnig v. Shulman</u>. He is to bring medical records on Dale Roehnig to the deposition. Use the subpoena in a civil case form provided in the back of the text or obtain a form from your local court. The deposition will be taken at the office of the plaintiffs' attorney on December 12, current year, at 3 p.m. Issue the subpoena one week prior to the date of the deposition. The doctor's address is 240 Central Avenue, Madison, Tennessee 37155. Phone: (615) 555-2177.

Project 3-6   Transcribe the notice of taking deposition in the <u>Roehnig v. Shulman</u> case.

Project 3-7   Transcribe the final judgment in the <u>Roehnig v. Shulman</u> case.

CHAPTER 4

PREPARING CORRESPONDENCE

OBJECTIVES

When you successfully complete this chapter, you will be able to:

➤ Transcribe letters for a legal office with subject lines, enclosures, and continuation-page headings

➤ Transcribe a letter addressed to three parties at different addresses

➤ Transcribe letters in block or modified block style

INTRODUCTION

The purpose of this chapter is to provide some guidelines for preparing correspondence for the legal office. The parts of a letter are listed and described and examples are displayed. This is not intended to be a complete coverage of all the correspondence rules. You will need to consult a good reference manual for any matters not addressed in this section; however, keep in mind that it is not unusual for reference manuals to disagree on specific details of letter placement.

Letters mailed out of the law office represent the attorney and the firm. They should be as complete and accurate as any other document the firm produces. It is the legal secretary's responsibility to transcribe a letter in an appropriate style, to check the content for accuracy, to punctuate correctly, to use the proper forms of address, and to choose appropriate closings.

STATIONERY

Standard paper (8 ½ x 11 inches) should be used for legal correspondence. The first page of a letter is usually printed on letterhead stationery, and continuation pages are printed on plain paper of the same color and quality.

One-inch margins are commonly used for letters because most word processing programs have default margins of one inch.

LETTERS

STYLES

Block style and modified block style (also called semiblock) are the letter styles most often used for business correspondence.

All letter parts begin at the left margin in the **block** style. This style is chosen if a firm wishes to portray a very efficient image — no time is wasted moving any part of the letter from the left margin to another location.

In the **modified block** style the date, closing lines, and the writer's typed signature and title begin at the horizontal center of the page, with all other letter parts beginning at the left margin. See Figures 4-1 and 4-3. Paragraphs may be blocked or indented. If paragraphs are indented, the law firm may choose to use either a five- or ten-space indention. Since many legal documents use ten-space paragraph indentions, some firms choose to indent paragraphs in the letters ten spaces also.

COMPONENTS

Refer to Figure 4-1 as you examine the following parts of a business letter:

- Letterhead
- Date
- Inside address
- Attention line
- Salutation
- Subject, Re, or In re line
- Body
- Complimentary closing
- Firm name
- Written signature
- Writer's name and business title
- Reference initials
- Enclosure
- Mailing notation
- Copy notation

Letterhead. Most letters will be printed on letterhead paper ordered from a printing company. However, occasionally a legal secretary may need to design a

---

BLOCK LETTER

All letter parts begin at the left margin.

MODIFIED BLOCK LETTER

All parts begin at the left margin except date, complimentary closing, and typed signature, which begin at center point.

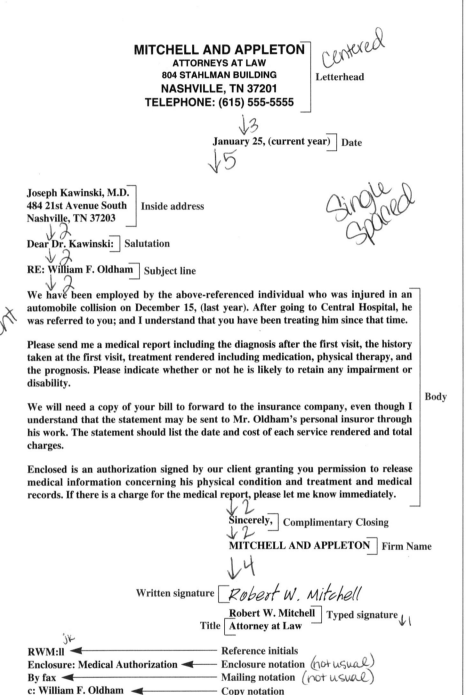

MITCHELL AND APPLETON
ATTORNEYS AT LAW
804 STAHLMAN BUILDING
NASHVILLE, TN 37201
TELEPHONE: (615) 555-5555   ⌐ Centered
                              └ Letterhead

↓3

January 25, (current year) ⌐ Date

↓5

Joseph Kawinski, M.D.   ⌐
484 21st Avenue South   Inside address
Nashville, TN 37203   └

↓2

Dear Dr. Kawinski: Salutation

↓2

RE: William F. Oldham ⌐ Subject line

↓2

We have been employed by the above-referenced individual who was injured in an automobile collision on December 15, (last year). After going to Central Hospital, he was referred to you; and I understand that you have been treating him since that time.

Please send me a medical report including the diagnosis after the first visit, the history taken at the first visit, treatment rendered including medication, physical therapy, and the prognosis. Please indicate whether or not he is likely to retain any impairment or disability.

We will need a copy of your bill to forward to the insurance company, even though I understand that the statement may be sent to Mr. Oldham's personal insuror through his work. The statement should list the date and cost of each service rendered and total charges.

Enclosed is an authorization signed by our client granting you permission to release medical information concerning his physical condition and treatment and medical records. If there is a charge for the medical report, please let me know immediately.

Body

↓2

Sincerely, ⌐ Complimentary Closing

↓2

MITCHELL AND APPLETON ⌐ Firm Name

↓4

Written signature ⌐ *Robert W. Mitchell*

Robert W. Mitchell ⌐ Typed signature ↓1
Title Attorney at Law

jk

RWM:ll ◄─────────── Reference initials
Enclosure: Medical Authorization ◄── Enclosure notation (not usual)
By fax ◄─────────── Mailing notation (not usual)
c: William F. Oldham ◄──────── Copy notation

Single Spaced

Date At Center

No Indent

FIGURE 4-1. Modified Block Style

MEDICAL AUTHORIZATION

This is to authorize any physician or representative of any hospital or clinic or any other health care provider to furnish **ROBERT W. MITCHELL, Attorney at Law, 804 Stahlman Building, Nashville, TN 37201,** any information or opinion that he may request regarding my physical condition and treatment which has been rendered to me and to allow him to see and copy any X-rays or medical records available regarding my condition and my treatment.

This authorization is valid for three (3) years following its date of execution.

_____

DATE: _____

_____

WITNESS

FIGURE 4-2. Enclosure

MITCHELL AND APPLETON
ATTORNEYS AT LAW
804 STAHLMAN BUILDING
NASHVILLE, TN 37201
TELEPHONE: (615) 555-5555 | Letterhead

January 25, (current year) | Date

Joseph Kawinski, M.D.
484 21st Avenue South | Inside address
Nashville, TN 37203

Dear Dr. Kawinski: | Salutation

RE: William F. Oldham | Subject line

We have been employed by the above-referenced individual who was injured in an automobile collision on December 15, (last year). After going to Central Hospital, he was referred to you; and I understand that you have been treating him since that time.

Please send me a medical report including the diagnosis after the first visit, the history taken at the first visit, treatment rendered including medication, physical therapy, and the prognosis. Please indicate whether or not he is likely to retain any impairment or disability. | Body

We will need a copy of your bill to forward to the insurance company, even though I understand that the statement may be sent to Mr. Oldham's personal insuror through his work. The statement should list the date and cost of each service rendered and total charges.

Enclosed is an authorization signed by our client granting you permission to release medical information concerning his physical condition and treatment and medical records. If there is a charge for the medical report, please let me know immediately.

Sincerely, | Complimentary Closing

MITCHELL AND APPLETON | Firm Name

Robert W. Mitchell | Written Signature
Robert W. Mitchell ◄———————— Typed Signature
Attorney at Law ◄———————— Writer's Title

RWM:ll ◄———————————— Reference Initials
Enclosure: Medical Authorization ◄——— Enclosure Notation
By fax ◄——————————— Mailing Notation
c: William F. Oldham ◄———————— Copy Notation

FIGURE 4-3. Block Style

letterhead. A letterhead should include information such as the firm name or attorney's name, address, telephone number, and fax number. With a word processing program and laser printer, it is possible to design attractive letterheads.

Date. The current date should be placed on each letter to be mailed out of the office. It is placed 2 to 2 ½ inches from the top of the paper but not less than three lines below the letterhead. Spell the name of the month and use figures for the day and year; for example, January 1, 19—.

Inside Address. The address of the person or business to receive the letter is the inside address. It is placed at the left margin four to six lines below the date and always includes the name of an individual or business, street and/or post office address, and city, two-letter state abbreviation, and ZIP code.

When writing to an attorney, either a personal title precedes the attorney's name **or** the abbreviation Esq. is placed after the attorney's name. If Esquire is used to identify an attorney, as is often done in the United States, it is placed after the name, preceded by a comma, and abbreviated Esq. Esquire can be used in addressing a male or female attorney. Do not use personal titles with Esquire.

Nancy Calgon, Esq.   (not Ms. Nancy Calgon, Esq.)

Anthony Wong, Esq.   (not Mr. Anthony Wong, Esq.)

Mr. is an appropriate title for a male attorney; Ms. is an appropriate title for a female attorney. If a married female attorney prefers Mrs. or an unmarried female attorney prefers Miss, let her preference be a guide. The signature block from a previous letter will indicate such a preference. Also include in the inside address a professional title, such as Attorney at Law or Attorney for the Plaintiff, after the attorney's name. Some examples of inside addresses for an attorney are shown below.

Janice Moss, Esq.
2400 Broadway
Cleveland, OH 84210-1901

Ms. Janice Moss
Attorney at Law
2400 Broadway
Cleveland, OH 84210-1901

Ms. Janice Moss
Attorney for the Plaintiff
2400 Broadway
Cleveland, OH 84210-1901

If a firm name is included in the inside address, it can be inserted after the name of the attorney or after the attorney's professional title. If the title is given after the name of the law firm, a plural form is used to indicate that all members of the firm are attorneys. The name of the law firm name is spelled and punctuated in the same style as shown on the firm's letterhead. If a letterhead or

other correspondence is not available, the listing in the telephone directory will
serve as a guide.

Ms. Janice Moss
Attorney at Law
Albers, Moss and Norman
2400 Broadway
Cleveland, OH 83210-1901

Ms. Janice Moss
Albers, Moss and Norman
Attorneys at Law
2400 Broadway
Cleveland, OH 83210-1901

If correspondence is addressed to more than one attorney at the same
address, place each attorney's name on a separate line with the common address
listed below.

Ms. Janice Moss
Mr. Harold Norman
Attorneys at Law
2400 Broadway
Cleveland, OH 83210-1901

If correspondence is addressed to two or more attorneys at different
addresses, place the complete name and address of each attorney one below the
other or side by side.

Ms. Janice Moss
Attorney at Law
2400 Broadway
Cleveland, OH 83210-1901

Mr. Albert Parker
Attorney at Law
Box 43809
Arlington, VA 02532-6755

or

Ms. Janice Moss	Mr. Albert Parker
Attorney at Law	Attorney at Law
2400 Broadway	Box 43809
Cleveland, OH 83210-1901	Arlington, VA 02543-6755

When writing a judge, justice, district attorney, attorney general, secretary
of state, and most other government and court officials, **The Honorable**
precedes the individual's name. The title **Hon.** is a less formal but acceptable
form. Examples are shown below.

The Honorable George Stone
Chief Justice of the
   Tennessee Supreme Court
1230 Capitol Boulevard
Nashville, TN 37201-2334

Hon. Ralph Stone
Judge of the United States District Court
   for the Middle District of Tennessee
2388 Broadway Boulevard
Nashville, TN 37223-3888

Attention Line. Place an attention line on a letter to direct it to a specific individual in the law firm or company. The attention line makes it clear that the letter is company business and can be handled by another person in the company. The first line of the inside address will be a company or law firm name. The attention line is placed at the left margin a double space below the inside address. A colon and two spaces follows the word "Attention." The line, including the word "attention," is displayed in full caps or with capital and small letters. Examples are:

Attention: Mr. Alberto Sanchez

ATTENTION: ALBERTO SANCHEZ

Attention: Office Manager

Salutation. The salutation is a greeting to the person receiving the letter. It placed at the left margin a double space below the attention line if one is used or a double space below the inside address. The following salutations are appropriate when writing to an attorney or law firm. The use of Esq. in the inside address does not affect the choice of a salutation.

Dear Mr. Mitchell: (when writing to a male attorney)

Dear Ms. Moss: (when writing to a female attorney)

Dear Mrs. Moss: (according to preference of the recipient)

Dear Miss Abernathy: (according to preference of the recipient)

Gentlemen: (when writing to a firm with all male attorneys)

Ladies: (when writing to a firm with all female attorneys)

Ladies and Gentlemen: **or** Gentlemen and Ladies: (when writing

   to a firm with male and female attorneys)

Ladies or Gentlemen: (when writing to a firm with the gender of

   the attorneys unknown)

Friendly salutations, such as Dear Bob and Dear Janice may be used when the attorney writes to those he knows as friends. The secretary should make a note of any friendly salutations the attorney uses, as the party receiving one letter with a friendly salutation and another with a more formal salutation may be offended and wonder why the change of tone.

Legal secretaries often address correspondence to clerks of the court, judges, justices, chief justices, and the secretary of state. Suggested salutations follow.

Clerk of the Court	Dear Sir: Dear Madam: Dear Mr. Coleman: Dear Ms. Coleman:
Judge	Sir: Madam: Dear Judge Simmons:
Justice	Sir: Madam: Dear Mr. Justice: Dear Madam Justice:
Chief Justice	Sir: Madam: Dear Mr. Chief Justice: Dear Madam Chief Justice:
Secretary of State	Sir: Madam: Dear Mr. Secretary: Dear Madam Secretary:

Two widely accepted punctuation styles are **standard** (also called mixed) and **open**. For mixed punctuation, place a colon after the salutation and a comma after the complimentary closing. No punctuation marks follow the salutation or complimentary closing when using open punctuation.

Subject, Re, or In re Lines. In legal correspondence, most firms use **Re** (meaning matter) or **In re** (meaning in the matter) to introduce the subject of a letter. The **Re** line is a double space below the salutation. The subject line can be placed at the left margin for any letter style; an alternative is to indent it to paragraph point in a letter style where the paragraphs are indented. A colon and two spaces follow the word "Re" or "In re." The line, including the word "Re" or "In re," is displayed in full caps or with capital and small letters. When a case name is the subject of a letter, the case name should be underscored. Examples are:

Re: <u>Jones v. Smith</u>   (case name)

Re: Probate of Will

RE: PROBATE OF WILL

Re: <u>Jones v. Smith</u>
    Case No. 3333

Re: <u>Jones v. Smith</u>
    Our File No. SM143-12
    Your File No. JO582-34

In re: <u>Sally Jones v. Leo Smith</u> — Slip and Fall Accident

Body. Begin the body of a letter a double space below the Re line; if no Re line is used, begin a double space below the salutation. Paragraphs are singled-spaced with a double-space between them. The section on "Letter Styles" in this chapter provides information on paragraph indentions.

Complimentary Closing. A complimentary closing is a courtesy word or phrase closing the body of a letter. It begins a double space below the body either at the left margin or at center point — the letter style will dictate the horizontal placement. For formal closings, use "Very truly yours" or "Respectfully yours"; for informal closings, use "Sincerely yours," "Sincerely," or "Cordially yours." Capitalize only the first letter of the first word of the closing.

Firm Name. If a firm name is included, it implies that the correspondence represents the firm, not the individual who signed it. It is placed a double space below the complimentary closing and at the same horizontal point as the complimentary closing. The name should be keyed in full caps, spelled exactly as shown on the firm's letterhead.

Writer's Name and Business Title. The writer's name is keyed four lines below the name of the firm or, if no firm name is included, four lines below the complimentary closing. The typewritten name should match the written signature; for example, James A. Jones should be keyed as James A. Jones, not J. A. Jones. Mr. is placed before a man's name only if it is not clear that the person signing the letter is a male; for example, Mr. Pat Alderson. A female has the option of including or omitting a personal title in the typed signature. For example:

Sincerely,   Sincerely,

Mrs. Janice Moss   Janice Moss

Reference Initials. Reference initials are placed a double space below the writer's name at the left margin. The reference may include the writer's and the typist's initials (in that order) or only the typist's. When both sets of initials are used, they can be separated with a colon or right diagonal. If father and son work in the same firm, an abbreviation for Jr. and III can be added to the reference initials to clarify whether the father or son is the author of the letter. Any of the following styles are appropriate.

    kk
    KK
    KK:filename
    NS:kk
    NS:KK
    CDB Jr/kk
    CDB III/kk

Enclosures. A notation indicating that items are to be enclosed with the letter should be placed at the left margin one line (some reference manuals recommend two lines) below the reference initials. Use the word "Enclosure" or "Enclosures" to indicate that an item or items are to be mailed in the same envelope with the letter. Items enclosed may also be listed as shown below.

    Enclosures:
    1. Complaint
    2. Summons

    Enclosures: Certified check for $150
                 Complaint for divorce

Mailing Notation. Special mail service for delivering a letter is noted one line (some reference manuals recommend two lines) below the Enclosure notation, if one is used, or below the reference initials. Type the word "By" followed by the type of service: By fax; By Airborne; By certified, return receipt.

Copy Notations. When people other than the addressee of a letter receive copies, they are listed at the left margin below the mailing notation, enclosure, or reference initials. The notation "c:" or "cc:," "c" or "cc," "pc," or "Copy" or "Copies" precedes the name or names. Names of those who are to receive copies should be arranged in order of importance, or in alphabetical order if rank is not important. Personal titles may be, but are not required to be, included. Place a check mark on each person's copy to identify the receiver.

    cc Dr. James Jones
        Ms. Nancy Richardson
        Mr. David Swartz

or

    cc J. Jones
        N. Richardson
        D. Swartz

CONTINUATION PAGE HEADINGS

Continuation page headings are to be placed one inch from the top of the second and subsequent pages. Each continuation page should have the name of the addressee, page number, and date arranged either in a block at the left margin or on one line across the top of the page. If the heading is arranged on one line, display the page number without the word "page." See the examples below.

Vincent Tischler, Esq.
Page 2
March 12, 1996

or

Vincent Tischler, Esq.   2   March 12, 1996

ENVELOPES

Many legal documents can be mailed in a No. 10 envelope, more commonly known as a large envelope. If the firm does not have envelopes with printed return addresses, the return address is typed in the upper lefthand corner. The mailing address is single-spaced and blocked beginning 2 to 2 ½ inches from the top and 4 inches from the left edge of the envelope. Notation of a special mailing service, such as certified or registered, is keyed in full caps below the stamp, a half inch from the right edge of the envelope. "Personal" or "confidential" notations are placed a triple space below the return address.

```
+-----------------------------------------------------------+
|  Mitchell and Appleton                          +-------+  |
|  804 Stahman Building                           |Postage|  |
|  Nashville, TN 37201                            +-------+  |
|                                                           |
|                                              CERTIFIED    |
|                                                           |
|           Dr. Joseph Kawinski                             |
|           Internal Medicine Associates                    |
|           484 21st Avenue South                           |
|           Nashville, TN 37203                             |
|                                                           |
+-----------------------------------------------------------+
```

If a firm chooses to use the full-caps, no-punctuation style of addressing envelopes recommended by the U.S. Postal Service, instructions for formatting the address are available by writing or calling the United States Postal Service and asking for Publication 28. The fact that a full-caps style is used on the envelope does not alter the way the inside address is keyed on the letter.

To prepare an envelope as recommended by the U.S. Postal Service, use these basic guidelines:

- Use FULL CAPS with no punctuation.

- Use abbreviations for directions — N, S, E, W, NE, NW, SE, SW.

- Abbreviate avenue, street, drive, road, place, circle, boulevard, and court as AVE, ST, DR, RD, PL, CIR, BLVD, CT.

- Abbreviate room, suite, and apartment as RM, STE, APT.

- Use two-letter state codes.

- Place the city, state, and ZIP code on one line.

- Leave one or two spaces between the state and ZIP code.

- Place a hyphen between the five-digit ZIP Code and the four-digit extended ZIP Code.

Mitchell and Appleton
804 Stahlman Building, Nashville, TN 37200

CERTIFIED

DR JOSEPH KAWINSKI
INTERNAL MEDICINE ASSOC
484 21ST AVE S
NASHVILLE TN 37203-3253

SUMMARY

- The legal secretary is responsible for transcribing correspondence, checking the content for accuracy, punctuating correctly, and using the proper form for addresses and closings.

- The two letter styles most frequently used for business correspondence are block and modified block (also known as semiblock). All parts of a letter in block style begin at the left margin. The date, complimentary closing, and writer's name and business title begin at the horizontal center in the modified block style, with all other parts at the left margin. Paragraphs may be blocked or indented in the modified block style. Block is the more efficient of the two styles.

- A letterhead should include the company name, address, telephone number, and fax number if available.

- A letter should be dated the day it is mailed. The format for the date is month, day, and year — January 1, 19—.

- When writing to an attorney, Esq. can be used after the name *or* Mr., Mrs., Ms., or Miss (as appropriate) can be used before the name. Never use both titles.

- When an attention line is included in a letter addressed to a business, it is clear that the letter is company business and can be handled by another person in the organization.

- Two styles of punctuating the salutation and complimentary closing of a letter are open and standard (mixed). For open punctuation, no end-of-line punctuation follows the salutation and complimentary closing; for standard punctuation, a colon is inserted after the salutation and a comma after the complimentary closing.

- Generally, law firms use "Re" or "In re" as the introductory words to the subject line of a letter.

- A firm name in the inside address of a letter should be spelled and punctuated as shown on the firm's letterhead. If a letterhead is not available, the form in the telephone directory can be used as a guide.

- If a letter has multiple inside addresses, the addresses are stacked vertically or placed side by side, or both.

- The typed signature on a letter should match the written signature, with the exception of personal titles.

- When the firm name is placed in full caps after the complimentary closing, the letter represents the firm.

- Reference initials, enclosures, mailing notations, and copy notations are placed at the left margin below the writer's name and business title.

- Continuation page headings should be placed at the top of the second and subsequent pages of correspondence and should include the name of the addressee, page number, and date. The information can be displayed in block format or on one line across the top of the page.

- Envelopes may be addressed in the same style as the inside address on the letter or in the full-caps, no-punctuation style recommended by the U.S. Postal Service.

REVIEW EXERCISES

T F 1. The date on a letter should be typed three inches from the top of the page.

T F 2. Every personal name in an inside address should be preceded by a title.

T F 3. "The Honorable" is the title used for a judge, justice, and secretary of state.

T F 4. In an attention line on a letter, a semicolon should follow the word "Attention."

T F 5. The salutation is typed a double space below the attention line or the inside address.

T F 6. "Dear Madam Justice" is an acceptable salutation for a female Justice of the Supreme Court.

T F 7. If "Esq." is used after an attorney's name, "Attorney at Law" should be the second line of the inside address.

T F 8. "Madam" is an appropriate salutation for a letter addressed to a firm of female attorneys.

T F 9. The body of a letter is single-spaced with double-spacing between paragraphs.

T F 10. If a letter were addressed to "Robert W. Mitchell, Esq.," the salutation would be "Dear Esq. Mitchell."

T F 11. Reference initials always include initials of the author and of the typist.

T F 12. The correct order for the notation lines at the end of a letter are enclosure, mailing notation, copy notation, and reference initials.

T F 13. When the firm name is placed in full caps after the complimentary closing, it is clear that the letter represents the firm.

TRANSCRIPTION RULES

CAPITALIZATION

In Correspondence

Names used in legal correspondence (letters, memoranda, etc.) are generally keyed with initial caps. More often than not, the terms "plaintiff" and "defendant" are keyed in lowercase letters. Names of documents, such as complaint, answer, and motion to dismiss, may be typed with lowercase letters or with initial caps. Consistently follow the capitalization pattern preferred by the attorney.

After going to *Central Hospital,* he was referred to you.

The *plaintiff* was injured on December 15, (current year).

Enclosed is a copy of the *Summons* and *Complaint.*

or

Enclosed is a copy of the *summons* and *complaint.*

COMMAS

Dependent Clauses — Essential

Do not place commas around a dependent clause that appears within or at the end of a sentence if it is essential to the meaning of the sentence. If an essential clause is omitted, it changes the meaning of the sentence.

The defendant stated to the plaintiff that he would be responsible for the future rent of the student *who was residing on the plaintiff's rental property.* (Without the "who" clause, this could mean any student, not just the one who was riding on the rental property.)

Dependent Clauses — Nonessential

Place commas around a dependent clause that appears within or at the end of a sentence if it is not essential to the meaning of the sentence. A nonessential clause can be omitted from the sentence and not change the meaning of the sentence; it simply provides additional information.

We will need a copy of your bill to forward to the insurance company, *even though the statement may be sent to Mr. Oldham's personal insurer through his work.*

The defendant stated to the plaintiff that he would be responsible for the future rent of Joseph Hill, *who was residing at the Plaintiff's rental property.*

(This could be only Joseph Hill; the other information does not change the meaning of the sentence if omitted.)

Et al.

"Et al." is often used in a case name. "Et" means *and;* "al." means *others.* Punctuate the expression as you would any other items joined by "and." If you have only one item followed by "et al.," no comma is required. If you have two or more items in a series followed by "et al.," a comma is needed. See the following examples:

<u>Baldwin's Furniture v. Appleton Shopping Center et al.</u> (No comma is needed — two items joined by "and" do not require a comma. It can be read as Appleton Shopping Center and others.)

<u>Baldwin's Furniture v. Albert Jones, Trucking Company, et al.</u> (Comma is needed because there are three items in a series — Albert Jones, Trucking Company, and others.)

Parenthetical Expressions

Parenthetical terms are explanatory words added by the writer. Such expressions that are introductory or interrupt the flow of the sentence are set off with commas. Examples are *in addition, in my opinion, of course, consequently, however, further, furthermore, nevertheless, besides,* and *however.* Voice inflection can be used to determine whether or not the element is essential. If the voice drops the expression is nonessential and should be set off with commas. If the voice rises, the expression is essential and should not be set off.

You, *I believe,* are a licensed physician.

Further, it is agreed that all formalities as to reading and signing of the deposition are waived.

Will you tell us, *please,* the purpose of the blood test?

<u>But</u>

It is *further* agreed that all formalities as to reading and signing of the deposition are waived.

HYPHENATION

Attorney at Law

It is common practice not to hyphenate "Attorney at Law"; however, some authorities show it hyphenated.

Mail a copy to Robert W. Mitchell, *Attorney at Law,* 804 Stahlman Building, Nashville, TN 37201.

Fractions

In letters, spell out and hyphenate fractions. Use numbers if the spelled-out form is long and awkward.

One-half
Two-thirds
42/100

Modifiers Before a Noun

When two or more words function together as one to modify a noun, use a hyphen to connect them. If the modifiers do not appear before a noun, generally do not insert the hyphens. Do not insert the hyphen if one of the words is an adverb (usually ending in *ly*).

Refer to the ***above-referenced*** case. The case is referenced above.
Use a ***six-inch*** line. The line is six inches.
He is a ***highly paid*** attorney. (ends in *ly*)
He purchased ***over-the-counter drugs.*** The drugs are sold over the counter.

NUMBER EXPRESSION

In legal correspondence, numbers ten and under are spelled out; numbers over ten are written in figures. Amounts of money are shown in numeric form only. Some attorneys may prefer to follow the method used in legal documents.

The facts should be admitted within ***30*** days after service.
My client is willing to agree to a settlement of ***$20,000.***

POSSESSION

Singular Possession

Show singular possession of a noun not ending in *s* by adding an apostrophe and s. Show possession of a singular noun ending with an *s*, *sh*, *z*, or *zh* by adding an apostrophe and s. If the word is hard to pronounce when adding an apostrophe and *s*, add an apostrophe only.

The defendant said that the ***child's*** actions caused the accident.

The defendant felt her ***boss's*** actions were the proximate cause of the accident.

The defendant felt that Mr. ***Phillips'*** response to the request for settlement was not satisfactory.

Plural Possession

Show possession of a plural noun not ending in *s* by adding an apostrophe and *s*. Show possession of a plural noun ending in *s* by adding an apostrophe.

The ***men's*** claims that they are joint owners of the property are totally incorrect.

My ***clients'*** documents were filed before the deadline.

SEMICOLON

Two Independent Clauses Joined by a Conjunctive Adverb

A conjunctive adverb is an adverb that connects two independent clauses.

Some conjunctive adverbs are the following: however, so, also, nevertheless, consequently, hence, otherwise, furthermore, therefore, accordingly. When two independent clauses are joined by these terms, place a semicolon before the conjunctive adverb and a comma after it.

Mr. Baldwin has waived all of his rights to a trial; *however,* we may be able to work out a settlement.

Barbara Harding did not retain counsel due to her financial condition; *therefore,* we request that the default judgment be dismissed.

Both "v." and "vs." can be used for "versus" in a case name. <u>Jones v. Smith</u> or <u>Jones vs. Smith</u>

Transcription Hints:

TRANSCRIPTION EXERCISES

1. Design a letterhead for Mitchell and Appleton, Attorneys at Law, 804 Stahlman Building, Nashville, TN 37200. The telephone number is (615) 555-5555. Save it on a diskette to use for the projects.

2. Design a letterhead for Warner C. Watkins, an attorney, 1612 14th Avenue North, Nashville, TN 37201. His telephone number is (615) 555-6666. Save it on a diskette to use for the projects.

3. Design a letterhead for Crockett, Mathis & Edison, Attorneys at Law, at 508 Gulf Shores Trust Building, 2000 Westgate Drive, Gulf Shores, Alabama 35721. The telephone number is (205) 555-6433. Save it on a diskette to use for the projects.

4. Design a letterhead for Taylor, Hatfield and Callahan, Attorneys at Law, on the 22d Floor of the Gulf Life Building, 1600 North Water Street, Gulf Shores, AL 35720. The phone number is (205) 555-3387. Save it on a diskette to use for the projects.

Use a secretarial reference manual and the rules presented in this and previous chapters to aid you in correctly transcribing the following material. The sentences are presented in lowercase letters without punctuation, as you would hear them on a transcriber.

5. re rhodes furniture v lajazz dance et al

6. in re harry bradley v honey cartwright frank bradley et al

7. the defendant at all times was acting in the scope of his employment furthermore all acts perpetrated by the defendant were done in furtherance of his employers business

8. the plaintiff parked her automobile at the parking area for state employees which is owned and operated by the defendant and proceeded to the concrete stairs that lead to the cordell hull building

9. the child took a step which placed his left foot under the lawn mower

10. robert w mitchell is an attorney at law

11. the plaintiff is asking for a ten thousand dollar settlement

12. the purchaser will pay an amount equal to 1/2 of the prorated taxes

13. further we feel that this settlement should be equally divided between the plaintiffs.

14. the plaintiffs have been next door neighbors to the defendant for 4 years

15. this is a formal application to construct a sewer line which i understand will be an 8 inch line from palm hill pike to lot 4

16. i have discussed your companys offer to settle for fifteen thousand dollars in the above styled matter

17. this settlement should be broken up with dales receiving 17000 dollars and his parents receiving 7500 dollars

Follow instructions given below:

18. Use the full-caps style and address a No. 10 envelope to: warner c watkins (he is an attorney) 1612 14th avenue north (use your city, state, and zip code)

19. Key the correct salutation for a woman who is the secretary of state.

20. Prepare the subject line for Pricknard v. Saint Stephens Memorial Hospital. Our file number is PR234-93; your file number is ST987-93.

21. Prepare a complimentary closing and signature block for Mr. Eugene Hollins of Crossley, Hollins & Ray.

RESEARCH ACTIVITIES

1. Consult two or three reference manuals and/or typing textbooks and compare the rules for letter placement presented in this chapter with the rules presented in the reference manuals and typing texts. Make a list of any differences.

2. Call the United States Postal Service and ask for Publication 28.

PROJECTS

Insert the cassette tape for Chapter 4 and transcribe the following projects.

Project 4-1   Transcribe a letter to Dr. Ben Hunt to schedule a deposition in the case of Roehnig v. Shulman. Use Mitchell and Appleton letterhead. Mr. Mitchell prefers the modified block style letter with indented paragraphs and standard punctuation.

Project 4-2   Transcribe a letter in the Roehnig v. Shulman case discussing the setting up of a deposition of Mr. Shulman. Use Warner Watkins letterhead. Mr Watkins uses modified block style for his letters with standard punctuation.

Project 4-3   Transcribe a letter for Mr. Watkins in the Roehnig v. Shulman case about 1 month after the one transcribed in Project 4-2, still discussing Mr. Shulman's inability to give a deposition.

Project 4-4   Transcribe a letter for Mr. Mitchell in the Roehnig v. Shulman case discussing an offer to settle out of court.

Project 4-5   Transcribe a letter for Mr. Watkins in the Roehnig v. Shulman case making a counteroffer to settle out of court.

Project 4-6   This is a long letter in the <u>Harry and Emory Bradley v. Honey Lou Cartwright et al.</u> case introduced in Project 2-4. This letter is written to the Department of Water and Sewerage to make an application to the city government to construct a sewer line. Use the Crockett, Mathis & Edison letterhead. Format the letter using modified block style with indented paragraphs and standard punctuation.

Project 4-7   This is a letter written to three attorneys, Mr. Eugene Hollins, Mr. Robert Taylor, and Mr. J. B. Merry, Jr., at different addresses. One of the attorneys involved in the case is attempting to schedule a deposition at a time that is suitable to all. Use Crockett, Mathis & Edison letterhead.

Project 4-8   This is a letter in <u>Bradley v. Cartwright</u>. One of the parties in the case may want to purchase an interest in the property over which the sewer line dispute arose. Use Taylor, Hatfield and Callahan letterhead. Use block style with open punctuation.

UNIT I
PERFORMANCE ASSESSMENT

A.   The following document has editorial, spelling, grammar, and punctu-
      ation errors. Mark each error, indicate the correction on the copy below,
      and key and print a corrected copy of the document.

      This is the body of a complaint in a personal injury lawsuit where the
      plaintiff, Daisy Mae Johnson, was injured when she fell on slick ceramic
      tile in front of the defendant's store. She is filing the lawsuit against
      Wallace A. Miller d/b/a Miller's Furniture Store in the Circuit Court for
      Biloxi, Mississippi. The attorney for the plaintiff is Patrick Hammer, 230
      Capitol Boulevard, Biloxi, Mississippi 33333, Case No. 32343, Phone:
      (601) 555-9192.

COMPLAINT

Plaintiff, DAISY MAE JOHNSON, a resident of Harrison County, Biloxi,
Mississipi, sues the defendant, WALLACE A. MILLER, the principle owner and
operator of Miller's Furnature Store in the sum of $50,000.00, and for cause of
action would show as follows:

1. Both the Plaintiff and Defendant are residence of Harrison County,
Mississippi, and all events that arose out of this suite occured in Harrison
County, Biloxi, Mississippi.

2. On December 23, last year, the Plaintiff, Daisy Mae Johnson was
walking on Irish Hill Drive intending to go into Miller's Furnature Store to do
some Christmas shopping. Directly in front of the Defendants store is a ceramic
tile logo of Defendant MILLER's head and face. As she stepped on this tile
logo, the Plaintiffs feet slipped and she was thrown to the ground, hitting the
concrete and tile violently.

3. The Plaintiff sustained serious injuries in that she landed on her hip
fracturing it. She was taken to the University of Mississippi Medical Center,
Biloxi Branch where she was treated. It was found that she had fractured her
right femur at the junction of the pelvic bone which required a new ball and
socket hip joint.

4. The Defendant, WALLACE A. MILLER, is guilty of negligence which
is the direct and approximate cause of the injuries to the Plaintiff. Upon
examination, it was found that the ceramic face of the Defendant had just been
mopped and was still wet. However, there was no signs of warning or
indications in anyway by the Defendant or his employees that the ceramic tile
was in a dangerous state for invitees of the store. Said negligence on the part of

the defendant and his employees were also gross and wantton and showed an indefference to the safety of customers and the general public.

WHEREFORE, the Plaintiff DAISY MAE JOHNSON, demands judgment against the Defendant WALLACE A. MILLER for damages in the amount of Fifty Thousand Dollars ($50,000.00) and further demands a jury to try this cause of action.

B.   Place the cassette tape for Performance Assessment I in the transcriber. Transcribe I-B, a complaint. Eric Wallace is the plaintiff; Richard Bannister and Jose Rodriguez d/b/a (this is the abbreviation for doing business as) Rodriguez Roofers are the defendants. This case is to be heard in the Circuit Court for Broward County, Florida. Beverly Ann Lyons (No. 47329) is the attorney for the plaintiffs. Her address is Prudential Building, Suite 222, 244 Las Olas Boulevard, Fort Lauderdale, Florida 21341. Phone: (305) 555-3254.

C.   Listen to the recorded instructions on the cassette tape for completing Item I-C. You will be instructed to retrieve a previously created document and will be given instructions for altering it to be used in the Wallace v. Banister case. The judge is Lisa Dianne Rose; the attorney is Sak F. Ewing.

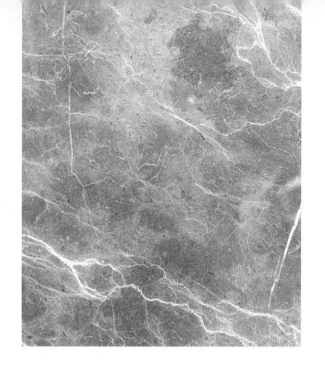

UNIT II
PROBATE

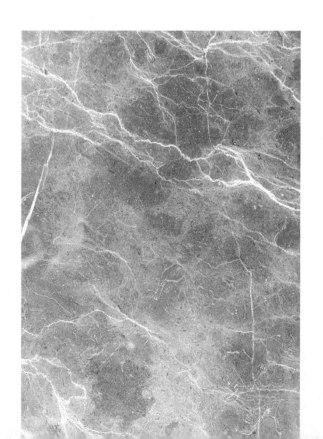

JOB DESCRIPTION

TRANSCRIPTION RESPONSIBILITIES

JOB TITLE: Legal Secretary

AREA OF PRACTICE: Probate

TRANSCRIPTION DUTIES:

1. Is responsible for the formatting, page numbering, spelling, and grammatical accuracy of all probate documents.

2. Is responsible for preparing affidavits to self-prove wills.

3. Drafts last wills and testaments from standardized paragraphs or previously transcribed wills, making adjustments in gender and proper names, as appropriate.

4. Knows the proper procedure for execution of wills and for copying and assembling wills in legal backs.

5. Knows the format for transcribing a living will or durable power of attorney for health care.

6. Is responsible for transcribing and correctly formatting all petitions and orders for probate, guardianships, conservatorships, and name changes.

7. Correctly formats inventories and final accountings for probate, guardianships, and conservatorships.

8. Is responsible for efficiently using a word processing software program or electronic typewriter to create and edit documents.

CHAPTER 5

WILLS

OBJECTIVES

When you successfully complete this chapter, you will be able to:

➤ Transcribe a last will and testament

➤ Prepare an affidavit to self-prove a will

➤ Participate in an execution-of-will meeting

➤ Transcribe a codicil

➤ Transcribe standardized paragraphs with variables to be used to later create wills

➤ Transcribe a living will and a durable power of attorney for health care

---

INTRODUCTION

Most people are concerned with what happens to their property after death. Many people desire to leave property to a spouse and, if the spouse is deceased, to provide for the care of minor children. There is also a growing concern about health-care matters. In order to ensure that one's wishes are honored, a person should contact an attorney and have him or her prepare the appropriate documents shown below:

LAST WILL AND TESTAMENT

AFFIDAVIT TO SELF-PROVE A WILL

CODICIL

LIVING WILL

DURABLE POWER OF ATTORNEY FOR HEALTH CARE

LAST WILL AND TESTAMENT

TYPES OF WILLS

Typewritten or Formal Will. The form of will the legal secretary most often deals with is the typewritten will. It may be dictated by the attorney or compiled by the attorney from standardized paragraphs altered to fit the needs of the client. Such a will contains the types of paragraphs discussed in the next section entitled "Purpose and Format" and includes all the formalities of execution and witnessing required by each state; namely, the testator/trix must sign the last will and testament in the presence of the witnesses, and the witnesses must sign in the presence of the testator/trix.

Holographic Will. A holographic will is one written in the testator/trix's own handwriting. Generally, these are the types of wills individuals choose to write for themselves rather than seeking the advice of an attorney. A holographic will may or may not be witnessed. If not, before the will can be **probated**, the handwriting must be proved by two or three witnesses. A limited number of states recognize this type of will as valid.

Oral or Nuncupative Will. An oral will is one spoken by the testator during his last days of illness before witnesses and afterwards reduced to writing. There may be a dollar limit set on distributions made by an oral will. Some states will honor an oral will as long as it does not change a written will and is made by someone who is in danger of or near death and who later dies as a result of the danger.

PURPOSE AND FORMAT

A **last will and testament** is an instrument in which a person states how property is to be distributed after death and names a person to handle his or her affairs after death. For the will to be **legally binding**, it must be executed (signed and witnessed) according to the required formalities of law. In order to make a will, a person must be of sound mind and legal age. Sound mind means that the maker of the will, called the **testator** (male) or **testatrix** (female), understands that a will is being made and that it is binding, knows how much personal and real property he or she owns, and knows who will receive property and their relationship to the maker of the will. Legal age is determined by each state; usually it is 18 years of age.

It is important that the following information be incorporated in a will so that legal requirements for making the will are satisfied and so that property is distributed according to the wishes of the maker. Failure to include certain wording will cause confusion and may lead to wrong interpretations of the will. Carefully examine each paragraph of John Blair Cook's will (Figures 5-1 and 5-2) as you read the following material.

Sound Mind, Legal Age, Revoke Former Wills. The opening paragraph of a will should establish a person's legal right to make a will. Note that the first paragraph reads, "I, JOHN BLAIR COOK, . . . being of sound mind and disposing memory . . . declare this instrument as my Last Will and Testament." The

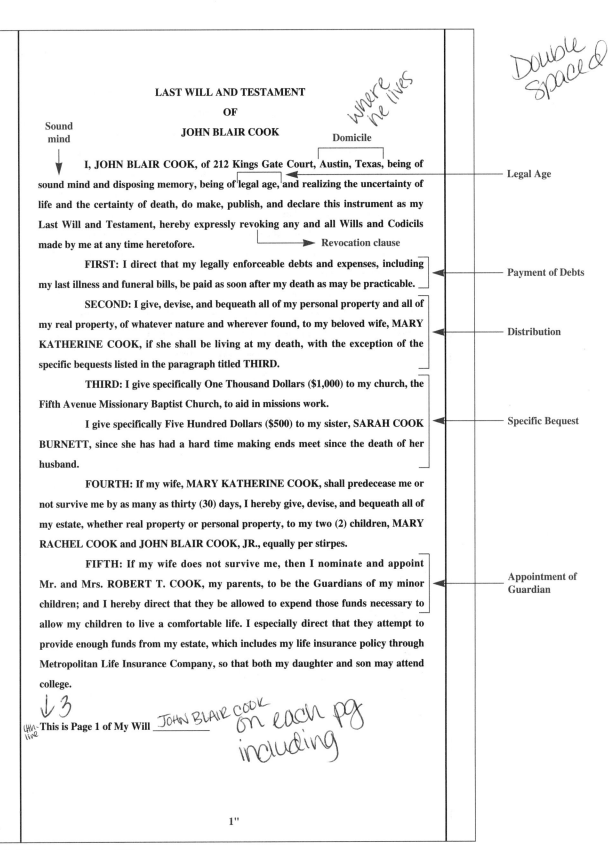

Double Spaced

LAST WILL AND TESTAMENT
OF
JOHN BLAIR COOK

Sound mind

where he lives   Domicile

I, JOHN BLAIR COOK, of 212 Kings Gate Court, Austin, Texas, being of sound mind and disposing memory, being of legal age, and realizing the uncertainty of life and the certainty of death, do make, publish, and declare this instrument as my Last Will and Testament, hereby expressly revoking any and all Wills and Codicils made by me at any time heretofore.

Legal Age

Revocation clause

FIRST: I direct that my legally enforceable debts and expenses, including my last illness and funeral bills, be paid as soon after my death as may be practicable.

Payment of Debts

SECOND: I give, devise, and bequeath all of my personal property and all of my real property, of whatever nature and wherever found, to my beloved wife, MARY KATHERINE COOK, if she shall be living at my death, with the exception of the specific bequests listed in the paragraph titled THIRD.

Distribution

THIRD: I give specifically One Thousand Dollars ($1,000) to my church, the Fifth Avenue Missionary Baptist Church, to aid in missions work.

I give specifically Five Hundred Dollars ($500) to my sister, SARAH COOK BURNETT, since she has had a hard time making ends meet since the death of her husband.

Specific Bequest

FOURTH: If my wife, MARY KATHERINE COOK, shall predecease me or not survive me by as many as thirty (30) days, I hereby give, devise, and bequeath all of my estate, whether real property or personal property, to my two (2) children, MARY RACHEL COOK and JOHN BLAIR COOK, JR., equally per stirpes.

FIFTH: If my wife does not survive me, then I nominate and appoint Mr. and Mrs. ROBERT T. COOK, my parents, to be the Guardians of my minor children; and I hereby direct that they be allowed to expend those funds necessary to allow my children to live a comfortable life. I especially direct that they attempt to provide enough funds from my estate, which includes my life insurance policy through Metropolitan Life Insurance Company, so that both my daughter and son may attend college.

Appointment of Guardian

↓3

4 lines — This is Page 1 of My Will _JOHN BLAIR COOK_ *on each pg including*

1"

FIGURE 5-1. Page 1 of a Will

Residuary of Estate →

       SIXTH: All the rest, residue, and remainder of the property which I may own at the time of my death, real, personal, and mixed, of whatsoever nature and wheresoever situated, I bequeath to my wife, MARY KATHERINE COOK.

Appointment of Executrix →

       SEVENTH: I hereby nominate and appoint my wife, MARY KATHERINE COOK, to be the Executrix of this my Last Will and Testament and direct that no bond be required for the faithful performance of her duties. I further vest my Executrix with full power and authority to sell, transfer, and convey any property, real or personal, which I may own at the time of my death at such time and price and upon such terms and conditions as she may determine and to do every other act necessary for the complete administration of this Will.

Testimonium →

       IN WITNESS WHEREOF, I have hereunto signed and subscribed my name to this my Last Will and Testament, consisting of this and one (1) preceding typewritten page; and for the purpose of identification, I have initialed each such page, all in the presence of the persons witnessing it at my request on this the _____ day of May, (current year), at Austin, Texas.

                                 _____

                                   JOHN BLAIR COOK, Testator

Attestation →

       The foregoing instrument, consisting of this and one (1) preceding page, was signed, sealed, published, and declared by JOHN BLAIR COOK, the Testator, to be his Last Will and Testament in our presence; and we, at his request and in his presence and in the presence of each other, have hereunto subscribed our names as witnesses and have made oath that he was of sound mind and disposing memory this the ___ day of May, (current year).

_____ residing at _____
WITNESS

_____ residing at _____
WITNESS

_____ residing at _____
WITNESS

This is Page 2 of My Will _____

FIGURE 5-2. Page 2 of a Will

first paragraph should also contain a revocation clause, which revokes all former wills or **testamentary instruments**. Even though the most recent date on a will is a determining factor when there is more than one will, failure to revoke a former will makes it difficult to determine which instrument to rely upon after death.

Domicile. A domicile is a person's true, permanent home where he or she plans to return even though residing elsewhere. A person may have several residences but can have only one domicile. It is important to specify the domicile in the will because the state named is the one where the will is to be probated upon death of the maker. In the first paragraph of Figure 5-1, Austin, Texas, is the domicile of John Cook. In cases where the testator has property in more than one state, the will may have to be administered in each state.

Payment of Debts. Most wills state that debts and expenses of the last illness are to be paid as soon as practicable after death; however, the statement is not necessary because state laws require that debts be paid before any of the decedent's estate can be distributed to persons named in the will. This section of the will may also address how taxes are to be paid. The wording in the payment of taxes clause will clarify whether taxes are to be paid by the person to inherit property or by the estate of the deceased. If not mentioned, taxes, like other debts, must be paid before any of the decedent's estate can be distributed.

Distribution of Real and Personal Property. The distribution clause in a will identifies the types of property to be distributed and the person or persons who are to receive the property. Two types of property are real property (land and anything attached to it) and personal property (everything that is not real property, such as cars, boats, furniture, and personal belongings).

Some terms and their definitions used in this portion of a will are as follows:

Beneficiary	Individual who receives property under the provisions of a will.
Bequeath (verb)	To give personal property.
Bequest	Personal property distributed by a will.
Devise (noun)	Real property.
Devise (verb)	To give real property.
Devisee	Person receiving real property.
Legacy	Real property.
Legatee	Person receiving real property.
Residuary estate	Portion of the deceased's estate after debts are paid and specific distributions are made.
Specific bequest	Specific items of personal property named in a will.

TESTAMENTARY INSTRUMENT

Any documents, such as a will or codicil, to take effect after the death of the maker.

DOMICILE

A person's true, permanent home, to which he or she plans to return though residing elsewhere.

Two ways that a portion of an estate, or the entire estate, can be distributed to classes of individuals, such as "to my children," are per stirpes or per capita.

Per stirpes means that a child gets a deceased parent's share. For example, John Blair Cook, Sr., had two children, Rachel Cook and John Blair Cook, Jr. Rachel Cook had no children and John Blair Cook, Jr., had one child, Robert. John Blair Cook, Jr. is deceased. After John Blair Cook, Sr.'s death, his estate is to be distributed per stirpes to his children. The result is that Rachel Cook would get one-half and Robert Cook, the grandson, would get one-half. See the diagram below.

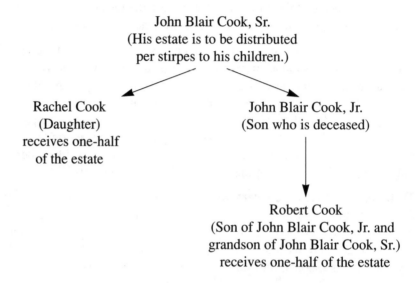

Per capita means that the property is divided among the living children. If John Blair Cook, Sr.'s will had stated that the estate was to be distributed to the children per capita, Rachel Cook (the daughter) would get the entire estate.

Name Executor/trix, Guardian, etc. The individual named in the will to administer the provisions of the will is known as the **executor** (male) or **executrix** (female). A more inclusive term used to identify the person who serves in that position is **personal representative**, and in some states that term is the only one used. The job of administration includes collection of assets of an estate and distribution of those assets. In naming a personal representative, one should select a trustworthy individual in whom he or she has a great deal of confidence. The personal representative should live in the state, and preferably the county, where the will is probated and where the property is located. Often a second person is named to serve as co-executor/trix or to serve as personal representative in case the first-named representative is unable or unwilling to serve.

A **guardian** should be named to take care of the needs of minor children or to take care of incompetent adults. The powers given to the guardian should be clearly outlined. For instance, a guardian should know whether to look after the person or to look after the person and his or her money. In a case where a child whose parents have died has inherited large sums of money through insurance, the child needs to be cared for and the child's money needs to be managed.

Waive Bond. Making **bond** is purchasing insurance to cover any losses if the executor acts dishonestly or irresponsibly in the administration of the will. Unless otherwise stated in the will, the personal representative must make bond in the amount of the total personal assets of the estate of the deceased. The testator has the option of stating in the will that "bond is waived" for the executor/trix, thus eliminating the need or expense of paying the bond premium. The cost of the bond is paid for out of the decedent's estate, and it would be a waste of money in situations where a wife is to inherit the entire estate anyway. If the bond is not waived, and the personal representative does not or cannot make bond, that person will not be allowed to serve; and another person will be appointed.

Trust Provisions. A **trust** is property or money held by one party for the benefit of another. A **testamentary trust** is one that is to take effect upon death of the one who makes the trust. A **trustee** is the party who is holding the property; a **trustor** is a person whose property is being held in trust and is the one who creates the trust. A trustee is named in the will, and detailed instructions outlining the powers and duties of the trustee are given.

A trust is needed in situations where a spouse is to inherit a large sum of money and who either is advanced in age, has never handled financial affairs, or is no longer able to handle financial matters because of health. The testator may be concerned that someone will take advantage of the situation. A simple solution is to appoint a third party (the trustee) in a will, such as an attorney, close friend, and often the trust department of a bank, to handle the money. The trustee would make payments to the beneficiary as needed or as specifically directed in the trust provisions of the will. Money can also be left to children in a trust.

Article VII of the will shown in Figure 5-3, creates a trust composed of the residuary estate and names the First Federal Bank of Fargo, North Dakota, as trustee to manage the funds. The trustee is to collect income from investing the trust fund and make monthly payments to the wife until she dies or remarries. Upon the occurrence of the death or remarriage of the wife, the balance of the trust fund is to be divided among the children. If any child is not yet 21 years of age when the balance of the fund is distributed, that child's share is to be held until age 21 with adequate provisions made for maintenance, education, and welfare of that child.

Testimonium Clause. The testimonium clause is the last paragraph of the will and begins with the words IN WITNESS WHEREOF, and includes a statement about the signing of the will and the date of signing. A signature line for the testator/trix is inserted after the paragraph. The testator must sign and have the required number of witnesses attest to the signing of the will.

If this is done improperly or the required number of witnesses has not signed the testimonium clause, the last will and testament may be invalid. If so, the property will pass as if there was no will.

Attestation Clause. This clause is a statement signed by witnesses to the will. The attestation clause follows the testator's signature and states that the

BOND

An insurance policy issued by a bonding company to ensure that duties are faithfully and honestly performed.

TRUST

Property or money held by one party for the benefit of another.

TESTAMENTARY TRUST

A trust to take effect upon death of the maker.

TRUSTEE

The party who is holding the property named in the trust.

TRUSTOR

The person whose property is being held in trust and the one who creates the trust.

ARTICLE VII

I direct that after all the above-stated bequests and devises have been fulfilled and after the payment of all debts, administration expenses, and death taxes have been paid, then my Executor shall deliver and convey all the remainder of my residuary estate, of whatever kind and nature and wheresoever situated, to the FIRST FEDERAL BANK OF FARGO, located in Fargo, North Dakota, as Trustee, to be held, managed, and controlled as a trust estate with all the rights and powers and subject to the limitations herein set out. I direct that this Trust be for the following uses and purposes:

A. The Trustee shall collect the income from the property comprising the trust estate and shall remit the net income in monthly installments to my wife, NANCY B. SCHMIDT, until her death or until the Trustee has actual knowledge of her remarriage.

B. Upon the death or when the Trustee has actual knowledge of the remarriage of my wife, the Trustee shall divide the principal of the trust estate into as many equal shares as there are children of mine then living and deceased children of mine leaving issue then surviving.

1. If any beneficiary shall be under twenty-one (21) years of age at the time the principal of any trust is required to be distributed to him or her under the above provisions, the share of such beneficiary shall be retained in trust by the Trustee until he or she attains such age. During such time, the Trustee shall pay to such beneficiary or expend on his or her behalf so much of the net income derived from his or her particular fund as the Trustee may deem necessary to provide adequately for the maintenance, education, and welfare of such beneficiary.

2. When each such beneficiary shall attain the age of twenty-one (21) years, the Trust shall terminate as to such beneficiary, and the Trustee shall distribute his or her fund to such beneficiary.

C. I hereby authorize and empower the said Trustee, FIRST FEDERAL BANK OF FARGO, in its sole discretion, at any time and from time to time, to disburse from the principal of any of the trust estates created under this ARTICLE VII such amounts of money as it may deem advisable to provide adequately for the health, support, maintenance, and education of my beneficiaries, including, but not limited to, expenses incurred by reason of illness and disability.

ARTICLE VIII

I hereby authorize my Executor and my Trustee, FIRST FEDERAL BANK OF FARGO, in exercise of reasonable discretion with respect to all property, real and personal, at any time forming part of my estate, to exercise any and all powers as set forth in North Dakota Century Code, Sections 35-50-101 to 105, all of which provisions and powers are incorporated herein by reference as fully as if copied herein verbatim.

FIGURE 5-3. Trust Paragraphs

testator signed in the presence of the witnesses and that the witnesses signed in the presence of the testator and each other. Signature and address lines are provided for the witnesses immediately following the clause. Some states require two witnesses; others require three. Legal secretaries are frequently called upon to serve as witnesses. Witnesses should be of legal age, should not be named in the will to serve as personal representative, guardian, or trustee, and should not be an heir.

The attestation clause that follows is for a testator. It can easily be revised for a testatrix by changing the personal pronouns to "her" and "testator" to "testatrix."

The foregoing instrument, consisting of this and four (4) preceding pages, was signed, published, and declared by (insert the name of the testator), the Testator, to be his Last Will and Testament in our presence, and we, at his request and in his presence and in the presence of each other, have hereunto subscribed our names as witnesses, this the _____ day of _____, 19___.

_____ residing at _____
WITNESS

_____ residing at _____
WITNESS

_____ residing at _____
WITNESS

Formatting Instructions for Wills

- Wills are often printed on high-quality **legal cap**, which is paper with ruled lines at the left and right margins. In addition to the rulings, many firms use a first sheet with **Last Will and Testament** printed as a title and use second sheets with no title for continuation pages.

- Print last wills and testaments and codicils on 8½- by 11-inch or 8½- by 14-inch paper, according to office practice.

- If plain paper is used, set 1-inch left and right margins. Add vertical ruled lines to unruled paper if a word processing program with line-draw capabilities is available.

- Set the margins two spaces inside the ruling lines when printing on legal cap. Do not cross over a line.

- Maintain at least a 1½-inch top margin on all pages to allow space for the legal back to be stapled over the pages at the top.

LEGAL CAP

Paper with ruled vertical lines at the left and right margins.

- The title is keyed in full caps, centered. The title may be placed on two or three lines for balance. Double-space between the lines and triple-space after the title.

- If will paper is used that has **LAST WILL AND TESTAMENT** printed on the form, center the testator/trix's name and double-space below it as shown here.

LAST WILL AND TESTAMENT

OF

NANCY WORTHINGTON CROSSLEY

- Double-space the body of a will unless instructed otherwise by your attorney.

- The body of the will is divided into sections called articles or items, which are numbered consecutively throughout the document. Some commonly used schemes for identifying the sections are shown below. Double- or triple-space before the section heading and double-space after it.

ARTICLE I

or

ITEM I

or

FIRST: (at paragraph point)
SECOND:

or

First: (at paragraph point)
Second:

or

1. (at paragraph point)
2.

Articles might have subsections labeled with (1), (2) or (a), (b).

- The testimonium clause should not be placed on a page by itself. At least two lines of text from the body of the will should be on the same page as the testimonium and attestation clauses — it continues the document in such a way that subsequent alterations would be difficult.

- Single-space or double-space the attestation clause, depending on the space available.

- Type the signature line for the first witness a triple space below the attestation clause. Allow about 2 ½ inches for the signature line, space once, type "residing at," space once, and type another 2 ½ inch line. Either one or two lines may be provided for the addresses. Leave three blank lines between witness lines.

_____ residing at _____

_____

_____ residing at _____

_____

or

_____   _____
WITNESS   ADDRESS

_____   _____
WITNESS   ADDRESS

- Number each page (including page 1) of a will using one of the following methods. The blank lines are provided so the testator/trix can initial each page to ensure that pages are not changed or inserted.

Page 1 of 5

Page 1 of the Last Will and Testament of Cherronda Brown _____
Page 1 of My Will _____
Page 1 of My First Codicil _____
This Is Page One of My Last Will and Testament _____
This Is Page 1 of My Will _____
Page 1 of 5

- Prepare an original and two copies of the will — an original, executed will for the testator to keep in a safe deposit box or safe location, a copy for the testator's files, and a copy for the office files. Copies are made after the will is executed.

SELF-PROVING AFFIDAVIT

Before a will can be probated, the witnesses to the will are to appear in court and swear that they witnessed the signing of the decedent's will. If a witness dies before the testator/trix dies, then two people who could testify to the authenticity of the witness's signature would be subpoenaed into court to testify. To eliminate this problem or the problem of locating a witness who cannot be found, most states have passed statutes that allow for self-proving a will. The witnesses sign an affidavit before a notary public (some states do not require the signing before a notary) usually at the time of the execution of the will. The will and affidavit are submitted for probate after the death of the testator/trix.

SELF-PROVING AFFIDAVIT

A sworn statement before a notary by the witnesses to a will.

Refer to Figure 5-4 as you review the parts and content of a self-proving affidavit.

- Title

- Venue

- Body

- Signature lines for the witnesses

- Jurat

- Signature line and commission expiration line for the notary

The venue is required on every affidavit. Without the state and county identification, the notary's seal would be null and void. The body states the facts to which the witnesses are taking oath. The witnesses sign the affidavit indicating that they saw the testator/trix sign the will. Note that the testator does NOT sign the affidavit. The jurat is included for the notary (in some states this would be omitted).

CODICIL TO A WILL

CODICIL

An addition or amendment to a will.

A **codicil** is an addition or amendment to a will. One or more codicils can be prepared adding provisions to the will, revoking articles in the will, or updating the will. Consequently, a codicil is most often prepared when the testator wants to add or remove something from an existing will without writing an entirely new will.

The title of a codicil should include the number of the codicil, such as First Codicil to the Last Will and Testament of (Testator's Name), Second Codicil to the Last Will and Testament of (Testator's Name). It should be prepared, dated, witnessed, self-proved, and executed with all the formalities of a complete will and then be kept with the will to which it relates.

EXECUTION-OF-WILL MEETING

EXECUTION

All the formalities of signing and delivering a document or contract.

After the will has been prepared, the testator or testatrix should be given adequate time to read the document before the witnesses and the notary public are called in for the execution of the documents. **Execution** is the legal term for signing and delivering any document, including a will. The testator signs the document on the signature line exactly as his name is typed within the document; for example, Harold Timothy Adkins would sign Harold Timothy Adkins, not Harold T. Adkins. The testator may be asked to sign or initial each page of the will. If each page is initialed rather than signed, the initials for Harold Timothy Adkins would be H.T.A., not H.A.

1½"

AFFIDAVIT OF WITNESSES TO PROVE WILL | Title — there is no
caption as this is
not part of a
litigation matter

STATE OF TEXAS)
| Venue
COUNTY OF CHEROKEE)

We, **ROBERT F. HART, CONA A. GIVAN,** and **DIANNE M. BERLIN,** after first being duly sworn according to law, make oath to the following:

1. That we are adult citizens of Cherokee County, Texas, and were so on the date of the signing of the Will of **JOHN BLAIR COOK.**

2. That we witnessed the execution of the Last Will and Testament of **JOHN BLAIR COOK,** dated May 13, (current year), to which this Affidavit is attached and that this Affidavit is being made at the request of the Testator according to Texas statutory law.

3. That our signatures are affixed to the said Last Will and Testament and that we signed our names at the request of the Testator, **JOHN BLAIR COOK,** in his presence and in the presence of each other at the place and on the date recited in the said Last Will and Testament. ← Body (Sworn Statement)

4. That the Testator, **JOHN BLAIR COOK,** signed said document as and for his Last Will and Testament in our sight and presence.

5. That at the time we witnessed said Last Will and Testament, the Testator, **JOHN BLAIR COOK,** was, in our opinion, of sound mind and disposing memory.

Further, Affiants saith not.

_____   _____
NAME OF WITNESS   ADDRESS

_____   _____
NAME OF WITNESS   ADDRESS ← Signature Lines for Witnesses

_____   _____
NAME OF WITNESS   ADDRESS

Sworn to and subscribed before me
this the ____ day of May, (current year). | Jurat

_____
NOTARY PUBLIC

My Commission Expires: _____ | Notary's Signature Line and Expiration Date

FIGURE 5-4. Affidavit to Self-Prove a Will

The witnesses are to watch the testator sign and then place their signatures on the last page with the testator looking on. The witnesses do not need to know the contents of the document, as they are signing a statement indicating that they believe the testator to be of sound mind and of legal age and that they are witnessing the signing of the will. If the document is to be self-proved, a notary public observes as all witnesses sign the affidavit, then signs on the line provided for the notary public, seals it, and enters the date of expiration of the notary commission. Only after everyone has signed is anyone allowed to leave the room.

After a new will for a client is executed, the testator or testatrix should destroy the old will by physically tearing up the previous will. This is often done immediately after signing the new will, while everyone is still present.

ASSEMBLING COPIES OF THE WILL

Only the original will is signed and witnessed. The secretary makes two copies of the executed will — the original and one copy are for the client and one copy is for the office files. The copies are clearly marked or stamped COPY or PHOTO-COPY. Care should be taken in assembling the original and copies because staple marks made when staples are removed should not appear on any documents as this could indicate that someone had tampered with the will. The completed will followed by the affidavit is placed in a covering about one inch longer and one-half inch wider than the will paper, known as a **legal back**. The packet is stapled two or three times across the top; and if legal-sized paper is used, it is folded in half twice and then placed in an envelope to be given to the client. Most attorneys provide the high-quality will paper, legal back, and envelope to create a professional look; however, it in no way affects the legality of the document. See Figure 5-5.

LEGAL BACK

A sheet of paper (sometimes colored) slightly larger and heavier than the paper on which a document is printed. It is a cover on documents.

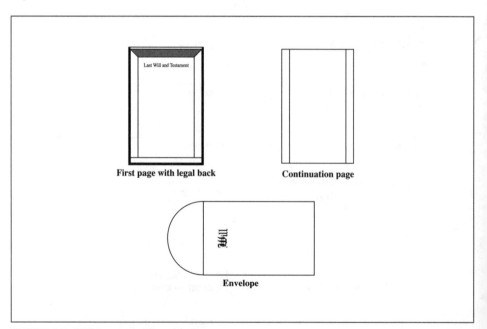

First page with legal back   Continuation page

Envelope

FIGURE 5-5. Will Paper and Envelope

LIVING WILL

A living will is a distinct and separate type of will from that previously discussed. A person can have a living will without having a formal will and vice versa. Its purpose is to instruct the medical profession in advance about the conditions under which to provide or withdraw medical treatment when there is no reasonable expectation of recovery. The document may instruct the doctors to allow a person to die and not be kept alive by life-support equipment, or it can instruct them not to withdraw life-support equipment. Living wills may also include a person's desire to donate organs for transplantation.

A living will is signed, witnessed, and notarized, just as is a formal will. It is signed by the **declarant**, the person making the declaration about life-support devices. Relatives, individuals who are to inherit, employees of the hospital, or the attending physician cannot serve as witnesses to the signing of the document. Refer to Figures 5-6 and 5-7, a living will of John Blair Cook, as you review the following elements:

- Title

- Body, including the name of the person making the living will and the desires of the declarant

- Testimonium clause

- Signature line for the declarant

- Witness statement followed by signature lines for the witnesses

- Statement signed by a notary that the document was subscribed (signed), sworn to, and acknowledged in his or her presence

DURABLE POWER OF ATTORNEY FOR HEALTH CARE

As an alternative or an addition to a living will, some states have passed statutes that allow an individual to sign a durable power of attorney for health care. It is a simple written instrument in which the maker (or principal) appoints someone as **attorney in fact**, rather than the physician, to make health-care decisions for the maker. Attorney in fact does not mean that the person appointed is necessarily an attorney at law. It is a term to describe anyone appointed as an agent to act for another person. It goes into effect only when the principal is unable to give informed consent. The attorney in fact (agent) must follow the directions that are stated in the document.

The principal, the person making the document, can terminate a durable power of attorney at any time by destroying the signed document or by making a written direction. A durable power of attorney is different from a formal will or from a living will, and one can have a durable power of attorney without either of the other types of wills.

LIVING WILL
Written instructions to the medical profession not to provide or to withdraw medical treatment when there is no reasonable expectation of recovery.

DECLARANT
Sometimes used as a party designation in living wills in which the person who signs makes declarations about life-support devices being used or not used.

DURABLE POWER OF ATTORNEY FOR HEALTH CARE
A written instrument in which the maker appoints someone other than the physician to make health care decisions for the maker.

ATTORNEY IN FACT
One who is appointed to act in the place of another.

LIVING WILL
OF
JOHN BLAIR COOK

Title

I, JOHN BLAIR COOK, willfully and voluntarily make known my desire that my dying shall not be artificially prolonged under the circumstances set forth below; and I therefore declare as follows:

If, at any time, I should have a terminal condition and my attending physician has determined that there can be no recovery from such condition and the application of medical care would serve only to artificially prolong the dying process, I direct that medical care be withheld or withdrawn and that I be permitted to die naturally with only the administration of medications or the performance of any medical procedure deemed necessary to provide me with comfortable care or to alleviate pain. I authorize the withholding or withdrawal of artificially provided food, water, or other nourishment or fluids.

Notwithstanding my previous declaration relative to the withholding or withdrawal of life-prolonging procedures, I express my desire to donate my organs and/or tissues for transplantation; and I direct my attending physician, if I have been determined dead according to Texas statutory law, to maintain me on artificial support systems only for the period of time required to maintain the viability of and to remove such organs and/or tissues.

Body

In the absence of my ability to give directions regarding my medical care, it is my intention that this declaration shall be honored by my family and physician as the final expression of my legal right to refuse medical care and accept the consequences of such refusal.

I understand the full import of this declaration, and I am emotionally and mentally competent to make this declaration.

Testimonium ➔ IN WITNESS WHEREOF, I do hereinafter affix my signature on this the _____ day of _____, (current year).

Signature line for declarant | _____
JOHN BLAIR COOK, Declarant

Sworn Statement by Witnesses ➔ We, the subscribing witnesses hereto, are personally acquainted with and subscribe our names hereto at the request of the Declarant, an adult, whom we believe to be of sound mind, fully aware of the action taken herein and its possible consequence.

We, the undersigned witnesses, further declare that we are not related to the Declarant by blood or marriage; that we are not entitled to any portion of the estate of the Declarant upon his decease under any will or codicil thereto presently existing or by operation of law then existing; that we are not the attending physicians, an employee

Page 1 of 2

FIGURE 5-6. Living Will, Page 1

of the attending physician or a health facility in which the declarant is a patient; and that we are not persons who, at the present time, have a claim against any portion of the estate of the declarant upon his or her death.

_____
WITNESS

_____
WITNESS

_____
WITNESS

STATE OF TEXAS   )

COUNTY OF CHEROKEE)

      Sworn to, subscribed, and acknowledged before me by **JOHN BLAIR COOK,** the Declarant, and sworn to and subscribed before me by _____, _____, and _____, witness, this the _____ day of _____, (current year).

      Sworn to by Declarant and Witnesses

_____
NOTARY PUBLIC

My Commission Expires: _____

FIGURE 5-7. Living Will, Page 2

Adapted from Tenn. Hospital Association's Living Will, 1991

The durable power of attorney is typed in the same format as a living will, including a statement similar to the one shown below for the notary public to sign. State statutes usually provide the appropriate terminology.

STATE OF _____

COUNTY OF _____

On this the _____ day of _____, 19___, before the undersigned Notary Public, personally appeared (name of principal), personally known to me (or proved to me on the basis of satisfactory evidence) to be the person whose name is subscribed to this instrument, and acknowledged that (he or she) executed it. I declare under penalty of perjury that the person whose name is subscribed to this instrument appears to be of sound mind and under no duress, fraud, or undue influence.

_____
NOTARY PUBLIC

My Commission Expires: _____

SUMMARY

- A last will and testament is an instrument stating how a person's property is to be distributed after death.

- A male who makes a will is a testator; a female, is a testatrix.

- Wills can be formal, holographic, or nuncupative. A formal will is prepared by an attorney and is executed and witnessed as required by state laws; a holographic will is handwritten by the testator; and a nuncupative will is oral.

- All wills should begin by stating that the maker is of sound mind and legal age, is making a will, and revokes former wills and codicils.

- Wills may include paragraphs dealing with payment of debts and taxes, distribution of real and personal property, distribution of the residuary estate, naming of a personal representative and guardian, and sometimes creation and description of a trust.

- The executor or executrix, also known as a personal representative, named in the will is responsible for collecting and distributing assets of the deceased according to the terms of the will.

- A guardian should be named in a will if provisions need to be made for the care of the person and/or property of minor children or incompetent adults.

- The last paragraph of a will is known as the testimonium clause and begins with the words "IN WITNESS WHEREOF."

- A will should be dated at the end, which is usually done in the testimonium clause.

- The attestation clause precedes the signature lines for the witnesses.

- Wills may include trust provisions if the testator/trix so desires.

- A codicil is an addition or amendment to a will and is executed with the same formalities of a last will and testament and should be kept with the will to which it relates.

- Wills and codicils to wills can be self-proved by preparing an affidavit.

- The name of the testator should be spelled exactly as he plans to sign his name on the last will and testament.

- A living will instructs the physician how to proceed when a patient has a terminal condition with no hope of recovery.

- Some states have passed statutes allowing an individual to sign a durable power of attorney for health care as an alternative or an addition to a living will. An attorney in fact is named to make health care decisions once the maker is unable to give informed consent.

REVIEW EXERCISES

T F 1. A person who makes a will should be of sound mind and legal age.

T F 2. A legal secretary would usually be involved in typing a holographic will.

T F 3. Domicile is a person's true, permanent home.

T F 4. The residuary estate would include specific items of personal property that are to go to beneficiaries.

T F 5. Per capita and per stirpes are terms that indicate how an estate will be distributed to children and/or grandchildren.

T F 6. An executor may also be known as a personal representative.

T F 7. An executor and guardian must always make bond.

T F 8. The attestation clause is the last paragraph of the body of the will before the testator's signature.

T F 9. When witnesses sign a will, they also indicate their residence.

T F 10. A self-proving affidavit is a separate document.

T F 11. It is a requirement that witnesses to a will appear in court and testify that they witnessed the will even though they signed a self-proving affidavit.

T F 12. An affidavit may be invalid if the venue is omitted.

T F 13. During an execution-of-will meeting, the testator, witnesses, and notary public are not to leave the room until everyone has signed the documents.

T F 14. All copies of a will should be clearly marked as copies.

T F 15. A legal secretary can feel free to destroy a former will of a client if a new one has been executed.

T F 16. Every page of a will should be numbered.

T F 17. The testimonium clause can be typed on a page by itself.

T   F   18.   As with other legal documents, do not number the first page of a will.

T   F   19.   The testimonium and attestation clauses can be single-spaced in order to keep them on the same page.

T   F   20.   A person who has a living will does not need a last will and testament.

TRANSCRIPTION RULES

The following punctuation rules have been presented in previous chapters. Additional examples are provided for your review.

CAPITALIZATION

Document Titles

Document titles for this chapter are:

Affidavit to Prove Will
Last Will and Testament
Living Will
Durable Power of Attorney
Will

Party Designation

Party designations for wills are:

Agent
Attorney in Fact
Declarant
Executor
Executrix
Guardian
Personal Representative
Principal
Testator
Testatrix
Trustee

COMMAS

Dependent Clauses — Nonessential

I give One Thousand Dollars ($1,000) to my sister, SARAH COOK BURNETT, *since she has had a hard time making ends meet since the death of her husband.* (nonessential)

Phrases — Interrupting

I, JOHN BLAIR COOK, *being of sound mind and disposing memory,* do publish this instrument as my Last Will and Testament.

The foregoing Last Will and Testament, *consisting of four (4) pages, including this page,* was signed by JOHN BLAIR COOK.

Phrases — Introductory

IN WITNESS WHEREOF, I have signed and subscribed my name to this my Last Will and Testament.

Series

I *give, devise, and and bequeath* all of my personal property and all of my real property to my beloved wife.

I, JOHN BLAIR COOK, being of sound mind, do *make, publish, and declare* this instrument as my Last Will and Testament.

The following rules have not been previously presented.

CITATIONS TO LEGAL MATERIAL

Section or §

Spell out the word "Section" when referring to section numbers in text.

The material can be found in the <u>General Statutes of North Carolina</u>, Section 24-4-208.

COMMAS

Series Joined by Conjunctions

If the items in a series are joined by conjunctions, do not separate them with commas.

I have signed and declared and published this to be my Last Will and Testament.

UNDERLINE OR ITALICIZE

Complete Published Works

The titles of books and magazines or any complete published legal materials are underlined or italicized.

This document is construed as a Durable Power of Attorney for Health Care according to the **<u>General Statutes of North Carolina</u>**.

TRANSCRIPTION EXERCISES

Use a secretarial reference manual and the rules presented in this and previous chapters to aid you in correctly transcribing the following material. The sentences are presented in lowercase letters without capitalization and punctuation and with misspelled words.

1. i john blair cook residing in the city of austin county of hays state of texas do make publish and declare this to be my last will and testament

2. any devises or legates or beneficiarys who shall contest this will shall not be entitled to share in my estate

3. the fore going instrument consisting of this and ten preceeding pages was signed sealed published and declared by the testatrix to be his last will and testament

4. i authorize my executor and my trustee first federal bank of fargo to exercise any and all powers as set fourth in north dakota century code sec. 35 50 101 to 35 50 105 all of which powers are incorporated here in by reference as fully as if copied here in verbatim (The executor and trustee had been named previously.)

5. we robert f hart cona a givan and dianne m berlin after first being duely sworn according to law make oath to the following 1 that we are adult citizens of cherokee county tx 2 that we witnessed the execution of the last will and testament of john blair cook and 3 that this affidavid is being made at the request of the testatrix

6. we the witnesses hereinafter signed declare that the principle signed this durable power of attorney

7. in anticipation of decisions that may have to be made about my dying if such a time occurs i make known my desire that my dying not be artificially prolonged

8. i have the right to revoke this living will either orally or in writing by communicating that choice to my family or doctor

Prepare the following portions of documents and save them to a glossary or file to retrieve into documents as needed. If a macro feature is available on your word processing program, you may want to create these as macros.

9. Prepare signature lines for witnesses to a will. Use the style that provides for two lines for the address. Name the macro wit.

10. Prepare your own legal cap with vertical lines three-quarters of an inch from each edge of the paper. See Figure 5-1. Name the macro vert.

11. Prepare any other macros you feel would speed the job of preparing wills. Write the name and descriptions on the lines below for future reference.

_____

_____

_____

RESEARCH ACTIVITIES

1. Consult your state statutes to determine if your state provides for self-proving of wills.

2. Consult your state statutes to determine the number of witnesses who are to sign a will.

3. Ask someone who works in a legal office to describe the format he or she uses for typing wills. Does the office use legal backs? printed first sheets? continuation sheets to match?

4. Look in the library for sample wills or sample paragraphs for wills. Read the wills to familiarize yourself with the terminology.

PROJECTS

Insert the cassette tape for Chapter 5 and transcribe the following projects.

Project 5-1   Transcribe the will of George Curtis Landers, who has a wife and five sons. Print the will on legal cap. Center the title on three double-spaced lines. Use centered article numbers for the divisions, i.e., ARTICLE I, etc. Use the following style for page numbering: Page 1 of My Will _____. Use the macro you created for inserting witness lines.

Using Figure 5-4, prepare a self-proving affidavit. Use the names of two of your classmates as witnesses. Ely, Minnesota is in St. Louis County.

Schedule a meeting with your classmates and have an execution-of-will meeting. You will need one attorney, one secretary who is also a notary, two or three witnesses, and a testator.

Project 5-2   Transcribe the first codicil of George Curtis Landers. Center the title on three double-spaced lines. Print the codicil on legal cap.

Paragraphs are indented, but sections of the codicil are not numbered. Number the pages.

Project 5-3   This project consists of paragraphs identified as "A. Exordium Clause" through "O. Attestation Clause." Save each paragraph; name the first one "A," second one "B," etc. These paragraphs can be recalled later to make a complete will. The paragraphs should be created so variable information can be inserted at a later time. Review the merge feature of your software and save each paragraph so it can be retrieved and variable information inserted.

Paragraph A will appear on the screen as follows if you are using WordPerfect:

I, testator's name~ a resident of city~, state~, being of sound mind and disposing memory, ...

Prepare a will for Ronald P. Hoffman by retrieving paragraphs A, B, C, D, E, J, K, N, and O. Add signature lines as needed. Insert the following information.

Paragraph A:	RONALD P. HOFFMAN Franklin North Carolina
Paragraph E:	JOHN J. HARRISON, my friend and business associate Bank Account No. 2D3867-7654 at First Union Bank, Main Branch, Franklin, North Carolina
Paragraph J:	three (3) sons
Paragraph K:	MELVIN C. JONES Executor him him Executor
Paragraph N:	(Insert No. of pages) August, 1994 Franklin, North Carolina
Paragraph O:	(Insert No, of pages) RONALD P. HOFFMAN Testator his August, 1994 Franklin, North Carolina

Project 5-4   Transcribe a living will for John David Robinson.

Project 5-5   Transcribe a durable power of attorney for health care for John David Robinson.

CHAPTER 6

PROBATE PROCEDURE

INTRODUCTION

Have you ever known anyone who lost a family member and had to determine what to do with the property of the deceased? Have you ever thought that someday you may be responsible for handling such matters? In the case we will be examining, Lucy Perez, the **decedent**, died leaving her husband and two children.

When someone dies, an estate is created consisting of everything the person owns. It is known as a **probate estate**. The probate laws of the state specify the procedures to be followed in handling the decedent's estate. Every person dies either **testate** (having made a valid will) or **intestate** (not having made a will). In the case of a testate procedure, the estate is distributed according to the terms of the will. In an intestate procedure, the **laws of succession** (also known as laws of descent and distribution) for each state determine who will receive the decedent's property, how much, and in what order. Whether the procedure is testate or intestate, someone will have to be appointed to administer the estate of the decedent. The duties of one who administers an estate are to:

- Carry out the desires of the decedent as stated in the will or, if there is no will, distribute property according to state laws

- Notify heirs

- Take an inventory of the assets of the estate

- Notify creditors by publishing a notice of death in the newspaper

- Pay all debts owed by the decedent

DECEDENT

A deceased person.

PROBATE ESTATE

All property to be distributed by will or by descent and distribution after death.

TESTATE

A procedure for settling an estate for a person who died after having made a will.

INTESTATE

A procedure for settling an estate for a person who died not having a will.

LAWS OF SUCCESSION

(also known as laws of descent and distribution) Laws that govern the way property passes if one dies without leaving a will.

- File all tax returns and pay all taxes due

- Distribute all specific bequests or, if there is no will, pay the heirs as set out in the laws of intestate succession

- Make an accounting of all estate receipts and payments and close out the estate when everything is completed

PROBATE PROCEDURES

Procedures for probating a will are the steps one follows to ensure that the estate is distributed in the manner desired by the decedent and/or according to the laws of the state. Once a person dies, the will is to be probated in the county where the testator had his usual residence at the time of death. The will may also have to be probated in each state where the decedent owned land.

This chapter focuses on the content and format of the following documents:

> **PETITION TO PROBATE A WILL**
>
> **ORDER ADMITTING WILL TO PROBATE**
>
> **AFFIDAVIT OF NOTIFICATION OF BENEFICIARIES**
>
> **INVENTORY**
>
> **RECEIPT OF SPECIFIC BEQUEST**
>
> **FINAL ACCOUNTING**
>
> **PETITION FOR LETTERS OF ADMINISTRATION**
>
> **ORDER FOR INTESTATE ADMINISTRATION**

PETITION TO PROBATE A WILL

PETITION TO PROBATE A WILL

A document asking that a will be admitted to probate court.

The purpose of the petition is to submit the will so it can be proved to be valid, to provide information about the deceased and the heirs, and to request that the judge appoint someone to administer the will. The first step in this process is to prepare a petition to probate a will. Refer to Figures 6-1 and 6-2, a petition to probate the will of Lucy Perez. Matthew Perez was named in the will as executor, and he is submitting the petition to probate her will. Any interested person can sign and file the petition, but it is most often done by the spouse, the closest heir, or the personal representative. Locate the following sections of the petition:

- Caption (venue, style of the case, file number, and title)

- Body

- Prayer clause

- Signature line for the petitioner and signature block for the attorney

- Verification

- Cost bond (in some states)

Caption. The centered court heading includes the court name, county, and state: IN THE PROBATE COURT FOR DEKALB COUNTY, GEORGIA. The style of a probate petition should begin with IN THE MATTER OF: _____, Deceased, or IN THE ESTATE OF: _____, Deceased, or IN RE: _____, Deceased, or PROBATE OF THE LAST WILL AND TESTAMENT OF _____, Deceased. "Deceased" is included in the style because a will cannot be probated unless the person is deceased. The individual petitioning the court is named and identified as petitioner in the style of the case. A line is provided to the right of the style of the case for inserting a file or docket number.

Body. Examine the body of the petition to probate the will of Lucy Perez and locate the following types of information:

- Name, relationship, and residence of the petitioner

- Name and relationship of the person named as personal representative

- Age, date of death, and residence of the deceased

- Date of the will

- Names of witnesses to the will

- Names of witnesses who signed an affidavit to self-prove the will

- Names, relationships, ages, and residences of heirs, if known

- Estimated value of the personal property and real estate of the deceased

- Bond waived

Prayer Clause. In the prayer clause Matthew Perez, the petitioner, prays that the will be admitted to probate, that **letters testamentary** (a document giving the personal representative power to manage the estate of the deceased) be issued, that the affidavits of witnesses to self-prove the will be accepted by the court, and that probate of the will be granted and ordered.

Signature Lines. A signature line is prepared for Matthew Perez along with a signature block at the left margin for the attorney.

Verification. A verification is placed at the bottom of the document. It has a venue, statement that the contents of the document are true to the best of the petitioner's knowledge, information, and belief, and a jurat for the notary to sign. When a vertification is included in a petition, the petition is referred to as a **sworn petition**.

LETTERS TESTAMENTARY

An instrument or document of authority issued to the executor or executrix of an estate of a person who dies leaving a will.

SWORN PETITION

A petition that contains a statement sworn to before a notary public by the petitioner that the contents of the document are true.

The petition is submitted to the clerk of the court and a time for a hearing is set. At the hearing before a judge (in some areas before an officer in the probate clerk's office known as a **probate master**) a statement is made to the court that the person is deceased and that the executor/trix is present and wants to qualify and submit the will for probate. The will is examined and, if it is authentic, the judge will order that it be admitted to probate.

ORDER ADMITTING THE WILL TO PROBATE

An **order** is a document signed by the judge, commanding or ordering that certain things be done. An order is generally prepared at the same time as the petition in anticipation of the judge's allowing the will to be probated or "admitted into probate." It restates much of the information in the petition and then orders that the will be admitted to probate, that the clerk of the probate court file and record the will, that a personal representative be appointed (usually the executor/trix named in the will), and that letters testamentary be issued. Note the following parts of the order as you examine Figure 6-3. The caption now identifies the petitioner, Matthew Perez, as executor because prior to the signing of the order, the judge officially appointed him as executor.

- Caption

- Body of the order

- Signature lines for the judge or probate master

- Approved-for-entry block for the attorney (the attorney signs indicating that she is satisfied with the contents of the document)

- Certificate signed by the attorney for the executor, stating that a copy of the order to probate is being sent to each heir (may be required in some states)

REPRESENTATIVE'S OATH

After the order was signed by the judge, Matthew Perez took an oath before the clerk of the probate court that he would administer the will of the deceased and faithfully perform the duties of the personal representative. Nothing can be done until and unless the oath is taken. The next step, unless it has been waived, is to make bond. The personal representative pays a premium to the insurance bonding company to ensure the "faithful performance of his or her duties." When the fee, which is based on the value of the personal property of the probate estate, is paid, the insurance company's representative signs the necessary bond book in the probate clerk's office. This usually delays the issuance of letters testamentary for a couple of days.

IN THE PROBATE COURT FOR DEKALB COUNTY, GEORGIA

IN THE MATTER OF:)
)
Probate of Last Will and Testament   )
of LUCY PEREZ, Deceased,   )   No. _____
)
MATTHEW PEREZ, Petitioner.   )

PETITION TO PROBATE A WILL

Your Petitioner, MATTHEW PEREZ, would respectfully show unto the Court:

1. That he is a resident of Dekalb County, State of Georgia, and an interested party in this estate.

2. That said LUCY PEREZ died on the 30th day of November, (current year), a resident of Dekalb County, State of Georgia, at the age of seventy (70), leaving a Last Will and Testament bearing the date of July 4, (ten years ago), and witnessed by JACK ADAIR and KAREN APPLEBY. The witnesses signed the attached Affidavit to Prove Will.

3. That Will nominates and appoints MATTHEW PEREZ, husband of the deceased and a resident of the State of Georgia, to serve as Executor without bond.

4. That the deceased left an estate to be administered and that the estimated value of the estate is Fifty Thousand Dollars ($50,000) in personal property and One Hundred Fifty Thousand Dollars ($150,000) in jointly owned real estate to be passed on to the surviving spouse.

5. That the names, relationship, ages, and residences of the beneficiaries named in the Will are:

Name	Relationship	Age	Residence
MATTHEW PEREZ	Husband	75	185 Briarcliff Road Atlanta, GA 30310
SIMON PEREZ	Son	45	338 Chamblee Tucker Road Atlanta, GA 30303
CHRISTINA MONTGOMERY	Daughter	40	605 Midway Circle Memphis, TN 38098

PREMISES CONSIDERED, PETITIONER PRAYS:

1. That the said Last Will and Testament of LUCY PEREZ be admitted to probate.

FIGURE 6-1. Petition to Probate a Will, Page 1

2. That the affidavits of subscribing witnesses to self-prove the Will be accepted by the Court.

3. That MATTHEW PEREZ be appointed Executor of the Last Will and Testament of LUCY PEREZ and that he be allowed to serve without bond.

4. That Letters Testamentary be issued to MATTHEW PEREZ as Executor.

↓4

_____
                    MATTHEW PEREZ, Petitioner

↓4

_____
MARILYN C. CANDISH (No. 89891)
Attorney for Petitioner
2000 Peachtree Towers
Atlanta, GA 30300
(404) 555-3333

↓3

STATE OF GEORGIA)   ⟩Make sure) line up
COUNTY OF DEKALB)

Your Petitioner, MATTHEW PEREZ, after being duly sworn, makes oath that the statements contained in the foregoing Petition to Probate a Will are true to the best of his knowledge, information, and belief.

↓4

_____
                    MATTHEW PEREZ, Petitioner

↓3
Sworn to and subscribed before me
this the _____ day of _____, (current year).

↓4

_____
NOTARY PUBLIC
↓2?
My Commission Expires: _____

- 2 -

FIGURE 6-2. Petition to Probate a Will, Page 2

IN THE PROBATE COURT FOR DEKALB COUNTY, GEORGIA

IN THE MATTER OF:	)	
	)	
Probate of Last Will and Testament	)	No. 75972
of LUCY PEREZ, Deceased,	)	
	)	
MATTHEW PEREZ, Executor.	)	

ORDER ADMITTING WILL TO PROBATE

This matter came on to be heard on the 27th day of February, (current year), before the Honorable CHRISTOPHER F. WOOLWINE, Judge of the Probate Court for Dekalb County, Georgia, upon a Petition to probate a paper writing purporting to be the Last Will and Testament of LUCY PEREZ and witnessed by JACK ADAIR and KAREN APPLEBY. After testimony in open court and a review of all documents submitted and it appearing to the Court from the Affidavits of the witnesses that the said paper writing was written in the lifetime of the deceased and signed by the witnesses in the presence and at the request of the deceased and in the presence of each other and as attesting witnesses thereto; that said instrument was executed by the deceased as and for the deceased's Last Will and Testament; that the deceased was at the time of sound mind and disposing memory; that the deceased died in Atlanta, Dekalb County, Georgia; and that the deceased's usual place of residence and domicile at the time of death was in the said county, all of which are the findings of the Court.

IT IS THEREFORE ORDERED, ADJUDGED, AND DECREED by the Court that the Last Will and Testament of LUCY PEREZ be and is hereby admitted into probate; that the Clerk of the Probate Court is hereby directed to file and record the same; that the named Executor, MATTHEW PEREZ, be appointed Executor with his being allowed to qualify without posting bond; and that Letters Testamentary be issued to MATTHEW PEREZ.

ENTERED this the _____ day February, (current year).

_____
CHRISTOPHER F. WOOLWINE, JUDGE

APPROVED FOR ENTRY:

_____
MARILYN C. CANDISH (No. 89891)
Attorney for Executor
2000 Peachtree Towers
Atlanta, GA 30300
(404) 555-3333

CERTIFICATE

I, MARILYN C. CANDISH, Attorney for Executor, do hereby certify that I have mailed a true and exact copy of this Order Admitting Will to Probate to each heir at his or her last known address on this the _____ day of February, (current year).

_____
MARILYN C. CANDISH

FIGURE 6-3. Order to Probate a Will

LETTERS TESTAMENTARY

Once the oath had been taken and the will had been probated, letters testamentary were issued by the probate clerk to Matthew. With the authority of the letters, Matthew can open a bank account in the name of the estate of the deceased, can take charge of the estate assets, pay all of the debts, and make sure the estate is distributed as stated in the will.

If Matthew had not been able to serve, the court would have issued **letters of administration, c.t.a.** (cum testamento annexo, meaning "with will attached") to someone else. In a case where someone not named as the personal representative in the will is appointed, bonding is normally required. Sometimes the courts will waive that bonding requirement when a bank or a financial institution has agreed to administer the estate c.t.a.

> **LETTERS OF ADMINISTRATION, c.t.a.**
>
> *(cum testamento annexo — with will attached) An instrument or document issued to a person who was not named executor or executrix in a will, giving the person to whom it is issued authority to administer the will.*

NOTIFICATION OF HEIRS

All heirs are normally notified in writing that administration of the estate has begun. This can be accomplished by sending each of the heirs a notice or a copy of the order admitting the will to probate. Along with the notice, a copy of the will should be sent to each beneficiary. Some states have specific notice documents, but in other states it is sufficient to mail a letter notifying heirs.

AFFIDAVIT OF NOTIFICATION OF BENEFICIARIES

Some courts require that the personal representative file an affidavit with the clerk of the probate court, providing the names and addresses of all beneficiaries who were notified and the names of any beneficiaries who were not notified, along with a reason they were not notified. Matthew Perez gave each of his children a copy of the will and then filed the sworn affidavit with the clerk of the court. See Figure 6-4.

Another method of assuring the clerk that all heirs have been notified is to have the heirs sign receipts for all personal property they receive. If a check is issued, a statement is typed above the endorsement area on the back of the check, such as —"I have received $5,000 from the estate of Lucy Perez and have no further claim to the estate." Endorsing the check serves not only as a receipt but also as evidence of notification.

NOTICE TO CREDITORS

It is required that a notice to creditors be published in a newspaper of general circulation. The notice runs for a period of time set by state statutes, usually three or four consecutive weeks, and is to inform all persons to whom the estate of the

IN THE PROBATE COURT FOR DEKALB COUNTY, GEORGIA

IN THE MATTER OF:)
)
The Estate of   )
LUCY PEREZ, Deceased,   )   No. 75972
)
MATTHEW PEREZ, Executor.   )

AFFIDAVIT OF NOTIFICATION OF BENEFICIARIES

STATE OF GEORGIA)

COUNTY OF DEKALB)

    Pursuant to <u>Georgia Code Annotated</u>, I hereby certify that I have notified SIMON PEREZ, 338 Chamblee Tucker Road, Atlanta, GA 30303, and CHRISTINA MONTGOMERY, 605 Midway Circle, Memphis, TN 38098, who are beneficiaries of the above estate by sending them a copy of the Will of LUCY PEREZ.

    I submit this Affidavit under oath for the purposes contained herein and state that the information is true.

_____

MATTHEW PEREZ, Executor

Sworn to and subscribed before me
this the _____ day of _____, (current year).

_____

NOTARY PUBLIC

My Commission Expires: _____

FIGURE 6-4. Affidavit of Notification of Beneficiaries

deceased owes money. The notice tells creditors to file **claims** with the clerk of the court, usually within six months from the date of the first publication of the notice. A copy of the notice should also be mailed to all known creditors.

Upon notice, a creditor of the deceased must file a written claim stating such information as the amount owed, when the debt was made, the creditor's name and address, and any other relevant information about the debt. Failure on the part of a creditor to file a claim within the required time will forever prevent the creditor from collecting the indebtedness. Once the claim is submitted by the creditor to the clerk of the court, the clerk notifies the attorney or personal representative of the estate.

When the personal representative receives the claim, he or she should verify that the amount of the claim is correct and pay the amount due within the time specified by state laws. If it is believed that the money is not owed or that the amount is incorrect, the representative should promptly file a document, known as an **exception**, stating that the creditor is not entitled to the claim. The judge will rule and the claim is either dismissed, modified, or must be paid.

INVENTORY

Unless waived by the will, a complete **inventory** of the personal property and real estate owned by the deceased at the time of death is filed with the clerk. Matthew filed the inventory shown in Figure 6-5. He included items such as cash on hand, money on deposit, stock and bonds, certificates of deposit, all household furnishings, money owed to the deceased, automobiles and trucks, boats, jewelry, etc.

Some items not to be included on the inventory are jointly owned real estate with **right to survivorship**, bank accounts or stocks and bonds owned jointly with right to survivorship, and retirement benefit plans and life insurance policies payable to a named beneficiary. These items are said to pass "outside" the probate process. It should be noted that even though this information is not included on the inventory, the attorney keeps a record of such property because other documents or reports prepared by the attorney for the estate or personal representative, such as state and federal tax reports, require that jointly owned assets be reported.

An estimated monetary value should be determined for each item listed on the inventory. The estimates are usually made by the attorney or the personal representative. The values on the inventory are also used for filing tax reports and should be fairly accurate, or the estate may be liable for additional inheritance or estate taxes (discussed in the next section).

The inventory is signed and sworn to by the personal representative.

(Caption is same as in Figure 6–4, page 153.)

INVENTORY

TO THE PROBATE COURT FOR DEKALB COUNTY, GEORGIA:

COMES the Executor in the Estate of LUCY PEREZ, deceased, and reports that the following assets belonging to the estate have come into his hands as of the date of appointment:

Personal Property	Value
1. Cash on Hand	$ 455.32
2. Money on Deposit	26,389.00
3. Stocks and Bonds	35,928.00
4. Household Furniture	6,300.00
5. Insurance Payable to Estate	5,000.00
6. Automobiles and Trucks	6,500.00
7. Jewelry	2,000.00
8. Miscellaneous Personal Property	500.00
TOTAL PERSONAL PROPERTY	$83,072.32

Real Property	Value
1. No Individually Owned Real Estate	

TOTAL VALUE OF ESTATE $83,072.32

STATE OF GEORGIA   )

COUNTY OF DEKALB)

The foregoing is a full, true, and perfect Inventory of all the goods and chattels, rights and credits of this estate at this date which have come into my possession to the best of my knowledge and belief.

_____
MATTHEW PEREZ, Executor

Sworn to and subscribed before
me this the _____ day of March, (current year).

_____
NOTARY PUBLIC

My Commission Expires:_____

_____
MARILYN C. CANDISH (No. 89891)
Attorney for Petitioner
2000 Peachtree Towers
Atlanta, GA 30300
(404) 555-3333

I, MARILYN C. CANDISH, Attorney for the Executor, certify that I have mailed a true and exact copy of this Inventory to each of the heirs listed in the Last Will and Testament to their addresses shown in the Petition to Probate on this the _____ day of March, (last year).

_____
MARILYN C. CANDISH

FIGURE 6-5. Inventory of Estate

Formatting Instructions for Money Columns on the Inventory

- Use a right tab, right align code, or decimal tab to keep decimal points aligned.

- Place a dollar sign next to the first and total amounts in a column. Align the dollar signs by placing them on the same horizontal space.

- Underline the last amount in a money column, extending it the full width of the column.

- Double underline the total amount.

TAX REPORTS

Various state and federal forms are to be prepared on behalf of the deceased for the personal representative of the estate to sign. The legal secretary may be responsible for typing the information in the forms from a draft copy prepared by the attorney. The size and complexity of the estate determine which and how many of the following forms must be prepared and whether or not taxes will have to be paid.

- Application for Employer Identification Number, Form SS-4

- Notice of Fiduciary Relationship, Form 56

- Federal Estate Tax, Form 706

- Income Tax Return, Form 1040, 1040A, or 1040EZ, for the last year of life

- Fiduciary Income Tax Return, Form 1041

- State Inheritance Tax Return

- State Income Tax Returns (if income is taxed at the state level)

File IRS Form SS-4, Application for Employer Identification Number, to get a tax identification number, which is necessary for filing federal tax forms for the estate of the deceased.

FIDUCIARY

One who manages money or property for another. In probate matters, this is the personal representative.

Form 56, Notice Concerning Fiduciary Relationship, is to be submitted to the Internal Revenue Service to notify it of the creation of the decedent's estate. Tax forms and notices will then be mailed to the executor, also known as the **fiduciary**, instead of the old address of the deceased.

FEDERAL ESTATE TAX

A federal tax imposed on the privilege of transmitting property at death.

Form 706, United States Estate Tax Return, is a 17-page booklet with Schedules A through Q for listing real estate, stocks and bonds, personal property, insurance benefits, retirement accounts, as well as debts and expenses. The **federal estate tax** is imposed on the privilege of transmitting property at death and is a tax on all assets owned by the decedent. As of 1993, if the gross taxable estate is worth $600,000 or more on the date of death, Form 706 must be filed with the Internal Revenue Service. Filing is not required if the value of the estate is less than $600,000. The return is due nine months after the date of death.

Form 1040, 1040A, or 1040EZ, U.S. Individual Income Tax Return, is to be filed for the year of death, reporting income earned before death, and covers the period of time from January 1 through the date of death.

Form 1041, U.S. Fiduciary Income Tax Return, is filed if the estate earns income of $600 or more from the date of death to 12 months later. Since a personal representative should not pay out money to beneficiaries until all claims from creditors are received and paid out, the decedent's money is usually put in an interest-bearing account. Large sums of money will earn more than $600 in interest income.

State inheritance taxes are imposed on the amounts received by benefici- aries. The state department should be consulted for information and forms. Often these parallel the federal forms, and some states allow the filing of Form 706, United States Estate Tax Return, in place of their state form. Unlike federal estate tax forms, often state inheritance tax forms must be filed even if no taxes are due. The state issues to the personal representative a tax waiver, which is a form that must be presented before selling any of the deceased's stock or bonds and before closing the estate.

STATE INHERITANCE TAXES

Taxes on the amounts received by beneficiaries.

State income tax laws vary, and if there is a state income tax, returns for the last year of life or any portion thereof must be filed.

ANNUAL ACCOUNTING, FINAL ACCOUNTING, OR STATEMENT IN LIEU OF ACCOUNTING

An **accounting** is a report of the income and expenses of an estate. Unless waived by the will, a final accounting must be submitted to close the estate. It summarizes all financial transactions: receipts and disbursements of the estate assets. Copies of all receipts, including receipts from the heirs showing they received their money, and canceled checks are kept to support the report.

ACCOUNTING

A report of the income and expenses of an estate.

Figure 6-6 is a receipt for a specific bequest and is the type of form each beneficiary signs upon receipt of money or personal property. Also refer to Figures 6-7 and 6-8 for the final accounting report of Matthew Perez, the executor. Note that all cash received is reported on the first page, including cash received from the sale of the estate assets. On the second page all disbursements are listed by date, amount, and check number. On the final accounting, all receipts must equal all disbursements. If the estate is extremely large, an annual accounting is made each year until the final accounting when the estate is closed.

Some states allow for the filing of a statement in lieu of accounting to replace the final accounting, provided all of the heirs are in agreement. The personal representative may file an affidavit, signed by the heirs, in which they swear that the debts have been paid, that they have received their shares, and that they waive an accounting. Along with the affidavit, the executor submits an order closing the estate and includes a receipt from the state inheritance tax division indicating that taxes have been paid or that there are no inheritance taxes. If no federal estate taxes are due, there is nothing filed from the federal estate tax division.

IN THE PROBATE COURT FOR DEKALB COUNTY, GEORGIA

IN THE MATTER OF:)
)
The Estate of LUCY PEREZ, Deceased,   )   No. 75972
)
MATTHEW PEREZ, Executor.   )

RECEIPT OF SPECIFIC BEQUEST

I, CHRISTINA MONTGOMERY, hereby state that I have received from the above-named estate a bequest in the amount of Ten Thousand Dollars ($10,000) made to me in the decedent's Will and have no further claim or interest in this estate.

Dated this the _____ day of _____, (current year).

_____
CHRISTINA MONTGOMERY
605 Midway Circle
Memphis, TN 38098

FIGURE 6-6. Receipt of Specific Bequest

ORDER CLOSING THE ESTATE

With final accounting, a final order for closing the estate is prepared. It releases the executor from his duties and any further liability. If bond was made, it is canceled, and no further premiums are due. The executor should obtain from the court a statement of court costs so payment can be made before closing the bank account and closing the estate. The court will not allow the entering of the order until all court costs have been paid.

INTESTATE PROCEDURE

If a person dies without leaving a will, the procedure is to file a petition for letters of administration. **Letters of administration**, rather than letters testamentary, are issued to the personal representative if a person dies without leaving a will. The person appointed by the court to administer the estate is known as the **administrator** (male) or **administratrix** (female) or, in some

IN THE PROBATE COURT FOR DEKALB COUNTY, GEORGIA

IN THE MATTER OF:)
)
The Estate of LUCY PEREZ, Deceased,) No. 75972
)
MATTHEW PEREZ, Executor.)

FINAL ACCOUNTING REPORT OF EXECUTOR

  I hereby submit for your approval my accounting in the above estate. I have received into the estate for this reporting period the following:

R E C E I P T S

Date	Payor and Type of Receipt	Amount
02/28/last yr.	Cash on Hand	$ 455.32
02/28/last yr.	Money on Deposit	26,389.00
03/31/last yr.	Interest Earned	1,583.00
05/12/last yr.	Insurance Paid to the Estate	5,042.81
05/30/last yr.	Income from Stock Dividend	2,875.00

From the sale of the following items, I received:

Date	Payor and Type of Receipt	Amount
05/30/last yr.	Stocks and Bonds	6,253.00
07/31/last yr.	Notes and Debts Owed the Deceased	2,000.00
08/15/last yr.	Automobiles and Trucks	7,500.00
Total Receipts		$52,098.13

FIGURE 6-7. Final Accounting, Page 1

I have paid out the following sums on behalf of the deceased's creditors and have a receipt or canceled check to verify each expenditure.

D I S B U R S E M E N T S

Date	Payee and Type or Payment	Amount
02/05/last yr.	Lawnhurst Memorial Gardens, Check 1001	$ 4,405.21
02/15/last yr.	Baptist Hospital, Check 1002	4,547.44
03/10/last yr.	Mid-State Medical Group, Check 1003	3,408.30
04/01/last yr.	Atlanta Gazette (publication), Check 1004	35.00
06/21/last yr.	Register of Deeds (recording deed), Check 1005	45.00
07/01/last yr.	Simon Perez (son), Check 1006	10,000.00
07/01/last yr.	Christina Montgomery (daughter), Check 1007	10,000.00
07/31/last yr.	Marylin C. Candish (attorney's fees), Check 1008 . .	2,000.00
08/01/last yr.	Probate Court (filing fees), Check 1009	150.00
08/31/last yr.	Matthew Perez (heir), Check 1010	17,507.18
	TOTAL DISBURSEMENTS	$ 52,098.13

STATE OF GEORGIA   )

COUNTY OF DEKALB)

I, MATTHEW PEREZ, make oath that the foregoing is a full, true, and just accounting of all the funds I have received and disbursed in this estate. I further state that I have mailed or delivered notice of the requirement to file claims to the creditors of the decedent who were known by, or reasonably ascertainable by, me.

_____
MATTHEW PEREZ, Executor

Sworn to and signed before me
this the _____ day of _____, (current year).

_____
NOTARY PUBLIC

My Commission Expires:_____

_____
MARILYN C. CANDISH (No. 89891)
Attorney for Executor
2000 Peachtree Towers
Atlanta, GA 30300
(404) 555-3333

(Add certificate to heirs. See example in Figure 6–12, page 165.)

- 2 -

FIGURE 6-8. Final Accounting, Page 2

states, the personal representative. The laws of succession vary from state to state, but usually they provide that assets of the deceased go to a surviving spouse and children, surviving parents, brothers or sisters, grandparents, and closest living relatives, in that order. If no living relatives can be located, the property will go to the state.

As you review the documents for probating an intestate matter, note that the names of the documents are petition for letters of administration (Figures 6-9 and 6-10) and order for intestate administration (Figures 6-11 and 6-12). Also note that since there is no will that waives bond, the administrator must go through the procedure of being bonded, as described earlier in this chapter, or having bond waived by having all beneficiaries sign a consent to waive that requirement.

Note that the style of the case is "IN THE MATTER OF: The Estate of PAUL D. RUBINSTEIN, Deceased." In the caption for the petition, Arthur P. Dudley is identified as the Petitioner, but in the caption for the order, he is identified as the Administrator. In the body of the order, the judge directs that letters of administration be issued.

IN THE PROBATE COURT FOR PHILADELPHIA COUNTY, PENNSYLVANIA

IN THE MATTER OF:)
)
The Estate of PAUL D. RUBINSTEIN,)
Deceased,) No. _____
)
ARTHUR P. DUDLEY, Petitioner.)

PETITION FOR LETTERS OF ADMINISTRATION

COMES NOW your Petitioner, ARTHUR P. DUDLEY, and would respectfully show unto the Court the following:

1. The decedent, PAUL D. RUBINSTEIN, died on June 27, (current year), at the age of eighty (80) years. The decedent's place of residence was the City of Philadelphia, County of Philadelphia, State of Pennsylvania.

2. The decedent is survived by the following heirs whose names, relationships, ages, and mailing addresses appear below:

Name	Relationship	Age	Residence
HATTIE E. RUBINSTEIN	Wife	82	2707 Concord Road Philadelphia, PA 04321
PAUL D. RUBINSTEIN	Son	50	127 West 25th Street Philadelphia, PA 04320
ZACKERY L. RUBINSTEIN	Son	48	1548 White Plain Road Camden, NJ 03211

3. The decedent owned real estate located at 2707 Concord Road, Philadelphia, Pennsylvania, along with his wife, HATTIE E. RUBINSTEIN, as tenants by the entirety; and his wife survives him.

4. The decedent owned certain personal property which your Petitioner believes to be worth approximately One Hundred Twenty-two Thousand Nine Hundred Twenty-seven Dollars ($122,927), and your Petitioner is prepared to make a full and exact Inventory of the personal property.

5. Your Petitioner and the wife of the decedent have made a full and thorough search for wills and codicils signed by the decedent, but no such wills or codicils have been found.

6. Your Petitioner, ARTHUR P. DUDLEY, is not the person with the highest statutory right to serve; however, he is a close personal friend, and those with higher rights to serve have asked him to serve as Administrator of this estate.

FIGURE 6-9. Petition for Letters of Administration, Page 1

7. Your Petitioner is qualified and stands ready to qualify and serve as the Administrator according to law if the Court sees fit to appoint him.

8. Each person who is a beneficiary of the estate of PAUL D. RUBINSTEIN is an adult, and each has signed a consent to the Personal Representative's bond being waived as evidenced by the Agreement to Waive Bond attached hereto and marked as Exhibit A.

9. For the purpose of the Pennsylvania Inheritance Tax, the gross value of the decedent's estate is approximately Two Hundred Forty-eight Thousand Dollars ($248,000).

PREMISES CONSIDERED, PETITIONER PRAYS:

1. That upon hearing of this cause, the Clerk of the Probate Court for Philadelphia County, Pennsylvania, be directed to administer the oath and otherwise qualify the Administrator and to issue proper Letters of Administration to the Petitioner.

2. That notice by publication be given to all creditors of the decedent as required by Pennsylvania Consolidated Statutes.

3. That notice be given the Pennsylvania Department of Revenue as required by Pennsylvania Consolidated Statutes.

4. That bond for the Personal Representative be waived.

5. For such other and further relief as the Court deems proper.

_____
ARTHUR P. DUDLEY, Petitioner

_____
ROGER M. McVEER (No. 5921)
Attorney for Petitioner
294 Curtiswood Office Complex
Philadelphia, PA 04320-1222
(215) 555-2068

STATE OF PENNSYLVANIA   )

COUNTY OF PHILADELPHIA)

I, ARTHUR P. DUDLEY, after first being duly sworn, make oath that the statements in this Petition for Letters of Administration are true to the best of my knowledge, information, and belief.

_____
ARTHUR P. DUDLEY, Petitioner

Sworn to and subscribed before me
this the _____ day of _____, (current year).

_____
NOTARY PUBLIC

My Commission Expires:_____

- 2 -

FIGURE 6-10. Petition for Letters of Administration, Page 2

IN THE PROBATE COURT FOR PHILADELPHIA COUNTY, PENNSYLVANIA

IN THE MATTER OF:)
)
The Estate of PAUL D. RUBINSTEIN,) No. 68339
Deceased,)
)
ARTHUR P. DUDLEY, Administrator.)

ORDER FOR INTESTATE ADMINISTRATION

This cause came on to be heard on the 1st day of August, (current year), before the Honorable PHILIP ALLEN, Judge of the Probate Court for Philadelphia County, Pennsylvania, upon a Petition for Letters of Administration, the sworn testimony of the Petitioner, ARTHUR P. DUDLEY, and the record as a whole upon which the Court finds:

1. The decedent, PAUL D. RUBINSTEIN, died on June 27, (current year), at the age of eighty (80) years;

2. The decedent's place of residence was the City of Philadelphia, County of Philadelphia County, State of Pennsylvania;

3. The decedent left no Will;

4. The Petitioner was a close friend and confidant of the decedent and all persons with higher right to serve as Administrator of the decedent's estate have waived their right in writing in favor of the Petitioner;

5. The decedent is survived by HATTIE E. RUBINSTEIN, wife of the decedent, PAUL D. RUBINSTEIN, son of the decedent, and ZACKERY L. RUBINSTEIN, son of the decedent; and

6. The decedent owned certain personal property that is subject to Court supervised administration, which your Petitioner believes to be worth approximately One Hundred Twenty-two Thousand Nine Hundred Twenty-seven Dollars ($122,927).

IT IS THEREFORE ORDERED, ADJUDGED, AND DECREED that the Clerk of the Probate Court for Philadelphia County, Pennsylvania, be and hereby is directed to administer the oath and otherwise qualify the Administrator and to issue proper Letters of Administration to ARTHUR P. DUDLEY.

FIGURE 6-11. Order for Intestate Administration, Page 1

      IT IS FURTHER ORDERED that bond be waived and that notice be issued
to the creditors and the Pennsylvania Department of Revenue as required by the
<u>Pennsylvania Consolidated Statutes</u>; and the Administrator has until October 1,
(current year), to file the necessary Inventory.

      ENTERED this the _____ day of August, (current year).

               _____

               PHILIP ALLEN, JUDGE

APPROVED FOR ENTRY:

_____

ROGER M. McVEER (No. 5921)
Attorney for Administrator
294 Curtiswood Office Complex
Philadelphia, PA 04320-1222
(215) 555-2068

               CERTIFICATE

      I, **ROGER M. McVEER,** Attorney for the Administrator, hereby certify that
I have mailed a copy of this Order for Intestate Administration to the Administrator,
the widow of the deceased, and to each son of the deceased at the addresses shown in
the Petition heretofore filed on this the 2d day of August, (current year).

               _____

               ROGER M. McVEER

FIGURE 6-12. Order for Intestate Administration, Page 2

SUMMARY

- Every person dies testate (with a will) or intestate (without a will).

- The first document prepared in a testate probate procedure is the petition to probate a will.

- The first document prepared in an intestate procedure is a petition for letters of administration.

- The petition consists of a caption, body, prayer clause, signature line for the petitioner, signature block for the attorney, and verification.

- Letters testamentary are issued to the person who is named as personal representative in a will. The letters give the personal representative power to manage the estate of the deceased.

- Letters of administration are issued to the person appointed as personal representative for an intestate estate.

- Letters of administration, c.t.a., are issued when a will exists and a personal representative is not named or is named and cannot serve.

- An order to probate a will is normally prepared at the same time as the petition to probate a will.

- The order has a caption, body in which the facts of the petition are restated and the order of the judge is enumerated, signature block for the judge or probate master, and approved for entry block for the attorney.

- A personal representative appointed to oversee an intestate estate is an administrator (male) or administratrix (female). The term personal representative can be used to identify anyone administering an estate.

- Before letters are issued by the court, the personal representative must make an oath that he or she will faithfully perform all duties required of a personal representative.

- Heirs should be notified that they are to inherit property from the deceased.

- A notice is published in a newspaper to inform creditors to file claims for any debts owed to them by the deceased. A copy of that notice is mailed to all known creditors. Usually claims are to be filed within six months of the publication of the first notice.

- An inventory is taken of all estate assets unless it is waived in the will or by agreement of all the beneficiaries. Even if it is waived, the attorney may request that the personal representative provide that information because it is needed for completing the tax forms.

- The personal representative, or the attorney for the representative, is responsible for filing state and federal income, inheritance, and estate tax forms for the estate when due.

- A final accounting is filed before closing the estate unless it has been waived in the will or by signed agreement of all of the beneficiaries. The final accounting lists receipts and disbursements of the estate.

REVIEW EXERCISES

T   F   1. Probate procedure is important only if a decedent has left a will.

T   F   2. An order admitting a will to probate is normally prepared when a petition to probate a will is prepared.

T   F   3. Sally Jones, Plaintiff v. Estate of Kathy Wong is an appropriate style of the case for a petition to probate a will.

T   F   4. The body of the petition includes information about the age, date and time of death, residence, and religious preference of the deceased.

T   F   5. Letters testamentary are issued to an executor of a will.

T   F   6. Letters testamentary are issued to an administrator, c.t.a.

T   F   7. Letters of administration are issued to an administratrix.

T   F   8. A personal representative can open a bank account in the name of the estate before taking oath and receiving letters from the court.

T   F   9. Heirs should receive copies of the decedent's will.

T   F   10. The usual maximum amount of time a creditor has to file a claim is 90 days after the publication of a notice in the newspaper.

T   F   11. An inventory is a listing of all the receipts and expenditures made by the personal representative of an estate.

T   F   12. The secretary most likely will not be involved in typing tax forms for a decedent's estate.

T   F   13. Form SS-4 is filed to get a tax number for submitting federal tax forms for the estate of the deceased.

T   F   14. Copies of all receipts and canceled checks must accompany the final accounting when it is filed with the court.

T   F   15. Money columns are aligned at the left on the inventory and final accounting.

TRANSCRIPTION RULES

CAPITALIZATION

Document Titles

Document titles for probate matters are:

Affidavit to Prove Will

Codicil

Last Will and Testament

Letters of Administration

Letters Testamentary

Petition for Letters of Administration

Petition to Probate a Will

Will

Party Designations

Party designations for probate documents are:

Administrator

Clerk

Court (meaning Judge)

Judge

Executor

Personal Representative

Petitioner

Phrases in Full Caps

Key the following and similar phrases in full caps. Note the colon following the phrase.

PREMISES CONSIDERED, PETITIONER PRAYS:

IT IS THEREFORE ORDERED, ADJUDGED, AND DECREED. . . .

COLON

Formal List

Use a colon to introduce a formal list; however, do not use a colon after a verb or preposition if the items are to continue on the same line.

The assets that have come into the hands of the Executor *are:*

Cash on Hand	$ 350.50
Stocks and Bonds	1,000.00

The assets that have come into the hands of the Executor *are* cash on hand and stock and bonds.

Introductory Statement

Use a colon after introductory words such as "following" or "as follows."

I have received into the estate for this reporting period the *following:* two (2) automobiles, one (1) boat, and money on deposit.

COMES NOW your Petitioner, ARTHUR P. DUDLEY, and would respectfully show unto the Court the *following:*

1. The decedent died on June 27, (current year).

2. The decedent is survived by three (3) heirs.

COMMAS

Phrases — Interrupting

Do not use commas to set off the phrase "be and is hereby." This phrase means that the Last Will and Testament be admitted and is admitted to probate by (or hereby) this order.

It is ordered that the Last Will and Testament of LUCY PEREZ *be and is hereby* admitted into probate.

To Wit

"To wit" is a term meaning *namely* or *that is.* Place a colon before and a comma after *to wit* if the emphasis is on the material that follows the expression. Place a comma before and a comma after *to wit* if the emphasis is on what precedes.

As Executor you have four (4) responsibilities: *to wit,* notifying heirs, paying debts, taking inventory, and preparing an accounting. (Emphasis is on what follows *to wit* rather than on the introductory statement.)

The Executor notified all of the beneficiaries, *to wit,* the three children and wife of the deceased. (Emphasis is on the fact that the beneficiaries were notified.)

NUMBER EXPRESSION

Ages

In legal documents, express ages in words and then in numerals; however, if the ages are shown in a table, use numerals only.

LUCY PEREZ died at the age of seventy (70).

The name, age, and relationship of my beneficiaries are:

Name	Relationship	Age
MATTHEW PEREZ	Husband	75
SIMON PEREZ	Son	45

SEMICOLONS

Series of Long, Parallel Dependent Clauses

Use semicolons to separate three or more long, parallel dependent clauses in a series.

After testimony in open court, the Judge determined that said paper writing was written and signed by the decedent; that said instrument was executed by the deceased as his Last Will and Testament; and that the deceased was at the time of sound mind.

TRANSCRIPTION EXERCISES

Use a secretarial reference manual and the rules presented in this and previous chapters to aid you in correctly transcribing the following material. The sentences are presented in lowercase letters without capitalization and punctuation.

1. the decedent is survived by the following heirs whose names relationships ages and addresses are as follows mrs barbara s gardner spouse adult 717 choata drive kalamazoo michigan 74431   vernon a gardner son 22 years 1712 east lansing road lansing michigan 74221 barbara w gardner-fritch daughter 28 years 1233 wausau place ann arbor michigan 74324 (HINT: Plan the tab settings for a table before you key the data.)

2. the decedents regular abode and residence was 717 choata drive kalamazoo michigan 74431

3. the following assets came into the hands of the coexecutors 1 cash on hand in wallet $231.50 2 national bank of kalamazoo—savings $86,997.29   3 american national bank—checking and savings $12,884.66

4. it is therefore ordered adjudged and decreed by the court that the last will and testament of philip e gardner be and is hereby admitted into probate that the clerk is hereby directed to file and record the will and that letters testamentary be issued

5. the court finds as follows

6. your petitioner will make a full and exact inventory upon qualifying as administratrix of the decedents estate

7. the decedent died on march 17 (current year) at the age of 76 years

8. each person who is a beneficiary has signed a consent to the administrators bond being waived

9. i have mailed a copy of this order to each of the decedents children to wit paul tatum timothy tatum and elizabeth tatum

10. attached is an affidavit to prove will

RESEARCH ACTIVITIES

1. Consult your state statutes under laws of succession or laws of descent and distribution to determine how property is distributed when a person dies without leaving a will.

2. If there is a probate court in your county, obtain locally designed forms used in probate matters. Discuss how to complete the blanks on those forms.

3. Call the Internal Revenue Service Forms Division and ask for a copy of Forms SS-4, 56, 706, 1040, and 1041. Familiarize yourself with the information requested on the tax forms.

4. Determine whether there is a state income tax or inheritance tax in your state. If so, obtain forms for filing those taxes.

5. Call your court clerk and/or consult the state statutes to determine if a form is available for creditors to use in submitting a claim against an estate.

PROJECTS

Insert the cassette tape for Chapter 6 and transcribe the following projects.

Project 6-1   Transcribe the petition to probate the will of Philip E. Gardner, who died and left a wife and three children, one of which is a minor. In the will, Philip E. Gardner appointed his attorney, Arthur P. Dudley, and a bank to serve as co-executors. There is an example of witness signature lines on page 269 of this text.

Project 6-2   Transcribe an order admitting the will of Philip E. Gardner to probate to accompany Project 6-1. The case no. is 93-P-423.

Project 6-3   Transcribe a petition for letters of administration. The decedent, Walter M. Tatum, died intestate, predeceasing a wife and three grown children. The wife is petitioning the court to be named administratrix and to serve without bond.

Project 6-4   Transcribe an order for intestate administration in the matter of Walter M. Tatum to accompany Project 6-3. The case no. is 93-P-122.

Project 6-5   Prepare an inventory of the estate of Philip E. Gardner. Data for preparing the inventory is provided on cassette tape. Follow the format shown in Figure 6-5.

Project 6-6   Prepare a final accounting for the estate of Philip E. Gardner. The estate is divided equally, four ways, among the wife and children. Data for preparing the final accounting is provided on cassette tape. Follow the format shown in Figures 6-7 and 6-8.

CHAPTER 7

GUARDIANSHIPS, CONSERVATORSHIPS, AND NAME CHANGES

INTRODUCTION

The three matters discussed in this chapter — guardianships, conservatorships, and name changes — are classified as probate matters. These matters would be heard in probate court or any court that has jurisdiction over probate matters. Practice varies greatly from state to state; however, the instructions presented in this chapter can be used as a guideline for preparing documents and can be altered to fit specific court rules.

This chapter presents samples of the documents shown in the box below. Models of petitions and orders for conservatorships are not shown because the format is identical to those prepared for guardianships. Inventories and accounting reports were shown in Chapter 6, and duplicate samples are not repeated in this chapter.

> **PETITION TO APPOINT A GUARDIAN**
>
> **NOTICE OF HEARING**
>
> **ORDER TO APPOINT A GUARDIAN**
>
> **PETITION FOR CHANGE OF NAME**

GUARDIANSHIPS

GUARDIAN

One appointed by the court to oversee and manage the affairs of one incapable of managing his or her own affairs, such as a minor child or incompetent adult.

CONSERVATOR

One appointed by the court to oversee and manage the affairs of a disabled or incompetent adult. In some states, synonymous with guardian.

MINOR

One who has not reached the age of majority as defined by law, usually 18 years of age.

WARD

One who is placed under the care of a guardian or conservator.

RESPONDENT

The minor child or disabled or incompetent adult in guardianship and conservatorship matters.

GUARDIAN AD LITEM

One appointed by the court to represent the interests of a minor child or disabled or incompetent adult at a court hearing.

A **guardian** or **conservator** is a person appointed by the court to oversee and manage the affairs of one who is unable to manage his or her own affairs. Some states use the term guardian to identify one who has been appointed to oversee the person and/or estate of both **minors** and incompetent or disabled adults. Other states use guardian to refer to a person who manages the affairs of a minor and conservator to refer to one who manages affairs for an incompetent or disabled adult. In this chapter we will assume the latter definition. Once a guardian or conservator is appointed, the minor or incompetent or disabled adult becomes a **ward** of the court; and an estate to be managed by the guardian or conservator is created.

In the case we will examine, the parents of a minor child, Virginia Meadows, were killed in an automobile accident. When such a tragedy occurs, normally someone in the family is willing to accept the responsibility of caring for the child. In Virginia's case, her uncle, Henry Ewing, wanted to care for her. He contacted an attorney to prepare the documents for establishing and for administering the guardianship.

Documents to establish a guardianship are:

- Petition to appoint a guardian

- Notice of hearing

- Order to appoint a guardian

- Inventory (unless waived)

Documents to administer a guardianship are:

- Annual accounting on the anniversary of the court order granting the guardianship

The first step in establishing a guardianship is to file with the clerk of the court a petition to appoint a guardian for the minor child. The minor child is referred to as the **respondent**. At the time of filing, a copy of the petition is left with the clerk of the court for a person, usually an attorney, to be appointed by the judge to look after the interests of the child at a court hearing. This person is known as a **guardian ad litem**. Judges keep lists of attorneys interested in serving as guardians ad litem. Notice of that appointment may be by a letter or phone call from the judge's office, and legal notice is completed when the attorney picks up a copy of the petition from the clerk's office. A minor child is not usually served with a petition because the guardian ad litem is responsible for representing his or her interest. It is a good idea to serve other interested parties, such as a relative the minor is living with or the closest living relative. The idea of service is to give notice to interested parties that a petition has been filed.

PETITION TO APPOINT A GUARDIAN

Refer to Figures 7-1 and 7-2 as you examine the petition to appoint a guardian in the matter of Virginia Ann Meadows, a minor. The petitioner usually is, but is not required to be, the person desiring to be appointed guardian. In this matter, Henry E. Ewing, the petitioner and the one seeking to be guardian, is submitting the petition.

Caption. In matters such as these, the parties are identified as petitioner and respondent. Notice that the caption begins: IN THE MATTER OF: Virginia Ann Meadows, a Minor, Respondent; Henry E. Ewing, Petitioner.

Body. The paragraphs in Figure 7-1 are labeled and provide the following information:

A. Establishes jurisdiction of the court and states the name and address of the minor

B. Establishes the necessity of appointing a guardian and states the age and date of birth of the minor

C. States the value of the real and personal property of the minor

D. States the name, age, relationship, and address of the proposed guardian

E. Establishes that the proposed guardian is ready, willing, and able to serve and provides reasons for wanting to be the guardian

Prayer Clause. The petitioner specifies his requests in the prayer clause (see Figure 7-2), including a request that the court set a time for a hearing to appoint him as guardian.

Signature block. The signature block can be prepared for the attorney to sign the document, with the petitioner's swearing to and signing the verification, as shown in Figure 7-2; or the petitioner can sign the petition, with the attorney's signature block being placed at the left margin as shown below. Both styles should have a verification.

_____

HENRY E. EWING, Petitioner

_____

VICTOR WILSON (No. 66723)
Attorney for Petitioner
1825 Spring Street
Alexandria, VA 22314
(804) 226-3272

IN THE PROBATE COURT FOR FAIRFAX COUNTY, VIRGINIA

IN THE MATTER OF:)
)
VIRGINIA ANN MEADOWS, a Minor,   )
)
        Respondent,   )   No. _____   **Caption**
)
HENRY E. EWING,   )
)
        Petitioner.   )

Tab indent!

PETITION TO APPOINT A GUARDIAN

COMES NOW your Petitioner, HENRY E. EWING, and would show unto the Court as follows:

A. **Court Jurisdiction.** The minor in this cause of action, VIRGINIA ANN MEADOWS, is a resident of Fairfax County, Virginia, living at 1243 Braddock Place, Alexandria, VA 22314.

B. **Necessity to Appoint Guardian.** VIRGINIA ANN MEADOWS, hereinafter referred to as the "Ward," is ten (10) years old, having been born on February 12, (ten years ago). On April 2, (current year), both of the Ward's parents died in a car wreck on McMillian Street while coming home after dinner.

C. **Ward's Estate.** The Ward has inherited interest in the real property located at 1243 Braddock Place with an estimated value of Two Hundred Forty-three Thousand Dollars ($243,000), along with personal property in an estimated value of One Hundred Forty-eight Thousand Dollars ($148,000). If the Petitioner is appointed Guardian in this action, he will fully determine the value of the Ward's interest in both personal and real property and file such in the form of an inventory as required by the <u>Code of Virginia Annotated</u>.   **Body**

D. **Identity and Relationship of Petitioner.** Your Petitioner is the maternal uncle of the Ward. Specifically, HENRY E. EWING is forty-eight (48) years of age, lives at 6213 Woodward Drive, Alexandria, VA 22314, and is the closest living relative of the Ward.

E. **Relief Sought.** Your Petitioner seeks to be appointed Guardian of the estate of VIRGINIA ANN MEADOWS and is ready, willing, and able to qualify and serve in this capacity. He is currently working as an internal auditor for the Jefferson Memorial Bank in Alexandria, Virginia, is a C.P.A., and has sufficient capacity to handle the financial affairs of the Ward. Further, he is married to HELEN PRESS EWING, and the parties have no children but are willing and desiring to care for VIRGINIA ANN MEADOWS personally.

FIGURE 7-1. Petition to Appoint a Guardian, Page 1

PREMISES CONSIDERED, PETITIONER PRAYS:

1. That the notice requirement be waived, since all necessary parties have joined as Petitioners and the Respondent is a minor.

2. That the Respondent, VIRGINIA ANN MEADOWS, the minor herein, be appointed a Guardian Ad Litem upon the filing of this Petition and that service of the Ward be accomplished by serving the Guardian Ad Litem.

3. That the Court set the date and time for a hearing for this cause; and at the hearing, the Petitioner, HENRY E. EWING, be appointed Guardian of the person and estate of VIRGINIA ANN MEADOWS with all powers and authority allowed by law.

4. That bond be waived pursuant to Section 34-2-203 of Code of Virginia Annotated.

5. That the Guardian be allowed thirty (30) days to qualify and file a specific Inventory.

6. That the fees for the Guardian and the Guardian Ad Litem be set by this Court and charged against the estate of VIRGINIA ANN MEADOWS.

Prayer

VICTOR WILSON (No. 66723)
Attorney for Petitioner
1825 Spring Street
Alexandria, VA 22314
(804) 555-3272

Signature Block

STATE OF VIRGINIA   )

COUNTY OF FAIRFAX   )

The Petitioner, HENRY E. EWING, after being duly sworn, makes oath that the foregoing statements in this Petition are true to the best of his knowledge, information, and belief.

HENRY E. EWING, Petitioner

Verification

Sworn to and subscribed before me
this the _____ day of May, (current year).

NOTARY PUBLIC

My Commission Expires: _____

- 2 -

FIGURE 7-2. Petition to Appoint a Guardian, Page 2

Verification. Whether the petitioner or attorney signs the document, the petitioner signs a verification. Following the verification is a jurat, signature line, and commission expiration line for the notary public. In some states the notary information is not required.

NOTICE OF HEARING

A notice of hearing is to notify the respondent that a petition has been filed and to inform the respondent of the time and place set for the court hearing. The notice in the case of Virginia Ann Meadows is shown in Figure 7-3. The notice has the same caption as the petition to appoint a guardian. It is addressed to the respondent, the minor, and is mailed to the guardian ad litem. In this particular case, the prayer clause of the petition states that "service of the ward be accomplished by serving the guardian ad litem." A copy should also be mailed by certified mail, return receipt, to the closest relative and person having custody if that person is someone other than the petitioner. The notice used in this case is to be signed by the clerk of the court. Rules in some states may allow the attorney to sign the notice.

ORDER TO APPOINT A GUARDIAN

At the hearing, the judge listens to testimony of the petitioner, guardian ad litem, and attorney for the petitioner. The judge determines whether to appoint the petitioner as guardian. If so, the order making the appointment is signed and entered as an order of the court.

See Figures 7-4 and 7-5 for an order appointing Henry Ewing as guardian of Virginia Meadows. Note that in the style of the case, the petitioner is now identified as the "guardian." Refer to the body of the order and notice that it:

- Names and appoints the guardian

- Sets the amount of bond

- Specifies that payments be made for upkeep and that funds be kept in a nonspeculative bank account

- Restricts expenditures over a set amount unless approved by the court

- Sets the fees for the attorney and guardian ad litem

The remaining portions of the order are a signature line for the judge's signature, signature lines for the attorney for the petitioner and the guardian ad litem to approve the contents of the order, and certificate of service to the guardian ad litem.

Copies are prepared as follows: an original to be filed with the court, a copy each for the guardian and guardian ad litem, and a file copy.

IN THE PROBATE COURT FOR FAIRFAX COUNTY, VIRGINIA

IN THE MATTER OF:)	
)	
VIRGINIA ANN MEADOWS, a Minor,)	
)	
Respondent,)	No. 96836
)	
HENRY E. EWING,)	
)	
Petitioner.)	

NOTICE OF HEARING

TO: VIRGINIA ANN MEADOWS
      1243 Braddock Place
      Alexandria, VA 22314

You are hereby notified that a Petition has been filed in the above-styled case, a copy of which is attached herein, in which it is alleged that you are incapable of caring for yourself or disabled from managing your property or both. The Petitioner seeks the appointment of a Guardian for your person or property or both. The Court, being satisfied that there is good cause for the exercise of jurisdiction as to the matters alleged in the Petition, has set a hearing on the 16th day June, (current year), at 9 a.m. in the offices or the courtroom of the Honorable BERRNARD F. COHEN, Judge of this court.

The Court has appointed a Guardian Ad Litem to investigate these matters and make a report to the Court. The Guardian Ad Litem is charged with asserting your best interests and making recommendations, consistent with law, as to what action should be taken in your best interests. The name and address of the Guardian Ad Litem is:

                ROGER C. WEBBER
                Guardian Ad Litem
                296 Court Square Building
                Alexandria, VA 22314

A list of your rights in connection with the above-described hearing is attached or printed on the reverse side of this notice.

IN WITNESS WHEREOF, I have hereunto set my hand and affixed the seal of the court at my office on the _____ day of _____, (current year).

                            _____
                            CLERK AND MASTER or CLERK

FIGURE 7-3. Notice of Hearing.
Adapted from the Third National Bank, <u>Tennessee Will's Manual</u>, Nashville, Tennessee.

IN THE PROBATE COURT FOR FAIRFAX COUNTY, VIRGINIA

IN THE MATTER OF:	)	
	)	
VIRGINIA ANN MEADOWS, a Minor,	)	
	)	
Respondent,	)	
	)	No. 96836
HENRY E. EWING,	)	
	)	
Petitioner.	)	

ORDER TO APPOINT A GUARDIAN

This cause came on to be heard on the 16th day of June, (current year), before the Honorable BERRNARD F. COHEN, Judge of the Probate Court for Fairfax County, Virginia, upon a Petition to Appoint a Guardian for VIRGINIA ANN MEADOWS, a minor; and after testimony in open court by the Petitioner, HENRY E. EWING, his wife, the minor Respondent, the statements by ROGER C. WEBBER, Guardian Ad Litem, and the record as a whole, the Court finds the following:

A. That the Ward, VIRGINIA ANN MEADOWS, has been duly notified in this proceeding by service of process on the duly appointed Guardian Ad Litem, ROGER C. WEBBER, and was properly represented at the hearing of this cause;

B. That the Ward is a resident of Fairfax County, Virginia, and is a minor owning real and personal property and is in need of proper supervision because of the death of both of her parents in an automobile wreck on April 2, (current year); and

C. That HENRY C. EWING is a fit and proper person to be named Guardian of the person and estate of VIRGINIA ANN MEADOWS.

IT IS THEREFORE ORDERED, ADJUDGED, AND DECREED that upon making the required bond, HENRY C. EWING be and is hereby appointed Guardian of the person and property of VIRGINIA ANN MEADOWS with the bond being set at One Hundred Forty Thousand Dollars ($140,000). Further, the Guardian has until July 16, (current year), to file the necessary Inventory.

IT IS FURTHER ORDERED that the Guardian shall maintain the upkeep of the Ward with the funds in the estate of the Ward, and the Court hereby authorizes the Guardian to make regular and periodic expenditures for said upkeep. Such funds that are not needed for the immediate upkeep of the Ward shall be maintained in bank deposits of a nonspeculative nature. Any expenditure over the amount of Two Thousand Five Hundred Dollars ($2,500) must be approved by the Court before such expenditure is made.

FIGURE 7-4. Order to Appoint a Guardian, Page 1

IT IS FURTHER ORDERED that the fee of the Attorney for the Guardian be set at Nine Hundred Dollars ($900) and the fee of the Guardian Ad Litem be set at Three Hundred Dollars ($300) and that the fees and costs of this cause be paid from the estate of VIRGINIA ANN MEADOWS.

ENTERED this the _____ day of June, (current year).

_____
BERRNARD F. COHEN, JUDGE

APPROVED FOR ENTRY:

_____
VICTOR WILSON (No. 66723)
Attorney for the Guardian
1825 Spring Street
Alexandria, VA 22314
(804) 555-3272

_____
ROGER C. WEBBER (No. 23441)
Guardian Ad Litem
296 Court Square Building
Alexandria, VA 22314
(804) 555-6790

CERTIFICATE

I, VICTOR WILSON, Attorney for the Guardian, hereby certify that I have mailed a copy of this Order to Appoint a Guardian to ROGER C. WEBBER, Guardian Ad Litem, 296 Court Square Building, Alexandria, VA 22314, on this the _____ day of June, (current year).

_____
VICTOR WILSON

FIGURE 7-5. Order to Appoint a Guardian, Page 2

INVENTORY

 After the guardian makes bond, unless waived, and takes oath, the **letters of guardianship** giving the guardian authority to act on behalf of the ward are issued by the clerk of the court. If the child has nothing of value, inventory will usually be waived. In cases where the child owns a considerable amount of property, an inventory will likely be required.

The format for filing an inventory with the court is the same as presented in Chapter 6 for probate matters. The inventory of the ward's estate includes not only the assets with an estimated value for each item but also information about regular income received by the ward. The total estimated amount is often used in determining the amount of the guardian's bond.

ANNUAL ACCOUNTING

The format for filing an accounting is the same as presented in Chapter 6 for probate matters. If the child has property or significant regular income, an accounting is filed annually during the continuation of the guardianship. Detailed records should be kept and submitted with the annual accounting.

TERMINATION OF A GUARDIANSHIP

Once the minor reaches the **age of majority** (usually 18), a petition to terminate the guardianship can be filed. A hearing is scheduled, and notice of that hearing is served on the parties. The guardian presents a final accounting, after which the judge orders the account settled and the guardian discharged. At this time the bond (unless it had already been waived) is terminated and any funds belonging to the former ward, who is no longer a minor or ward of the court, are turned over to him or her.

Documents to terminate a guardianship are:

- Petition to terminate the guardianship
- Notice of hearing
- Order terminating the guardianship

CONSERVATORSHIPS

If your grandmother became disabled because of a stroke or heart attack, she would need someone to care for her financial matters and to see that her physical needs were met. A family member or other responsible person willing to accept the responsibility of becoming a conservator would see an attorney, who would prepare documents to create the conservatorship. Documents for establishing, administering, and terminating a conservatorship are similar to those used for guardianships.

A conservatorship is different from a guardianship in that all powers are removed from the ward when a guardian is appointed, and only identified powers are removed when a conservator is appointed. For example, an aging grandmother may be physically able to take care of herself and live alone but unable to manage her checkbook or the cattle farm she owns. The only power the conservator would be given would be authority to manage the farm and the checkbook.

A petition and an order for conservatorship include the same types of information as a petition and an order for guardianship, plus additional information as follows:

- A description of the disability

- The name and address of the person with whom or institution where the respondent lives

- The name and address of a living spouse, child, parent, or sibling

- A sworn medical examination report by a physician or a psychologist, verifying and explaining the disability

- An explanation of the rights to be removed from the respondent and a list of powers given to the conservator and taken from the respondent

When a conservator is appointed, the clerk issues **letters of conservatorship** to give authority to the conservator to handle the specified duties.

LETTERS OF CONSERVATORSHIP

An instrument or document giving authority to manage the property of a disabled or incompetent adult.

A conservator can be discharged from the assigned responsibilities or have them modified for failing to properly care for the ward. Any interested person or the disabled person can petition the court to conduct a hearing to consider negligent or improper actions by the conservator. The court can order any relief considered in the best interest of the disabled person.

Conservatorships terminate when the ward dies or when the ward regains mental or physical capacity.

In the case of death, the conservator files a final accounting. Once the court approves the final accounting, the conservator delivers all the ward's property to the personal representative of the estate. The personal representative gives a receipt for the property to the conservator, and it is filed with the court. In many cases the conservator is appointed personal representative of the estate, since he or she is already handling the affairs of the ward. The conservatorship still must be closed through the accounting process, then reopened by the personal representative of the estate of the deceased.

If the ward regains mental or physical capacity, a petition to terminate the conservatorship is filed. A hearing is scheduled, and a notice of hearing is served on the parties. At the hearing, evidence of the ward's improved condition and ability to manage affairs is presented. A final accounting is submitted. Signing of an order by the judge terminates the guardianship.

Formatting Instructions for Guardianship and Conservatorship Documents

- Use paper the size required by your court rules. Use the same margins, spacing, indentions, and page numbering as on other court documents as described in Chapter 1.

NAME CHANGES

Have you ever thought you would like your name changed? Give the judge a reason, and you can probably have a new name in a few days.

A person's legal name is the name given at birth. Most often, people desire name changes when they have gone by a different name for many years, such as a nickname. A stepchild may want to legally have and use the name of a stepfather without being adopted. It is common to have a name changed to one's stage name. Courts usually allow name changes so long as they are not for any wrongful reason, such as avoiding creditors.

A person can change a name as part of another action, such as an adoption or divorce, or can change it because he or she desires to have a different name. If the change of name is part of another action, the demand for a new name is made in the prayer clause of the documents prepared for that action. See Chapter 9, Figure 9-8. Here the name remains the same.

If a name change is desired and is not related to another matter, the procedure is to file a petition with the court, verified by the applicant, stating the current name, desired name, and a reason for desiring the change. See Figures 7-6 and 7-7 for a petition for change of name where a mother, as next friend, is requesting a surname change for her son to his stepfather's surname.

An order for change of name must be signed by the judge to make it official. The order should include a statement by the court ordering the name changed and ordering the Department of Vital Statistics to change the birth certificate.

IN THE PROBATE COURT FOR SAN DIEGO COUNTY, CALIFORNIA

IN RE:)
)
The Name Change of   )
CARLOS JOSE ROMARIZ, a Minor,   )
)   No. _____
By: MARIA ROMARIZ DAVIDSON,   )
    As Next Friend,   )
)
              Petitioners.   )

PETITION TO CHANGE NAME

COMES your Petitioner, CARLOS JOSE ROMARIZ, a minor, by and through MARIA ROMARIZ DAVIDSON, the natural mother as next friend of the minor Petitioner, and would respectfully petition the Court to change CARLOS JOSE ROMARIZ's name to CARLOS JOSE DAVIDSON.

Petitioner and the minor, CARLOS JOSE ROMARIZ, are both residents of the City of San Diego, County of San Diego, State of California, residing at 1249 El Prado, San Diego, CA 92101.

Petitioner would show that CARLOS JOSE ROMARIZ was born to her out of wedlock; and since that time, she has married WILLIAM HENRY DAVIDSON. They have been living as husband and wife for two (2) years now, since July 19, (two years ago). CARLOS JOSE ROMARIZ is now six (6) years of age, having been born on May 1, (six years ago); and since the marriage of his mother, he has been going by the surname of his stepfather, DAVIDSON. Petitioner is now ready to enroll the minor child in school and would like to change his surname to be that of his natural mother and stepfather.

Petitioner would show that CARLOS JOSE ROMARIZ owns no real or personal property and that this Petition is not made in an attempt to avoid debts or creditors.

PREMISES CONSIDERED, PETITIONER PRAYS that this Court order the name of the minor, CARLOS JOSE ROMARIZ, be changed to CARLOS JOSE DAVIDSON.

_____
MARIA ROMARIZ DAVIDSON, As
Next Friend

_____
MARY C. SOLOMON (No. 24521)
Attorney for Petitioners
Suite 1432
713 Space Park North
San Diego, CA 92101
(619) 555-1885

FIGURE 7-6. Petition for Change of Name, Page 1

STATE OF CALIFORNIA)

COUNTY OF SAN DIEGO)

         MARIA ROMARIZ DAVIDSON, after first being duly sworn, makes oath that the statements in the foregoing Petition are true to the best of her information, knowledge, and belief and that the Petitioners are residents of San Diego County, California, and have been residents herein for more than one (1) full year before the filing of this Petition.

                         _____
                         MARIA ROMARIZ DAVIDSON, Petitioner

Sworn to and subscribed before me
this the _____ day of August, (current year).

_____
NOTARY PUBLIC

My Commission Expires:_____

- 2 -

FIGURE 7-7. Petition for Change of Name, Page 2

SUMMARY

- Guardianships, conservatorships, and name changes are probate matters.

- A guardian is appointed to manage the affairs of a minor, and a conservator oversees affairs for an incompetent or disabled adult. Some states identify both responsibilities as guardianships.

- A guardianship or conservatorship is initiated by filing a verified petition to appoint a guardian or a conservator.

- The individual who files the petition is known as the petitioner, and the minor or disabled adult is the respondent.

- A guardian ad litem, usually an attorney, is appointed by the court to represent the interests of a minor at the court hearing.

- Written notice of a court hearing is mailed to the closest relative and the person having custody in a guardianship and to the respondent in a conservatorship.

- An order to appoint a conservator or guardian is signed and entered as an order of the court after the judge hears the matter at a court hearing and determines that the appointment is appropriate.

- After the order is signed, the guardian or conservator makes oath and bond, unless waived, after which the clerk of court issues letters of guardianship or letters of conservatorship.

- Once a guardian or conservator is appointed, the minor or disabled adult becomes a ward of the court and an estate to be managed by the appointee is created.

- The guardian or conservator must file an inventory listing assets and estimated values unless it has been waived because the individual owns no property.

- If conservatorship or guardianship estates have property or significant income, the person administering the estate files annual accounting reports with the court.

- Documents for the establishment and administration of a guardianship or conservatorship are a petition to appoint a guardian or conservator, notice of hearing, order to appoint a guardian or conservator, inventory, and accounting.

- Documents to terminate a guardianship are petition to terminate a guardianship, notice of hearing, and order terminating the guardianship.

- A conservatorship can be terminated when the ward dies or when the ward regains mental or physical capacity.

- A petition to appoint a guardian or conservator has a caption, body, prayer clause, signature block for the petitioner and/or attorney, and verification signed by the petitioner.

- A notice provides information about the date, time, and place of the hearing to appoint a guardian or conservator.

- The order to appoint a guardian or conservator names and appoints one to oversee the affairs of another, sets the amount of bond, and provides guidelines for administering the estate. It has a caption, body, signature line for the judge, approved-for-entry line for the attorney and guardian ad litem, and a certificate of service to the guardian ad litem.

- Two documents are needed to change one's name: a petition to change name and an order changing name.

- If a request for a name change is part of another legal action, it is requested in the documents for that action, and a separate petition and order are not needed.

REVIEW EXERCISES

T   F   1. A guardian must be appointed by the court, but a family member can be a conservator without obtaining court permission.

T   F   2. A verified petition means that the document is signed by the attorney.

T   F   3. Guardianships are usually terminated when a minor reaches the age of majority.

T   F   4. The parties to a guardianship proceeding are the plaintiff and the respondent.

T   F   5. The first document prepared when one wishes to be appointed as a guardian is a notice to interested parties stating the date, time, and place of a scheduled hearing.

T   F   6. The order signed by the judge is the official document that makes the appointment of a guardian or conservator.

T   F   7. A petition to appoint a guardian provides detailed information about the person to be appointed, the minor, the closest relative, and property of the minor.

T   F   8. Some states use the term guardianship to include management of the affairs and estate of minors and disabled or incompetent adults.

T   F   9.   A notice does not have to be signed.

T   F   10.   Documents required for conservatorships are similar to those
               prepared for guardianships.

T   F   11.   Name change is not a probate matter.

T   F   12.   A petition to change name is the only document needed to change
               one's name.

T   F   13.   The court appoints a conservator to represent a minor's interests
               during a legal proceeding.

T   F   14.   The documents that must have a verification or oath in a guardian-
               ship matter are the petition and order.

T   F   15.   The prayer clause in a petition to appoint a conservator would
               request that a conservator be appointed, a time be set for a
               hearing, and notice be given to persons required by state law.

T   F   16.   The petitioner signs the order for name change.

T   F   17.   An accounting is a list of the names and values of assets.

T   F   18.   A person's legal name is the one given at birth.

TRANSCRIPTION RULES

CAPITALIZATION

Document Titles and Party Designations

Document titles and party designations used in petitions for conservatorships, guardianships, and name changes are:

Conservator

Guardian

Guardian Ad Litem

Notice of Hearing

Order to Appoint a Guardian

Order to Appoint a Conservator

Petition

Petition to Appoint a Guardian

Petition to Appoint a Conservator

Petition for Change of Name

Petitioner

Respondent

Ward

Do not capitalize beneficiary or decendent.

PERIOD

Run-In Heading

Place a period after a run-in heading, which is a heading on the same line as the paragraph it describes. The heading should be either boldfaced or underlined. The preferred style for word processing is boldface. Leave two spaces after the period.

Court Jurisdiction. The minor in this cause of action is a resident of Fairfax County, Virginia, living at 1243 Braddock Place, Alexandria, VA 22314.

SEMICOLON

Series of Long, Parallel Dependent Clauses (This rule was presented in Chapter 6; additional examples are shown below:)

IT IS FURTHER ORDERED that the fee of the Attorney for the Petitioner be set at Five Hundred Dollars ($500); that the fee of the Guardian Ad Litem be set at Three Hundred Dollars ($300); and that these fees and costs be paid from the estate of the Ward.

IT IS FURTHER ORDERED that the fee of the Attorney for the Petitioner be set at Five Hundred Dollars ($500) and that the fee be paid from the estate of the Ward. (There is not a series of three or more clauses, so no semicolon is needed.)

TRANSCRIPTION EXERCISES

Refer to Appendix A and review the rules entitled "Comma — Parenthetical Expressions," "Comma — Phrases Within a Sentence," and "Period — Enumerated Paragraphs Beginning with That."

Use a secretarial reference manual and the rules presented in this and previous chapters to aid you in correctly transcribing the following material. The sentences are presented in lowercase letters without capitalization and punctuation.

1. A. wards estate   the ward owns real property appraised at 125,000 dollars and personal property with an estimated value of 75 thousand dollars

2. the petitioner prays that the notice requirement be waived that the respondent camille benavides the minor be appointed a guardian ad litem that the court set the date and time for a hearing that the court costs and bond be waived and that the fees be set by this court and charged against the estate of camille benavides

3. it is ordered adjudged and decreed that it is proper for the name of the petitioner to be changed and that the birth certificate of lucinda twyford be changed to read lucy ford

4. the ward has been duly notified in this proceeding by service of process on the guardian ad litem

5. the petitioner makes oath that the foregoing statements in this petition are true

6. in fact a total of ten children were given the surname twyford

7. the ward has been notified specifically through service of process on the guardian ad litem

8. further the guardian has until the last day of april to file the inventory and accounting

9. the petitioner after being duly sworn makes oath that the statements in the petition are true to the best of her knowledge information and belief

10. the court being satisfied that there is good cause for the hearing has notified the attorneys and petitioner to appear on december 15 (current year)

11. ferline mentz is four years of age having been born november 11 (4 years ago) and has been going by the surname of her stepfather

12. the conservator is charged with asserting your best interests consistent with the law in determining whether to sell or invest your stocks and bonds

13. petitioner would show: 1 that the court has jurisdiction because the ward and petitioner live within the boundaries of the county 2 that the ward is

in need of someone to care for him as he is a minor and unable to care for his physical and financial needs 3 that the minor has real and personal property worth approximately 200 thousand dollars 4 that the proposed guardian is ready willing and able to serve.

RESEARCH ACTIVITIES

1. Consult your state codes to determine what the age of majority is in your state.

2. Consult your state codes to determine the court(s) in which guardianships, conservatorships, and name changes are filed. Determine whether guardianships and conservatorships are separate matters in your state or whether they are combined under the topic of guardianships.

3. Contact a legal secretary in your state and compare the documents described in this chapter with the documents required in your state.

4. Contact the clerk of the probate court in your county to obtain forms used in guardianship and conservatorship proceedings.

PROJECTS

Insert the cassette tape for Chapter 7 and transcribe the following projects.

Project 7-1   Transcribe a petition to appoint a guardian in the matter of Yang Feng Yeh and Seung Ho Yeh, minors. The petitioner is Caroline A. Yoshizawa. This is a petition to appoint a guardian and guardian ad litem where two minor children's parents have died and an aunt wants to be guardian. The attorney is Nugen C. Lee, 2621 Beach Front Boulevard, Kailua, Hawaii 96708.

Project 7-2   Transcribe an order for the appointment of a guardian. This is an order to accompany Project 7-1.

Project 7-3   Transcribe a petition to appoint a conservator. Marguerite D. Maartin is the petitioner; Ramon Juarez Maartin is the ward. The ward is an eighty-two-year-old man who is suffering from Alzheimer's disease. The case is to be filed in the County Court of Doña Ana County, New Mexico. The attorney's address is in Las Cruces, NM.

Project 7-4   Transcribe an order appointing a conservator to accompany Project 7-3.

Project 7-5   Transcribe a petition to change the name of a Native American. He is an adult.

Project 7-6   Transcribe an order to change a name for Project 7-5. There is no certificate since there is no adverse party to serve.

UNIT II
PERFORMANCE ASSESSMENT

A. The following document has spelling, grammar, punctuation, and word-choice errors. Mark each error on the copy below using proofreaders' symbols. Key and print a corrected copy of the document for the attorney's approval. Prepare a caption.

This is an Order for Intestate Administration of the estate of Millie Faye Brono, Deceased. Andrew John Brono is being named personal representative of the estate. The case is in the Probate Court of Hennepin County, Minnesota, Case No. 92-P-1253.

IN THE PROBATE COURT OF HENNEPIN COUNTY, MINNESOTA

IN THE MATTER OF:	)
	)
THE ESTATE OF MILLIE FAYE BRONO,	)
	)
Deceased,	) No. 93-P-1253
	)
	)
ANDREW JOHN BRONO,	)
	)
Petitioner.	)

ORDER FOR INTESTATE ADMINISTRATION

This cause came on to be heard on the 2nd day of December, current year, before the HONORABLE JOHN W. ROBINSON, Judge of the Probate Court of Hennepin County, Minnesota upon a Petition for letters of administration, the testimony in open court from the Petitioner, ANDREW JOHN BRONO, and statements by council for the Petitioner, from all of which the Court find:

1. That the decedent, MILLIE FAYE BRONO, died on November 20, current year, at the age of 71 years;

2. That the decedents place of residents was 1233 Lowry Avenue, North East, Minneapolis, MN;

3. That to the best of the petitioners knowledge, the decedent left no Last Will and Testiment and that the petitioner has made a due and diligent search for any such Will;

4. That the decedent is survived by a husband, your petitioner herein, ANDREW JOHN BRONO, along with four grown children whose name and addresses are correctly listed in the Petition for Intestate Administration;

5. That the decedent owned, along with her husband, the house located at 1233 Lowry Avenue, North East, Minneapolis, Minnesota, as tenents by the entirety;

6. That the decedent owned certain personel property subject to probate administration which was soully in the decedents' name in a value not to exceed Ten Thousand Dollars ($10,000);

IT IS THEREFORE ORDERED, ADJUDGED, AND DECREED that the Clerk and Master of the Probate Court of Hennepin County, Minnesota administer the oath and otherwise qualify the Administrator, ANDREW JOHN BRONO, and issue proper Letters Testamentary upon the Administrator securing bond in the amount of Ten Thousand Dollars ($10,000.00).

IT IS FURTHER ORDERED that the Clerk and Master give proper notice to the creditors' of the deceased as required by law and that the Administrator file the necessary Inventory within sixty (60) days of the date of this order.

Entered this the _____ day of December, (current year).

_____
JOHN W. ROBINSON, JUDGE

Approved for Entry:

_____
STEVEN B. COUNTS (No. 3765)
Attorney for Administrator
4431 Minnehaha Avenue
St. Paul, Minnesota 55101
(314) 555-0092

B. Place the cassette tape for Performance Assessment II in the transcriber. Transcribe II-B, a Petition to Probate a Will and to Grant Letters Testamentary. James Sidney Bowker is the petitioner; James Forrest Bowker is the deceased. This case is to be heard in the Probate Court for Roanoke County, Virginia. The attorney is Leon R. Sensing (No. 87822), 552 Dominion Bank Building, Roanoke, Virginia 10341. Phone: (502) 555-9166. The witnesses are Silvia A. Porter, Fred L. Beasley, and Winnie H. Short.

C. Listen to the recorded instructions on the cassette tape for completing Item II-C. You will be instructed to retrieve a previously created document and will be given instructions for altering it to be used In the Matter of James Forrest Bowker, Deceased.

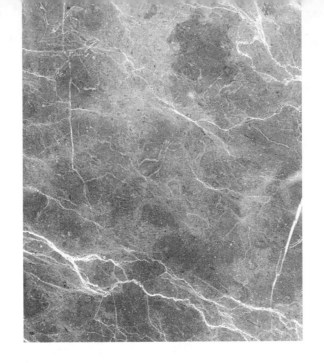

UNIT III
FAMILY LAW

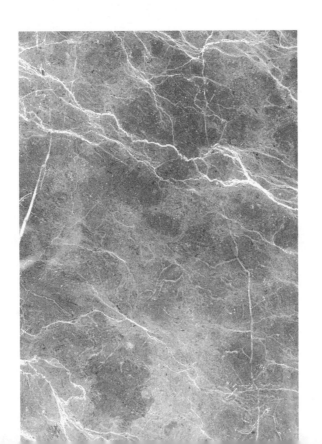

JOB DESCRIPTION
TRANSCRIPTION RESPONSIBILITIES

JOB TITLE: Legal Secretary

AREA OF PRACTICE: Family Law — Divorce, Adoption, and Paternity

TRANSCRIPTION DUTIES:

1. Is responsible for the transcription, formatting, and grammatical accuracy of all family law documents.

2. Is responsible for preparing a statistical page to retrieve and use for divorce complaints.

3. Retrieves and alters previously created family law documents according to instructions from the attorney.

4. Prepares divorce summonses.

5. Is familiar with the documents needed for divorce, adoption, and paternity matters.

6. Knows when to include a certificate of service on documents.

CHAPTER 8

TERMINATION OF MARRIAGE

OBJECTIVES

When you successfully complete this chapter, you will be able to:

➤ Transcribe a divorce complaint and prepare a summons

➤ Transcribe an answer to a divorce complaint

➤ Transcribe a marital dissolution agreement

➤ Transcribe a final decree of divorce

INTRODUCTION

Divorce is a procedure for terminating a marriage. Divorce is a matter that affects not only the parties who are ending a marriage but also the lives of children and other concerned family members. It is likely that you can name friends or family who have had to deal with the stress of going through a divorce.

This chapter discusses grounds for divorce, terminology used in divorce matters, the types of divorce proceedings, and documents used in divorce cases.

DIVORCE

A process for terminating a marriage, usually based on legal grounds as defined in the state statutes.

GROUNDS FOR DIVORCE

The reasons a divorce is granted are called **grounds**. Each state has passed laws stating the grounds on which divorces can be granted, and those laws vary significantly from one state to another. There are fault grounds and no-fault grounds for divorce.

Fault Grounds. Some typical grounds for divorce in states where fault divorces are granted are cruel and inhuman treatment (also known as inappropriate marital conduct), abandonment and nonsupport, desertion, habitual drunkenness, living apart from each other for a period of time, being convicted of certain crimes, and adultery.

No-Fault Grounds. The basis on which a no-fault divorce is granted is known as **irreconcilable differences** or **irretrievable breakdown**. It allows two people to agree to terminate a marriage with neither party being charged with wrongdoing.

GROUNDS

The state-approved legal reasons a divorce can be granted.

IRRECONCILABLE DIFFERENCES

A no-fault ground for terminating a marriage; also irretrievable breakdown.

IRRETRIEVABLE BREAKDOWN

A no-fault ground for terminating a marriage; also irreconcilable differences.

TERMINOLOGY

In states where fault divorces are granted, the party initiating the divorce action is a plaintiff or complainant, and the opposing party is the defendant. The termination of the marriage is a divorce, and the documents filed are a complaint and an answer.

In states that allow for no-fault divorces, the party initiating the action is the petitioner, and the answering party is the respondent. The termination of the marriage is a **dissolution**, and the documents filed are a petition and a response.

It is common practice to use the terminology interchangeably in states where both fault and no-fault divorces are granted.

DISSOLUTION

A process for terminating a marriage, usually on a no-fault basis.

TYPES OF DIVORCES

Uncontested. Uncontested means the opposing party takes no legal action to stop the divorce. An uncontested divorce can be (1) based on fault grounds or (2) based on irreconcilable differences.

An uncontested case based on fault grounds **might** proceed as follows: The plaintiff files a complaint for divorce. The defendant does not file an answer within the required time period. The plaintiff's attorney files a motion for default and prepares an order for default judgment in anticipation that the judge will sign it. A date is set for hearing the motion; and at that hearing, the judge rules on whether to grant the default. At the hearing the judge is mainly concerned with whether the defendant has been legally notified of what is happening. If the default judgment is granted, a hearing date is set to hear the plaintiff's side of the divorce action. At the divorce hearing, the judge rules on whether to grant the divorce. Before a final decree of divorce is signed, the judge requires that property be equitably divided.

In an uncontested case where fault grounds are alleged, the following documents are prepared:

- Summons for divorce

- Petition or complaint for divorce

- Motion for default judgment

- Order for default judgment

- Marital dissolution agreement, also called property settlement agreement

- Final decree of divorce

- Certificate of divorce for the state's records

An uncontested case on no-fault grounds **might** proceed as follows: The petitioner files a petition of divorce, stating that the grounds are irreconcilable differences or irretrievable breakdown. Both parties sign the marital dissolution agreement, which is attached to the petition for divorce. A short hearing takes place before the judge, after which the judge signs a final decree of divorce. The documents to be prepared are:

- Petition for divorce

- Marital dissolution agreement

- Final decree of divorce

- Certificate of divorce

Contested. Contested means that the defendant attempts to have the divorce dismissed or granted in favor of the defendant. A contested case can be based on fault grounds or on irreconcilable differences. After being served with a petition for divorce, the defendant answers the complaint, denying the grounds. The case then proceeds as any other civil litigation matter (as presented in Chapters 1 through 3). The attorney may need to prepare all of the documents listed above for an uncontested divorce and litigation documents studied in Chapters 1 through 3. The details of the case determine the types of documents needed.

DOCUMENTS USED IN DIVORCE CASES

The content and format of the documents filed in a contested divorce case where Yolanda McKissick is filing an action against her husband, Lawrence Byron McKissick are as follows:

SUMMONS

COMPLAINT FOR ABSOLUTE DIVORCE

ANSWER AND COUNTERCLAIM

FINAL DECREE OF DIVORCE

SUMMONS

The summons in this case is prepared by Yolanda's attorney to notify her husband, Lawrence, that she is filing for a divorce.

The summons is prepared and attached to the front of the complaint for divorce. A divorce summons is similar to the summons prepared for other types of litigation; however, the attorney often includes a statement demanding the defendant to appear at a given day and time for a court hearing to explain why or show cause why a particular order should not be issued by the court. See Figure 8-1.

COMPLAINT OR PETITION

Complaints or petitions for divorce, whether contested or uncontested, should have these basic elements:

- Caption

- Statistical information

- Body

- Prayer clause

- Signature block

- Verification

- Pauper's oath (if applicable)

- Fiat (if applicable)

Caption. See Figure 8-2. In this case, Yolanda McKissick is identified as the complainant and Lawrence McKissick as the defendant.

Statistical information. Paragraph I of the petition consists of statistical information about the husband and wife, such as full names (including the maiden name for the wife), race, residence, length of residence, date and place of birth, place of employment, number of prior marriages, husband's or wife's membership in the Armed Services, the date and place of the marriage, the date and place of the separation, and the names and ages of children of the marriage.

Body. The grounds are listed at the end of paragraph I, as shown in Figure 8-2, and are restated as an allegation in the language of the state statutes in the second paragraph, numbered with the roman numeral II. See Figure 8-3, page 2 of the complaint.

The grounds for divorce and specific charges of wrongful actions may be included in the allegations. Some states allow for quoting the grounds for divorce from the state **statutes** with no further statement of wrongdoing.

Prayer. Refer to Figures 8-3 and 8-4 and read the ten enumerated items in the prayer clause.

Sometimes in complaints for divorce actions (as in <u>McKissick v. McKissick</u>), the plaintiff asks the court to order that the defendant stop abusing and harassing the plaintiff or begin paying support payments. (See Figure 8-4, paragraph 5.) This type of protection is called **extraordinary relief**. Extraordinary relief means that the plaintiff is asking for this relief **before** there

EXTRAORDINARY RELIEF

A plaintiff's request for relief from the defendant before there is a hearing, such as requiring the defendant to support the children, stop harassing, etc.

CIRCUIT COURT SUMMONS   **BOULDER, COLORADO**

STATE OF COLORADO, COUNTY OF BOULDER

YOLANDA McKISSICK,   )
)
    Complainant,   )
)
vs.   )
)   No. _____
LAWRENCE BYRON McKISSICK,   )
)
Serve at: 408 Main Street, Apt. 4   )
        Boulder, CO 80306   )
)
    Defendant.   )

TO THE ABOVE-NAMED DEFENDANT:

    You are summoned to appear and defend a civil action (Complaint for Divorce) filed against you in Circuit Court, Boulder County, Colorado, and your defense must be made within thirty (30) days from the date this summons is served upon you. You are further directed to file your defense with the Clerk of the Court and send a copy to the Plaintiff's attorney at the address listed below. Also, you are summoned to appear at 9 a.m. on the 8th day of February, (current year), and show cause, if any you have, why you should not commence supporting your wife and minor children and further show cause why you should not be enjoined from coming around your wife and minor children for the purpose of physically abusing them or causing them any bodily harm.

    In case of your failure to defend this action by the above date, judgment by default will be rendered against you for the relief demanded in the complaint.

ISSUED: _____, 19____

                          CIRCUIT COURT CLERK
                          Boulder County, Colorado

SUSAN DALE-ROGERS (No. 82385)
Attorney for Complainant
308 Veterans Memorial Building, Suite 400
1000 Veterans Boulevard
Boulder, CO 80304
(303) 453-6666

TO THE SHERIFF:

    Please execute this summons and make your return hereon as provided by law.

                          CIRCUIT COURT CLERK

Received this summons for service the _____ day of _____, 19____.

                          SHERIFF

Adapted from Tenn. Circuit Court Divorce Summons

Show cause hearing (annotation)

FIGURE 8-1. Divorce Summons. The terminology in this form is taken from the Tennessee Circuit Court summons form.

Caption ———→

IN THE FIRST CIRCUIT COURT FOR BOULDER COUNTY, COLORADO

YOLANDA McKISSICK,   )
)
         Complainant,   )
)
vs.   )   No. _____
)
LAWRENCE BYRON McKISSICK,   )
)
         Defendant.   )

COMPLAINT FOR ABSOLUTE DIVORCE

THE COMPLAINANT WOULD MOST RESPECTFULLY SHOW UNTO THE COURT:

I.

Pursuant to the provisions of <u>Colorado Revised Statutes</u>, the Complainant submits the following statistical information.

<u>**COMPLAINANT**</u>

Full Name:	YOLANDA McKISSICK
Race:	African American
Residence:	2707 Sharon Hill Drive, Boulder, CO 80306
Length of Residence:	4 years
Date and Place of Birth:	May 1, (24 years ago), Boulder, Colorado
Employed:	Unemployed
Number of Prior Marriages:	None
Member of Armed Services:	No

<u>**DEFENDANT**</u>

Statistics ———→

Full Name:	LAWRENCE BYRON McKISSICK
Race:	African American
Residence:	408 Main Street, Apt. 4, Boulder, CO 80304
Length of Residence:	3 years
Date and Place of Birth:	June 21, (28 years ago), Fort Collins, Colorado
Employed:	Unknown at this time
Number of Prior Marriages:	None
Member of Armed Services:	No

DATE & PLACE OF MARRIAGE: February 12, (four years ago), Boulder, Colorado

DATE & PLACE OF SEPARATION: January, 8, (current year), Boulder Colorado

NAME AND AGES OF CHILDREN BORN OF THIS MARRIAGE:

       Chinequa Deresa McKissick, born March 23, (two years ago)
       Lawrence Byron McKissick, Jr., born November 24, (four years ago)

GROUNDS:

1.   **Irreconcilable differences**
2.   **Cruel and inhuman treatment**
3.   **Abandonment and nonsupport**

FIGURE 8-2. Divorce Complaint, Page 1. Form used by Circuit Court in Davidson County, Tennessee.

II.

Your Complainant would show that since the separation, the Defendant-Husband has exhibited violent behavior, including kicking over furniture; he has broken the chain lock off the front door; and his activities became so violent on one occasion that he shot a pistol in the direction of the house where one of their minor children was sleeping. A criminal warrant was taken out for his arrest. The Defendant-Husband has threatened the Wife and cursed her on many occasions.

III.

Your Complainant therefore would show that there have arisen such irreconcilable differences between the parties as to allow them to obtain an absolute divorce under Section 36-4-103 of the <u>Colorado Revised Statutes</u>.

Body ◄————

IV.

Further, the Wife would charge that the Husband has been guilty of such cruel and inhuman treatment or conduct towards her as to render further cohabitation unsafe and/or improper.

V.

Further, the Wife would charge that the Husband has abandoned her and has failed and refused to provide for her since the separation of the parties; and since she is unemployed and is taking care of the parties' two (2) minor children, she would ask that a Show Cause Order be issued directing the Husband to appear and show cause, if any he has, why he should not commence supporting the wife and minor children, pending a final hearing of this cause.

PREMISES CONSIDERED, COMPLAINANT PRAYS:

1. That proper process issue and be served upon the Husband and that he be required to answer this Complaint, with oath being expressly waived.

2. That at the hearing of this cause, the Wife be awarded an absolute divorce from the Husband and that she be restored to all the rights and privileges of an unmarried person.

Prayer ◄————

3. That at the hearing of this cause, the custody of the two (2) minor children of the parties be vested in the Wife, with reasonable rights of visitation being reserved for the Husband.

4. That the Wife be awarded child support and alimony, both pendente lite and permanent, as well as her reasonable attorney's fee in this cause.

- 2 -

FIGURE 8-3. Divorce Complaint, Page 2

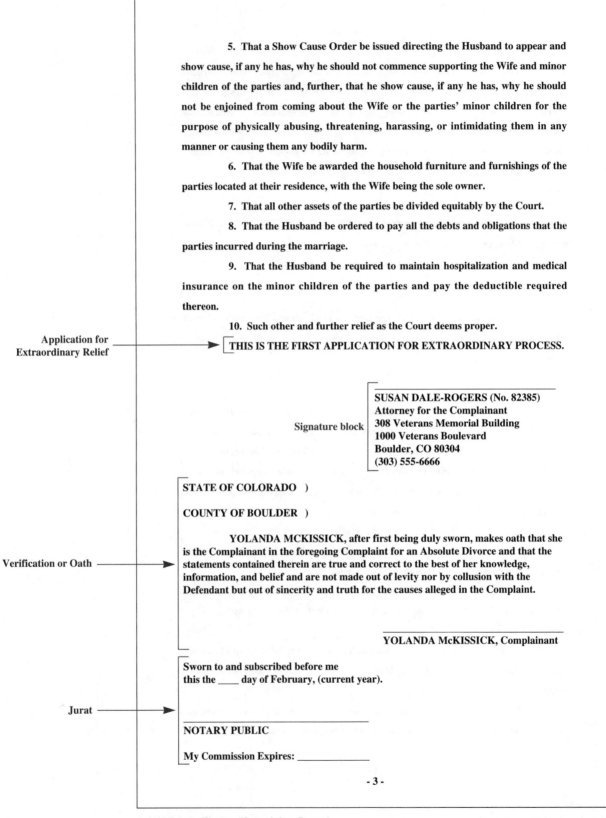

5. That a Show Cause Order be issued directing the Husband to appear and show cause, if any he has, why he should not commence supporting the Wife and minor children of the parties and, further, that he show cause, if any he has, why he should not be enjoined from coming about the Wife or the parties' minor children for the purpose of physically abusing, threatening, harassing, or intimidating them in any manner or causing them any bodily harm.

6. That the Wife be awarded the household furniture and furnishings of the parties located at their residence, with the Wife being the sole owner.

7. That all other assets of the parties be divided equitably by the Court.

8. That the Husband be ordered to pay all the debts and obligations that the parties incurred during the marriage.

9. That the Husband be required to maintain hospitalization and medical insurance on the minor children of the parties and pay the deductible required thereon.

10. Such other and further relief as the Court deems proper.

Application for Extraordinary Relief → ⌐ THIS IS THE FIRST APPLICATION FOR EXTRAORDINARY PROCESS.

Signature block

SUSAN DALE-ROGERS (No. 82385)
Attorney for the Complainant
308 Veterans Memorial Building
1000 Veterans Boulevard
Boulder, CO 80304
(303) 555-6666

STATE OF COLORADO   )

COUNTY OF BOULDER   )

Verification or Oath → YOLANDA MCKISSICK, after first being duly sworn, makes oath that she is the Complainant in the foregoing Complaint for an Absolute Divorce and that the statements contained therein are true and correct to the best of her knowledge, information, and belief and are not made out of levity nor by collusion with the Defendant but out of sincerity and truth for the causes alleged in the Complaint.

_____

YOLANDA McKISSICK, Complainant

Sworn to and subscribed before me
this the ____ day of February, (current year).

Jurat →

_____
NOTARY PUBLIC

My Commission Expires: _____

- 3 -

FIGURE 8-4. Divorce Complaint, Page 3

FIAT

TO THE CLERK OF THE CIRCUIT COURT:

  Issue a Show Cause Order directing the Defendant, **LAWRENCE BYRON MCKISSICK**, to appear before the Court on the ____ day of March, (current year), at 9 a.m., to show cause, if any he has, why he should not commence supporting the Complainant-Wife and the parties' minor children, pending a final hearing of this cause, and why, if any he has, he should not be enjoined from coming about the Wife or the parties' minor children for the purpose of physically abusing, threatening, harassing, or intimidating them in any manner whatsoever, pending a final hearing of this cause.

  ENTERED this the _____ day of February, (current year).

           ——————————————
           JUDGE

                  — Fiat

- 4 -

FIGURE 8-5. Divorce Complaint, Page 4

is a trial on the divorce. It refers to having a court hearing on important matters, such as requiring the defendant to move out of the house, to quit abusing or harassing, or to begin making payments to the spouse. The "extraordinary" refers to having an early hearing. The prayer must not only state the extraordinary relief desired but also pray that a hearing on the matter be set at an early date. If extraordinary relief is prayed for, the full-caps statement THIS IS THE FIRST APPLICATION FOR EXTRAORDINARY PROCESS is included at the end of the prayer.

Verification. The verification is a part of the complaint and states that the contents of the complaint are true and that the statements are not made out of levity or collusion with the defendant. For example, an elderly couple who agrees to get a divorce so one or the other can collect a larger retirement payment from social security would be guilty of collusion.

PAUPER'S OATH

A statement under oath that the party is unable to pay court costs.

Pauper's Oath. A **pauper's oath** states that due to poverty, the party filing the action is unable to pay the costs of the lawsuit. The statement can be included in the verification (see the verification in Figure 8-8) or as a separate section entitled "Pauper's Oath." The oath does not appear in the complaint filed for Yolanda McKissick because she has funds to cover the costs of the suit.

FIAT

A court order within a document, such as a complaint for divorce.

Fiat. A **fiat** is a court order setting a time and date for an early court hearing. If the plaintiff requests extraordinary relief (as in the McKissick complaint), not only is it justified in the allegations in the body of the complaint and listed in the prayer clause but also a fiat is added at the end of the complaint following the signature line for the attorney. (See Figure 8-5.)

Formatting Instructions for the Complaint

- See Chapter 1, pages 28-29, Formatting Instructions for a Complaint.
- Single-space the statistical material with double spacing between items as shown in Figure 8-2.

ANSWER TO COMPLAINT FOR DIVORCE

Answers to divorce complaints may include the following:

- Caption
- Introductory statement
- Denials or admissions
- Counterclaims
- Prayer clause
- Signature block for the attorney

- Verification if a counterclaim is included (jurat in some states)

- Certificate of service

Refer to Figures 8-6 through 8-8 as you examine the answer and counterclaim filed on behalf of Lawrence Byron McKissick.

Caption. The No. 93 D 789 has been assigned to the case.

Introductory statement. The introductory statement following the caption often contains phraseology such as "COMES NOW the defendant and for answer to the Complaint for Divorce filed against him or her, says:" The attorney for Lawrence used a similar statement.

Denials or admissions. Compare the answer to complaint in Figure 8-6 to the allegations in the complaint in Figures 8-2 and 8-3. The defendant denies all allegations except he admits the statistical data and admits that the parties have irreconcilable differences.

Counterclaim. A counterclaim is made by Lawrence McKissick, charging that the petitioner has been guilty of cruel and inhuman treatment and that the parties have irreconcilable differences (see Figure 8-7). With the filing of the counterclaim, the process reverses and the defendant becomes the counter-complainant (or counterclaimant). Since a counterclaim is included, the document name is Answer to Complaint and Counterclaim for Absolute Divorce. If the defendant/countercomplaintant is successful at trial, the court will grant the divorce to the defendant/countercomplainant instead of the complainant.

Prayer. In the document filed for Lawrence McKissick, a prayer is included at the end of the answer and another at the end of the counterclaim. The prayer at the end of the answer asks that the complaint filed against him be dismissed. The prayer at the end of the counterclaim asks that the divorce be granted to Lawrence, that the court divide the property, and that he get custody of the children.

Signature block. A standard signature block for the attorney for the defendant and countercomplainant is included.

Verification. When a counterclaim is part of the document, a verification should be included.

Formatting Instructions for the Answer and Counterclaim

- Follow the same directions for margins, spacing, and paragraph indentions as for preparing a complaint. Use Figures 8-6 to 8-8 as a guide for preparing the answer to a divorce complaint.

- Prepare an original copy to file with the court. After the original is signed, make a copy to serve on the complainant and a copy for the files.

IN THE FIRST CIRCUIT COURT FOR BOULDER COUNTY, COLORADO

YOLANDA McKISSICK,	)	
	)	
Complainant,	)	
	)	
vs.	)	No. 93-D-789
	)	
LAWRENCE BYRON McKISSICK,	)	
	)	
Defendant.	)	

ANSWER TO COMPLAINT AND COUNTERCLAIM FOR ABSOLUTE DIVORCE

ANSWER TO COMPLAINT

COMES NOW the Defendant, LAWRENCE BYRON McKISSICK, and for answer to the Complaint for an Absolute Divorce heretofore filed against him states as follows:

1. Defendant admits all of the statistical data in paragraph I of the Complaint but would show that the Complainant is employed and has a part-time job at Scott Woolen Mills, 126 Brandon Street, Boulder, Colorado. He would further deny that he has been guilty of any grounds for a divorce as stated in paragraph I of the Complaint.

2. Defendant specifically denies that he is or has been violent to the Complainant or the parties' minor children and demands strictest proof thereof.

3. Defendant would admit that the parties have irreconcilable differences as defined by the Colorado Revised Statutes.

4. Defendant denies the allegations in paragraph IV and demands strictest proof thereof.

5. Defendant denies the allegations in paragraph V and demands strictest proof thereof.

6. The Defendant, having answered the Complaint for Absolute Divorce filed against him, specifically denies each and every other allegation in the Complaint and demands strictest proof thereof.

WHEREFORE, the Defendant, LAWRENCE BYRON McKISSICK, would pray that the Complainant for an Absolute Divorce filed against him be dismissed and that the costs be adjudged against the Complainant.

FIGURE 8-6. Answer and Counterclaim, Page 1

COUNTERCLAIM FOR ABSOLUTE DIVORCE

NOW COMES the Defendant and assumes the role of a Counter-complainant and states as follows:

I.

Your Countercomplainant would charge that the Counterdefendant, YOLANDA McKISSICK, has been guilty of cruel and inhuman treatment or conduct towards the Countercomplainant as to render further cohabitation unsafe and/or improper.

II.

Countercomplainant would show that the parties have experienced such irreconcilable differences as to allow the Countercomplainant to obtain an absolute divorce under Colorado Revised Statutes, Section 36-801(2).

III.

Countercomplainant would show that he is the fit and proper person to have the custody and care of the parties' two minor children.

PREMISES CONSIDERED, THE COUNTERCOMPLAINANT PRAYS:

1. That proper process issue and be served on the Counterdefendant by sending a copy of this Counterclaim to Ms. SUSAN DALE-ROGERS, Attorney for Plaintiff, 308 Veterans Memorial Building, Suite 400, 1000 Veterans Boulevard, Boulder, CO 80304, requiring the Counterdefendant to answer, but her oath is hereby expressly waived.

2. That upon the hearing of this cause, the Countercomplainant be awarded an absolute divorce with all the rights and privileges of an unmarried person being restored.

3. That in lieu of a written Marital Dissolution Agreement between the parties, the Court, considering the entire record and the best interest of the parties hereto, determine a fair and equitable distribution of the parties' property.

4. That the Countercomplainant be awarded the custody of the parties' two minor children and that the the Counterdefendant be required to pay a reasonable amount of child support.

5. Such other and further relief as the Court deems proper.

PAUL L. FRANCIS (No. 22435)
Attorney for Defendant and
Countercomplainant
208 South Lake Parkway
Boulder, CO 80302
(303) 555-5000

- 2 -

FIGURE 8-7. Answer and Counterclaim, Page 2

STATE OF COLORADO   )

COUNTY OF BOULDER   )

Verification →

COMES the Countercomplainant, **LAWRENCE BYRON McKISSICK**, and makes oath that the foregoing statements in the Counterclaim for Absolute Divorce are true to the best of his knowledge, information and belief and that his Counterclaim is not made out of levity nor in collusion with the Counterdefendant but in sincerity and truth and for the causes mentioned therein. Further, that owing to his poverty, he is unable to bear the expense of this suit, and he is justly entitled to the redress sought to the best of his knowledge, information, and belief.

_____

LAWRENCE BYRON McKISSICK

Sworn to and subscribed before me
this the ____ day of March, (current year).

_____

NOTARY PUBLIC

My Commission Expires: _____

CERTIFICATE

I, **PAUL L. FRANCIS**, hereby certify that I have mailed a copy of this Answer to Complaint and Counterclaim for Absolute Divorce to Ms. SUSAN DALE-ROGERS, Attorney for Complainant, 308 Veterans Memorial Building, 1000 Veterans Boulevard, Boulder, CO 80304, on the _____ day of March, (current year).

_____

PAUL L. FRANCIS

FIGURE 8-8. Answer and Counterclaim, Page 3

FINAL DECREE

The final decree of divorce is a document signed by the judge who officially grants the divorce. In the <u>McKissick</u> case, the judge dismissed the complaint filed by the wife and signed a final decree granting the divorce to the husband. The judge also ordered an equitable division of property.

Refer to Figures 8-9 and 8-10, a partial final decree of divorce for the McKissicks, and note that it recites many of the facts and orders listed below. The facts appear before the statement IT IS ORDERED, and the actual court order appears after IT IS ORDERED.

FACTS

- States the hearing date, name of the court, and judge before whom the case was heard

- Verifies that process of service was completed (unless irreconcilable differences)

- States the grounds for the divorce

- States that the wife or husband is entitled to a divorce

- Affirms the marital dissolution agreement or states that the judge will divide the property equitably

ORDERS

- That the bonds of matrimony be forever dissolved

- That the marital dissolution agreement is made a judgment of the court or states how the property is divided

- That the named party be given custody of the children

- That the maiden name of the wife be restored

- That child support be paid

- That the parent who does not have custody of the children has visitation rights

- That the named party pay court costs

The final decree is formatted in the same style as the final judgment presented in Chapter 3, Figures 3-11 and 3-12. Since the original of the final decree is usually signed by the judge after the court hearing, no one actually gets a signed copy unless one is obtained from the clerk of the court. The original is filed with the court along with the certificate of divorce discussed in the next section.

IN THE FIRST CIRCUIT COURT FOR BOULDER COUNTY, COLORADO

YOLANDA McKISSICK,	)	
	)	
Complainant,	)	
	)	
vs.	)	No. 93-D-789
	)	
LAWRENCE BYRON McKISSICK,	)	
	)	
Defendant.	)	

FINAL DECREE OF DIVORCE

This cause came on to be heard on August 2, (current year), before the Honorable ALLEN V. DARNELL, Judge of the First Circuit Court of Boulder County, Colorado, upon the Complaint for Absolute Divorce filed by the Wife, the Answer and Counterclaim filed by the Husband, and upon the testimony in open court by the parties and their witnesses along with the entire record as a whole, it appears by the preponderance of the evidence that the Complaint filed by the Wife should be dismissed and that the Counterclaim filed by the Husband for an Absolute Divorce should be granted in that the Court finds the Wife has been guilty of such cruel and inhuman treatment as to render further cohabitation unsafe or improper and the Husband is entitled to an absolute divorce.

IT IS THEREFORE ORDERED, ADJUDGED, AND DECREED by the Court that the bonds of matrimony now subsisting between the Husband and Wife be and the same is forever dissolved. Husband is granted an absolute divorce with all the rights and privileges of an unmarried person restored.

IT IS FURTHER THE ORDER OF THE COURT that there be a distribution of the parties' property in the following manner:

a. That the parties be granted joint custody of their two (2) minor children with the principal custody being placed in the mother. Further, both parties shall be prohibited from taking the children out of the jurisdiction of this Court without prior Court approval, with the exception of summer vacation and spring break.

b. That the Husband be granted liberal visitation with the parties' minor children upon reasonable notification ahead of time that he wishes to visit with them.

FIGURE 8-9. Final Decree of Divorce, Page 1

k. That each party be responsible for paying one half (1/2) of the outstanding debts listed by the Wife, said list being made Exhibit No. 1 to her testimony and that the other party be held harmless for the other's half.

l. That all title, right, and interest the Wife may have in the 19-- Oldsmobile Cutlass be divested from the Wife and vested solely in the name of the Husband. That all title, right, and interest that the Husband may have in the 19-- Toyota Corolla be divested out of the name of the Husband and vested solely in the name of the Wife and that the Wife shall be solely responsible for all financial obligations and liens on the Toyota.

IT IS FURTHER ORDERED, ADJUDGED, AND DECREED that the Husband shall pay the costs in this cause for which execution be issued if necessary.

ENTERED this _____ day of August, (current year.)

_____
ALLEN V. DARNELL, JUDGE

APPROVED FOR ENTRY:

_____
PAUL L. FRANCIS (No. 22435)
Attorney for Defendant and Countercomplainant
208 South Lake Parkway
Boulder, CO 80302
(303) 555-5000

_____
SUSAN DALE-ROGERS (No. 82385)
Attorney for Complainant and Counterdefendant
308 Veterans Memorial Building
1000 Veterans Boulevard
Boulder, CO 80304
(303) 555-6666

2nd one not in assignment

CERTIFICATE

I, PAUL L. FRANCIS, hereby certify that I have mailed a copy of this Final Decree of Divorce to Ms SUSAN DALE-ROGERS, Attorney for the Complainant and Counterdefendant, 308 Veterans Memorial Building, 1000 Veterans Boulevard, Boulder, CO 80304, on the _____ day of August, (current year).

_____
PAUL L. FRANCIS

- 2 -

FIGURE 8-10. Final Decree of Divorce, Last Page

CERTIFICATE OF DIVORCE

The certificate of divorce varies from one state to another. It normally requests statistical data and is recorded and filed with the vital records division of the state. Blanks are provided on the form for data such as names, addresses, states, and dates of birth of the husband and wife, date of marriage, date of separation, number of children, date the marriage was dissolved, party to whom the divorce was granted, grounds, and signature of the court official. Confidential information about race, number of marriages, how marriages ended, and education is also requested on the form.

MARITAL DISSOLUTION AGREEMENT

There was no marital dissolution agreement in the <u>McKissick</u> case; the judge ordered the distribution of property as the husband had requested in the counterclaim. In another case, where Casandra Baker is filing for divorce from her husband, Joshua Baker, we will examine the

MARITAL DISSOLUTION AGREEMENT

MARITAL DISSOLUTION AGREEMENT

An agreement between parties to a divorce about such matters as property division, alimony, child support, child custody, etc. Also referred to as a property settlement agreement.

ALIMONY

Payments to support spouse or ex-spouse; also called spousal support, spousal maintenance.

CHILD CUSTODY

The primary care and maintenance of a child.

CHILD SUPPORT

The money paid by one party to the other for the support of the minor child no longer in that party's custody.

A **marital dissolution agreement**, often referred to as a property settlement agreement or property and support agreement, deals with issues such as property division, alimony, child support, child custody, visitation rights, continued insurance coverage, payment of debts, and restoration of a former or maiden name. It is a contract between the parties.

Property division is the distribution of property acquired by both parties during their marriage, and sometimes of property acquired before the marriage. The property may be real estate, household furnishings, certificates of deposits, stock, bonds, or retirement accounts. It can be divided according to agreement of the parties with the judge's approval, or it can be divided by the judge according to the equity of the situation. Some states have a community property law, which requires that all property be divided equally.

Payments to a wife by the husband or to the husband by the wife may be known as **alimony**, spousal support, spousal maintenance, or a similar term. Where alimony is an issue, an expense statement usually is submitted to aid the judge in determining the amount of alimony payment or in approving the monthly payment requested. Alimony can be a fixed, one-time sum (in solido), periodic payments (in futuro), or rehabilitative. Rehabilitative alimony is awarded to allow the divorced party an opportunity to go back to school to develop skills needed to enter or re-enter the job market.

Child custody and child support are parallel topics. **Child custody** is an award of the primary care of the child, usually to one of the parents. **Child support** is the money paid by one parent to the other for the continued support of a minor child. Custody is most often determined on the basis of what is in the best interest of the child and may be sole custody, joint custody, or split custody. **Sole custody** gives one parent the total responsibility of caring for the child or children. **Joint custody** gives the parents equal input into decisions about schools, church, surgery, or other matters. In a true joint custody, one spouse has the child part of the time and the other spouse has the child the other part of the time. The division of time may be nine months with one parent and three months with the other, six months with one and six months with the other, or any other division of time. **Split custody** gives one parent custody for a portion of time and the other parent custody for the remaining time. The custodial parent makes all decisions during the time he or she has custody. Custody of different children may be divided also. It is possible that custody of one child can be awarded to one parent and of another child to the other parent.

Visitation rights of the parents are spelled out as part of the custody arrangement. The noncustodial parent is customarily given visitation rights.

Read the partial marital dissolution agreement (paragraphs 4 through 8 have been omitted) between Joshua Baker, the husband, and Casandra Baker, the wife, shown in Figures 8-11 through 8-13. The agreement has the following parts:

- Caption or title

- Body — gives details of the agreement

- Signature lines

- Acknowledgment

Body. The details of the agreement between the husband and wife are addressed in the body of the document.

Signature lines.   Two signature lines are provided — one for the husband and one for the wife.

Acknowledgment. An **acknowledgment** is a statement, signed by a notary public, that the person who signed the document did so as his or her free act and deed. In Figures 8-12 and 8-13, a separate acknowledgment is included for each party. If both parties are scheduled to sign the document at the same time, it is acceptable to prepare one acknowledgment with both names.

SOLE CUSTODY

Custody in which one parent has the total responsibility of caring for the child. See also split and joint custody.

JOINT CUSTODY

Custody in which the parents have equal input into decisions about the welfare and care of a child. See also split and sole custody.

SPLIT CUSTODY

Custody in which the child is awarded to one parent for a portion of the time and to the other parent for the remaining time with the custodial parent making all decisions.

ACKNOWLEDGMENT

A statement by the person who signs a document that it was done as his or her free act and deed.

Formatting Instructions for the Marital Dissolution Agreement

- Triplicate original copies are made of the agreement. All three copies are signed by the parties. Original signatures are on the agreement filed with the clerk of the court and on each party's copy. The attorney who prepares the agreement keeps a file copy and provides a copy for the defendant's attorney.

IN THE FIRST CIRCUIT COURT FOR BOULDER COUNTY, COLORADO

CASANDRA BAKER,	)	
	)	
Petitioner,	)	
	)	
vs.	)	No. 93-D-1244
	)	
JOSHUA BAKER,	)	
	)	
Respondent.	)	

MARITAL DISSOLUTION AGREEMENT

THIS AGREEMENT is entered into this the 15th day of May, (current year), by and between CASANDRA BAKER, hereinafter referred to as "Wife," and JOSHUA BAKER, hereinafter referred to as "Husband."

WHEREAS, certain difficulties have arisen between CASANDRA BAKER and her Husband, JOSHUA BAKER, relative to their marital relations;

WHEREAS, the parties have been and are now living separate and apart and do not have expectations of resuming a marital relationship at this time;

WHEREAS, there appears no possibility of a reconciliation between the parties and it now has been determined that it is impossible for the parties to live happily in a marital state and that the Wife has filed a Complaint for an Absolute Divorce in the First Circuit Court of Boulder County, Colorado, with the Husband having duly filed an Answer and a Counterclaim; and

WHEREAS, the parties desire to enter into a Marital Dissolution Agreement at this time;

NOW, THEREFORE, for the consideration as herein set out, the parties do enter into this Marital Dissolution Agreement to settle all disputes as to all respective property rights. It is specifically understood and agreed by both parties hereto and they have been so advised that any Marital Dissolution Agreement entered into by and between them is made subject to the approval and ratification of the Court, in the event that the Court should see fit to grant a divorce at the hearing of this cause. In the event of such approval and ratification by the Court, the same may be incorporated within the Final Divorce Decree. The parties hereto agree and covenant as follows:

1. The parties shall have joint custody of the parties' minor children; however, the minor children shall live and reside with the Wife, and the Husband shall have reasonable visitation privileges with his giving reasonable notification ahead of time that he wishes to visit and exercise said visitation privileges.

2. To assist with the care, support, and maintenance of the minor children, Husband shall pay directly to Wife the sum of Sixty Dollars ($60) per week. In addition,

FIGURE 8-11. Marital Dissolution Agreement, Page 1

Husband shall maintain and provide medical and hospitalization insurance for the minor children, and said insurance shall be maintained until each child reaches his or her majority.

3. Each party shall have the responsibility and obligation to pay his or her own outstanding bills and debts that were made during the marriage. Further, each party shall hold the other party harmless on their respective debts and charge nothing in the name of the other party.

9. Each party shall pay his or her own attorney.

10. The parties hereto agree and acknowledge that this Marital Dissolution Agreement is entered into by each of them with full knowledge on the part of each the extent and probable value of all property and estate of the parties, jointly and personally, and each of the parties hereby forever releases and surrenders all of his or her right, title, and interest, marital or otherwise, in and to all of the estate whether real, personal, intangible, or mixed, now owned or hereinafter acquired by the other party.

11. The parties agree that this Marital Dissolution Agreement is subject to the approval of the Court in the event a divorce is granted to either party herein. If approved by the Court, then this Agreement is the full, final, and complete settlement of the rights and interests of the parties in and to the personal and other property of the same and is entered into by them of their own free will and accord and will be incorporated into any Final Decree for Divorce which shall be rendered by the Court.

IN WITNESS WHEREOF, the parties hereto set their signatures on the ____ day of May, (current year).

_____
CASANDRA BAKER, Wife

_____
JOSHUA BAKER, Husband

STATE OF COLORADO   )

COUNTY OF BOULDER   )

I, _____, a Notary Public of the aforesaid State and County certify that CASANDRA BAKER, with whom I am personally acquainted, personally appeared before me this date, and I acknowledge the due execution of the foregoing Marital Dissolution Agreement for the purposes therein expressed.

WITNESS my hand and official seal this the ____ day of May, (current year).

_____
NOTARY PUBLIC

My Commission Expires: _____

Acknowledgment for Wife

- 2 -

FIGURE 8-12. Marital Dissolution Agreement, Page 2

Acknowledgment
for Husband

STATE OF COLORADO)

COUNTY OF BOULDER)

I, _____, a Notary Public of the aforesaid State and County, certify that JOSHUA BAKER, with whom I am personally acquainted, personally appeared before me this date, and I acknowledge the due execution of the foregoing Marital Dissolution Agreement for the purposes therein expressed.

WITNESS my hand and official seal this the ____ day of May, (current year).

_____

NOTARY PUBLIC

My Commission Expires: _____

FIGURE 8-12. Marital Dißssolution Agreement, Last Page

- Include a court caption on the agreement if it is to be used in court as a separate document. If it is to be attached to the complaint, the caption can be omitted. It would begin with a centered title in full caps.

- When a marital dissolution agreement is included in the final decree of divorce, the signature lines should indicate that the parties have signed the original marital dissolution agreement. This is known as **conforming** the document. To indicate that Casandra Baker and Joshua Baker signed the agreement shown in Figure 8-12, key /s/ to indicate "signed," then key the name. To show that the notary signed, conform her signature and insert the notary expiration date. For example:

CONFORMING

Adding notations of signatures to a copy of a document to indicate that the parties have signed the original; for example, "/s/ Casandra Baker" on a signature line means she signed the original document.

CONFORMED COPY OF THE WIFE'S AND HUSBAND'S SIGNATURES

/s/ Casandra Baker
CASANDRA BAKER, Wife

/s/ Joshua Baker
JOSHUA BAKER, Husband

CONFORMED COPY OF A NOTARIZED DOCUMENT

/s/ Susan V. Jordan
NOTARY PUBLIC

My Commission Expires: 4/5/95

SUMMARY

- Divorce is a method for terminating a marriage.

- Divorce, complaint, answer, plaintiff, and defendant are terms used in states where fault grounds for divorce are recognized.

- Dissolution, petition, response, petitioner, and respondent are terms used in no-fault actions to terminate marriages.

- Any divorces may be contested or uncontested.

- Contested or uncontested cases may be based on fault grounds or irreconcilable differences (when state laws provide both options).

- A complaint for divorce has a caption, statistical information, allegations, prayer clause, signature block, verification, pauper's oath (if applicable), and sometimes a fiat.

- No summons is required in an uncontested, irreconcilable differences case where both parties have signed a marital dissolution agreement.

- If a case is uncontested, the respondent may choose not to answer the complaint, which is a basis for the plaintiff to obtain a default judgment.

- A marital dissolution agreement is a contract between the parties as to matters such as property division, alimony, child support, child custody, visitation, continued insurance coverage, payment of debts, and restoration of former or maiden name.

- A final decree of divorce orders that the bonds of matrimony be dissolved, as well as other issues related to the divorce, and is signed by the judge who grants the divorce.

- A certificate of divorce is attached to the final decree when it is filed. The certificate becomes a permanent record filed with the vital records division of the state.

REVIEW EXERCISES

T F 1. The first document to prepare in a divorce proceeding is the certificate of divorce.

T F 2. The secretary would prepare fewer documents for a contested divorce than an uncontested case.

T F 3. In a no-fault marital dissolution, the party starting the action is the plaintiff and the answering party is the defendant.

T   F   4. An uncontested divorce case can be based on fault grounds or can be based on irreconcilable differences.

T   F   5. In a contested case, the defendant would not file an answer to the complaint for divorce.

T   F   6. A summons is attached to the back of every complaint for divorce.

T   F   7. If the plaintiff needs extraordinary relief because of threats by the defendant, it should be justified in the allegations in the complaint and listed in the prayer cause.

T   F   8. The first page of a divorce complaint includes statistical information about the plaintiff and the defendant.

T   F   9. Only one thing, the divorce, should be requested in the prayer clause.

T   F   10. A fiat is a court order at the end of a complaint setting a time and date for an early court hearing.

T   F   11. If a party cannot pay court costs, a pauper's oath is made a part of the complaint.

T   F   12. The answer should have a certificate of service.

T   F   13. When a counterclaim is filed, the defendant becomes a counterdefendant.

T   F   14. Marital dissolution agreements are also known as property settlements or property and support agreements.

T   F   15. Payments made to the wife or husband to cover expenses for the children are called alimony.

T   F   16. Child custody and child support are matters that are addressed in the marital dissolution agreement.

T   F   17. The marital dissolution agreement is the document that officially dissolves the marriage.

T   F   18. An acknowledgment is signed by a notary public.

T   F   19. If there is more than one item in the prayer clause, number each item in the prayer with a centered roman numeral.

T   F   20. A marital dissolution agreement is signed by the attorney.

TRANSCRIPTION RULES

CAPITALIZATION

Phrases in Full Caps

Key the following and similar phrases appearing at the beginning of a paragraph in full caps:

IN WITNESS WHEREOF,

THIS AGREEMENT

NOW, THEREFORE,

WHEREAS,

WITNESS

COMMA

"And" Omitted Between Two Adjectives

Use a comma between two or more consecutive adjectives not joined by "and" that modify the same noun. If the first adjective modifies the combined thought of the second adjective and noun, do not separate the adjectives with a comma. TEST: If inserting the word "and" between the adjectives makes sense, the comma is placed between the adjectives.

The Wife charges that the Husband has been guilty of cruel, inhuman treatment. (Comma needed — cruel and inhuman clearly describes the treatment.)

The Petitioner prays that the Court approve the property settlement and make it a part of a final divorce decree. (No comma needed between final and divorce — It is not a final and a divorce decree; it is a divorce decree that is final.)

COLON

Hours and Minutes

Place a colon between hours and minutes when expressing time. Use figures with a.m. and p.m. Also use figures with o'clock, except in formal correspondence. Do not use a.m. or p.m. and o'clock together. With even hours, omit the zeros.

8 a.m. (not 8:00 a.m.)

8:25 a.m. (not 8:25 a.m. o'clock or 8:25 o'clock a.m.)

6 o'clock (not 6:00 o'clock)

SEMICOLON

Independent Clauses — No Conjunction

Use a semicolon between two closely related independent clauses not joined by a conjunction. Each clause should be a separate sentence if the clauses are not closely related.

The Complainant would show that the Husband has kicked over furniture; he has broken the chain lock off the front door. (These clauses both relate to the husband's behavior.)

The parties shall have joint custody of the minor children. Each party shall pay his or her own attorney. (These clauses are addressing separate, unrelated matters.)

TRANSCRIPTION EXERCISES

Refer to Appendix A and review the rules entitled "Commas — Apposition" and "Underlining."

Use a secretarial reference manual and the rules presented in this and previous chapters to aid you in correctly transcribing the following material. The sentences are presented in lowercase letters without capitalization and punctuation.

1. the grounds for this action can be found in colorado revised statutes section 36 801 (2)

2. the wife shall be granted the divorce she shall be restored to all the rights and privileges of an unmarried person

3. the defendant struck the plaintiff several times in her face causing black swollen eyes

4. file this complaint and cite the defendant to appear before me at nine am on tuesday the twenty-third day of august (current year)

5. whereas in a certain action pending in the circuit court for boulder county colorado the plaintiff prayed for and obtained a show cause order

6. i tamara kreeper declare that the statements and facts contained herein are true

7. the wife will ask for extraordinary relief the husband will be restrained from encumbering any of the assets of the parties

8. beth squires the minor child resides with her mother and has done so since birth

9. pursuant to the california rules of civil procedure the defendant must file an answer within thirty days

10. she drives a mazda mercury automobile

RESEARCH ACTIVITIES

1. Refer to your state codes to determine whether your state allows no-fault divorces. What are the grounds for divorce in your state?

2. After reading this chapter, interview a legal secretary who types divorce documents in your state. Make a list of the documents he or she types and ask about the contents of those documents.

3. Contact your state department that records vital records and ask for a blank copy of a certificate of divorce.

4. Obtain a copy of a summons for a divorce and any other forms used for divorce documents from the clerk of the court in your county. Use your local form for the projects to be transcribed.

PROJECTS

Insert the cassette tape for Chapter 8 and transcribe the following projects.

Project 8-1   Prepare a **form** for the first page of a divorce complaint to use for inserting statistical information. Refer to Figure 8-2 and insert input codes at each point where information would vary from one case to another. Save this form. You will be asked to retrieve it in Unit III Performance Assessment C.

Project 8-2   Transcribe the complaint for divorce in Seneca County, New York. Use the form prepared in Project 8-1. Sandra Vensa Jandreski is the complainant, and Rolfe Ernest Jandreski is the defendant. The attorney is Evelyn A. Lefkowitz. The parties have two children. The wife is asking for extraordinary relief. A fiat is included on the complaint for divorce to set a hearing on support for the wife and children, prohibiting the husband from being intoxicated around the wife or children, and attempting to put the husband out of the parties' home.

Project 8-3   Transcribe an answer and counterclaim. The husband, Rolfe Ernest Jandreski, denies most of the allegations and then charges the wife, the counterdefendant, with grounds for divorce and prays that the divorce be granted to him.

Project 8-4   Transcribe the marital dissolution agreement for the parties in Project 8-2. WITNESSETH should be on a line by itself, followed by a colon, and indented to paragraph point, as shown on page 265. This document is to be signed by each party and notarized. It is to be saved and will be used in its entirety in the final decree of divorce.

Project 8-5   Transcribe the final decree of divorce. This is the final decree for the divorce for which a complaint was filed in Project 8-2. An answer and counterclaim filed by the defendant (not shown) was withdrawn when the parties agreed on the terms of the marital dissolution agreement. As you transcribe Project 8-5, you will be retrieving Project 8-4 into the final decree.

ADOPTIONS AND PATERNITY

OBJECTIVES

When you successfully complete this chapter, you will be able to:

➤ Transcribe a petition for adoption and identify the parts

➤ Transcribe an order of reference

➤ Transcribe an order of abandonment

➤ Transcribe a final order of adoption

➤ Transcribe petitions, motions, and orders for paternity cases

---

ADOPTION

Adoption is an exciting area of work for a legal secretary because people are usually happy and thrilled about becoming parents. Adoption involves at least two people — one who is to be adopted, known as an **adoptee**, and one who wishes to adopt. A person must be 18 years of age or older to adopt, and a person of any age can be adopted.

ADOPTEE
One who is adopted.

Adoption laws have been and likely will continue to be changing, giving more rights to the various parties to adoption. As a result, some of the procedures and contents of documents outlined in this chapter are likely to change. Adoption laws also vary from state to state.

Once the person who wishes to adopt a child contacts an attorney, the process generally includes:

- Filing a document with the appropriate court to begin the procedure

- Obtaining consent from the proper person(s) or agency or proving that the child has been willfully deserted and forsaken by the parents **(abandoned)**

ABANDON
To willfully desert, leave, or forsake a child or an adult.

- Conducting an investigation of the child and the prospective home, unless waived by the judge

- Obtaining temporary placement in a home during a waiting period, unless waived by the judge

- Ordering of the final adoption by the judge

The documents most often used in adoption proceedings are shown below.

> **PETITION FOR ADOPTION**
>
> **ORDER OF REFERENCE**
>
> **AFFIDAVIT OF CONSENT**
>
> **ANSWER AND CONSENT**
>
> **ORDER OF ABANDONMENT**
>
> **INTERLOCUTORY DECREE OF ADOPTION**
>
> **FINAL DECREE OF ADOPTION**

PETITION FOR ADOPTION

An adoption procedure begins by filing a petition for adoption. Its purpose is to provide information to the court about the child and petitioners, to inform the court about others who must give consent, and to request that the court grant the adoption.

A petition for the adoption of Lena Sue Kemp by her stepfather, Dwayne Anthony Abernathy, with her father, William Harold Kemp, consenting to the adoption is shown in Figures 9-1 through 9-3.

The parts of the petition are:

- Caption

- Body

- Prayer clause

- Signature block for the attorney

- Verification of the petitioners

- Verification of the respondent

NATURAL PARENT

A biological, or birth, parent.

RESPONDENT

One who is a party to a legal action; thus, petitioner and respondent.

Caption. The caption in Figure 9-1 is for an adoption in which a stepparent is filing a petition to adopt a stepchild. The **natural mother** (also called the birth mother) joins her husband as a party to the action. In this case, the natural father (also called the birth father) is also joining in the petition, as **respondent**, by signing a verification giving consent to the adoption. The true name of the child is the name given at birth and is the name used in this petition.

The illustration on page 234 is a caption for a petition for adoption where a child-placement agency is involved. The differences between this and the caption in Figure 9-1 are that the name used in the child-placement agency adoption is

IN THE CIRCUIT COURT FOR DAVIDSON COUNTY, TENNESSEE

IN THE MATTER OF: *or male*)	
)	
The Adoption of a Female Child)	
Whose Name for the Purpose of)	
this Proceeding is)	
)	
LENA SUE KEMP)	
)	
BY:)	
)	No. _____
DWAYNE ANTHONY ABERNATHY and)	
ELLEN SUE ABERNATHY,)	
)	
Petitioners,)	
)	
vs.)	
)	
WILLIAM HAROLD KEMP,)	
)	
Respondent.)	

PETITION FOR ADOPTION

Your Petitioners, DWAYNE ANTHONY ABERNATHY and wife, ELLEN SUE ABERNATHY, would respectfully show to the Court as follows:

1. They are adult citizens and residents of Davidson County, Tennessee, and have been citizens and residents of the State of Tennessee for one (1) year next preceding the filing of this Petition.

2. Your Petitioner ELLEN SUE ABERNATHY would show that she was formerly married to WILLIAM HAROLD KEMP and that one child was born to this union, namely, LENA SUE KEMP, who was born June 27, (two *2008* years ago), in Nashville, Davidson County, Tennessee. On August 23, (two years ago), she and WILLIAM HAROLD KEMP were divorced in the Fifth Circuit Court of Davidson County, Tennessee; and she was granted sole custody and control of LENA SUE KEMP. On October 30, (two years ago), she married DWAYNE ANTHONY ABERNATHY in Daytona Beach, Florida. Since the birth of LENA SUE KEMP, she has had custody of her daughter and her present husband, DWAYNE ANTHONY ABERNATHY, has been supporting and helping support the said child and has been just like a father to her ever since she and DWAYNE ANTHONY ABERNATHY married.

FIGURE 9-1. Petition for Adoption by a Stepparent, Page 1

3. WILLIAM HAROLD KEMP acknowledges and represents to the Court by signing this verified Petition that he surrenders all parental rights and responsibilities for the minor child and consents to the adoption of the child by DWAYNE ANTHONY ABERNATHY.

4. It is the desire of your Petitioners that the relationship of parent and child be established between DWAYNE ANTHONY ABERNATHY and said child. It is their desire that said child's name be changed to LENA SUE ABERNATHY.

5. Your Petitioners state that said child has no real or personal property.

6. Your Petitioners are fit and proper persons to have the care and custody of the child, and they are financially able to support the child.

7. There has been full compliance with the law in regard to consent to adoption to the best of the Petitioners' knowledge, information, and belief.

PREMISES CONSIDERED, THE PETITIONERS PRAY:

1. That they be allowed to file this Petition for Adoption.

2. That all necessary references be made.

3. That an interlocutory decree, probationary waiting period, and Order of Reference in this case be dispensed with as your Petitioners have a relationship of mother and stepfather to the child to be adopted and that a Final Decree be entered in this case as soon as the report is obtained from the Tennessee Department of Human Services.

4. That upon final hearing of this cause, the relationship of parent and child be established between DWAYNE ANTHONY ABERNATHY and said child in accordance with Chapter 202 of the Public Acts of Tennessee.

JOHN S. CURTIS (No. 22466)
Attorney for Petitioners
126 Clement Towers
1440 West End Avenue
Nashville, TN 37201
(615) 555-2335

- 2 -

FIGURE 9-3. Petition for Adoption by a Stepparent, Page 2

STATE OF TENNESSEE   )

COUNTY OF DAVIDSON   )

       DWAYNE ANTHONY ABERNATHY and wife, ELLEN SUE ABERNATHY, make oath that the statements in the foregoing Petition are true to the best of their knowledge, information, and belief.

_____
DWAYNE ANTHONY ABERNATHY

                 ← Verification by Petitioners

_____
ELLEN SUE ABERNATHY

Sworn to and subscribed before me
this the _____ day of August, (current year).

_____
NOTARY PUBLIC

My Commission Expires:_____

STATE OF TENNESSEE   )

COUNTY OF DAVIDSON   )

       I, WILLIAM HAROLD KEMP, after having been duly sworn, make oath that I have read the foregoing Petition for Adoption, which consists of three (3) pages, including verifications, and that it is truthful in all respects and that I give my consent to the adoption of LENA SUE KEMP by DWAYNE ANTHONY ABERNATHY and that the parental relationship be established between them and that I further agree to release and surrender the parental relationship currently existing between LENA SUE KEMP and me.

                 ← Verification of Consent by Birth Father

_____
WILLIAM HAROLD KEMP

Sworn to and subscribed before me
this the _____ day of August, (current year).

_____
NOTARY PUBLIC

My Commission Expires: _____

- 3 -

FIGURE 9-3. Petition for Adoption by a Stepparent, Page 3

the new name of the child after the adoption and that there is no respondent because the parent or parents had previously given up parental rights when they surrendered the child to the agency.

IN THE CIRCUIT COURT FOR DAVIDSON COUNTY, TENNESSEE

IN THE MATTER OF:)) The Adoption of a Female Child) Whose Name for the Purpose of) this Proceeding is)) DANA KAY MORSE)) BY:)) RICHARD M. MORSE and) SHARON L. MORSE,)) Petitioners.)	No. _____

PETITION FOR ADOPTION

Caption for an Agency Adoption

Various phrases are used in the style of the case for an adoption, such as "In the Matter of the Adoption Petition of: _____ and _____, Adopting Parents," or "In Re Adoption of:"

Body. Read the body of the petition in Figures 9-1 and 9-2 and locate the following information: the names and residence of the petitioners, the ages and date of marriage of the petitioners, and the date and place of birth of the child. The petition also states that the birth father has surrendered parental rights; that a parent and child relationship between the child and stepfather be established; that the child be given the family name; that the child has no interest in property; and that the petitioners are fit persons and are financially able to adopt the child.

Prayer. To understand the prayer clause, the purpose of some documents and procedures discussed later in this chapter should be explained here. State laws generally require a waiting period before an adoption is finalized. In addition, unless waived, an investigation of the child and home is conducted. A document called an order of reference is prepared to order that investigation. Also, unless waived, an interlocutory (temporary) decree of adoption is issued, after which another waiting period is required before a final decree of adoption is signed by the judge.

Read the prayer on page 2 of the adoption petition for Lena Sue Kemp. The petitioners pray that the waiting period, interlocutory decree, and order of reference be waived; that a relationship of parent and child be established; and that the child's name be changed.

Signature Block. The attorney signs the petition.

Verifications. The petitioners sign a verification that the statements in the document are true. One verification, including the names of both the husband and the wife, is shown in the petition for Lena Sue. Another verification for the birth father, William Harold Kemp, is placed at the end of the petition for him to sign, stating that the contents of the petition are true and that he is giving up parental rights and consenting to the adoption.

ORDER OF REFERENCE

An **order of reference** is an order of the judge that the appropriate state department or child-placement agency conduct an investigation to determine whether the child is a proper subject for adoption and whether the prospective home is suitable for the child. The director of the agency is to submit a report to the court, for the judge's use only, within a stated period of time.

ORDER OF REFERENCE

The document that orders an investigation of a proposed adoptive home by the welfare department of the state.

The order of reference in Figure 9-4 is for an adoption requiring an investigation. The original name of the child, Dana Kay Smith, not the proposed new name, Dana Kay Morse, is used on the order and in the report submitted to the judge by the director of the agency. The reason for using the original name of the child on this document is that all records the investigator uses in preparing the report are filed under the child's birth name.

CONSENT DOCUMENTS

An important requirement of every adoption is that proper consent be given by the birth parents or the child-placement agency that has custody of the child. Written consent from the parent or parents is normally obtained in one of three ways: an affidavit of consent, verification giving consent on the petition for adoption, or answer and consent. In some states, a child of 14 years of age or older also gives consent.

Affidavit of Consent. An affidavit of consent is a document signed and sworn to by the birth parent or parents who are willing to give up parental rights and responsibilities. It is normally used in cases where the birth parent(s) gives consent before the petition is filed. In such cases, service of the petition on the parent who has signed the consent is not necessary. The document is an affidavit

AFFIDAVIT OF CONSENT

A sworn document by a birth parent or parents giving consent to adoption.

IN THE CIRCUIT COURT FOR DAVIDSON COUNTY, TENNESSEE

IN RE:	)	
	)	
The Adoption of a Female Child	)	
Whose Name for the Purpose of	)	
this Proceeding is	)	
	)	
DANA KAY SMITH	)	No. 6914
	)	
BY:	)	
	)	
RICHARD M. MORSE and	)	
SHARON L. MORSE,	)	
	)	
Petitioners.	)	

ORDER OF REFERENCE

In this cause, it appearing to the Court that the Petitioners, RICHARD M. MORSE and wife, SHARON L. MORSE, have filed a Petition seeking to adopt a child referred to in said Petition.

IT IS THEREFORE ORDERED, ADJUDGED, AND DECREED pursuant to Section 16 of Chapter 202 of the <u>Public Acts of Tennessee</u> that the Director of Tennessee Human Services for Davidson County, Tennessee, investigate the conditions and antecedents of the child sought to be adopted for the purpose of ascertaining whether she is a proper subject for adoption, to make appropriate inquiry to determine whether the proposed adoptive home is a suitable one for said child, and to investigate any other circumstances or conditions that may have a bearing on the adoption and of which the Court should have knowledge. Upon said investigation being completed, the said Director is to make a report to the Court within the time prescribed by law; and until the receipt of said report, all other matters are reserved.

ENTERED this the _____ day of _____, 19____.

_____
CHRISTINE A. BOYKIN, JUDGE

APPROVED FOR ENTRY:

_____
JOEL M. SULLIVAN (No. 2433)
Attorney for Petitioners
1233 Thompson Place
Nashville, TN 37221
(615) 555-2424

(Add certificate to Department of Human Services.)

FIGURE 9-4. Order of Reference

and is formatted in the same style as shown in Chapter 2, Figure 2-2. The caption may be omitted if the affidavit is attached to the petition when it is filed.

Verification of Consent. The verification of consent serves the same purpose as the affidavit of consent. Rather than being a separate document, it is a sworn statement placed at the end of the petition.

Answer and Consent. The answer and consent is a document used in cases where the **noncustodial** birth parent is willing to give consent to the adoption but did not do so prior to being served with the petition for adoption. After being served, the parent files an answer to the petition and gives consent to the adoption, thus, answer and consent. The document has a caption, body, signature block for the attorney, verification for the respondent, and certificate of service.

ORDER OF ABANDONMENT

When a child has been abandoned by a parent or parents, the child can be adopted without parental consent. An **order of abandonment** is a document signed by the judge, ruling that the child has been abandoned.

Abandonment can be obtained by:

- Presenting evidence of abandonment in the petition and requesting an order of abandonment in the prayer

- Presenting evidence at a court hearing to support the abandonment charge and requesting that the judge issue an order of abandonment

- Serving the natural parent whose whereabouts are not known by publication and if there is no response, obtaining a judgment by default

If a child has been abandoned and turned over to a child-placement agency, the director of that agency can give consent to adoption without abandonment proceedings.

Read the order of abandonment in Figures 9-5 and 9-6. This is an order of abandonment in a case where Thomas Aaron Gillette has abandoned his daughter, Jan Nicole Gillette. In the body of the order is a restatement of the evidence presented in the petition, followed by the court order that parental rights be terminated.

ADOPTION DECREES

Interlocutory Decree. An interlocutory decree temporarily assigns child care and custody to the petitioners without making the adoption final. The child is still under the authority of the court during this period of time. In certain cases, the judge may waive the interlocutory decree and sign a final decree. The decree restates much of the information contained in the body of the petition.

VERIFICATION OF CONSENT

A sworn statement by a birth parent giving consent to adoption. A verification is a statement at the end of a document.

ANSWER AND CONSENT

A verified document answering a petition and consenting to the adoption of one's birth child, thus giving up parental rights.

NONCUSTODIAL PARENT

The parent who does not have custody of a child.

ORDER OF ABANDONMENT

An order of the court stating that a child has been abandoned.

INTERLOCUTORY DECREE

A temporary order, such as the temporary assignment of the child care and custody of a child to the petitioners.

IN THE CIRCUIT COURT FOR DAVIDSON COUNTY, TENNESSEE

IN RE:)	
)	
The Adoption of a Female Child)	
Whose Name for the Purpose of)	
this Proceeding is)	
)	
JAN NICOLE GILLETTE)	
)	
BY:)	
)	No. 9079
GREGG LEE MOLINA and)	
SARAH ELLEN MOLINA,)	
)	
Petitioners,)	
)	
vs.)	
)	
THOMAS AARON GILLETTE,)	
)	
Respondent.)	

ORDER OF ABANDONMENT

This cause came on to be heard on the 20th day of October, (current year), before the Honorable CHRISTINE A. BOYKIN, Judge of the Circuit Court of Davidson County, Tennessee, upon the original Petition for Adoption and service by publication upon the Respondent, THOMAS AARON GILLETTE, a Judgment by Default having been duly taken against the Respondent, and the testimony of the witnesses heard in open court, from all of which appears to the Court that the Respondent has abandoned the child sought to be adopted in this cause for more than four (4) consecutive months immediately preceding the filing of this Petition in this Court, has legally and willfully abandoned JAN NICOLE GILLETTE; and GREGG LEE MOLINA and wife, SARAH ELLEN MOLINA, are the sole support and maintenance of the child.

IT IS THEREFORE ORDERED, ADJUDGED, AND DECREED that the child sought to be adopted, JAN NICOLE GILLETTE, is declared to be an abandoned child.

IT IS FURTHER ORDERED that all parental rights and responsibilities of the Respondent with respect to this child shall be and are fully terminated.

IT IS FURTHER ORDERED that this cause is referred to the Davidson County Director of the Tennessee Department of Human Services pursuant to Section 36-102 of <u>Tennessee Code Annotated</u> to investigate the conditions and

FIGURE 9-5. Order of Abandonment, Page 1

antecedents of the said child sought to be adopted for the purpose of ascertaining whether she is a proper subject for adoption, ...

ENTERED this the _____ day of _____, 19___.

_____
CHRISTINE A. BOYKIN, JUDGE

APPROVED FOR ENTRY:

_____
JOHN S. CURTIS (No. 22466)
Attorney for Petitioners
126 Clement Towers
1440 West End Avenue
Nashville, TN 37201
(615) 555-2335

CERTIFICATE

I, JOHN S. CURTIS, hereby certify that I have mailed a copy of this Order of Abandonment to the last known address of the Respondent, THOMAS AARON GILLETTE, 274 Blue Sky Road, Goodletsville, TN 37144, on this the ____ day of October, (current year).

_____
JOHN S. CURTIS

- 3 -

FIGURE 9-5. Order of Abandonment, Page 2

Final Decree of Adoption. The final decree of adoption, also called a final order of adoption, includes the same information as the interlocutory decree but makes the adoption final. It may address such matters as waiving the order of reference, investigation, waiting period, and interlocutory decree; releasing parental rights by the birth mother or father; creating parental rights between the petitioner and the adoptee; ordering the appropriate bureau or agency to prepare a new birth certificate; and changing the surname of the child. The final order should include the following sections:

- Caption
- Body
- Signature line for the judge
- Approved-for-entry block
- Certificate of service (if a respondent or agency is involved)

After the final order is signed, the clerk of the court submits a copy of the order and application for new birth certificate to the appropriate department to have a new birth certificate issued. Sometimes this involves changing the surname of the child; in other cases, the birth certificate is issued with the new name of the child and with the names of the new parents as true parents.

TYPES OF ADOPTIONS

Generally adoptions fall into one of three categories: stepparent adoptions, agency adoptions, and independent or private adoptions. Not all documents presented in this chapter are used in every adoption proceeding. The type of adoption determines the types and complexity of the documents.

Stepparent Adoption. The transcriptionist will most likely prepare the following documents for a stepchild adoption:

- Petition for adoption
- Order of abandonment (if the noncustodial parent has abandoned the child) or
- Affidavit of consent (if the noncustodial parent agrees and joins in the proceedings) or
- Answer and consent (if the noncustodial parent is served with the petition and consents to the adoption)
- Final decree of adoption

A stepparent who wishes to adopt a child is the petitioner. The petitioner's spouse, who would be the birth parent of the child, may join in the petition or give consent. Once abandonment has been proven or consent has been obtained, the noncustodial parent no longer possesses any rights as a parent. When a child is blood related, an order of reference, investigative report, waiting period, and interlocutory decree required in other types of cases are usually waived by the judge. The signed final order of adoption creates a parent-child relationship between the adoptee and petitioner.

Agency Adoption. The documents normally prepared for a state department or child-placement agency adoption are as follows:

- Petition for adoption

- Order of reference

- Answer and consent from the state department responsible for child placement

- Interlocutory decree

- Final decree of adoption

Two types of agencies involved in child placement are each state's department named to deal with child placement and child-placement agencies licensed by the state.

An agency may have custody of a child for any number of reasons — the birth parents abandoned the child, an unmarried parent or parents surrendered the child to the agency for adoption, or children were taken from their parents for abuse or neglect. When the state agency receives a child, the child is supported at public expense and becomes a **public charge**. A child is placed in a **foster home** until suitable adoptive parents can be located. Licensed child-placement agencies place children who have been surrendered to them for adoption.

PUBLIC CHARGE

One who is supported at public expense.

An individual or couple who wishes to adopt a child files an application with the agency. When a child becomes available for adoption, the child is placed in the prospective home. After a waiting period, a petition for adoption can be filed with the court. The court issues an order of reference to the state agency or licensed child-placement agency that placed the child to conduct an investigation. If the investigative report is favorable, the director of the agency files a consent to adoption. An interlocutory decree is prepared giving custody to the petitioners and instructing the agency to continue to supervise and report to the court. If the report is favorable, after another waiting period the judge will likely issue a final decree of adoption.

FOSTER HOME

A home where a child lives and is cared for before being adopted.

Private Adoption. In a private adoption a child is surrendered directly to the adoptive parents by the birth parent or parents. The following documents are prepared:

- Petition for adoption

- Surrender of the child by birth parents and agreement of adoptive parents (forms provided by the court clerk's office)

- Order of reference

- Interlocutory decree

- Final decree of adoption

In a private adoption, an agreement between the birth parents and adoptive parents is completed. The parties appear before a judge, and all parties sign the document; the judge signs a statement on the document that all actions were taken freely and voluntarily. The state department conducts an investigation, submits a report, and either gives or withholds consent. The report from the child-placement agency provides needed information to the court upon which to base a decision. If consent is given, an interlocutory decree and, after a waiting period, a final decree of adoption may be granted.

ADOPTION RECORDS

Adoption records are placed under seal in a fireproof vault and can be opened only upon court order. State laws vary, but usually certain types of nonidentifying information about the adoptee or the biological family are available to a child after reaching 18 years of age. If requested, the adoptee will usually be told the ages of parents at the time of his or her birth, the educational level of the parents, the sex and ages of other children of the parents, and the health history of the biological parents or relatives.

Formatting Instructions for Adoption Documents

- The instructions for margins, spacing, and pagination in Chapter 1, page 28, for formatting a complaint also apply to formatting a petition.

- Arrange the lines of the caption as shown in Figure 9-1 or the illustration under the topic "Caption" on page 234 in this chapter.

- Include a verification for the petitioners to sign.

- Include a certificate of service on every document where there is a respondent or an agency to be notified.

- File the petition in triplicate with the court clerk.

- Attach an order of reference, unless waived, to each petition.

- Prepare copies of the affidavit of consent, answer and consent, order of reference, order of abandonment, interlocutory decree, and final decree as follows: one original for the court, one copy for the respondent, one copy for the state agency, and one for the office files.

PATERNITY

Paternity is a procedure to establish fatherhood and to require the father to support, educate, and pay expenses for his child born out of wedlock, as well as the expenses of the mother during pregnancy.

Paternity suits are usually initiated by the mother (petitioner) against the person charged with being the biological father, referred to as the **alleged father** and defendant. The child's mother can file a petition while she is pregnant or after the child is born. If the child is likely to become supported by public welfare funds, the state department responsible for making payments to the unwed mother may file the petition to bring the alleged father to court.

The documents prepared by the plaintiff's attorney for a paternity suit are:

> **PETITION TO ESTABLISH PATERNITY**
>
> **AFFIDAVIT IN SUPPORT OF THE PETITION**
>
> **SUMMONS OR ATTACHMENT**
>
> **MOTION AND ORDER FOR A BLOOD TEST**
> **(IF REQUESTED BY EITHER PARTY)**
>
> **ORDER OF PATERNITY AND SUPPORT**

PATERNITY
A procedure to establish fatherhood.

ALLEGED FATHER
One who is charged with being the biological father of a child.

PETITION TO ESTABLISH PATERNITY

The petition to establish paternity provides information about the child and parents, establishes that the child was born out of wedlock, charges that the defendant is the father, and asks the judge to order the defendant to pay child support.

Read the petition to establish paternity in Figures 9-7 through 9-9. In this case, Dena Marie Sullivan is the mother of the child, Ketrea Arndra Sullivan. Lawrence Leroy Jenkins is the alleged father.

Caption. The style of the case begins with IN THE MATTER OF: followed by the name of the child, who is identified as being under the age of 18. The case is filed in a juvenile court, which hears matters affecting children under 18 years of age. It also identifies the petitioner as the mother, and the defendant as the alleged father.

Body. The body of the petition provides facts about the conception and birth of the child.

Prayer. In the prayer clause the petitioner requests that the defendant be brought into court, that he be declared to be the father, and that he pay child support. If a name change is desired, it is requested in the prayer. The birth certificate number of the child must be included in the petition if the name change is requested.

Verification. Following the body of the petition is a verification to be signed by the petitioner.

AFFIDAVIT

The petition may be supported by an affidavit attached to the petition rather than by a verification on the document itself.

SUMMONS OR ATTACHMENT

The attorney for the petitioner files a summons to be served, along with a copy of the petition, upon the alleged father to demand that he appear at a hearing. If that method is unsuccessful, the attorney prepares a document known as an **attachment**, which is signed and issued by the judge, to "attach the body" of the defendant. The defendant would then have to make bond or wait in jail until the hearing.

At the hearing evidence is presented, and often the father and child are ordered to take blood grouping tests to determine that the defendant is or is not the father of the child. Of course, other evidence is considered. Because of the sensitive nature of testimony at the hearing, proceedings are normally closed to the public.

ATTACHMENT

A method and also a document used to "attach the body" or property of a defendant.

MOTION AND ORDER FOR A BLOOD TEST

If either party wants a blood test before the hearing, one approach is to request it by written motion. In the motion the petitioner requests the court to issue an order that the defendant and child submit to **blood grouping tests**. An order for a blood test is a separate document in which the judge orders that blood tests be performed.

BLOOD GROUPING TESTS

Tests to determine the father of a child born out of wedlock.

ORDER OF PATERNITY AND SUPPORT

Once a judge has ruled that the defendant is the natural father, an order is entered establishing a father and child relationship, establishing the responsibility of the father to support the child and the right of the child to inherit from the father. If the judge rules that the defendant is not the natural father, the case is dismissed.

The order covers such matters as:

- The defendant is the natural father of the child.

- The father must pay for the support and education of the child.

IN THE JUVENILE COURT FOR McLENNAN COUNTY, TEXAS

IN THE MATTER OF:)
)
KETREA ARNDRA SULLIVAN   )
)
A Child Under the Age of   )
Eighteen (18) Years   )
)
DENA MARIE SULLIVAN,   )   No. _____
)
      Petitioner,   )
)
vs.   )
)
LAWRENCE LEROY JENKINS,   )
)
      Defendant.   )

PETITION TO ESTABLISH PATERNITY

COMES your Petitioner, DENA MARIE SULLIVAN, and would respectfully show the Court that on December 19, (two years ago), KETREA ARNDRA SULLIVAN was born to her as the natural mother in McLennan County, Waco, Texas, and that the said minor child was born out of wedlock. Nine (9) months before the birth of KETREA ARNDRA SULLIVAN, your Petitioner had been living with the Defendant, LAWRENCE LEROY JENKINS. She and the Defendant had been living in the same household for over two (2) years, and the parties continued to live together until the Defendant abruptly moved out on November 12, (two years ago).

During the period before and after conception of the minor child, your Petitioner had been with no other man except the Defendant, LAWRENCE LEROY JENKINS.

WHEREFORE, your Petitioner would show that LAWRENCE LEROY JENKINS is the true and accurate natural father of KETREA ARNDRA SULLIVAN and that upon hearing of this cause, he should be so declared by this Honorable Court.

PREMISES CONSIDERED, PETITIONER PRAYS:

1. That proper process be issued requiring the Defendant to appear and answer this Petition, but oath to such answer is expressly waived.

2. That upon hearing of this cause, the Defendant, LAWRENCE LEROY JENKINS, be declared the natural father of KETREA ARNDRA SULLIVAN and that the relationship of father-child be established.

FIGURE 9-7. Petition to Establish Paternity, Page 1

3. That the Court set child support in an amount reasonable for the upkeep and maintenance of the minor child.

4. That the Court order the Defendant to submit to a blood grouping test by an acceptable physician.

5. That there be no name change for the minor child in that the Petitioner wishes the child to continue to go by her maiden name, which the child has done since birth.

6. That the Petitioner be granted such other and further relief as the Court deems fit and proper.

_____

JUAN S. CARLOS (No. 5466)
Attorney for Petitioner
1346 San Jacinto Way
Waco, TX 43211
(915) 555-9909

- 2 -

FIGURE 9-8. Petition to Establish Paternity, Page 2

STATE OF TEXAS   )

COUNTY OF McLENNAN)

      I, DENA MARIE SULLIVAN, make oath that the statements in the foregoing Petition to Establish Paternity are true to the best of my knowledge, information, and belief.

                              _____

                              DENA MARIE SULLIVAN

Sworn to and subscribed before me
this the _____ day of May, (current year).

_____
NOTARY PUBLIC

My Commission Expires:_____

                            - 3 -

FIGURE 9-9. Petition to Establish Paternity, Page 3

- The child's name is changed (if desired).

- The father must pay a stated sum of money periodically until the child reaches 18 years of age.

- The father must pay expenses of the mother during pregnancy.

- The father must pay expenses incurred by the child before the order of paternity was signed.

Formatting Instructions for Paternity Documents

- Use 8½ by 11-inch paper, unless the court having jurisdiction in your state requires another size.

- Follow the format in Figures 9-7 through 9-9, for the petition; Figure 1-8 (Chapter 1) for the motion; and Figure 6-3 (Chapter 6) for the order.

SUMMARY

- Documents for adoption proceedings are the petition, order of reference, affidavit of consent or answer and consent, order of abandonment, interlocutory decree, and final decree.

- The petition has a caption, body, prayer clause, signature block, and verification.

- The caption for a stepparent adoption includes the child's original name, the petitioners' names, and the name of the noncustodial birth parent as a respondent.

- A petition for adoption is to be verified by the petitioners.

- If a noncustodial birth parent joins in the petition to give consent, a verification for his or her signature stating that parental rights are being surrendered is placed at the end of the petition.

- Written consent for adoption is normally obtained by filing an affidavit of consent, verification of consent, or answer and consent.

- To obtain an order of abandonment, present evidence of abandonment in the petition and request an order of abandonment in the prayer; present evidence at a court hearing and request that the judge issue an order; or serve the parent whose whereabouts are unknown by publication and, if there is no response, obtain a judgment by default.

- An order of reference signed by the judge orders the appropriate state department to investigate and determine whether a child is a proper subject for adoption and whether the prospective home is suitable for the child.

- The final order of adoption creates a parent and child relationship between the adoptee and the petitioner.

- After the final order is signed in a child-placement agency adoption, a new birth certificate is issued in the new name of the child with the names of the new parents as true parents.

- Three types of adoptions are stepparent, agency, and independent or private adoption.

- Adoption records are placed under seal and placed in a fireproof vault and can be opened only upon court order. Nonidentifying information can be obtained under certain circumstances.

- The purpose of a paternity proceeding is to establish fatherhood of a child born out of wedlock and require the father to support, educate, and pay expenses for his child.

- The alleged father in a paternity action may be brought into court with a summons or an attachment.

- The petition to establish paternity is supported either by a verification on the document or by an attached affidavit.

- The judge often orders that blood grouping tests be performed on the child and defendant in paternity cases.

REVIEW EXERCISES

T F 1. A person must be under 18 years of age to be adopted.

T F 2. A petition for adoption is required in stepparent and agency adoptions but not in private adoptions.

T F 3. The order of reference is normally waived in a stepparent adoption.

T F 4. Abandonment can be an issue in an adoption proceeding.

T F 5. The final order of adoption creates a parent and child relationship that did not previously exist.

T F 6. An adopted child has a right to inherit from the birth father after being adopted by a stepfather.

T F 7. In private adoptions, the appropriate state agency usually conducts an investigation.

T F 8. A petition for adoption must be verified by the petitioners.

T F 9. The caption on an adoption must always include the original name of the child and the new name requested after adoption.

T F 10. A caption in an adoption proceeding may include the name of the birth father as respondent.

T F 11. The order of reference is signed by the petitioner.

T F 12. Adoption records are closed, and the adopted child can never know whether he or she has siblings.

T F 13. A paternity proceeding is conducted to prove that the defendant is the father of a child born out of wedlock.

T F 14. Blood groupings are used as proof that the defendant is or is not the father of a child.

T F 15. An alleged father is always notified by an attachment that he has been charged with fathering a child out of wedlock.

TRANSCRIPTION RULES

COMMAS

Contrasting Expressions

A contrasting expression provides a thought different from the original statement and usually begins with *but* or *not*. Separate contrasting expressions from the rest of the sentence with a comma or commas.

The Petition for Adoption, ***not the Order of Reference***, consists of three pages.

He was willing to pay child support, ***but only on his own terms***.

Omitted Word or Words

If a repetitive word or words are omitted in a compound sentence, use a comma where the word or words are omitted.

Mitchell and Mitchell had a reputation for representing its clients competently; Ernst & Jordon, for questionable competence. (The repetitive words omitted are ***had a reputation***.)

Refer to Appendix A and Review the Following Rules:

Comma — Date
Comma — Geographic Locations
Comma — Independent Clauses Joined by a Conjunction
Hyphenation — Compound Adjectives Before a Noun
Possession — Singular
Possession — Plural
Semicolon — Independent Clauses with Commas Joined by a Conjunction

TRANSCRIPTION EXERCISES

Use a secretarial reference manual and the rules presented in this and previous chapters to aid you in correctly transcribing the following material. The sentences are presented in lowercase letters without capitalization and punctuation.

1. the mother was awarded custody but only temporarily when her divorce was granted

2. the petitioner is older than twenty one years of age the adoptee less than twenty one

3. the petitioner has no knowledge of the defendants present residence (There is one defendant.)

4. the petitioners have no knowledge of the defendants residence (There are two defendants.)

5. the minor childrens address is 161 harpeth haven drive peagram illinois

6. this cause came on to be heard on the seventeenth not the sixteenth day of july (current year)

7. the court has jurisdiction over the above described child named claude leslie

8. petitioners are fit persons to have the care and custody of the child and they are financially able to provide for her support and maintenance

9. petitioners are fit persons to have the care and custody of the child and are financially able to provide for her support and maintenance

10. petitioners mark pezzi and wife beth pezzi are fit persons to have the care and custody of the child and they are financially able according to their financial statement to provide for her support and maintenance

11. the petitioner has shared his home and cared for the child since his marriage to the childs mother

12. it is the desire of the petitioners that a parent child relationship be established between the child and stepfather

13. petitioners prayers for relief are as follows (There are two petitioners.)

14. the petitioners are citizens and residents of the city of cheyenne county of henry state of wyoming

RESEARCH ACTIVITIES

1. Consult your state codes and list information that can be obtained by an adopted child.

2. What are the time periods allowed by your state from the time when the petition for adoption is filed until an interlocutory decree can be granted? How long from the time the interlocutory decree is signed until a final decree can be granted? Are there any exceptions?

3. What court(s) in your state has jurisdiction over adoptions?

4. What court(s) in your state has jurisdiction over paternity cases?

PROJECTS

Insert the cassette tape for Chapter 9 and transcribe the following projects.

Project 9-1   Transcribe the petition for adoption where a minor boy is surrendered to an agency at birth. The petitioners are Larry C. Cherry and Estelle D. Cherry, and the child is identified as Bobby Ray Cherry. The agency placed the baby with the adoptive petitioners immediately upon his leaving the hospital. The birth father is unknown, and the whereabouts of the birth mother are unknown, even though she signed surrender papers at birth. Label the parts of the petition.

Project 9-2   Transcribe an order of reference for the case described in Project 9-1.

Project 9-3   Transcribe a final decree of adoption for the case described in Project 9-1.

Project 9-4   Transcribe an order of abandonment for a child known as Jamal Samuel Johnson, by Reginald Dorrae Wills and wife, Jacquelyn Ann Wills, Petitioners. The child has been abandoned by his parents, Twana Seredia Johnson and Anthony James Shelton. The parents have been served by publication. A copy of the order of abandonment was mailed to the Maryland Department of Human Services, 253 West Chesapeake Avenue, Annapolis, MD 18031.

Project 9-5   Transcribe a petition for paternity in a case where the father, David Fred Gupton, paid hospital bills for the child and mother, lived with the mother for two years, then left the mother, Lynn Ann Church, when the child was two years old.

Project 9-6   Transcribe a motion for blood test for the matter described in Project 9-5. The attorney for David Fred Gupton is Andrew John Phillip.

Project 9-7   Transcribe an order for blood test for the matter described in Project 9-5.

Project 9-8   Transcribe an order for paternity for the matter described in Project 9-5. The father has filed an answer.

UNIT III
PERFORMANCE ASSESSMENT

A. The following document has spelling, grammar, punctuation, and word-choice errors. Mark each error on the copy below using proofreaders' symbols. Key and print a corrected copy of the document for the attorney's approval.

This is an Order of Abandonment in an Adoption.

IN THE FAMILY COURT FOR SAGINAW COUNTY, MICHIGAN

IN RE:　　　　　　　　　　　　)
　　　　　　　　　　　　　　　)
The Adoption of a Female Child)
Whose Name for the Purpose　　)
of this Proceeding is　　　　　)
　　　　　　　　　　　　　　　)
TYSON RANDY LANDCASTER　　)
　　　　　　　　　　　　　　　)　No. 93-A-8331
BY:　　　　　　　　　　　　　)
　　　　　　　　　　　　　　　)
CRAIG W. KNOWLES and　　　　)
Wife, VIRGINIA L. KNOWLES　　)
　　　　　　　　　　　　　　　)
　　　　Petitioners,　　　　　)
　　　　　　　　　　　　　　　)
LYNN ANNE LANDCASTER　　　)
　　　　　　　　　　　　　　　)
　　　　Respondent.　　　　　)

ORDER OF ABANDONMENT

This cause came on to be heard on the 13th day of October, current year, before the Honorable CHRISTOPHER F. DOTEN, Judge of the Family Court of Saginaw County Michigan, and it appearing to the Court that the Petitioners, CRAIG W. KNOWLES and wife, VIRGINIA L. KNOWLES, has filed a Petition seeking to adopt the child refered to in their Petition; that the natural mother of the miner child have been duely served the Petition of Adoption of the miner child by publication run four consecutive weaks as required by law; that the miner child was born out of wedlock, and the identity of the natural father is unknown; that a Judgment by Default has been duely taken against LYNN ANNE LANDCASTER, the mother of the miner child; and upon testamony of witnesses in open court, the Court finds that the natural mother has willfully and legally abandoned the child for more than four (4) consecutive months immediately preceeding the filing of this Petition and that CRAIG W. KNOWLES, and wife, VIRGINIA L. KNOWLES, have been the sole support and maintainance of the child sense they were given physical possession of the child from the Department of Welfare Services for the state of Michigan. That the natural mother has abandened him and left him as a ward of the state of Michigan.

IT IS THEREFORE ORDERED, ADJUDGED, AND DECREED that the child sought to be adopted, TYSON RANDY LANDCASTER, is declared to be an abandoned child.

IT IS FURTHER ORDERED that all parental rights and responsibilities of the childs natural mother, LYNN ANN LANDCASTER, shall be and are here by fully terminated.

Entered this the _____ day of October, current year.

_____
CHRIS DOTEN, JUDGE

APPROVED FOR ENTRY:

_____
MARSHALL C. LINDSEY (No. 59887)
Attorney for Petitioners
LINDSEY and Associates
392 Lapeer Street
Saginaw Michigan 67120
(423) 555-8894

B. Place the cassette tape for Performance Assessment III in the transcriber. Transcribe III-B, a Marital Dissolution Agreement. Mia Tucon Xuan is the petitioner; Hui Xuan is the respondent. The case number is No. 93-D-90881 and is to be heard in the District Court of Alameda County, California.

C. Listen to the recorded instructions on the cassette tape for completing Item III-C. You will be instructed to retrieve the form you created in Project 8–1 and will be given instructions for altering it to be used in the Xuan case. The attorney for the complainant is Mary Ann Maracek (No. 56290), Maynard, Sacks and Maracek, 524 96th Avenue, Oakland, California 90611. Phone (819) 889-6545. The attorney for the defendant is Sidney D. James, 731 Mission Blvd., Oakland, California 90611.

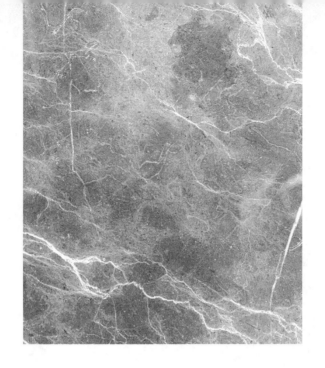

UNIT IV
LEGAL
INSTRUMENTS

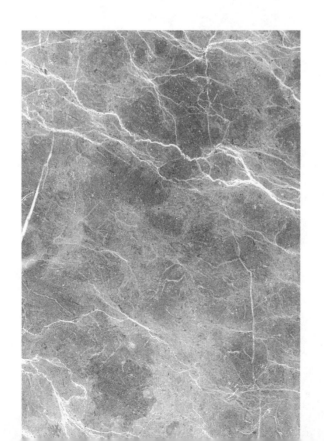

JOB DESCRIPTION

TRANSCRIPTION RESPONSIBILITIES

JOB TITLE: Legal Secretary

AREA OF PRACTICE: Contracts, Partnerships, Corporations, and Real Estate

TRANSCRIPTION DUTIES:

1. Is responsible for correctly transcribing a variety of contracts, partnership agreements, and lease agreements.

2. Supplies the appropriate number and type of signature lines for parties and witnesses to contracts and agreements, based on the content of the documents.

3. Prepares the appropriate number of copies of contracts and agreements and assembles copies.

4. Is responsible for transcribing documents for organizing a corporation.

5. Composes transmittal letters to the secretary of state's office or other offices where corporate documents are registered.

6. Drafts bylaws and minutes from a standardized copy for the attorney's approval.

7. Prepares stock certificates.

8. Prepares a standardized computer form with codes for variable information to use for deeds and mortgage instruments.

9. Transcribes or prepares deeds on a word processor. Is able to compose the derivation clauses on deeds and deeds of trust.

10. Is familiar with the content of settlement sheets to the extent that information can be adequately checked for accuracy.

CHAPTER 10

CONTRACTS

OBJECTIVES

When you successfully complete this chapter, you will be able to:

➤ Transcribe various types of contracts using the "Guidelines for Formatting Contracts" provided in this chapter

➤ Transcribe lease agreements

➤ Transcribe partnership agreements

➤ Provide the appropriate form of signature block based on information in the testimonium

➤ Identify the title, body, testimonium, and signature block of a contract

INTRODUCTION

Have you ever signed a written contract? If you are renting an apartment, you probably signed a lease agreement before moving in. If you purchase a car, buy a house, start a small business with a friend as partners, you most likely will be asked to sign a written contract or agreement.

In this chapter you will learn to format all types of contracts; however, the focus will be on two types:

LEASE AGREEMENTS
PARTNERSHIP AGREEMENTS

Contracts are agreements between two or more persons that are enforceable by law. To be enforceable, contracts must contain five basic elements:

• Offer
• Acceptance
• Competent parties
• Consideration
• Lawful purpose

One party must **offer** to enter into a contract with another, and the second party must **accept** for the contract to be valid. **Competence** refers to the age and mental ability to enter a contract. **Consideration** is whatever (often a monetary value) is paid as a price for a promise. The amount of the consideration is not important in a contract, only the fact that consideration exists. The contract must be made for a **lawful purpose** and will not be enforceable if its purpose is to commit a crime, to defraud someone, or to do harm to someone.

Contracts that must be in writing to be legally binding and enforceable are leases of real estate, sales of real estate, sales contracts when the selling price is over $500, and contracts that cannot be performed within one year.

In addition to leases and partnership agreements discussed in this chapter, an attorney is called upon to write many types of contracts, such as employment contracts, sales of autos, and sales of products. The instructions for formatting contracts presented below can be applied to all types of contracts.

Formatting Instructions for Contracts

- Prepare enough original copies of a contract for each party to have a signed original. Make a photocopy from a signed original to keep in the files.

- Use 8½ by 14-inch paper unless instructed otherwise. Letter-size paper can be used; however, legal-size adds distinction to the document.

- Set 1-inch left, right, and bottom margins. The top margin on page 1 should be 1½ or 2 inches, and top margins on other pages should be one inch. If the contract is bound at the top, additional 1/2 inch to the top margin on all continuation pages. Some attorneys prefer to place contracts in legal backs. (See Chapter 5, Figure 5-5.)

- Key the title in full caps, boldfaced, centered. Leave a triple space after the title. Multiple-line titles are double-spaced.

- Indent paragraphs either 1/2 or 1 inch from the left margin.

- Double-space the body unless instructed otherwise; some attorneys prefer that contracts be single-spaced. Property descriptions and quotations are single-spaced and indented from both margins. The indentions should match the paragraph indention, either 1/2 inch or 1-inch.

- Some contracts begin with the phrase KNOW ALL MEN BY THESE PRESENTS: The phrase is keyed in full caps, is placed at the left margin, appears on a line by itself, and is followed by a colon.

KNOW ALL MEN BY THESE PRESENTS:

That the undersigned, ALBERTO O. OKAFOR, who is

temporarily residing in the City of Dover, County of Kent, ...

- Place identifying terms such as Lessor and Lessee within quotation marks in the first paragraph where they are defined, but without quotation marks when used subsequently in the document.

- The word WITNESSETH after the introductory paragraph can be placed on a line by itself beginning at paragraph point or spread centered or centered in full caps. It may be placed on the same line where a new paragraph begins.

  Note in the first illustration below that the first paragraph ends with a comma because the opening paragraph is not a complete sentence.

ILLUSTRATION I

THIS AGREEMENT, made and entered into this 23d day of

January, 1994, by and between SUPERB APARTMENTS, INC.,

hereinafter referred to as the "Landlord," and JOSHUA

CRONIN, hereinafter referred to as the "Tenant,"

WITNESSETH:

1. The Landlord hereby leases to the Lessee the following

property located in Dover, Delaware:

In the second illustration, the opening paragraph is a complete sentence and ends with a period. The material following WITNESSETH is a dependent clause; therefore, a comma is placed after the term and it is placed on the same line as the paragraph. The letter T in "that" can be lowercase or capital.

ILLUSTRATION II

THIS AGREEMENT is made and entered into this 23d day

of January, (current year), by and between SUPERB APARTMENTS,

INC., hereinafter referred to as the "Landlord," and JOSHUA

CRONIN, hereinafter referred to as the "Tenant."

WITNESSETH, That the Landlord hereby leases to the

Lessee the following property located in Dover, Delaware:

- Paragraphs in the document may be enumerated. They may be enumerated with arabic numerals (1, 2, 3) or ordinals (FIRST:, SECOND:, THIRD:). Follow the instructions of the attorney. See the illustration below:

THIS AGREEMENT is made and entered into this 23d day

of January, (current year), by and between SUPERB APARTMENTS,

INC., hereinafter referred to as the "Landlord," and JOSHUA

CRONIN, hereinafter referred to as the "Tenant."

WITNESSETH,

FIRST: That the Landlord hereby leases to the

Lessee the following property located in Dover, Delaware:

- If enumerated paragraphs have paragraph headings, boldface or underline the run-in heading. Leave two spaces after the period. For example:

1. **Term**. The lease shall last . . . .

or

1. Term. The lease shall last . . . .

- If the terms of the contract are presented in articles, double-space before and after the article number. Article numbers are generally centered and shown in roman numerals. Boldface and capitalize as shown in the example below:

ARTICLE III

Term of Operation. It is agreed that the partnership shall

be for a term of three (3) years commencing on the date signed.

- Paragraphs in contracts often begin with WHEREAS and continue that pattern until the last paragraph, which begins with NOW, THEREFORE. Capitalize the terms and place a comma after WHEREAS and commas before and after THEREFORE. Place semicolons after each paragraph until the last, which ends with a period or colon (as in the illustration), depending on the sentence structure.

WHEREAS, Buyer is in the process of purchasing the ABC Company, of Paducah, Kentucky;

WHEREAS, Seller is ready and willing to sell the company for a reasonable fee to one qualified to continue operations of the company; and

WHEREAS, it would be advisable for Purchaser in the acquisition of such a company to hire a consultant to help organize the business;

NOW, THEREFORE, in consideration of the above premises, the parties agree as follows:

- Add the appropriate number and types of signature lines based on the testimonium clause. If an individual is to sign the document and the testimonium clause states that it is sealed, the abbreviation **L.S.**, for locus sigilli, meaning in the place of a seal, is placed at the end of the signature line. The practice of sealing documents came from an old English common law that required the person signing to impress his personal seal on the document. People today do not have seals, but in some states sealing a document carries a legal significance. For those states that require an individual's seal, the notation "L.S." is added to the signature lines. For signature lines, use one of the following formats:

L.S.

An abbreviation for locus sigilli, meaning in the place of a seal.

FOR UNSEALED INDIVIDUAL SIGNATURES

IN WITNESS WHEREOF, the parties have hereunto set their hands this
_____ day of _____, (current year).

_____
ALBERT SWARTZ, Lessor

_____
KAREN KINKO, Lessee

FOR SEALED INDIVIDUAL SIGNATURES

IN WITNESS WHEREOF, the parties have set their hands and seals the day
and year first above written.

_____ L.S.
ALBERT SWARTZ, Lessor

_____ L.S.
KAREN KINKO, Lessee

WITNESS

*One who observes the signing
of a document and adds his
or her name on a line
prepared for the witness.*

FOR WITNESSED INDIVIDUAL SIGNATURE LINES

_____   _____
Witness as to Lessor   ALBERT SWARTZ, Lessor

_____   _____
Witness as to Lessee   KAREN KINKO, Lessee

**FOR A CORPORATE SIGNATURE
AND AN UNSEALED INDIVIDUAL SIGNATURE**

IN WITNESS WHEREOF, the parties hereunto have set their hands the day and date first above written.

COMPUTER REPAIR CORPORATION

By _____
KEN CHUN, President and Lessor

_____
ALMA MOORE, Lessee

- Keep at least two lines of the document with the signature lines.

- On the line below the signature line, key the name of the party in full caps, followed by a comma and the identification, such as Lessor, Lessee, General Partner, Limited Partner, Partner, and the like.

- Number the pages at the bottom center of each page. Do not number page 1.

LEASES

A **lease** is a contract between a landowner, known as a **landlord** or **lessor**, and a person who agrees to pay for the use of the property for a period of time, known as a **tenant** or **lessee**. A lease is sometimes called an indenture, a contract, or an agreement. There can be short-term leases of apartments or residences or long-term leases, which cover a longer period of time. Either personal property, such as a vehicle or furniture, or real property can be leased.

Execution, acknowledgment (a statement signed by a notary public that the person who signs a document does so as his or her free act and deed), and recording of a lease are determined by state laws, attorney preferences, and local practice. The lessor and lessee both sign a lease, and sometimes it is witnessed by one who observes the contract being signed and adds his or her name on a line prepared for the witness. Leases are not usually recorded at the county register's office; however, local rules of practice should be consulted.

A lease has the following elements:

- Title

- Body

LEASE

A contract between a landowner and a tenant; also called an indenture, contract, or agreement.

LANDLORD OR LESSOR

One who owns property and rents or leases it to another person.

TENANT OR LESSEE

One who rents or leases real property from another person.

- Testimonium

- Signature lines

Read the lease agreement between the First National Bank, the lessor, and Jimmy and Carol McDonald, the lessees, shown in Figures 10-1 and 10-2.

Title

The title is usually a description of the type of lease, such as Commercial Lease, Property Lease, Timber Lease, Apartment Lease, or Automobile Lease. Leases do not have captions because they are not prepared to file in a court case; they are simply agreements between two or more parties.

Body

The first paragraph of the lease begins with words such as THIS AGREEMENT, THIS INDENTURE, THIS LEASE, or THIS LEASE CON- TRACT and provides the date and names the parties. Parties are often identified as lessor and lessee, party of the first part and party of the second part, first party and second party, landlord and tenant, and sometimes by name.

After the introductory paragraph, the word WITNESSETH is often used to introduce the facts that are the basis for the agreement, and the facts are followed by enumerated paragraphs listing provisions of the lease agreement.

The lease agreement between the parties spells out in detail the provisions of the agreement. It may provide information such as a description of the leased property, amount of payment, period of time the lease will run, provisions for renewal, security deposit, payment of rent, grace period in case of default of payment, responsibility for repairs, amount of payment required to cancel the lease, assignment or sublease of the premises, insurance coverage, alteration of the premises by the lessee, alteration of the premises by the landlord for the tenant, and restoration of the properties at the end of the lease.

Period of time. Leases can be set up to expire after a stated period of time or to terminate by mutual agreement of the parties at any time.

Renewal provisions. Leases often provide for automatic renewal at the end of the stated period of time unless either party notifies the other that he or she will not renew.

SECURITY DEPOSIT

An amount of money paid to the landlord to cover any damages caused by the tenant or to cover loss of rent if the tenant does not pay.

Security deposit. A **security deposit** is an amount of money paid to the landlord to cover any damages caused by the tenant or to cover loss of rent if the tenant does not pay. The tenant should clearly understand the amount and terms of the deposit before signing the agreement. Because of problems that have arisen over this issue, many states have passed laws governing landlords' use of security deposits and tenants' rights in reclaiming those deposits.

Rent payments. The amount and time of payment should be clearly stated. Usually a rent payment is made at the beginning of each month.

PROPERTY LEASE AGREEMENT

THIS LEASE AGREEMENT, made this the _____ day of December, (current year), by and between FIRST NATIONAL BANK of Las Vegas, hereinafter called the "Lessor," and JIMMY McDONALD and wife, CAROL, hereinafter call the "Lessees," both of Clark County, Nevada,

W I T N E S S E T H :

FIRST: The Lessor, for and in consideration of the rents, covenants, and agreements of the Lessee hereinafter set out, hereby leases to the Lessee for the term of twelve (12) months, commencing the first day of January, (next year), and ending on the 31st day of December, (next year), the following described property:

> House and lot located at 324 12th Street, Las Vegas, Nevada. The lot fronting approximately sixty (60) feet on said street and running back approximately one hundred twenty (120) feet, said property to be used for residence exclusively.

[handwritten annotation: Hanging paragraph]

[handwritten annotation: Not Bold]

[handwritten annotation: Full caps]

SECOND: The Lessees expressly agree to pay to Lessor for the use of said property the sum of Five Hundred Dollars ($500) per month rental in advance each month, the first payment falling due on the 1st day of January, (current year), and the remaining consecutively on the first day of each succeeding month until and including the first day of December, (current year). Payments are to be made at the FIRST NATIONAL BANK of Las Vegas at the offices for Rental Property, without demand or further notice, said demand and notice are hereby expressly waived.

THIRD: Should this property be destroyed by fire during this lease, this contract will be void as of the destruction.

FOURTH: Lessees will not keep anything in or on said property which will void the insurance policy on the property or structure thereon.

FIFTH: Lessees will not sublease or subrent the property rented or covered by this Lease, during the term of this Lease, without written permission from the Lessor.

SIXTH: Lessor or his agent will be permitted to enter at all reasonable times to view the premises, and within thirty (30) days of the expiration of the term of this Lease, Lessor is permitted to label the premises for rent and to show the same to other parties.

FIGURE 10-1. Lease, Page 1

TENTH: Should this Lease be placed in the hands of an attorney, after such default or breach, for the enforcement of any rights herein, the Lessees agree to pay reasonable attorney's fees of the Lessor.

ELEVENTH: The entire contract between the parties is contained in this instrument; and this contract shall be binding upon them, their heirs, successors, personal representatives, and assigns.

IN WITNESS WHEREOF, the parties hereunto have set their hands this the _____ day of December, (current year).

FIRST NATIONAL BANK

By _____
    KEN CHUN, President and Lessor

_____
JIMMY McDONALD, Lessee

_____
CAROL McDONALD, Lessee

- 2 -

FIGURE 10-2. Lease, Page 2

Grace period. The period of time within which the lease will not be terminated for late rent payments is the grace period.

Repairs. The contract should clearly state who is responsible for making repairs. Most often the landlord accepts the responsibility for making major repairs, with the tenant accepting responsibility for repairs needed as a result of wear and tear.

Assignment or sublease. To **assign** or **sublease** is to transfer the right to use the premises to a third party, known as the **assignee** or **sublessee**. Landlords usually do not allow assignment or subletting of property without their prior approval, and some do not allow it at all.

Testimonium

The testimonium clause begins with IN WITNESS WHEREOF and states whether the document is to be sealed. It gives guidance to the secretary in determining the types of signature lines to prepare.

Signature Lines

The number of signature lines varies depending on what the number of parties is, whether they are individuals or corporate officers, and whether the document is to be sealed, as well as what the attorney's preference in arrangement of the lines is. Refer to pages 264-269 of this chapter, entitled "Formatting Instructions for Contracts."

The attorney will instruct the secretary as to whether signatures are to be witnessed. If so, signature lines for witnesses are placed at the left margin, and signature lines for parties begin at center and extend to the right margin.

PARTNERSHIP AGREEMENTS

When persons wish to start a business, they usually discuss the possibility of doing so with one another and then consult an attorney to get advice as to the type of business to organize. After a discussion of the pros and cons of each type of business organization, the attorney helps the clients make the choice that fits their needs. One of the types of business organization is a partnership.

Partnerships are created when two or more persons, as co-owners, agree to carry on a business for profit. Partnerships may be general or limited. **General partners** are personally liable for all debts of the partnership and have equal voice in making partnership decisions. **Limited partners** are personally liable for the debts of the partnership only up to the amount they invest and have no say in running the business; they are basically investors. All members of a general partnership are general partners. A limited partnership has at least one general and one limited partner.

The document to create a partnership is a contract referred to as a partnership agreement.   The partnership agreement must have all the basic

---

GRACE PERIOD

The period of time within which a debt, such as a lease, will not be terminated for late payments.

ASSIGN

To give legal right to another party, such as to sublease real property.

SUBLEASE

To transfer the right to use property to a third party.

SUBLESSEE

One who subleases property from another.

PARTNERSHIP

An arrangement where two or more persons, as co-owners, agree to carry on a business for profit.

GENERAL PARTNERS

Partners who are personally liable for all debts owed by a partnership, share in the profits, and have equal voice in making partnership decisions.

LIMITED PARTNERS

Partners who are personally liable for the debts of a partnership only up to the amount they invest, share in the profits, but have no voice in making partnership decisions.

elements of a contract: offer, acceptance, competent parties, consideration, and lawful purpose. The body is generally very extensive because all sorts of possible things that may happen within the partnership business need to be addressed.

Examine the partnership agreement in Figures 10-3 and 10-4 and locate the title, body, testimonium, and signature lines.

Title. The title of the document usually includes the words Partnership Agreement or Articles of Partnership.

Body. The introductory paragraph begins with THIS AGREEMENT, THIS PARTNERSHIP AGREEMENT, or THIS CONTRACT and provides the date and names of the parties. The paragraphs often address the following issues:

Names of the partners.

A clear description of the nature of the business.

Term of the agreement. The partners can agree on a length of time for the partnership to continue or it can continue until they agree to terminate the agreement. Death or withdrawal of a partner at any time will terminate the partnership; however, a new partnership can be created to carry on the business activity.

Capital contributions. The amount of cash, assets, or services to be contributed by each partner is stated.

Sharing of profits. The agreement should clearly state the percentage of profits and losses to be shared by the partners.

Name of the partnership. Any name can be used, but it should not be deceptively similar to another business. If a partnership chooses to name itself McDonald's Burgers, the name would be deceptively similar to the McDonald's hamburger chain. Many states require that partnership names be registered with the secretary of state or appropriate public office.

Location of the business.

Accounting method.

Rights and duties of partners.

Withdrawal of partners.

Methods of dissolving the partnership.

Procedure upon the death of a partner for purchasing a deceased partner's share.

GENERAL PARTNERSHIP AGREEMENT

OF

THE COMPUTER TRAINING COMPANY

THIS AGREEMENT, which is executed this the 12th day of November, (current year), by and between RODNEY L. ENGLISH and HAMID EL BERRY is as follows:

1. We, RODNEY L. ENGLISH and HAMID EL BERRY, on this date agree to become partners in the selling of computer programming techniques in a business to be carried on in Mountain View, California, under the name of THE COMPUTER TRAINING COMPANY.

2. The parties began operating as a business pursuant to an oral agreement on July 1, (current year), and it is their desire to continue the business under the same name and to solidify their agreement by placing it into writing.

NOW, THEREFORE, intending to be legally bound hereby, the parties agree to continue the partnership under the laws of the State of California under the following terms and conditions:

ARTICLE I

Name and Place of Business. The name of the partnership shall be THE COMPUTER TRAINING COMPANY, and its principal place of business shall be 4233 Webster Street, Mountain View, California.

ARTICLE II

Purpose of the Business. The partnership shall engage in the business of training employees of client companies on methods of programming and computer use compatible with the client's business. It is further agreed that the Partners may, from time to time, expand the purpose of the business in the field of general computer use and training.

ARTICLE III

Term of Operation. It is agreed that the partnership shall be for a term of three (3) years commencing on the date signed as stated below, and this term may be renewed upon agreement of the Partners at the end of this term.

FIGURE 10-3. Partnership Agreement, Page 1

ARTICLE IV

Capital Contributions. It is agreed that each Partner will contribute Five Thousand Dollars ($5,000) as advanced capital with each contribution due and payable upon the signing of this General Partnership Agreement. Except as agreed to the contrary, the capital contributions of each Partner shall not be subject to withdrawal unless the partnership is dissolved. Periodic payment of wages or distribution of profit will not be considered as withdrawal of capital contributions.

ARTICLE V

Profits and Losses. The net profits of this partnership shall be paid out in the percentage of fifty-fifty (50% - 50%). It is also agreed that each party shall bear all losses equally fifty-fifty (50% - 50%). Further, it is agreed that neither Partner shall take out any profit on any month where expenses exceed income.

ARTICLE XI

Management. It is agreed that each party shall have an equal decision in the management of the partnership business. All decisions shall be by both parties. Each party agrees to devote his full time, energy, and attention to the partnership business to the exclusion of other businesses.

ARTICLE XV

Miscellaneous. There shall be one set of books, and either party has the expressed right to examine, inspect, and copy the books at reasonable business hours. Further, once a year the book shall be examined by an independent Certified Public Accountant agreed upon by both Partners.

Each party agrees to execute further instruments that from time to time may become necessary to perform the duties of the partnership business.

IN WITNESS WHEREOF, the above-named parties have signed their names in assent thereof on November 12, (current year).

_____

RODNEY L. ENGLISH, Partner

_____

HAMID EL BERRY, Partner

- 2 -

FIGURE 10-4. Partnership Agreement, Page 2

SUMMARY

- Contracts are agreements between two or more persons that are enforceable by law.

- Contracts must contain five basic elements to be enforceable by law: offer, acceptance, competent parties, consideration, and lawful purpose.

- Contracts dealing with real estate, contracts for sale of goods over $500, and those that cannot be performed within one year must be in writing to be legally binding.

- Leases are contracts between a landowner, known as the landlord or lessor, and a person who agrees to use the property for a period of time, known as a tenant or lessee.

- A contract has a title, body, testimonium, and signature lines.

- The body of a lease usually consists of an introductory paragraph naming and identifying the parties, paragraphs giving the facts that serve as a basis for the agreement, and a series of paragraphs giving details of the agreement.

- The testimonium clause gives guidance to the secretary in determining the format of the signature lines. The body of the contract gives guidance as to how many signature lines are needed and whether they are for individuals or corporations.

- Partnerships are created when two or more persons, as co-owners, agree to carry on a business for profit. Partnerships may be general or limited.

REVIEW EXERCISES

T F 1. Leases and partnership agreements are both contracts.

T F 2. Signature lines in contracts should always be witnessed or sealed.

T F 3. The size of paper on which a partnership agreement is printed determines the legal enforceability of the agreement.

T F 4. The last paragraph of a contract normally states the date, names of the parties, and identification of the parties, such as lessor and lessee.

T F 5. A colon or semicolon is used after the introductory paragraph in a contract, depending on whether the paragraph is a complete sentence or a sentence fragment.

T   F   6. The term WHEREAS is often used to introduce paragraphs in contracts.

T   F   7. Leases are always recorded in the county registrar's office.

T   F   8. A partnership agreement would contain paragraphs about security deposits, rent payments, grace period, and repairs.

T   F   9. A limited partnership agreement does not need to be in writing since the limited partner assumes no liability for the partnership debts.

T   F   10. Contracts may be single-spaced or double-spaced depending on the preferences of the attorney.

TRANSCRIPTION RULES

CAPITALIZATION

Phrases in Full Caps

Key the following introductory terms in full caps:

IN WITNESS WHEREOF,
IT IS FURTHER AGREED
KNOW ALL MEN BY THESE PRESENTS:
NOW, THEREFORE,
THIS AGREEMENT
THIS CONTRACT
THIS INDENTURE
THIS LEASE AGREEMENT
TO HAVE AND TO HOLD
WITNESSETH:

Party Designations

The following terms identify parties to contracts, leases, or partnerships:

First Party
Landlord
Lessor
Lessee
Partner
Party of the First Part
Party of the Second Part
Second Party
Tenant

NUMBER EXPRESSION

Days Preceding the Month

Days that precede the month can be expressed in ordinals (first, second, third, or 1st, 2d, 3d). Avoid the spelled-out version if it is more than one word.

The *first* day of December 19—
The *1st* day of December 19—
The *21st* day of December 19—

TRANSCRIPTION EXERCISES

Use a secretarial reference manual and the rules presented in this and previous chapters to aid you in correctly transcribing the following material.

1. Show two methods for transcribing the first day of January for the year 19—.

2. Show the signature lines for an unwitnessed lease agreement in which the landowner is Swartz Apartments, Inc., Thomas Swartz is the owner and president, and the tenant is Kiang Davidson.

3. You are to transcribe a contract with paragraphs enumerated with arabic numerals and run-in headings. Show two ways the following items could be transcribed. The run-in headings and text are as follows: Item 1, period of time. This lease agreement shall be effective for a period of one year; Item 2, security deposit. The security deposit of $150 will be returned if no repairs are required because of excessive damage to the apartment; Item 3, grace period. The lease will be terminated if late payments are not made within 30 days of the due date.

Transcribe the following sentences, which contain spelling errors. The sentences are presented in lowercase letters without capitalization and punctuation.

4. first the lessor for and in consideration of the rents covnants and agreements of the lessor hereinafter set out here by leases to the lessee for the term of twelve months the following described property

5. in witness whereof the above named parties have signed their names in ascent thereof on august 15 (current year).

6. this agreement made the seventh of march (last year) between guy downing doing business as steak and grits hereinafter referred to as the seller and albert swartz hereinafter referred to as the buyer

7. whereas LaMore commenced an action against priority book publishers in the district court of washington whereas priority raised certain counterclaims in that action against lamore whereas lamore and priority have agreed to settle the above described action in accordance with the following terms and subject to the following conditions

8. know all men by these presents that computer services inc hereinafter known as client herewith employs cully babbit hereinafter known as attorney as their attorney at law to represent them in a civil action based on negligence

9. this agreement is by and between first national bank party of the first part and jimmy mcdonald party of the second part

10. witnesseth: first that the client has this day employed the attorney to represent the client in a divorce case

second if the divorce is uncontested and there is a property settlement the client agrees to pay the attorney 100 dollars an hour for all services rendered

third if the divorce is stopped any time after the divorce complaint is filed the client agrees to pay the full amount of the fee

RESEARCH ACTIVITIES

1. Locate a copy of a lease agreement and partnership agreement in your library. Business law texts, attorney's forms books, legal procedures books, or legal reference manuals may have copies of lease and partnership agreements. Read the documents to familiarize yourself with the format and the content.

2. Consult your state codes to determine if specific wording is required on lease contracts. Many require exact words on topics such as security deposits. Make a copy of the requirements for future use.

PROJECTS

Insert the cassette tape for Chapter 10 and transcribe the following projects.

Project 10-1   Transcribe a lease agreement where Irwin Grigor and wife, Beth Grigor, are leasing a restaurant operated as Krispy Chicken from Ted Kuzawinski, the owner.

Project 10-2   Transcribe a general partnership agreement for Heritage Antiques, jointly owned by Ann L. Tilley, Michelle F. Grissom, and Janice E. Spears, where they have previously operated an antique store under an oral partnership agreement.

Project 10-3   Transcribe a security agreement for the Bald Tire Company. In this project, Bald Tire Company (the client of your attorney) has asked your attorney to draw up a sales contract that includes a security agreement and warranties. The text on the tape consists of the wording for the security agreement and the warranties. Your attorney requests that you design a form to be used by the Bald Tire Company as a sales invoice. The form will then be sent to a printer. Use your creativity in arranging the data in a usable format. The general information to be included is shown below. Normally such a form is designed with plenty of space for inserting the quantity, description of item, price, etc. At the bottom of the form (almost always in very small type) are the security agreement and warranties.

The client of the law firm is:
BALD TIRE COMPANY
1228 U.S. Highway 1
Cocoa Beach, FL 22042

Name _____

Address _____

City _____

State _____ ZIP _____

Phone _____

Provide columns for Quantity, Description/Service, Unit Price, and Extended Price. At the bottom of the form, provide a place for Total Price. As many lines as possible should be provided for inserting sales information.

Project 10-4   Transcribe a power of attorney. This is a document where Alberto O. Okafor is giving authority to his Attorney in Fact, Gozeal Zurike, to handle his banking transactions and do anything else necessary to protect Alberto's interests.

Project 10-5   Transcribe a release of claims agreed to as a settlement in an automobile accident. It is a contract between two parties, with one paying $12,000 and the other releasing him from all claims. This is a typical insurance company release, even though they are not mentioned, where they are paying for the damage caused by their insured, Richard M. Wayne.

Project 10-6   Transcribe the attorney retainer agreement in which the attorney is agreeing to represent the estate of Joseph P. Simpson's deceased mother, and Simpson is agreeing on the amount of the fee. The retainer agreement should be placed on the attorney's letterhead and is written as if it were the client dictating the contents of the agreement. Design a letterhead for R. L. Reed, Reed and Leahew, Attorneys at Law, 442 Sprague Avenue, Spokane, WA 82111. Phone: (509) 555-2211

CHAPTER 11

CORPORATIONS

OBJECTIVES

When you successfully complete this chapter, you will be familiar with the documents and procedures for organizing corporations. You should be able to:

➤ Create and complete an application to reserve a corporate name

➤ Prepare a cover letter for the articles of incorporation to the secretary of state

➤ Transcribe articles of incorporation, minutes, and bylaws with correct punctuation, capitalization, and formatting

➤ Prepare stock subscription agreements and stock certificates

---

INTRODUCTION

When persons are interested in organizing a corporation, they generally contact an attorney and discuss the best method of business organization. Many choose the corporate form because, among other things, chances of losing money are limited to the amount of the investment and transfer of ownership is easy.

A **corporation** is a legal entity separate and apart from the persons who own and control it. It can sue or be sued, establish bylaws, conduct business, and make contracts in its own name.

Corporations can be classified as domestic, foreign, or alien. A corporation is **domestic** in the state where it was organized or incorporated. A corporation is **foreign** to all states except the state in which it was organized. An **alien** corporation is one organized out of the country and doing business within the United States.

Corporations may also be categorized as **public** (cities, towns, or government-owned), **not for profit** (religious, social, or charitable), **for profit** (organized for the purpose of making a profit), or **professional** (licensed individuals, such as doctors and certified public accountants).

To organize a corporation, a person or persons must act as incorporators. The number required varies from state to state, usually ranging from one to three. The responsibility of the **incorporators** is to do all things necessary, under the state's laws, to establish a valid corporation. This usually involves signing documents to establish the corporation. Once the corporation has been legally

CORPORATION

A legal entity separate and apart from the persons who own and control it.

DOMESTIC CORPORATION

A corporation operating in the state where it was organized or incorporated.

FOREIGN CORPORATION

A corporation is foreign to all states except the state in which it was organized and officially incorporated.

ALIEN CORPORATION

A corporation organized out of the country and doing business within the United States.

PUBLIC CORPORATION

Cities, towns, or government-owned corporations.

FOR-PROFIT CORPORATION

Corporation organized for the purpose of making a profit.

NOT-FOR-PROFIT CORPORATION

Religious, social, or charitable corporation that is set up for benevolent purposes and not to make a profit.

PROFESSIONAL CORPORATION

Licensed individuals, such as doctors and certified public accountants, who incorporate themselves as a business.

INCORPORATORS

Those who do all things necessary to form a corporation.

STOCKHOLDERS

People who own shares of stock of a corporation; also shareholders.

SHAREHOLDERS

People who own shares of stock of a corporation; also stockholders.

BOARD OF DIRECTORS

Elected representatives of a corporation who are given authority to establish policy for the corporation.

established, the incorporators cease to function. Legal secretaries are often called on to serve as incorporators and to sign the articles of incorporation, as well as other documents to establish the corporation.

Whether small or large, a corporation has stockholders, a board of directors, and officers. **Stockholders**, also called shareholders, are the owners of the corporation. Their role is to provide capital by purchasing shares of stock, to attend annual shareholder's meetings, and to vote on matters presented at such meetings, including the election of members of the board of directors. The **board of directors** are elected at the first annual meeting of shareholders and at intervals thereafter. The board, at regular and/or special meetings, establishes policy for the corporation. A corporation has **officers**, usually appointed by the board of directors, whose function is to carry out policy established by the board. Most corporations have at least a president and secretary — other officers may be appointed.

To organize a for-profit corporation, the following documents are prepared:

APPLICATION FOR RESERVATION OF CORPORATE NAME

ARTICLES OF INCORPORATION

DESIGNATION OF REGISTERED AGENT FOR SERVICE OF PROCESS

TRANSMITTAL LETTER TO THE SECRETARY OF STATE

BYLAWS

MINUTES OF FIRST MEETINGS

SUBSCRIPTION AGREEMENTS

STOCK CERTIFICATES

CORPORATE MINUTE BOOK

Additional forms that are usually required are:

APPLICATION FOR EMPLOYER IDENTIFICATION NUMBER

SALES AND USE TAX APPLICATION

SUBCHAPTER S ELECTION FORM

APPLICATION FOR RESERVATION OF CORPORATE NAME

Every corporation needs a name different from the name of any other corporation. A corporate name should contain the word "corporation," "company," or "incorporated," or an abbreviation of the term, except when a corporation plans to conduct an insurance or banking business. The name of an insurance company or bank should indicate the type of business it is conducting.

A corporate name is reserved by contacting the designated government official who is responsible for licensing corporations. In most states that government official is the **secretary of state**. The initial contact is usually made by a phone call to the secretary of state's office. The desired name is provided, and someone in the office scans a database to determine if the name is available. If it is, a letter requesting the name or an application for reservation of the name is completed and mailed to the office. The name can be reserved for a period of time, usually from four to twelve months, depending on the state, by completing a form similar to Figure 11-1.

To complete the form used in the state of Indiana, insert the proposed name, name and address of applicant (who would be the incorporator or attorney for the corporation being organized), and a printed signature as indicated on the form.

ARTICLES OF INCORPORATION

The **articles of incorporation**, also called a **charter**, certificate of incorporation, or articles of association, is a document that states that the corporation has complied with all the legal requirements for setting up a corporation, as outlined in the state statutes. Once approved, it gives the corporation legal authority to function.

Refer to Figures 11-2 and 11-3, the articles of incorporation of Rental Ventures, Incorporated, and locate the following information:

- Name of the corporation

- Number of shares of stock the corporation is authorized to issue

- Address (including county) and zip code of the initial registered office

- Name and address of the initial registered agent for service of process (this may be a separate document)

- Name, address, and zip code of each incorporator

- Street address and zip code of the principal office of the corporation

- Statement that the corporation is for profit or not for profit

- Purpose for which the corporation is organized

The incorporators sign the articles of incorporation. The original copy of the articles and a check covering the recording fee are filed with the secretary of state. If an application for reservation of name was previously filed, the

---

OFFICERS

Elected individuals whose function is to carry out policy of a corporation. Example, president and secretary.

SECRETARY OF STATE

A government official whose duties include licensing corporations.

ARTICLES OF INCORPORATION

Also known as a charter.

CHARTER

A document filed with the secretary of state to organize a corporation; also a charter.

**APPLICATION FOR RESERVATION
OF EXCLUSIVE USE OF CORPORATE NAME**
State Form 26233 (R/ 1-88)
Approved by the State Board of Accounts, 1988

INDIANA SECRETARY OF STATE
CORPORATIONS DIVISION
302 W. WASHINGTON ST., RM. E018
INDIANAPOLIS, IN 46204
(317) 232-6576
Indiana Code 23-1-23-2
FILING FEE $20.00

*INSTRUCTIONS: Present original and one copy to the address in the upper
right corner of this form.*

Proposed name to be reserved:
Rental Ventures, Incorporated

Name of applicant:
Fritz M. Mueller, Attorney at Law

Address of applicant:
4204 Indiana Boulevard, Moorehead, IN

ZIP Code
51201

Signature
Fritz M. Mueller

Printed Name
Fritz M. Mueller

FOR USE BY SECRETARY OF STATE OFFICE ONLY

☐   The name is available and reserved for 120 days from the date stamped on this application.

☐   The name is indistinguishable from a name on the records of the Secretary and is therefore

     unavailable.

NOTE: The owner of the reserved name may transfer the reservation to another person by delivery

         to the Secretary of State a signed notice of the transfer. The notice must state the name and

         address of the transferee and the original approval date or have an attached copy of the

         original file - marked application for reservation of a corporate name.

FIGURE 11-1. Application for Reservation of Corporate Name

ARTICLES OF INCORPORATION

OF

RENTAL VENTURES, INCORPORATED

We, the undersigned incorporators, being of legal age and for the purpose of forming a corporation under the provisions of the Indiana General Corporation Act, as amended, do hereby adopt the following Articles of Incorporation:

ARTICLE I. NAME

The name of the Corporation shall be Rental Ventures, Incorporated.

ARTICLE II. PURPOSES

The Corporation shall have the general business purposes of engaging in the real estate leasing business.

ARTICLE III. REGISTERED OFFICE

The location and post office address of the registered office of the Corporation in this state shall be 126 Sperry Street, Sperry Business Park, Moorehead, IN 51201.

ARTICLE IV. FOR PROFIT

The Corporation is for profit.

ARTICLE V. DURATION

The duration of the Corporation shall be perpetual.

ARTICLE VI. CAPITAL STOCK

The Corporation shall have authority to issue one thousand (1,000) shares of common stock having no par value. Owners of these shares of common stock shall have the right at every meeting of the shareholders to one vote for each share of stock listed in their names on the books of the Corporation as of the date of the meeting. No shares of stock held in the name of the Corporation or not issued by the Corporation shall be entitled to any voting rights.

ARTICLE VII. REQUIREMENTS PRIOR TO DOING BUSINESS

The Corporation will not begin business until consideration of at least One Thousand Dollars ($1,000) has been received by the Corporate Treasurer for the issuance of shares of stock.

FIGURE 11-2. Articles of Incorporation, Page 1

ARTICLE VIII. RIGHTS OF SHAREHOLDERS

(a) **Voting Rights.** At each meeting of the shareholders and with respect to any matter upon which the shareholders shall have a right to vote, each holder of record of shares of common stock shall be entitled to one (1) vote for each share of common stock so held. No shareholder shall have the right to cumulate his/her votes for the election of directors, and there shall be no cumulative voting for any purpose whatsoever.

ARTICLE XII. BYLAWS

The Board of Directors is hereby expressly given the authority to make and alter the Bylaws of this Corporation, except that after the adoption of the initial Bylaws by the first Board of Directors, the Board may not make or alter any Bylaws without first the vote of the shareholders.

ARTICLE XIII. INCORPORATORS

The names and addresses of the incorporators are Upton A. Esmond, 3266 Belmont Avenue, Moorehead, IN 51205 and Jessica M. Moss, 120 South Seventh Street, Moorehead, IN 51201.

IN TESTIMONY WHEREOF, we, the undersigned incorporators, have set our hands this the 21st day of January, (current year).

_____
Upton A. Esmond, Incorporator

_____
Jessica M. Moss, Incorporator

STATE OF INDIANA   )

COUNTY OF WABASH   )

Before me on this the 21st day of January, (current year), personally appeared Upton A. Esmond and Jessica M. Moss, to me known to be the persons described in the foregoing Articles of Incorporation, and acknowledged that they executed the same as their free act.

_____
NOTARY PUBLIC

My Commission Expires: _____

4

FIGURE 11-3. Articles of Incorporation, Last Page

application is attached to the front of the articles so the secretary of state knows that name was reserved by the applicant. When the articles of incorporation are approved, the secretary of state returns a signed corporate charter, along with the articles. The signed charter is often framed and hung on the wall in the corporate office.

In addition to filing the articles with the secretary of state, some states require that the documents also be recorded in the public records at the office of the **register**, also known as a recorder or registrar. The articles are sent to the register's office with a recording fee attached. After being recorded, the original articles are returned to the applicant and are kept in a safe place, usually in a plastic protective cover in the corporate notebook with other important documents.

REGISTER OR REGISTRAR

One responsible for filing public records.

Formatting Instructions for Articles of Incorporation

- Use 8 ½ x 11-inch paper.

- Use 1-inch left, right, top, and bottom margins on all pages except page 1, which should have a 2-inch top margin.

- Key the title in full caps, centered, and either single- or double-spaced on three lines — ARTICLES OF INCORPORATION on the top line, OF on the second line, and the name of the corporation on the third line. Add boldface for emphasis.

- Indent paragraphs ½ inch from the left margin.

- Double-space or single-space the articles with double spacing between paragraphs. Many firms are trying to reduce the length of documents and are single-spacing more often than double-spacing.

- Names of the corporation and individuals are generally keyed with initial caps; however, they may be displayed in full caps.

- Capitalize the term Corporation when it refers to the corporation being organized. References to "the Corporation" or "this Corporation" are capitalized. References to "a corporation" are not capitalized. Also capitalize Charter (or any other name used for the document), Board of Directors, the Directors, the Board, and Bylaws.

- If the document has articles, the title, such as ARTICLE I. NAME, is centered. If the document is single-spaced, triple-space before and double-space after the centered heading. If the document is double-spaced, double-space before and after the centered heading. Boldface can be added.

- Add a 3-inch signature line for each incorporator, beginning at the horizontal center of the page and extending to the right margin. Place the name of the incorporator below the line, followed by a comma, space, and the word "Incorporator."

- Page numbers are centered horizontally at the bottom of each page, except page 1, which is not numbered.

DESIGNATION OF REGISTERED AGENT FOR SERVICE OF PROCESS

AGENT FOR SERVICE OF PROCESS

A person named to accept service of document if a corporation is sued.

A person is named to serve as the corporation's **agent for service of process**. This means that if a lawsuit is filed against the corporation, the summons and complaint are served on the person named as registered agent at the address provided for that individual. There is much flexibility in choosing the agent — often the person named is the principal officer of the corporation, whose business office address is used as the registered office address of the corporation. Sometimes the attorney for the corporation serves as the registered agent. There are also companies who are in the business of serving as registered agents for corporations; and for a fee, a representative of the company can be named as the agent.

The procedure for naming an agent for service of process varies from state to state. In some states, the agent is named in the articles of incorporation; and in other states, a separate certificate appointing a registered agent is filed with the secretary of state. See Figure 11-4.

TRANSMITTAL LETTER TO THE SECRETARY OF STATE

If the articles of incorporation and fees are to be mailed to the secretary of state, a transmittal letter similar to the one shown in Figure 11-5 should accompany the documents. On the envelope and inside address, "The Honorable" is the title to use for the secretary of state. The formal salutation is "Sir" or "Madam"; the informal salutation is "Dear Mr. Secretary" or "Dear Madam Secretary." The formal closing is "Very truly yours"; informal is "Sincerely yours." Choose the style of salutation and closing preferred by your attorney by reviewing correspondence from the office files.

BYLAWS

BYLAWS

The basic rules and regulations adopted by the board of directors for running a corporation.

Bylaws are the rules and regulations for the corporation and are adopted by the board of directors. The bylaws are filed in a notebook with the other corporate records. The bylaws are not normally filed with a public official, as are the articles of incorporation.

Read the bylaws of Rental Ventures, Incorporated, shown in Figures 11-6 through 11-8. Bylaws generally contain the following types of information:

- Place and time of stockholders' meetings

- Who may call special meetings

DESIGNATION OF REGISTERED AGENT

FOR

RENTAL VENTURES, INCORPORATED

To the Secretary of State of the State of Indiana:

Pursuant to the provisions of Section 48-5-1201 of the Indiana General Corporation Act, the undersigned incorporators of a domestic corporation being organized under the Act submit the following statement for the purpose of designating the registered agent for the Rental Ventures, Incorporated, in the State of Indiana:

1. The name of the Corporation is Rental Ventures, Incorporated.

2. The name and street address of its registered agent in the State of Indiana shall be The CTS Corporation, 225 North Second Street, Indianapolis, IN 52201.

Signed this the _____ day of January, (current year).

RENTAL VENTURES, INCORPORATED

By _____
Incorporator

_____
Incorporator

FIGURE 11-4. Designation of Registered Agent

FRITZ M. MUELLER
ATTORNEY AT LAW
4204 Indiana Boulevard
Moorehead, IN 51201

January 31, (current year)

The Honorable John B. Tubbs
Secretary of State
Corporate Division
Capitol Building
Indianapolis, IN 52201

Re: Incorporation of Rental Ventures, Incorporated

Dear Mr. Secretary:

Enclosed are the Articles of Incorporation of Rental Ventures, Incorporated. I am also
enclosing a check in the amount of $100 for the filing fee for this document.

Please return the Articles of Incorporation and Corporate Charter to me at the address
shown above as attorney for the proposed corporation.

Very truly yours,

Fritz M. Mueller, Attorney

Reference initials

Enclosures 2

FIGURE 11-5. Letter to the Secretary of State

BYLAWS

OF

RENTAL VENTURES, INCORPORATED

ARTICLE I

Offices and Location of Corporate Seal

1. **Offices.** The principal office and the location of the corporate seal is at 126 Sperry Street, Sperry Business Park, Moorehead, IN 51201, and the corporate Board of Directors have the right to change this location from time to time as required in the course of business.

2. **Seal.** The corporate seal shall reside at the principal office location.

ARTICLE II

Meetings of Shareholders

1. **Annual Meetings.** The annual meetings of the shareholders who are entitled to vote shall be held at such time and place as may be designated by the Board of Directors under Indiana Code, Section 48-17-10(a), either within or without the State of Indiana, within the month of March of each year.

2. **Notice of Meetings.** Written notice stating the date, time, and place of the annual meeting and, in the case of a special meeting, the purpose or purposes for which the meeting is called shall be mailed at least ten (10) days prior to the date of the meeting. In the case of a special meeting, the purpose or purposes for the special meeting shall be confined to the purpose or purposes set forth in the notice for the special meeting.

3. **Delivery of Notice of Meetings.** Written notice of said meetings shall be delivered either personally or by mail by or at the direction of the President, Secretary, officer, or person calling the meeting to each shareholder entitled to vote at the meeting. Deposit of the notice of the meetings shall be deemed to be delivered when deposited in the United States mail postpaid and correctly addressed. The person giving such notice shall certify that notice required by this paragraph has been given in accordance with Indiana Code, Section 48-11-202.

FIGURE 11-6. Bylaws

4. Quorum Required. For the purpose of any annual or special meeting of the stockholders, a majority of all shares outstanding entitled to vote shall constitute a quorum for the transaction of business whether in person or by proxy. In case there is not a sufficient number of shares outstanding, the meeting shall be adjourned until the requisite number of voting shares shall be represented.

5. Voting and Proxies. If a quorum exists, action on a matter shall be approved if the votes favoring the action exceed the votes opposing the action. Any shareholder may vote his or her shares either in person or by written proxy, with such proxy being effective when received by the Secretary or other person authorized to tabulate votes.

6. Suggested Order of Business. The suggested order of business at the annual meeting shall be as follows:

(a) Roll call of Board of Directors;
(b) Proof of due notice of the meeting as set out above;
(c) Determination of whether a quorum exists;
(d) Reading of the minutes of the prior meeting;
(e) Approval or disapproval of minutes of prior meeting;
(f) Report of the officers and committees;
(g) Election of directors;
(h) Appointment of Certified Public Accounting firm;
(i) All unfinished business;
(j) New business;
(k) Adjournment.

ARTICLE III

Board of Directors

1. Powers. The conduction of business of the Corporation shall be by management of the Board of Directors.

2. Qualification and Election. Directors need not be residents of this state nor shareholders in this Corporation. The shareholders, at their annual meeting, shall determine the number of directors required to constitute the Board of Directors. Each director shall be elected by a plurality of all the votes cast at any meeting at which a quorum is present and shall hold office until the expiration of the term for which that director is elected and shall remain until a successor has been elected in the case of early resignation.

2

FIGURE 11-7. Bylaws, Page 2

3. **Number of Directors.** The number of directors shall be fixed at a minimum of five (5) with the Board of Directors having the authority to increase the number of directors upon a plurality of all votes cast at any meeting at which a quorum is present and where notice of the increase has been given as provided for in ARTICLE II herein.

ARTICLE IX

Fiscal Year

1. **Fiscal Year.** Rental Ventures, Incorporated, shall be operated on a fiscal year which shall end the last day of March of each year.

CERTIFICATE

I, William F. Forrester, Secretary of Rental Ventures, Incorporated, hereby certify that these initial Bylaws were duly adopted as by the Bylaws of Rental Ventures, Incorporated, by the incorporators and shareholders at the initial meeting held on March 1, (current year), as provided for in Indiana Code, Section 48-2-401.

_____
William F. Forrester, Secretary

3

FIGURE 11-8. Bylaws, Page 3

- Time when notice of meetings should be given

- Shares of stock represented to constitute a quorum

- Voting and proxy requirements

- Qualification and election of the board of directors

- Number of directors

- When meetings of directors are to be held

- When notices of directors' meetings are to be given

- What constitutes a quorum at directors' meetings

- Election and duties of officers

- Procedure for handling resignations, removals, and vacancies of officers

- Issuance and transfer of shares of stock

Bylaws have a title, body organized into articles and subdivided into sections, certificate for the secretary of the corporation to sign, and signature line for the designated officer to sign (if required in the bylaws).

Formatting Instructions for Bylaws

- Use the same size of paper, vertical spacing, paragraph indentions, capitalization, and page numbering style as for the articles of incorporation.

- Use a 1 ½ inch left margin to allow space for punching holes in the left margin. If the bylaws are to be kept in a topbound notebook, add an additional half inch to the top margin of each page.

- Capitalize President, Secretary, Treasurer, and other references to officers of the corporation.

- Any of the following forms may be used in setting up the format for the articles.

ARTICLE I

ARTICLE I. CORPORATE POWERS

ARTICLE I

Corporate Powers

ARTICLE I

Corporate Powers

1. **Offices.** The principal office and the location of the corporate seal is at 126 Sperry Street . . . .

ARTICLE II

Meetings of Shareholders

1.1 **Annual Meetings.** The annual meetings of the shareholders who are entitled to vote . . . .

1.2 **Notice of Meetings.** Written notice stating the date, time, and place . . . .

- Prepare a signature line for the officer of the corporation who is to sign the bylaws.

MINUTES OF FIRST MEETINGS

Minutes are a written record of the business conducted at a meeting. The legal secretary may prepare the first set of minutes relating to the organization of a corporation. Once the corporation is organized, the corporate secretary is responsible for preparing minutes.

MINUTES

A written record of the business conducted at a meeting.

Several groups may conduct meetings relating to the organization of the corporation: directors, incorporators, or shareholders.

If the initial directors are named in the articles of incorporation, they hold an organizational meeting to complete the organization of the corporation. If the initial directors are not named in the articles, then the incorporators hold an organizational meeting to elect directors and complete the organization of the corporation. Minutes of all meetings are taken, whether meetings of directors, meetings of incorporators, meetings of shareholders, or special meetings.

At the first meeting of incorporators, the filing date of the original articles is recorded, directors are elected, and authorization to issue stock is given to the board of directors.

At the first meeting of directors, officers are elected, acts of incorporation are approved, a corporate seal may be adopted, a form of stock certificate is approved, authority is given to open a bank account, and any other matters related to the organization of the business are handled.

Approval of the directors' actions is the subject matter of the first meeting of shareholders.

Minutes are signed by the secretary of the corporation and may be signed by other officers of the corporation, depending on the requirements of the bylaws. A copy is always made for the **minute book**; the number of additional copies may vary from none in very small corporations to one for each director in large corporations.

Notice of meetings is usually required several days before a scheduled meeting. An alternative to giving the required notice is to have the members sign a waiver of notice of meeting and include it in, or attach it to, the minutes.

Read the minutes of the first organizational meeting of Rental Ventures, Incorporated shown in Figures 11-9 and 11-10.

MINUTE BOOK

A notebook where minutes of a corporation are filed.

Formatting Instructions for Minutes of Meetings

These rules apply to notices of meetings, waivers of notices of meetings, and minutes of any type.

- Use the same size of paper, vertical spacing, paragraph indentions, capitalization, and page numbering style as for the articles of incorporation.

- Use a 1 ½ inch left margin to allow space for punching holes in the left margin. If the minutes are to be kept in a topbound notebook, add an additional half inch to the top margin of each page.

- Minutes may be formatted with subject headings in full caps and bold at the left margin or arranged in standard paragraph form. Figures 11-9 and 11-10 show the standard paragraph format.

- Capitalize President, Secretary, Treasurer, and other references to officers of the corporation.

- Indent names of those present an additional half inch. See Figure 11-9.

- A **resolution** is a formal written statement of an opinion or intention adopted by the group. Resolutions are single-spaced and indented one-half inch from each margin. Some writers indent the first line of resolutions an additional one-half inch; others block the first line of the resolution. Resolutions begin with the word RESOLVED followed by a comma or colon. Almost always the next word is "that." "That" begins

RESOLUTION

A formal written statement of an opinion or intention adopted by a group.

MINUTES OF THE FIRST ORGANIZATIONAL MEETING

OF THE BOARD OF DIRECTORS

RENTAL VENTURES, INCORPORATED

The first organizational meeting of the Board of Directors of Rental Ventures, Incorporated, was held at 12 noon on the 1st day of March, (current year), at the law offices of Fritz M. Mueller, 4204 Indiana Boulevard, Moorehead, IN 51201. The following persons were present, all of which were incorporators or other persons interested in the formation of this Corporation:

Fritz M. Mueller
Upton A. Esmond
Jessica M. Moss
William F. Forrester

At this first meeting, all four (4) of the above-named persons were elected to the corporate Board of Directors with Upton A. Esmond being elected Chairman of the Board, Jessica M. Moss being elected Vice Chairman of the Board, William F. Forrester being elected Secretary of the Corporation, and Fritz M. Mueller being elected Attorney for the Corporation.

The chairman then brought forth the Charter for the Corporation that had been received back from the Secretary of State of the State of Indiana showing that the Corporate Charter had been issued and duly recorded on the 15th day of February, (current year), by the Secretary of State. The Charter was voted on and unanimously accepted by the incorporators and other persons present. It was

RESOLVED, that the proposed Charter of Rental Ventures, Incorporated, as presented to this first meeting be and the same is hereby adopted as and for the Charter of this Corporation and the same be filed in the official Corporate Record Book.

The chairman also brought forth a set of Bylaws prepared by Fritz M. Mueller, attorney; and a motion was entertained that the proposed Bylaws be accepted; and upon unanimous vote, the Bylaws were adopted and signed by William F. Forrester as Secretary. It was

RESOLVED, that the proposed Bylaws in the form presented to this first meeting be and the same are hereby adopted as and for the Bylaws of this Corporation and that the same be filed in the Corporate Record Book.

The next item of business was salaries of the officers and the Board of Directors; and after several minutes of discussion, it was decided that this matter would be reintroduced at the next Board of Directors' meeting to be held on April 1, (current year).

FIGURE 11-9. Minutes of First Organizational Meeting, Page 1

William F. Forrester, the Corporation's newly elected Secretary, then presented forms of corporate stock certificates that were supplied by Fritz M. Mueller that are to be used as the corporate stock certificates. A motion was then made and carried that the said stock certificates be adopted as the official stock certificates of this corporation.

A motion was then made, seconded, and carried as follows:

RESOLVED, that the Secretary of this Corporation is hereby authorized to and is hereby directed to issue the following stock certificates in the named amount: Fritz M. Mueller, one thousand (1,000) shares; Upton A. Esmond, one thousand (1,000) shares; Jessica M. Moss, one thousand (1,000) shares); and William F. Forrester, one thousand (1,000) shares.

The last business discussed was the attorney's fees and expenses incidental to the incorporation. It was therefore unanimously

RESOLVED, that the Secretary of the Corporation is hereby authorized to pay all fees and expenses incidental and necessary to the organization of this Corporation out of the first profits realized by the Corporation.

There being no further business, upon motion, the meeting adjourned.

_____
Upton A. Esmond, President

APPROVED:

_____
William F. Forrester, Secretary

2

FIGURE 11-10. Minutes of First Organizational Meeting, Page 2

with a capital *T* if a colon follows the term RESOLVED; *"that"* begins with a lowercase t if a comma follows the term RESOLVED. See Figure 11-9.

- When typing resolutions, the following words and phrases, as well as similar words and phrases, are typed in full caps followed by a comma:

  WHEREAS,
  RESOLVED,
  RESOLVED FURTHER,
  BE IT FURTHER RESOLVED,

SUBSCRIPTION AGREEMENT

Individuals who invest in corporations own shares of stock and are known as **stockholders**. A certificate is issued to represent that ownership. A **subscription agreement** is a signed agreement that the party signing will purchase stock of a corporation. Preincorporation subscription agreements are signed prior to the completion of the incorporation process, and subscription agreements are signed after the corporation is organized.

See Figure 11-11, a preincorporation subscription agreement, and Figure 11-12, a subscription agreement. Individual subscription agreements for each party interested in purchasing stock or a joint agreement can be prepared. For an individual subscription, a signature line for the individual is placed at the bottom of the agreement; for a joint agreement, signature lines for several subscribers are provided.

The articles of incorporation state the type, value, and number of shares of stock that can be issued by the corporation. Stock is classified as **common** or **preferred**. In the event the corporation is dissolved, preferred stockholders are paid with the assets of the corporation before common stockholders. Preferred stockholders also get paid the profits of the corporation in the form of dividends before common stockholders.

Stock can be issued at par value or no par value. **Par value** stock has a value per share shown on the certificate and cannot be issued for less than the amount set. **No par** stock does not have a value placed on the stock certificate and can be issued for any amount.

STOCK CERTIFICATES

A **stock certificate** is issued by a corporation to indicate that the person named on the certificate is the owner of the number of shares stated on the face of the instrument.

SUBSCRIPTION AGREEMENT

A contract for the purchase of securities or of stock in a corporation.

COMMON STOCK

A type of stock whose owners are paid last in case a corporation dissolves; represents ownership in a corporation.

PREFERRED STOCK

A type of stock whose owners are paid first in case a corporation dissolves or goes out of business.

PAR VALUE

Stock that shows a value per share on a stock certificate.

NO PAR STOCK

Stock that does not state a value on the face of the stock certificate.

STOCK CERTIFICATE

A certificate issued to a stockholder, providing written evidence of ownership in a corporation.

PREINCORPORATION SUBSCRIPTION AGREEMENT

I, Upton A. Esmond, do hereby subscribe and agree to purchase one hundred (100) shares of the common stock at the par value of Ten Dollars ($10) per share in the Rental Ventures, Incorporated, a corporation to be organized under the laws of the State of Indiana for the purpose of renting real estate property; and I further agree to pay to the said Rental Ventures, Incorporated, in cash for the shares One Thousand Dollars ($1,000) as follows: fifty percent (50%) of the total amount upon signing of the prescription and the balance of fifty percent (50%) in the amount of Five Hundred Dollars ($500) thirty (30) days later.

SIGNED: This the _____ day of January, (current year).

_____
Upton A. Esmond

FIGURE 11-11. Preincorporation Subscription Agreement

SUBSCRIPTION AGREEMENT

       We, the undersigned, each subscribe and agree to purchase one hundred (100) shares each of no par value common stock at the purchase price of Ten Dollars ($10) per share in Rental Ventures, Incorporated, a stock corporation, created and existing under the laws of the State of Indiana for a total amount of One Thousand Dollars ($1,000) each. We agree to pay to the Corporation the above-stated amount by March 31, (current year), and the Corporation agrees to issue to each subscriber certificates for shares of stock in Rental Ventures, Incorporated, upon payment in full.

Names	Residences	No. of Shares
_____	_____	_____
_____	_____	_____
_____	_____	_____
_____	_____	_____

FIGURE 11-12. Subscription Agreement after Creation of a Corporation

Companies usually order commercially printed certificates with much of the needed information printed on the certificate. The secretary may need to type only the name of the purchaser and the number of shares.

Information on the certificates includes:

- A statement that the corporation is organized under the laws of this state

- The name of the corporation

- The name of the person to whom stock is issued

- The number and class of shares of stock

- The par value or statement that the shares are issued at no par

- Date of issuance

Figure 11-13 can be used as a guide for preparing a stock certificate.

In some states, it is not a requirement that a certificate to show ownership of stock be issued. Often in small corporations and Subchapter S corporations (discussed later in this chapter), there are no certificates, and the record of stock ownership is simply carried on the corporate books in what is called "book entry form."

CORPORATE MINUTE BOOK

CORPORATE MINUTE KITS OR OUTFITS

A binder, minute paper, corporate seal, dividers, stock certficates, and stock ledger for a corporation.

CORPORATE SEAL

A seal used by a corporation, which imprints stock certificates and other legal documents of a corporation.

STOCK LEDGER

A form used for keeping a record of the names and addresses of shareholders and of the issuance and transfer of stock certificates.

Corporate minute kits or outfits are available from various companies. Attorneys often order these for their corporate clients. The kit consists of a binder, minute paper, corporate seal, dividers, stock certificates, and a stock ledger.

The binder looks like a three-ring notebook with the name of the corporation inscribed on the front cover. Minute paper is high-quality paper on which minutes of meetings of the directors, shareholders, and incorporators are printed. The **corporate seal** is used to impress the official seal of the corporation on stock certificates and other legal documents of the corporation. The stock certificates would be similar to the one shown in Figure 11-13, except the name of the corporation would already be printed on the form. The **stock ledger** is provided for listing names of stockholders and the number of shares owned and for recording any transfers of ownership.

A less expense method of preparing corporate records is to purchase a corporate record binder and make one's own tabs, use good-quality bond paper instead of the more expensive, hard-to-match minute paper, and purchase blank stock certificates.

The material in a corporate minute book is usually organized as follows: the seal in front, the charter, minutes of incorporators, stock specimen (a sample

FIGURE 11-13. Stock Certificate

copy of the stock certificate), balance sheet, minutes of meetings of shareholders, minutes of meetings of directors, bank resolution (document giving authority to open a bank account in the name of the corporation), bylaws, stock transfer ledger, and stock certificates.

The incorporation documents, including the corporate charter issued by the state, are usually kept in the corporate office. The attorney usually keeps a copy of all documents related to the organization of the corporation. The corporate seal is kept at the office of the corporation, where it is used to imprint stock certificates or to seal other corporate documents.

APPLICATION FOR EMPLOYER IDENTIFICATION NUMBER

FEDERAL TAX NUMBER

A number required by the Internal Revenue Service for businesses.

The Internal Revenue Service requires that a corporation have a **federal tax number**. Form SS-4 and instructions for applying for the employer identification number (EIN) can be obtained by calling a toll-free number listed in the phone book under IRS. The corporation must periodically file forms with the IRS that require the tax number (corporate income tax and payroll tax forms); therefore, it is important to obtain this number while incorporating.

When completing the form:

- Always read instructions on the form and on any accompanying instruction sheets.

- Use lower-case x's to select a choice within a box and make sure they fit within the boxes on the original form and on the copies.

- Descenders, letters extending below the line of type (such as g, p, q), should be printed above the line provided on the form, not touching the line.

- Use 10-point type (if your printer defines type size in points) or 12-pitch or 12 cpi (if your printer defines type size in pitch or characters per inch).

SALES AND USE TAX APPLICATION

If a corporation plans to sell products or services that are taxable, a sales and use tax application should be obtained from the states, counties, or cities where business will be conducted. Instructions are generally provided with the forms. The application is submitted to the appropriate department where taxes are to be submitted. If taxes are not paid in a timely manner, the charter will be revoked and other consequences are likely to follow.

SUBCHAPTER S ELECTION FORM

Form 2553, election by a small business corporation (often called **Subchapter S**), should be filed with the Internal Revenue Service (IRS) if a corporation wishes to establish a special tax status that is the closest thing possible to a partnership. The corporation files information tax returns, but no tax assessment is made on the corporation — corporate income is shown as income to the stockholders. Subchapter S allows an individual or stockholder to avoid double taxation (paying a corporate tax and also paying a tax on any stock dividends issued) and is often used by individuals beginning a new corporation.

      Instructions for completing Form 2553 are on the form. An accompanying instruction sheet is also available.

SUBCHAPTER S

A type of small business organization that is incorporated and allows the owners to be taxed individually rather than as a corporation.

SUMMARY

- Corporations are classified as domestic, foreign, or alien. Domestic corporations do business where incorporated; a corporation is foreign to all states except the state where incorporated; an alien corporation is organized out of the country and does business within the United States.

- Corporations have stockholders, a board of directors, and officers.

- A corporate name is reserved by submitting a letter requesting a name reservation or an application for reservation of corporate name to the secretary of state.

- Articles of incorporation are submitted to the office of the secretary of state; and once approved, the articles are returned with a signed corporate charter. That corporate charter gives the corporation authority to function.

- Bylaws are the rules adopted by the board of directors to govern the corporation. They include information about meetings, officers, stock, and voting. Bylaws are usually organized into articles and subdivided into sections.

- Minutes are to be kept of all meetings. If proper notice of a meeting has not been given, the members can sign a waiver of notice and continue with the meeting. The waiver is included in the minutes or attached to the minutes of the meeting.

- Stock subscription agreements are contracts for the purchase of stock and are signed by prospective purchasers.

- Stock may be classified as common or preferred and is issued at par or no par value.

- Corporate minute books can be purchased from printing companies and are used for organizing corporate records.

- An application for employer identification number (Form SS-4) is completed to obtain a federal tax number.

- A state and local tax number is obtained by completing a sales and use tax application. Application should be made for any local, city, or county business tax permits.

- Form 2553, Subchapter S, is completed and submitted to the Internal Revenue Service to establish a tax status that avoids double taxation.

REVIEW EXERCISES

T   F   1. An alien corporation is one organized out of the state but doing business within the state.

T   F   2. The board of directors establishes policy for a corporation.

T   F   3. The word "corporation" must be used in a corporate name.

T   F   4. A city or town is an example of a not-for-profit corporation.

T   F   5. The officers of a corporation are usually appointed by the stockholders.

T   F   6. If the articles of incorporation are to be mailed to the secretary of state, a transmittal letter should be prepared.

T   F   7. The signed corporate charter gives the corporation power to function.

T   F   8. The original copy of the articles of incorporation is mailed to the county court clerk's office.

T   F   9. The president of the corporation might sign the bylaws.

T   F   10. The rules that govern the corporation are called subscription agreements.

T   F   11. If a corporation plans to sell taxable goods or services, it must complete a Subchapter S election form.

T   F   12. Most bylaws provide that notice of meetings of corporations be given or that a waiver of those meetings be signed by the members of the group.

T   F   13. One of the items in a corporate outfit is the corporate seal.

T   F   14. A charter may also be called a corporate agreement.

T   F   15. A charter is normally typed on 8 ½ by 14-inch paper.

T   F   16. A stock certificate is a contract for the purchase of securities.

T   F   17. The divisions and subdivisions of bylaws are articles and sections.

TRANSCRIPTION RULES

SEMICOLON

Series Containing Commas

Set off items in a series containing commas with a semicolon.

The nature of the business is to construct and distribute cabinets; to lease, purchase, or sell all such property; and to engage in any lawful act for which a corporation is organized.

COMMA

Phrases — Interrupting

The interrupting phrase rule was presented in Chapter 3. An interrupting phrase may be essential information that interrupts the flow of the sentence from the subject to the verb or from the verb to the object. Additional examples are shown below. Remember! When you set material off with commas, you should be able to read a complete sentence when omitting the phrase.

The Corporation may dispose of all property, *real and personal,* as is deemed necessary.

The undersigned persons, *having capacity to contract,* adopt the following Charter.

The meeting shall be at such time and place, *either within or without this state,* as may be designated by the directors.

NUMBER EXPRESSION

Numbers in Legal Documents

In legal documents, express fractions in written and numeric form.

Not less than *one-tenth (1/10th)* of the directors must vote.

TRANSCRIPTION EXERCISES

Use a secretarial reference manual and the rules presented in this and previous chapters to aid you in correctly transcribing the following material. There are misspelled words in the sentences.

1. Prepare the inside address, salutation, and complimentary closing for a letter to the secretary of state. Assume the name of the secretary of state is Alice Reno and her office is located in the Capitol Building, Suite 350 in your city and state. (Your attorney prefers the informal style.)

2. Transcribe this resolution: upon motion duly made it was resolved that the corporation proceed to carry on the business for which it was incorporated and it was further resolved that the signing of these minutes shall constitute full ratification thereof and waiver of notice of the meeting by the signatory

3. Prepare signature lines for four stockholders to sign. The stockholders are foster schleiker, demetreus schlieker, renita schleiker, and bradley schleiker.

Transcribe the following sentences:

4. the attorney still needs to draft the articles of corporation order a corporate seal stock register and minute book and conduct the organizational meeting

5. persuant to waiver of notice the first meeting of the stockholders was held at the attorneys office

6. in no event shall the total amount of cash plus the value of property donated or recieved exceed twenty thousand dollars

7. foster schleiker is to receive one third of the common stock of the corporation

8. there being no farther business to come before the meeting of shareholders upon motion duly made and seconded the meeting was adjourned

9. the board of directors must get a two thirds majority vote to pass a resolution

10. the stock certificates were issued to f m meuller 1000 shares upton a esmond 1000 shares jessica m moss 1000 shares and william forrester 1000 shares

RESEARCH ACTIVITIES

1. Consult your state codes to determine how much money is required for starting a corporation.

2. Consult your state codes to determine the number of incorporators needed to organize a corporation.

3. In your state, what is the secretary of state's name and address?

4. Obtain a copy of the application for sales tax for your state.

5. Write or call your secretary of state's office to request a form to reserve a corporate name.

6. Use resources available to you to try to determine the cost of a corporate minute outfit.

PROJECTS

Insert the cassette tape for Chapter 11 and transcribe the following projects.

Project 11-1   Design a form using Figure 11-1 as a guide, and prepare an Application for Reservation of Corporate Name for the company in Project 11-2. Ann Tilley at Heritage Antiques, Incorporated, 634 Ala Moana, Honolulu, HI 92022, is the applicant.

Project 11-2   Transcribe articles of incorporation for Heritage Antiques, Incorporated. These are the same parties who formed a partnership in Project 10-2. Now they have decided to incorporate. Prepare a cover letter to the secretary of state.

Project 11-3   Transcribe the designation of registered agent for Heritage Antiques, Incorporated.

Project 11-4   Transcribe the bylaws for the corporation organized in Project 11-2.

Project 11-5   Prepare a stock subscription agreement for the parties in Project 11-2.

Project 11-6   Prepare stock certificates for the corporation organized in Project 11-2.

Project 11-7   Transcribe minutes for the corporation organized in Project 11-2.

CHAPTER 12

REAL ESTATE

OBJECTIVES

When you successfully complete this chapter, you will be able to:

➤ Prepare forms with merge codes for warranty deeds

➤ Prepare a warranty deed by merging variable information

➤ Transcribe a sales contract

➤ Transcribe a deed of trust note

➤ Prepare a settlement sheet for a real estate transaction

INTRODUCTION

Purchasing homes or condominiums is a part of our everyday lives. Purchases of land and things attached to land are referred to as **real estate** transactions. Transfers of real estate are required to be in writing; the written instrument that transfers title from one person to another is a **deed**.

In this chapter you will follow a real estate transaction from the creation of a warranty deed through the final settlement. Two additional types of deeds will also be presented. The following documents will be analyzed:

REAL ESTATE

Land and anything attached to it.

DEED

A written instrument by which title to real estate is conveyed from one person to another.

> **WARRANTY DEED**
> **DEED OF TRUST**
> **DEED OF TRUST NOTE**
> **SETTLEMENT SHEETS**
> **INSTALLMENT DEED**
> **QUITCLAIM DEED**

The parties to a deed are the **grantor**, or seller, and the **grantee**, or purchaser, and the parts of a deed are:

- Premises

- Habendum

- Warranties

- Testimonium

The **premises** of a deed include (1) the names of the grantors and grantees, (2) the **consideration**, an amount of money or something of value, (3) a **granting clause** stating that the property was "conveyed," and (4) a **property description**, which is a legal description of the boundaries of a piece of property. Following the property description and also included in the premises is a **derivation** clause naming the people from whom the sellers purchased the property. The word "derivation" comes from the root word "derive"; thus, the property was derived from the previous owners. The clause is quite helpful in tracing ownership of property.

The **habendum** generally begins with the words "To have and to hold." The clause defines the extent of interest conveyed, such as fee simple, life estate, tenancy in common, or tenancy by the entirety. Fee simple is a total ownership; the owner can sell or transfer the property at any time. It is the most desirable type of ownership. A life estate is the ownership and use of property during one's lifetime; upon death, ownership transfers back to the grantor or someone else named in the deed. Tenants in common own real estate jointly, but each owns an unidentified portion of land — four people may own a piece of land jointly, but each one-fourth is unidentified. Tenancy by the entirety creates an ownership between husband and wife in which each holds title to the entire piece of property; upon death of one partner, the survivor is the owner of the entire piece of property.

Warranties are promises or guarantees made by the grantor. They might include warranties against encumbrances, of the right to quiet enjoyment and possession, or of the right to convey the property. Encumbrances are claims or rights against the property. For instance, a **lien** can be placed against property for nonpayment of an indebtedness for which the property is used as security. If a person borrows money to pay for a house, the lender has a claim (**mortgage**) against the property until the indebtedness is paid in full. A lien can also be placed against property as a result of a court judgment or nonpayment of property or federal taxes. The right to quiet enjoyment and possession means the land cannot be claimed by someone having a better title. The right to convey the property means the owner has the right to sell the property.

The **testimonium** clause begins with IN WITNESS WHEREOF or IN TESTIMONY WHEREOF and states the date when the grantors signed the deed. The testimonium includes the grantor's written signature and an acknowledgment.

Deeds must be recorded at the register's office to be good against others who may make claims of ownership. There is a charge for recording the document and a transfer tax based on the value of the property. To be recorded, a deed should include the following:

- Name and address of the new owner

- Address of the property

- Name and address of the party to get a tax notice

- Oath as to value or consideration

- Map and parcel number

- Acknowledgment

When the purchaser of real property does not pay for it fully in cash, the following three documents are prepared simultaneously: warranty deed, deed of trust, and deed of trust note.

LIEN

A claim against property to secure a debt.

MORTGAGE

A lien against real estate.

TESTIMONIUM

A clause that begins with "IN WITNESS WHEREOF," OR "IN TESTIMONY WHEREOF," and includes the grantor's signature and an acknowledgment.

Formatting Instructions for a Deed

- Prepare the original for the grantee, a copy for the grantor, and a copy for the office files.

- Use 8 ½ x 14-inch paper unless instructed otherwise.

- If a form is used, set the left and right margins to align with the words already printed copy on the form.

- If plain paper is used for preparing a deed, use 1-inch side and bottom margins. The top margin on page 1 should be 2 inches; continuation pages may be 1 inch unless the document is to be bound at the top, in which case an additional ½ inch is added to the top margin for binding.

- Set two tabs — one for a 1-inch paragraph indention and another at center for the signature lines.

- Deeds may be double-spaced or single-spaced.

- Indent property descriptions 1 inch from the left and right margins. It is acceptable to use the full width of the margins for property descriptions when typing on a form. Single-space the property descriptions with double spacing between paragraphs. In property descriptions:

    Write North, Northeast, South, West, and the like, with initial caps, but do not capitalize northerly, southerly, etc.

    Write directions of property lines as follows: "South thirty (30) degrees, thirty-three (33) minutes, twenty-five (25) seconds West." A single quotation mark represents minutes; a double quotation represents seconds. It is preferable not to use figures, symbols, and abbreviations, but if space is limited, the previous direction could be written as S 30° 33' 25" W. On most word processing systems, the degree symbol can be made by holding down the alt key and entering the number 248 on the ten-key pad. It looks like this: °

Write lengths of property lines in words and in numbers. For example, "one hundred fifty-two and twenty-five one hundredths (152.25) feet." If expressed in symbols, the apostrophe (') represents feet. The previous property line could be written as 152.25'.

- To ensure accuracy, proofread property descriptions by having someone read *aloud* from the original copy as another person checks the printed copy, spelling any unusual terms and clearly identifying numerals. In proofreading the length of the property line 152.25 feet, read it as one five two point two five feet.

WARRANTY DEED

WARRANTY DEED

A deed that contains general warranties.

A **warranty deed** is the most desirable type of deed because it contains general warranties that the seller will warrant and defend the title against any claims by previous owners.

Use these guidelines to examine the warranty deed in Figures 12-1 and 12-2, in which Kurt and Lisa Ambrose transfer a house and lot to Shalom and Mary Shanlever. Then compare the warranty deed in Figures 12-1 and 12-2, a form provided by Chicago Title Insurance Company, with Figures 12-3 and 12-4, a typewritten version of the same deed.

A. Names and address of new owners.

B. Name and address of the person or organization who will pay the taxes on the property. This may be a mortgage company if taxes are included in the monthly payments; or it may be the new owner.

MAP AND PARCEL NUMBERS

Numbers assigned to each parcel of land, which can be obtained from the trustee's office or from the register's (known as registrar in some areas) office.

C. Map and parcel numbers. These numbers are assigned to each parcel of land and can be obtained from the register's office or from the county office where tax records are kept.

D. Consideration. Consideration here refers to an amount of money or something of value exchanged for the transfer of land. State laws usually require that some consideration be stated in the deed. Often a nominal amount is stated here rather than the full amount paid.

E. Names of grantors.

F. Conveyance clause or granting clause.

G. Names of grantees.

H. Land description.

WARRANTY DEED

B.

ADDRESS NEW OWNER(S) AS FOLLOWS:	SEND TAX BILLS TO:	MAP PARCEL NUMBERS
SHALOM SHANLEVER et ux.	CITY MORTGAGE COMPANY	Map 111-1
(NAME)	(NAME)	
576 Amberwood Circle	P.O. Box 2850	Par. 222
(STREET ADDRESS OR ROUTE NUMBER)	(STREET ADDRESS)	
Nashville, TN 37209	Nashville, TN 37219	
(CITY) (STATE) (ZIP)	(CITY) (STATE) (ZIP)	

A. → SHALOM SHANLEVER et ux.   **C.** → Map 111-1

FOR AND IN CONSIDERATION of the sum of - - - - - - - - - -Ten and 00/100 (10.00)- *Dollars,*   **D.**

cash and other good and valuable consideration, the receipt of which is hereby acknowledged, including the assumption by the said Grantees of the unpaid balance of a certain indebtedness secured by a Deed of Trust to CITY MORTGAGE COMPANY in the original principal amount of Fifty Thousand Dollars ($50,000) as of record in Book 1111, page 2345, Register's Office of Davidson County, Tennessee.

E. → KURT AMBROSE and wife, LISA K. AMBROSE,

F. → *have this day bargained and sold, and do hereby transfer and convey unto the said* SHALOM SHANLEVER and wife, MARY SHANLEVER,   **G.**

the Grantees herein, their (successors), heirs and assigns, certain real estate in Davidson County, Tennessee as follows:

H. → Land in Davidson County, Tennessee, being Lot No. 2, and described according to a survey made by Susan Boundary, surveyor, dated June 1, (current year), as follows:

Beginning at an iron pin at the corner of Lots 1 and 2 on the westerly margin of Amberwood Circle; thence in a southwesterly direction South five (05) degrees, thirty (30) minutes West two hundred twenty-five (225) feet to an iron pin; thence in a westerly direction South eighty-five (85) degrees, thirty (30) minutes eleven hundred (1,100) feet, more or less, to an iron pin; thence in a northeasterly direction North four (04) degrees, forty (40) minutes East twelve and seventy-five one hundredths (12.75) feet to an iron pin; thence in an easterly direction North eighty-four (84) degrees, ten (10) minutes East twelve hundred (1,200) feet, more or less, to the point of beginning containing five and three one hundredths (5.03) acres, more or less.

I. → Being the same property conveyed to KURT AMBROSE and wife, LISA K. AMBROSE, by deed from CHARLES OLSON and wife, BARBARA OLSON, of record in Book 1001, page 111, Register's Office for Davidson County, Tennessee.

K. → STATE OF TENNESSEE
COUNTY OF DAVIDSON }   *The actual consideration or value, whichever is greater, for this transfer is* $ 100,000.00
Subscribed and sworn to before me this the _____ *day of* _____
_____ 19 _____   *Affiant*
My commission expires: _____
(Affix Seal)   *Notary Public*

unimproved ( )
This is improved (X) property, known as 576 Amberwood Circle   Nashville, TN 37209   **J.**
(House Number)   (Street)   P.O. Address: (City or Town)

L. → *TO HAVE AND TO HOLD said real estate, with the appurtenance, estate, title, and interest thereto belonging, to the Grantees, their (successors), heirs and assigns forever we covenant that we are lawfully seized and possessed of said real estate in fee simple, have a good right to convey it, and that the same is unencumbered.*

M. → *We further covenant and bind ourselves, our heirs and representatives, to warrant and forever defend the title to said real estate to said Grantees, their (successors), heirs, and assigns, against the lawful claims of all persons.*

Whenever used, the singular number shall include the plural, the plural the singular, and the use of any gender shall be applicable to all genders.

Witness our hands this _____ *day of* _____, 19 ___, *the corporate party, if any, having caused its name to be signed hereto by its duly authorized officers on said day and date.*

N. → KURT AMBROSE

LISA K. AMBROSE

FIGURE 12-1. Warranty Deed, Page 1

STATE OF TENNESSEE
COUNTY OF DAVIDSON

Personally appeared before me ___ , the undersigned, _____ , *a Notary Public in and for said County and State* __KURT AMBROSE and wife, LISA K. AMBROSE,__ _____

_____

O. → *the within named bargainor* s_____ , *with whom I am personally acquainted (or proved to me on the basis of satisfactory evidence), and who acknowledged that* __they__ *executed the within instrument for the purposes therein contained.*

Witness my hand and official seal at __Nashville,__ _____ *Tennessee,* *this* _____ *day of* _____, 19 _____.

_____*Notary Public*

*Commission expires*_____

STATE OF TENNESSEE
COUNTY OF DAVIDSON

Before me, _____ , *a Notary Public of the State and County aforesaid, personally appeared* _____ , *with whom I am personally acquainted (or proved to me on the basis of satisfactory evidence), and who, upon oath,*

P. → *acknowledged* _____*self to be* _____ *of the* _____ , *the within named bargainor, a corporation, and that* _____ *he as such* _____ *being authorized so to do, executed the foregoing instrument for the purpose therein contained, by signing the name of the corporation by* _____*self as* _____ .

Witness my hand and seal, at office in _____ , *this* _____ *day of* _____, 19 _____.

_____*Notary Public*

*Commission expires*_____

Q. → This instrument was prepared by:
Larry Lawyer
Law Associates
2400 River Road, Suite 400
Nashville, TN 37217

WARRANTY DEED

FROM
KURT AMBROSE and wife, LISA K. AMBROSE

TO
SHALOM SHANLEVER and wife,
MARY SHANLEVER

Compliments of
Chicago Title Insurance Company
First Floor — First American Center
Phone 255-4631
NASHVILLE, TENNESSEE 37238

FIGURE 12-2. Warranty Deed, Page 2

PREPARED BY:

Larry Lawyer, Law Associates
2400 River Road, Suite 400
Nashville, TN 37217

W A R R A N T Y   D E E D

NEW OWNER:	SEND TAX BILLS TO:	MAP AND PARCEL NO.
SHALOM SHANLEVER et ux.	CITY MORTGAGE COMPANY	Map 111-1
576 Amberwood Circle	P.O. Box 2850	Par. 222
Nashville, TN 37209	Nashville, TN 37219	

FOR AND IN CONSIDERATION of the sum of Ten and 00/100 Dollars ($10.00) cash and other good and valuable consideration, the receipt of which is hereby acknowledged, including the assumption by the said Grantees of the unpaid balance of a certain indebtedness secured by a Deed of Trust to CITY MORTGAGE COMPANY in the original principal amount of Fifty Thousand Dollars ($50,000) as of record in Book 1111, page 2345, Register's Office of Davidson County, Tennessee, KURT AMBROSE and wife, LISA K. AMBROSE, have this day bargained and sold, and do hereby transfer and convey unto the said SHALOM SHANLEVER and wife, MARY SHANLEVER, the Grantees herein, their (successors), heirs and assigns, certain real estate in Davidson County, Tennessee, as follows:

> Land in Davidson County, Tennessee, being Lot No. 2, and described according to a survey made by Susan Boundary, surveyor, dated June 1, (current year), as follows:

> Beginning at an iron pin at the corner of Lots 1 and 2 on the westerly margin of Amberwood Circle; thence in a southwesterly direction South five (05) degrees, thirty (30) minutes West two hundred twenty-five (225) feet to an iron pin; thence in a westerly direction South eighty-five (85) degrees, thirty (30) minutes eleven hundred (1,100) feet, more or less, to an iron pin; thence in a northeasterly direction North four (04) degrees, forty (40) minutes East twelve and seventy-five one hundredths (12.75) feet to an iron pin; thence in an easterly direction North eighty-four (84) degrees, ten (10) minutes East twelve hundred (1,200) feet, more or less, to the point of beginning containing five and three one hundredths (5.03) acres, more or less.

> Being the same property conveyed to KURT AMBROSE and wife, LISA K. AMBROSE, by Deed from CHARLES OLSON and wife, BARBARA OLSON, of record in Book 1001, page 111, Register's Office for Davidson County, Tennessee.

This is improved property, known as 576 Ambrose Circle, Nashville, TN 37209.

TO HAVE AND TO HOLD said real estate, with the appurtenance, estate, title, and interest thereto belonging to the Grantees, their (successors), heirs and assigns, forever we covenant that we are lawfully seized and possessed of said real estate in fee simple, have a good right to convey it, and the the same is unencumbered.

FIGURE 12-3. Typed Warranty Deed, Page 1

(

We further covenant and bind ourselves, our heirs and representatives, to warrant and forever defend the title to said real estate to said Grantees, their (successors), heirs and assigns, against the lawful claims of all persons.

Whenever used, the singular number shall include the plural, the plural the singular, and the use of any gender shall be applicable to all genders.

WITNESS our hands this the _____ day of _____, 19 ____.

_____
KURT AMBROSE

_____
LISA K. AMBROSE

STATE OF TENNESSEE)

COUNTY OF DAVIDSON)

Personally appeared before me, the undersigned, a Notary Public in and for said County and State, KURT AMBROSE and wife, LISA K. AMBROSE, the within named bargainors, with whom I am personally acquainted, or proved to me on the basis of satisfactory evidence, and who acknowledged that they executed the within instrument for the purposes therein contained.

WITNESS my hand and official seal at Nashville, Tennessee, this the _____ day of _____, 19 ____.

_____
NOTARY PUBLIC

My Commission Expires: _____

STATE OF TENNESSEE)

COUNTY OF DAVIDSON)

The actual consideration or value, whichever is greater, for this transfer is $100,000.

_____
AFFIANT

Subscribed and sworn to before me
this the ____ day of _____, 19 ___.

_____
NOTARY PUBLIC

My Commission Expires: _____

- 2 -

FIGURE 12-4. Typed Warranty Deed, Page 2

I. Derivation clause. This clause identifies the previous owner and the book and page number where the previous deed was recorded and is useful in tracing ownership of the property.

In composing Part I, the derivation clause in Figure 12-1, the secretary would have a copy of the previous deed. Each deed has a derivation clause, which includes the names of the previous owners and also refers to a book and page number where the deed is recorded at the county register's office. That book and page number is an index for finding the document. The derivation clause would show Charles and Barbara Olson as the grantors and Kurt and Lisa Ambrose as the grantees. It would read as follows:

> Being the same property conveyed to Charles Olson and wife, Barbara Olson, by deed from John Jones and wife, Sally Jones, of record in Book 950, page 788, Register's Office for Davidson County, Tennessee.

In the derivation clause in the deed in Figure 12-1, a copy of which is duplicated below, Kurt and Lisa Ambrose are transferring the property to the new owners; the Joneses are dropped off and the Ambroses are added.

> Being the same property conveyed to Kurt Ambrose and wife, Lisa K. Ambrose, by deed from Charles Olson and wife, Barbara Olson, of record in Book 1001, page 111, Register's Office for Davidson County, Tennessee.

It is normally the secretary's responsibility to update the derivation clause when preparing the deed. The exact words shown above are not required, but the names of the parties and book and page numbers where the deed is recorded are essential.

J. Address of property. This is the actual street address of the purchased property. Property with a building is improved real estate; property without buildings is unimproved.

K. Affidavit of value. This affidavit states the value of the property or the amount paid, whichever is greater. The value of the property is on file in the office of the county tax assessor, a county official who assigns values to real estate. The affidavit should appear somewhere on the face of the instrument to establish the amount of transfer tax due. A tax based on the value shown on the deed is assessed when the deed is recorded.

AFFIDAVIT OF VALUE

An affidavit stating the value of the property or amount paid, whichever is greater.

L. Habendum. This clause defines the extent of interest conveyed.

M. Warranties. In this deed, the grantors warrant that they own the land in fee simple and have a right to convey it, that there are no encumbrances, and that they will forever defend the title.

N. Grantors' signatures. The signature of the grantor must appear on the deed. If the grantor is a corporation, an authorized officer must sign. If the grantor is a partnership, any of the general partners may sign.

O. Acknowledgment for an individual. To be valid, this must include the county and state. The notary's commission cannot have expired, and all signatures must be notarized. The notary must sign the acknowledgment and affix his or her seal.

P. Acknowledgment for a corporation.

Q. Name and address of the person who prepared the instrument. This information establishes legal responsibility for the preparation of the instrument.

DEED OF TRUST

DEED OF TRUST

An instrument conveying ownership of property to a trustee to secure a debt; a mortgage.

A **deed of trust** is similar to a mortgage; however, there is a distinction between a mortgage and a deed of trust. A mortgage gives a creditor a lien against the real estate, and a deed of trust conveys the real estate to a third party, a **trustee**, for the benefit of the creditor.

The transfer is from the purchaser (who becomes the grantor in the deed of trust) to the trustee, who holds the property in trust until the full amount of money the purchaser owes for the property is paid in full. The deed of trust spells out what will happen if the purchaser stops making payments.

When the debt is paid, the deed of trust is released, and the release document is recorded at the office of the register of deeds.

As you read the following descriptions, examine the elements of a deed of trust in Figures 12-5 and 12-6. Notice that the affidavit of value is not required on the deed of trust and neither are map and parcel numbers. The transfer tax charged on a deed of trust is based on the amount of the loan, not the value of the property. Map and parcel numbers can be obtained from the warranty deed and need not be repeated.

A. Name and address of person who prepared the instrument.

B. Consideration. As in the warranty deed, a nominal dollar amount may be stated.

C. Grantors. The grantee in a warranty deed is the new owner of the property, who becomes the grantor in the deed of trust. The purchaser of the property is granting or conveying it to the trustee.

D. Conveyance clause.

E. Property description. This is identical to the property description in the warranty deed.

F. Derivation clause. Notice that the progression of ownership moves up one step because the property was conveyed by the warranty deed prepared

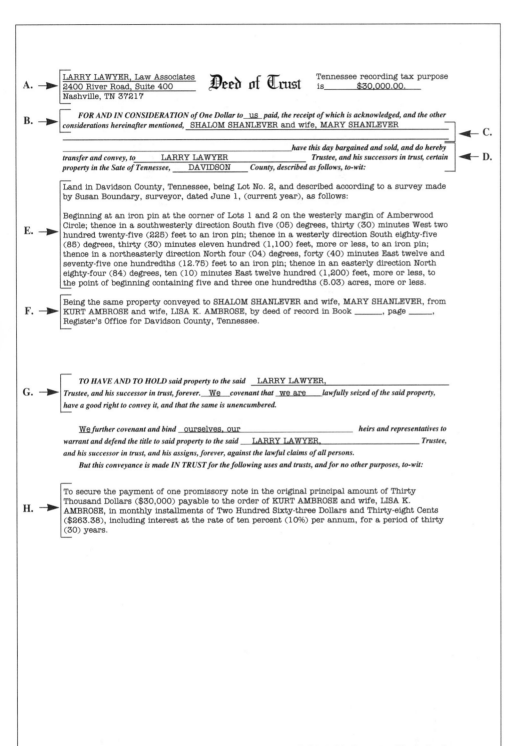

A. → LARRY LAWYER, Law Associates   𝕯eed of 𝕿rust   Tennessee recording tax purpose
2400 River Road, Suite 400   is_____$30,000.00._____
Nashville, TN 37217

B. → *FOR AND IN CONSIDERATION of One Dollar to__us__ paid, the receipt of which is acknowledged, and the other considerations hereinafter mentioned,* SHALOM SHANLEVER and wife, MARY SHANLEVER   ← C.

_____*have this day bargained and sold, and do hereby*   ← D.
transfer and convey, to   LARRY LAWYER   *Trustee, and his successors in trust, certain property in the Sate of Tennessee,*   DAVIDSON   *County, described as follows, to-wit:*

E. → Land in Davidson County, Tennessee, being Lot No. 2, and described according to a survey made by Susan Boundary, surveyor, dated June 1, (current year), as follows:

Beginning at an iron pin at the corner of Lots 1 and 2 on the westerly margin of Amberwood Circle; thence in a southwesterly direction South five (05) degrees, thirty (30) minutes West two hundred twenty-five (225) feet to an iron pin; thence in a westerly direction South eighty-five (85) degrees, thirty (30) minutes eleven hundred (1,100) feet, more or less, to an iron pin; thence in a northeasterly direction North four (04) degrees, forty (40) minutes East twelve and seventy-five one hundredths (12.75) feet to an iron pin; thence in an easterly direction North eighty-four (84) degrees, ten (10) minutes East twelve hundred (1,200) feet, more or less, to the point of beginning containing five and three one hundredths (5.03) acres, more or less.

F. → Being the same property conveyed to SHALOM SHANLEVER and wife, MARY SHANLEVER, from KURT AMBROSE and wife, LISA K. AMBROSE, by deed of record in Book _____, page _____, Register's Office for Davidson County, Tennessee.

G. → *TO HAVE AND TO HOLD said property to the said*   LARRY LAWYER,
*Trustee, and his successor in trust, forever.*__We__*covenant that*__we are__*lawfully seized of the said property, have a good right to convey it, and that the same is unencumbered.*

__We__*further covenant and bind*__ourselves, our__*heirs and representatives to warrant and defend the title to said property to the said*__LARRY LAWYER,__*Trustee, and his successor in trust, and his assigns, forever, against the lawful claims of all persons.*
But this conveyance is made IN TRUST for the following uses and trusts, and for no other purposes, to-wit:

H. → To secure the payment of one promissory note in the original principal amount of Thirty Thousand Dollars ($30,000) payable to the order of KURT AMBROSE and wife, LISA K. AMBROSE, in monthly installments of Two Hundred Sixty-three Dollars and Thirty-eight Cents ($263.38), including interest at the rate of ten percent (10%) per annum, for a period of thirty (30) years.

As part of the consideration for the execution of this instrument, and of the indebtedness secured hereunder, the undersigned agree to keep all buildings now on, or to be hereafter erected on said property, insured in some reliable fire insurance company, or companies, for the sum of $__value__,or at least the maximum insurable value, until the indebtedness herein secured is fully paid, and to have the loss, if any, made payable on the policy, or policies, to said trustee for the benefit of the lawful owner or holder of said indebtedness as his interest may appear.

FIGURE 12-5. Deed of Trust, Page 1

Undersigned further agree to pay all taxes and assessments thereon, general or special, and to pay them when due, and, upon demand of said Trustee or the lawful owner and holder of said indebtedness, to pay, discharge, or remove, any and all liens which may be hereafter placed against said property and which shall adversely affect the lien of this instrument or enforcement of the terms and provisions hereof, to keep the improvements on said property in good repair and preservation, and in case the Trustee or his successors or the lawful owner and holder of said indebtedness shall hereafter be required to appear in any court or tribunal to enforce this deed of trust, or the terms thereof, or to defend the title to, or possession of, said property, or the lien of this instrument, all the costs and expenses of such appearance or proceedings, together with a reasonable attorney's fee shall be allowed, and if paid by the Trustee or the lawful owner and holder of said indebtedness, shall bear six (6) percent interest from the date of payment and shall be and become a part of the indebtedness secured hereby.

I. ▸

Now, if the undersigned Grantors shall pay said indebtedness, and all instruments thereof, when due, according to the terms hereof, or of any note or notes evidencing the same, and pay taxes, keep up repairs, keep said premises insured, and perform the other and foregoing obligations and agreements then this trust conveyance shall be of no further force or effect. But if Grantors fail to pay said indebtedness, or any part or installment thereof, promptly at maturity, or if, failing to pay taxes, keep up repairs, keep said premises insured, or perform said other obligations and agreements as herein provided, Grantors fail to reimburse the Trustee or lawful owner and holder of said indebtedness for all sums, with interest, so expanded by said Trustee, or lawful owner and holder of said indebtedness, within thirty days from date of such payment, this trust conveyance shall remain in full force and effect and at the option of the lawful owner and holder of said indebtedness or part or installments thereof then past due and unpaid, all remaining unpaid indebtedness shall become due and payable at once, without notice, and the said Trustee, or his successor in trust, is hereby authorized and empowered upon giving twenty (20) days' notice by three publications in any newspaper, daily or weekly, published in Davidson County, Tennessee, to sell said property at the front door of the courthouse in said county to the highest bidder for cash, at public outcry, free from statutory right of redemption, homestead, dower, and all other exemptions of every kind, which are expressly waived, and the said Trustee or his successor in trust, is authorized and empowered to execute and deliver a deed to the purchaser. The creditor may bid at any sale under this trust conveyance. Grantors agree that the Trustee may, at any tie after default in the payment or any part of said indebtedness, enter and take possession of said property, and shall only account for the net rents actually received by him. Grantors further agree that, in the event the Trustee fails, before selling said property as herein provided, to enter and take possession thereof, the purchase shall be entitled to immediate possession thereof upon delivery to him by the Trustee of a deed for said property.

In the event of the death, absence, inability, or refusal to act of the said Trustee at any time when action under the foregoing powers and trust may be required, the owner of the debt herein secured is hereby authorized to name and appoint a successor to execute this trust, and the title herein conveyed to the above-named Trustee shall be vested in said successor.

In the event of a sale of said property under and by virtue of this trust, the Grantors and all persons holding under them shall be and become the tenants at will of the purchaser from and after the execution and delivery of a deed to such purchaser upon five (5) days' written notice.

Upon any sale under this Deed of Trust, the proceeds will be applied by the Trustee.

First: To pay all the costs and charges of executing this trust, including attorney's fees and the expenses of any litigation which may arise on account of the execution and enforcement of this trust, or in connection therewith as above provided.

Second: To pay said debt, or any balance thereof then remaining unpaid.

Third: The residue to be paid to Grantors, or their order.

WITNESS ___our___ hand _s_ this _____ day of ___September___, 19 ____, the corporate party, if any, having caused its name to be signed herein by all duly authorized officers on said day and date.

J. ▸

MARY SHANLEVER	SHALOM SHANLEVER

STATE OF TENNESSEE
COUNTY OF DAVIDSON

Personally appeared before me, ___the undersigned_____. a Notary Public in and for said County and State_____SHALOM SHANLEVER and wife, MARY SHANLEVER,_____

K. ▸

the within named bargainor _s_____, with whom I am personally acquainted (or proved to me on the basis of satisfactory evidence), and who acknowledged that___they____ executed the within instrument for the purpose therein contained.

Witness my hand and official seal at _____Nashville,_____Tennessee, this _____ day of _____, 19_____.

_____Notary Public

Commission expires_____

STATE OF TENNESSEE
COUNTY OF DAVIDSON

Before me,_____, a Notary Public of the State and County aforesaid, personally appeared_____, with whom I am personally acquainted with (or proved to me on the basis of satisfactory evidence), and who, upon oath, acknowledged _____ self to be _____ of the _____, the within named bargainor, a corporation, and that _____ he as such _____ being authorized so to do, executed the foregoing instrument for the purpose therein contained, by signing the name of the corporation by _____ self as _____.

Witness my hand and seal, at office in _____, this _____ day of _____, 19_____.

_____Notary Public

Commission expires_____

DEED OF TRUST

FROM

SHALOM SHANLEVER and wife,

MARY SHANLEVER

TO

LARRY LAWYER, TRUSTEE

Compliments of
Chicago Title Insurance Company
First Floor — First American Center
Phone 255-4631
NASHVILLE, TENNESSEE 37238

FIGURE 12-6. Deed of Trust, Page 2

earlier. Now you describe from whom the current owner purchased the property, giving book and page number where it is recorded. Note that in Figure 12-5, the Olsons, who appeared in the derivation clause in the previous warranty deed, were dropped off and the Shanlevers were added. Since the warranty deed and deed of trust may be recorded at the same time, a blank is provided for inserting the missing information at the time of recording, or terminology such as "Being the same property conveyed to the Grantors herein by Deed recorded simultaneously herewith" can be used.

G. Habendum.

H. Description of why the conveyance is being made.

I. Description of what will take place if payments are not made.

J. Signatures of grantors.

K. Acknowledgment.

DEED OF TRUST NOTE

A promissory note is a document in which the buyers promise to pay to the sellers a sum of money, which may be paid monthly, quarterly, semiannually, on some other schedule, or in one lump sum. A rate of interest is usually stated on the promissory note. A **deed of trust note** is a promissory note that accompanies a deed of trust. Read the deed of trust note in Figure 12-7 in which Shalom and Mary Shanlever (the buyers) agree to pay to Kurt and Lisa Ambrose (the sellers) $30,000 in monthly installments of $263.27 for 30 years with interest accumulating at the rate of 10 percent per year. The body of a deed of trust note indicates where payments are to be made, states that it is secured by a deed of trust, and provides a place for the signatures of the buyers who are the makers of the note.

DEED OF TRUST NOTE

A promissory note; a document in which the maker promises to pay to the lender a stated sum of money.

Once the term (number of years), interest rate, and total amount of the note are known, a monthly payment schedule (shown on page 327) can be used to determine the amount of equal monthly payments required to pay the loan. A booklet containing interest rates from 5 to 25 percent, amounts of loans from $500 to $500,000, and terms from 1 to 40 years, entitled *The Consumers Amortization Guide* can be ordered from Dugan Publishers, Inc., Gordensville, TN 38563. Many such booklets are published and can be found in most libraries and bookstores.

The procedure is to find the page with the interest rate (see the table on page 327), look down the left column to the total amount of the loan and follow the row to the column showing the total number of years to pay on the loan. The point at which the amount and years intersect is the monthly payment. Locate the amount of payment for $30,000 at 10 percent for 30 years; $263.27 is the amount shown as a monthly payment in the deed of trust note in Figure 12-7.

DEED OF TRUST NOTE

Amount: $30,000   Nashville, Tennessee   November 22, (current year)

Final Payment Due: December 1, (30 years from now)

     1. FOR VALUE RECEIVED the undersigned, hereinafter referred to as "Borrowers," promise to pay to the order of KURT AMBROSE and wife, LISA K. AMBROSE, hereinafter referred to as "Lenders," on or before the due date, the principle sum of Thirty Thousand and 00/100 Dollars ($30,000.00) in monthly installments as follows: On the 1st day of December, (current year) the sum of Two Hundred Sixty-three Dollars and Twenty-seven Cents ($263.27) and thereafter Two Hundred Sixty-three Dollars and Twenty-seven Cents ($263.27) the first day of each succeeding month, the last installment being due on the first day of December, (30 years from now). The unpaid principal will bear interest at the rate of ten percent (10%) per annum for a period of thirty (30) years.

     7. Upon default for any reason and under any circumstance, the Borrowers promise to pay all costs of collection, including but not limited to, reasonable attorney fees and all expenses incurred in the collection, whether or not suit is filed thereon.

     8. The Borrowers hereby waive demand, notice, and protest for the nonpayment or dishonor of this Note and failure to the Lenders, owners or holders of this Deed of Trust Note, to enforce any right herein granted shall not preclude the right of enforcement in any subsequent default or dishonor of payment. Any delay or omission on the part of the Lenders to exercise or enforce any right herein shall not operate as a bar to future actions on their part.

     9. All agreements and covenants between the Lenders and the Borrowers are expressly limited to those stated herein and any representations by the Lenders or their agent are not binding unless contained herein.

     10. The privilege of prepayment or repayment, in whole or in part, is reserved for the Borrowers without any penalty attaching.

     WITNESS the following signature of the Borrowers as of this the _____ day of November, (current year).

                                        _____

                                        SHALOM SHANLEVER

                                        _____

                                        MARY SHANLEVER

FIGURE 12-7. Deed of Trust Note

If the amount is not shown in the amount column, it can be computed; for example, if a loan is $37,000 for 25 years at 10 percent, the sum of the monthly payment for $35,000 for 25 years at 10 percent and the monthly payment for $2,000 for 25 years at 10 percent is the total monthly payment.

The monthly payment can also be determined by using a business calculator. With the calculator in financial mode, enter the number of payments (number of years x 12), the interest per period (10% ÷ 12 if payments are monthly), the total amount of the loan (as future value), then press PMT (for payment) and the amount of each monthly payment will be displayed. Various arrangements of payments can be made depending on agreements between the parties; for example, a large down payment may be made, with smaller monthly payments.

Monthly Payment Schedule
10 Percent Interest

Amount	24 Yrs.	25 Yrs.	28 Yrs.	29 Yrs.	30 Yrs.	35 Yrs.
20000	183.48	181.75	177.60	176.50	175.52	171.94
30000	275.22	272.62	266.39	264.75	263.27	257.91
35000	321.09	318.05	310.79	308.87	307.15	300.89
40000	366.96	363.49	355.19	353.00	351.03	343.87
50000	458.69	454.35	443.98	441.24	438.79	429.84
75000	688.04	681.53	665.97	661.86	658.18	644.75
100000	917.39	908.70	887.96	882.48	877.57	859.67

SETTLEMENT SHEETS

A **settlement sheet** is a statement showing all costs involved in a real estate transaction.

Information for preparing the settlement sheets is obtained from the **sales agreement**, a contract between the buyers and sellers, specifying the terms of the sale. A sales agreement is often supplied by a real estate agent but is a simple contract as discussed in Chapter 10.

Separate settlement sheets are prepared for the sellers and for the buyers. The sellers' settlement sheet shows all credits and charges to the sellers; the buyers', all credits and charges to the buyers.

SELLERS' SETTLEMENT SHEET
Items that increase the amount of cash the seller is to receive are credits to the seller's statement, and everything that decreases the amount of cash (something for which the seller pays or something that reduces what is received) is a debit or a charge.

SETTLEMENT SHEET

A statement showing all costs involved in a real estate transaction.

SALES AGREEMENT

A contract between the buyer and seller, specifying the terms of the sale.

Refer to Figure 12-8, the Sellers' Settlement Sheet, and locate the following information.

REAL ESTATE CLOSING

A meeting where all parties sign the documents and transfer money as outlined in the settlement sheets.

Real estate closing date. One must know the date the documents will be signed and the transaction completed, the **real estate closing** date, before preparing the settlement sheets. November 22, 19—, is the closing date for this transaction.

Property sold. The selling price is placed in the sellers' credit column.

Property taxes. Property taxes are usually paid yearly at the end of the year. If the sellers have owned the property for a portion of the year and have not paid property taxes, they owe a proportional share of the taxes.

Taxes are based on the assessed (estimated) value of the property, which is estimated by a public official known as a tax assessor. Tax rates, as well as assessed values, change from time to time. For this exercise, the tax rate is $4.81 per $100 based on 25 percent of the assessed value. The assessed value of the property is $80,000; 25% of the assessed value (25% x $80,000) is $20,000. Divide $20,000 by 100 = 200 to determine the number of 100s; multiply 200 x $4.81 to get total taxes of $962. To compute the amount of daily taxes, divide $962 by 365 = $2.6356. Divide by 366 if it is a leap year.

Calculate the number of days for which the sellers owe taxes. They owned the real estate from January 1 to November 22, which is 326 days, as shown below. Multiply 326 by $2.6356 to get $859.21, the amount the sellers owe for property taxes. Debit the sellers' account.

January	31
February	28
March	31
April	30
May	31
June	30
July	31
August	31
September	30
October	31
November	<u>22</u>
TOTAL DAYS	326

The Ambroses have not paid property taxes. If they had been paid, the sellers' account would have been credited for the unexpired portion (39 days at $2.6356 = $102.79 — it is 39 days from November 22 through December 31). The buyers' account would have been debited for the same amount.

Tax information is kept in the office of the trustee or public official who is designated to collect taxes. In many parts of the country, tax information can be accessed by anyone who wishes to use a computer in the trustee's office. It may also be possible to call the office to request tax information.

SELLERS' SETTLEMENT SHEET

DATE: November 22, 1993
SELLERS: KURT AMBROSE and wife, LISA K. AMBROSE
BUYERS: SHALOM SHANLEVER and wife, MARY SHANLEVER
PROPERTY: Davidson County, Tennessee

	Debits	Credits
Property Sold		$100,000.00
Prorata Current Year's Taxes		
1993 ($2.6356 per day — 326 days)	$ 859.21	
Earnest Money in Hands of "Seller"	1,000.00	
Vendor's Lien Retained by Seller	30,000.00	
Loan assumed: Superb Lending Company	50,000.00	
Attorney's Fee	220.70	
Title Policy — Titles, Inc.	500.00	
Closing Fee — Titles, Inc.	100.00	
Commission to Agent — Super Realtors	6,000.00	
Total Deductions	$ 88,679.91	
Proceeds to Seller (Difference between		
Deductions and Total Credits)	$ 11,320.09	
TOTALS	$100,000.00	$100,000.00

FIGURE 12-8. Sellers' Settlement Sheet

Earnest money. An amount of money deposited by the prospective buyer to ensure a good-faith intent to buy is referred to as **earnest** money. The earnest money is usually put in the care of a real estate agent when an offer to purchase real estate is made. Since the amount being held is the sellers' money and will be given to the sellers at closing, it is shown as a debit (reduction to the amount to be received). If the buyers are unable to obtain financing, they may lose this money.

Deed of trust note. Show the $30,000 deed of trust note as a reduction in cash dollars to be received by debiting the sellers' account.

Mortgage assumption. Show the amount of the mortgage assumed as a reduction in the cash dollars to be received by the sellers.

Attorney's fee. The attorney's fee is to be paid by the sellers, thus it is recorded as a debit. This is determined by the terms of the sales agreement.

Title insurance. It is customary for the sellers to pay for the title insurance; therefore, debit the account for $500.

Closing fees. Closing fees are expenses that must be paid in addition to the purchase price of the real estate and may include fees for title examination, appraisals, surveys, etc. The closing fee of $200 was split, with the sellers paying $100 and the buyers paying $100 — debit the sellers' account for their portion and debit the buyers' account for their portion. The terms of the sales agreement specify who is to pay each of the closing fees.

Commission. The sellers pay the $6,000 real estate commission fee. In this illustration, the fee charged by the real estate agent for selling the property is 6 percent of the selling price. If two real estate agents are involved in the transaction — one as a listing agent and one as selling agent — the fees are usually split, with 3 percent to one and 3 percent to the other.

Total. The expenses or debits are totaled, $88,679.91, and subtracted from the credits, $100,000. The resulting amount, $11,320.09, is the amount of cash the sellers will receive at closing.

BUYERS' SETTLEMENT SHEET

The selling price of the real estate plus each item the buyer is to pay are placed in the buyer's debit column, and any reductions (or credits) to those amounts go in the credit column.

Refer to Figure 12-9, the Buyers' Settlement Sheet, and locate the following information:

Selling price. The buyers' account is debited for the selling price of the house — an item they will pay.

Earnest money. The buyers' account is credited for the $1,000 earnest money, an amount already paid and held by the real estate agent.

Property taxes. See explanation of taxes under Sellers' Settlement Sheet. The taxes of $859.21 are not to be paid by the buyers.

BUYERS' SETTLEMENT SHEET

DATE: November 22, 1993
SELLERS: KURT AMBROSE and wife, LISA K. AMBROSE
BUYERS: SHALOM SHANLEVER and wife, MARY SHANLEVER
PROPERTY: Davidson County, Tennessee

	Debits	Credits
Property Purchased	$100,000.00	
Earnest Money deposited with Agent or "Seller"		$ 1,000.00
Prorata Current Year's Taxes 1993 ($2.6356 per day — 326 days)		859.21
Recording Deed — $9.00, Tax — $370.00	379.00	
Recording Mtg. — $9.00, Tax — $32.20	41.20	
Closing Fee — Titles, Inc.	100.00	
Mortgage assumed Superb Lending Company		50,000.00
Vendor's lien retained by Seller		30,000.00
Transfer Fee	45.00	
Cash to be Paid by Buyer		18,705.99
TOTALS	$100,565.20	$100,565.20

FIGURE 12-9. Buyers' Settlement Sheet

TRANSFER TAX

The charge for transferring property from one owner to another.

Deed recording and transfer fees. The buyers normally pay for recording the deed. There is a charge per page for recording the document plus a charge for transferring property from one owner to another, called a **transfer tax**. For this illustration, the cost of recording the document is $4 per page and a $1 fee for collecting the transfer tax — the minimum is $9. The transfer tax is 37 cents per $100 of value shown on the affidavit of value in the deed. (Divide $100,000 by 100 to get the number of 100s in the selling price. Multiply 1,000 x .37 to get the tax amount — $370.) A shortcut is to divide the .37 by 100 (.0037) and multiply by the value of the property, $100,000 x .0037.

Deed of trust recording fee and taxes. The charge for recording the deed of trust or any type of mortgage instrument is $4 per page plus a $1 fee for collecting the transfer tax — the minimum is $9. The tax is 11.5 cents per hundred with a $2,000 exemption. In our example, $30,000 minus $2,000 = $28,000 divided by $100 = 280 times 11.5 cents = $32.20. The amount can also be calculated by multiplying $28,000 by .00115.

Closing fees. The payment of the closing fee was split half and half. The buyers' account is debited for $100.

Transfer fee. The buyers are responsible for paying the $45 transfer fee for assuming the $50,000 mortgage from Superb Lending Company.

Loan assumption and deed of trust note. The reductions from the amounts to be paid are shown as credits; namely, $50,000 for a loan assumption, and $30,000 for a deed of trust note.

Total. The debits and credits are totaled, and the difference, $18,705.99, is placed in the credit column under "Cash to be paid by the Buyer."

Balancing the Sheets and Making Payment

The secretary is responsible for checking to see if the statements balance — making sure the amount of money received equals the amount of payments to be made.

The amount of money to be received from the buyers is $18,705.99.

Payments to be made as part of the closing procedure are as follows.

Proceeds to Sellers	$11,320.09
Attorney's fee	220.70
Title insurance	500.00
Closing fee	200.00
Real estate agent's fee	6,000.00
Recording deed	379.00
Recording deed of trust	41.20
Transfer fee	45.00
TOTAL	$18,705.99

The new owners will pay taxes when they receive the tax bill at the end of the year.

REAL ESTATE CLOSING

A real estate closing is a meeting where all parties sign the documents and money is transferred as outlined in the settlement sheets. For the Ambrose/Shanlever closing, Larry Lawyer (the seller's attorney), Kurt and Lisa Ambrose (the sellers), Shalom and Mary Shanlever (the buyers), and the legal secretary were present. The attorney not only directed all matters at the closing but also served as a third party, known as an **escrow agent**, to collect and distribute funds. The buyers brought a check to pay the amount due, as shown on the buyers' settlement sheet. They also signed a deed of trust and deed of trust note. The sellers signed the warranty deed. The secretary notarized the signatures and wrote a check, for the attorney's signature, to the sellers for the amount due them. The secretary was also responsible for writing all other checks as outlined on the previous page for handing the documents as follows:

ESCROW AGENT
One who holds funds and distributes them according to the contract.

- Original deed of trust note to the sellers, one copy to the buyers, and one copy for the files

- Buyer's settlement sheet to the buyers, one copy for the files

- Seller's settlement sheet to the sellers, one copy for the files

- Original deed to register's office; after recording, original to the buyers, one copy for the files

- Original deed of trust to register's office; after recording, original to the trustee, one copy for the files

INSTALLMENT DEED

Installment deeds are commonly used when the seller finances the unpaid balance owed by the buyer on a piece of property. The **installment deed** used as an illustration in this chapter is an instrument that transfers property from the seller to the buyer then to a trustee until the value of the property is paid in full with interest. All of this is accomplished in one document. The buyer takes possession of the property, agrees to keep the property in good repair, and pays taxes. When the loan is paid in full, the trustee releases title to the buyer.

INSTALLMENT DEED
The type of deed in which the seller finances the unpaid balance owed by the buyer on a piece of property.

Read the installment deed in Figures 12-10 through 12-13, in which Dale Makens is transferring a piece of property to Matthew and Angela Snyder. The Snyders then transfer the property to Larry Lawyer, the trustee.

QUITCLAIM DEED

A **quitclaim** (or quit-claim) deed transfers whatever interest the grantor has in property to the grantee. It has no guarantees to protect the grantee from claims by previous owners.

QUITCLAIM DEED
A deed that transfers only the ownership that one has in property with no further warranties.

Installment Deed

ADDRESS NEW OWNER(S) AS FOLLOWS:	SEND TAX BILLS TO:	MAP PARCEL NUMBERS
MATTHEW SNYDER et ux.	SAME	MAP 81-15
(NAME)	(NAME)	
601 Deer Lake Drive		PAR. 150
(STREET ADDRESS OR ROUTE NUMBER)	(STREET ADDRESS)	
Nashville, TN 37207		
(CITY) (P.O. ZONE) (ZIP)	(CITY) (ZONE) (ZIP)	

FOR AND IN CONSIDERATION of the sum of - - - - - - - - Ten Thousand (10,000) - - - - - - - - *Dollars,*

of which - Three Thousand (3,000) -

- *Dollars, has been paid in cash,*

the receipt of which is hereby acknowledged, and for the remainder - - - - - - Seven Thousand (7,000) - - - - -

- *Dollars,*

MATTHEW SNYDER, and wife, ANGELA SNYDER ....*have executed*

their joint promissory note of even date herewith in the amount of Seven Thousand Dollars ($7,000) with interest from date at the rate of nine percent (9%) per annum payable to the order of DALE MAKENS in 36 monthly installments of principal and interest of Two Hundred Twenty-two Dollars and Sixty Cents ($222.60) beginning January 31, (current year), and continuing with one successive monthly installment falling due on the first day of each succeeding month thereafter until said note and interest are paid in full, the last monthly installment for the balance then remaining unpaid falling due January 31, (three years from now),

and providing for payment of attorney's fees, and to secure the payment of said indebtedness, principal, interest, and

attorney fees, a lien is expressly retained on the land herein conveyed,..

I, DALE MAKENS, unmarried,

have this day bargained and sold, and do hereby transfer and convey unto the said..............................

MATTHEW SNYDER, and wife, ANGELA SNYDER, their

....*(successors), heirs and assigns,*

certain real estate in Davidson County, Tennessee, as follows:

Being the northerly 56 feet of the southerly 100 feet of lot Nos. 120 and 121 on the Map of Treetop Acres as of record in Book 377, page 208, Register's Office for said County. Said part of Lots Nos. 120 and 121 fronts 56 feet on the westerly side of Treetop Drive and runs back between parallel lines 100 feet, more or less, to a dead line.

Being the same property conveyed to the within-named Grantor by deed of RAYMOND SPAULDING et ux. as of record in Book 8926, page 331, said Register's Office. This conveyance is made subject to restrictive covenants of record.

STATE OF TENNESSEE COUNTY OF DAVIDSON } The actual consideration or value whichever is greater, for this transfer is $10,000.00
Subscribed and sworn to before me, this the _____ day of
_____ 19 ____.   _____
Affiant
My commission expires: _____   _____
(Affix Seal)   **Notary Public**

FIGURE 12-10. Installment Deed, Page 1

unimproved ( )
This is improved (X) **property, known as** .... 313 Treetop Drive .... Nashville, TN 37207 ....

                        (House Number)   (Street)   **P. O. Address:**   (City or Town)

TO HAVE AND TO HOLD said real estate with the appurtenances, estate, title and interest thereto belonging, to
the said.......... MATTHEW SNYDER, and wife, ANGELA SNYDER, ...

..........*(successors)*,

heirs and assigns forever. ...We....*covenant that* ......we are.... *lawfully seized and possessed of said real estate in fee*
simple, have a good right to convey it, and that the same is unencumbered

except taxes for (current year), which have been prorated between the parties and
assumed by the grantees.

     I.........*further covenant and bind* ....myself, my.......... *heirs and representatives, to*
warrant and forever defend the title to said real estate to said ....MATTHEW SNYDER, and wife, ANGELA SNYDER,
their..........

(successors), heirs and assigns, against the lawful claims of all persons.

    And now, for the purpose of better and more effectually securing the payment of said lien indebtedness; rendering
unnecessary court proceedings for the enforcement of said lien in the event of the non-payment of said indebtedness and
installments thereof, as they mature, as hereinafter provided, and for the consideration of one dollar paid in cash,
receipt of which is acknowledged, the said ....MATTHEW SNYDER, and wife, ANGELA SNYDER,..........,

....

hereinafter referred to as trustors, hereby transfer and convey unto ....LARRY LAWYER..........,
Trustee, his successors and assigns, the real estate hereinbefore described, with the appurtenances, estate, title and
interest thereto belonging upon the following uses and trusts:

    Trustors agree to keep all buildings now on, or to be hereafter erected on said property, insured in some reliable
fire insurance company, or companies, for the sum of $ ....N/A.........., *or at least the maximum insurable value, until*
the indebtedness herein secured is fully paid, and to have the loss, if any, made payable on the policy, or policies, to said
trustee for the benefit of the lawful owner or holder of said indebtedness as his interest may appear.

    Trustors further agree to pay all taxes and assessments thereon, general or special, and to pay them when due,
and, upon demand of said trustee or the lawful owner and holder of said indebtedness, to pay, discharge, or remove,
any and all liens which may be hereafter placed against said property and which shall adversely affect the lien of this
instrument or enforcement of the terms and provisions hereof; to keep the improvements on said property in good
repair and preservation, and in case the trustee or his successors or the lawful owner and holder of said indebtedness
shall hereafter be required to appear in any court or tribunal to enforce, or defend the title to, or possession of, said
property, or the lien of this instrument, or appear in any court to prove the above indebtedness, all the costs and

FIGURE 12-11. Installment Deed, Page 2

by trustors upon demand of the trustee or lawful owner or holder of said indebtedness, and, upon failure to do any of these things, then said trustee, or the lawful owner and holder of said indebtedness may do any or all of these things and the amounts so paid shall bear 6 percent interest from the date of payment and shall be and become a part of the indebtedness secured hereby.

Now if trustors shall pay the indebtedness aforesaid when due, according to its terms, and pay taxes, keep up repairs, and keep said premises insured, and pay any and all other sums when due, as aforesaid, then this trust conveyance shall be of no further force of effect. But if said indebtedness, or any installment thereof, or interest thereon, is not paid promptly at maturity, or if, failing to pay taxes, keep up repairs or keep said premises insured, or pay said other sums when due, as herein provided, trustors fail to reimburse the trustee, or lawful owner and holder f said indebtedness for all sums, with interest, so expended by said trustee, or lawful owner and holder of said indebtedness, within thirty days from date of such payment, this trust conveyance shall remain in full force and effect, and at the option of the lawful owner and holder of said indebtedness then past due and unpaid, all remaining unpaid indebtedness, and installments thereof, shall become due and payable at once, without notice, and the said trustee, or his successor in trust, is hereby authorized and empowered, upon giving twenty days' notice by three publications in any newspaper, daily or weekly, published in Davidson County, Tennessee, to sell said property at the front door of the Court House in said County to the highest bidder for cash, at public outcry, free from the equity of redemption, homestead, dower and all other exemptions of every kind, which are hereby expressly waived; and the said trustee, or his successor in trust, is authorized and empowered to execute and deliver a deed to the purchaser. The creditor may bid at any sale under this trust conveyance. The trustee may, at any time after default in the payment of any said indebtedness, enter and take possession of said property, and shall only account for the net rents actually received by him. It is further agreed that, in the event the trustee fails, before selling said property, as herein provided, to enter and take possession thereof, the purchaser shall be entitled to immediate possession thereof upon the delivery to him by the trustee of a deed for said property. In case of sale hereunder, the proceeds will be applied by the trustee as follows:

1st. To the payment of all costs, charges and expenses of executing this conveyance and enforcing said lien as herein provided; also reasonable attorney's fees for advice in the premises, or for instituting or defending any litigation which may arise on account of the execution of this conveyance, or the enforcement of said lien; also the expenses of any such litigation

2nd. To the payment of all taxes which may be unpaid on said premises.

3rd. To the payment of all unpaid indebtedness herein secured, and any and all sums expended in the protection of said property, as herein authorized.

4th. The residue, if any, will be paid to trustors, their order, representatives or assigns.

In case of the death, absence, inability, or refusal to act of said trustee at any time when action under the foregoing power and trusts may be required, the lawful owner and holder of said indebtedness, or, if more than one when said indebtedness is represented by notes, then of the first-maturing unpaid note, or upon his refusal or failure so to do, then the holder in order of the next maturing notes, is hereby authorized and empowered to name and appoint a successor to execute this trust by an instrument in writing to be recorded in the Register's Office for Davidson County, Tennessee, and the title herein conveyed to the above named trustee shall be vested in said successor.

The word "Trustors" when used herein shall apply to parties both singular and plural.

IN WITNESS WHEREOF the parties to this instrument have signed their names, and the corporate party has caused its name to be signed hereto by its duly authorized officers, on this the .... day of ...., 19........

....
DALE MACKENS
....

....
MATTHEW SNYDER
....

....
ANGELA SNYDER
....

STATE OF TENNESSEE }
COUNTY OF DAVIDSON

Personally appeared before me, ... the undersigned ...., *a Notary Public in and for said County and State,* ..... DALE MACKENS, MATTHEW SNYDER and wife, ANGELA SNYDER, ...

....

....

the within named bargainor ...^s....., *with whom I am personally acquainted, and who acknowledged that* .... they ......

executed the within instrument for the purposes therein contained.

Witness my hand and official seal at ..... Nashville, ... *Tennessee,*

this the .... *day of* ...., 19............

....*Notary Public*

Commission expires..

FIGURE 12-12. Installment Deed, Page 3

STATE OF .... }

COUNTY OF.................................. }

    Personally appeared before me, ..., a Notary Public in and

for said County and State, ...

the within named bargainor..............., with whom I am personally acquainted, and who acknowledged that ....

executed the within instrument for the purposes therein contained.

    Witness my hand and official seal at...,

this the .... day of ...., 19................

                                                   ..Notary Public

                                Commission expires..

STATE OF TENNESSEE }
COUNTY OF DAVIDSON }

    Before me, ..., a Notary Public of the State and

County aforesaid, personally appeared ....,

with whom I am personally acquainted, and who, upon oath, acknowledged ....self to be................................

.. of the ....,

the within named bargainor, a corporation, and that ....he as such ....,

being authorized so to do, executed the foregoing instrument for the purpose therein contained, by signing the name of

the corporation by ....self as ....

    Witness my hand and seal, at office in ....,

this the .... day of ...., 19................

                                                   ..Notary Public

                                Commission expires..

INSTALLMENT DEED

FROM

DALE MACKENS

TO

MATTHEW SNYDER and wife,

ANGELA SNYDER

Chicago Title Insurance Company
First American Center — Phone 255-4631
NASHVILLE, TENNESSEE 37238

FIGURE 12-13. Installment Deed, Page 4

Some attorneys use quitclaim deeds in divorce settlements to transfer real property from both to one of the parties. By using a quitclaim deed, the grantor has no involvement in rectifying subsequent claims against the property.

The quitclaim deed shown in Figures 12-14 and 12-15 conveys ownership from a married couple, Michael Wayne Queener and Victoria Ann Queener, to a trustee, Larry Lawyer, then from the trustee to Victoria. Notice that the parts to the deed are similar to those in the warranty deed, except the quitclaim deed has no warranties and no habendum. Two acknowledgments are provided — one for the grantors and one for the trustee.

QUITCLAIM DEED

ADDRESS NEW OWNER(S) AS FOLLOWS:	SEND TAX BILLS TO:	MAP PARCEL NUMBERS
VICTORIA ANN QUEENER	FIRST NATIONAL SAVINGS AND LOAN	MAP 51-4
(NAME)	(NAME)	
555 Oak Valley Drive	353 Church Street	PAR. 2
(STREET ADDRESS OR ROUTE NUMBER)	(STREET ADDRESS)	
Madison, TN 37115	Nashville, TN 37219	
(CITY) (STATE) (P.O. ZIP)	(CITY) (STATE) (ZIP)	

FOR AND IN CONSIDERATION of love and affection (and no monetary consideration) and for the express purpose of making a re-conveyance to ___ VICTORIA ANN QUEENER, ___

We, ___ MICHAEL WAYNE QUEENER and VICTORIA ANN QUEENER ___

by these presents do hereby quitclaim and convey unto ___ LARRY LAWYER ___ ,

Trustee, his successors and assigns, the following described tract or parcel of land, to wit:

Land in Davidson County, Tennessee, being Lot No. 30 in the Map of Horseshoe Bend, Section II, of record in Book 8442, page 60, Register's Office for said County.

Said Lot No. 30 fronts one hundred thirty-three and twenty-two one hundredths (133.22) feet on the West side of Oak Valley Drive and runs back three hundred (300) feet on the North line and three hundred twenty-five and fifteen one hundredths (325.15) feet on the South line, to a dead line measuring one hundred twenty (120) feet.

Being the same property conveyed to MICHAEL WAYNE QUEENER and wife, VICTORIA ANN QUEENER, by Warranty Deed from FRANK FRISCH and wife, KAY S. FRISCH, of record in Book 3629, page 1, Register's Office for Davidson County, Tennessee.

STATE OF TENNESSEE }
COUNTY OF DAVIDSON }   The actual consideration or value whichever is greater, for this transfer is $ none
Subscribed and sworn to before me, this the _____ day of
_____, 19___.   Affiant _____

My commission expires: _____
                        (Affix Seal)   Notary Public

unimproved ( )
This is improved (x) property, known as ___ 555 Oak Valley Drive Madison, TN 37115 ___
                    (House Number) (Street) P.O. Address: (City or Town) (Postal Zone)

Said property is conveyed subject to such limitations, restrictions, and encumbrances as may affect the premises.

And now, I, the said ___ LARRY LAWYER ___ , *Trustee, for the express purpose of carrying out the intent of this conveyance, as above set out, do hereby quitclaim and convey unto* ___ VICTORIA ANN QUEENER ___

_____ *heirs and assigns, the same property hereinabove described and set forth, to which reference is here made, and said property is conveyed subject to the same limitations, restrictions and encumbrances as may affect the premises, as above set forth.*

IN WITNESS WHEREOF we have hereunto set our hands on this the _____ day of _____, 19___.

_____
MICHAEL WAYNE QUEENER

THIS INSTRUMENT WAS PREPARED BY:
LARRY LAWYER   _____
Law Associates   VICTORIA ANN QUEENER
2400 River Road, Suite 400
Nashville, TN 37217   _____
                       LARRY LAWYER   *Trustee*

FIGURE 12-14. Quitclaim, Page 1

STATE OF TENNESSEE }
COUNTY OF DAVIDSON

Personally appeared before me, ...undersigned.. , a Notary Public in and for said County and State, the within named, MICHAEL WAYNE QUEENER and VICTORIA ANN QUEENER, the Bargainors, with whom I am personally acquainted, and who acknowledged that they executed the within instrument for the purposes therein contained.

WITNESS my hand and official seal at Nashville, Tennessee, this the .... day of ...., 19..........

....Notary Public

My commission expires:.....................................

STATE OF TENNESSEE }
COUNTY OF DAVIDSON

Personally appeared before me,...the undersigned...................................., a Notary Public in and for said County and State, the within named....LARRY LAWYER...................................., Trustee, the bargainor, with whom I am personally acquainted, and who acknowledged that he, as Trustee, executed the within instrument for the purposes therein contained.

WITNESS my hand and official seal at Nashville, Tennessee, this the .... day of ...., 19..........

....Notary Public

My commission expires:.....................................

QUITCLAIM **Deed**

From: MICHAEL WAYNE QUEENER et ux.

to: LARRY LAWYER, Trustee.

AND

From: LARRY LAWYER, Trustee.

to: VICTORIA ANN QUEENER

Compliments of
Chicago Title Insurance Company
S.W. Corner Third & Union
Phone 256-2656
NASHVILLE, TENNESSEE 37201

FIGURE 12-15. Quitclaim, Page 2

SUMMARY

- A deed has premises, habendum, warranties, and testimonium. The premises include four parts — names of grantors and grantees, consideration, conveyance clause, and property description with a derivation clause.

- Deeds must be recorded at the county register's office.

- Most deeds are typed on 8 ½ by 14-inch paper and may be double- or single-spaced. Property descriptions are indented and single-spaced.

- Deed forms are often used for preparing deeds. This allows the secretary to fill in blanks where variable information is needed.

- Four types of deeds are warranty deed, deed of trust, installment deed, and quitclaim deed.

- A deed of trust transfers ownership of property to a trustee to secure a debt until it is paid in full.

- A warranty deed is the most desirable type of deed because it contains general warranties that the seller will warrant and defend the title against any claims by previous owners.

- Installment deeds are commonly used where the seller finances the unpaid balance owed on a piece of property. The buyer makes installment payments to the seller, keeps the property in good repair, and pays taxes.

- Quitclaim deeds transfer only the ownership that one has or may have in property, with no warranties.

- The secretary is usually responsible for constructing the derivation clause in a deed. As property is transferred from one owner to the other, the clause has to be changed to identify the most recent previous owner.

- A deed of trust note should be prepared for the amount owed to the lender by the borrower. The amount of the indebtedness, interest rate, monthly payments, and term should be stated on the note.

- A settlement sheet should be prepared for the buyer and for the seller to list all charges and credits to the parties' accounts. The amount of money to be collected from the buyer and distributed to the seller and to pay expenses for the transaction must balance.

REVIEW EXERCISES

T   F   1.   The testimonium clause begins with "To have and to hold."

T   F   2.   A fee is charged for recording a warranty deed and a deed of trust.

T   F   3.   Property descriptions should be proofread very carefully by having one person read aloud from the original as the other checks the typed copy.

T   F   4.   In property descriptions, key northerly, southerly, easterly, and westerly with initial caps.

T   F   5.   Property descriptions should be single-spaced and indented except when printed forms are used.

T   F   6.   The full amount to be paid for a piece of property must be inserted on a warranty deed after the words "For and in consideration of the sum of."

T   F   7.   The seller is the grantee.

T   F   8.   The acknowledgments for an individual and for a corporation are identical.

T   F   9.   It is important to include the name and address of the person who prepared a deed or deed of trust on the instrument so as to establish legal responsibility for its content.

T   F   10.   A deed of trust is identical to a mortgage.

T   F   11.   An affidavit of value should be included on the deed of trust.

T   F   12.   One can determine the equal monthly payment required to pay off a loan if the amount of a loan and the interest rate are known.

CALCULATION AND TRANSCRIPTION EXERCISES

Answer the following questions. Show your calculations for Questions 1, 2, and 4.

1. Assuming the date of sale is August 25 and it is not a leap year, for how many days must the seller be charged for unpaid taxes?

2. If a person has a $75,000, 30-year, 10 percent loan, what is the amount of each monthly payment? Use the schedule on page 327 of this chapter.

3. For how many days are the sellers of property responsible for paying taxes if the date of sale is April 22, 19—? (19— is not a leap year.)

4. What is the cost of recording a deed and paying the transfer tax if the charge is $4 per page plus a $1 fee for collecting the tax (your deed has three pages and the minimum amount is $9)? The tax is 37 cents per $100, and the value of the property is $85,000.

Use a secretarial reference manual and the material presented in this and previous chapters to aid you in correctly transcribing the following material. There are incorrectly used terms and misspelled words in the sentences. Hint: Make sure the correct parties are identified.

5. (An old deed contains the derivation clause shown below. The Gentrys are conveying the property to a new owner, Hunter McCulloch and wife, Marie McCulloch. Prepare the derivation clause for the new deed.)

   Being the same property conveyed to Hal Gentry and wife, Susan Gentry, by Deed from Al Smith and wife, Susan Smith, of record in Book 213, page 404, of the Register's (or Registrar's) office for (Your County), (Your State).

6. (Spell out all references in the following property description): thence leaving said harding street south 56 degrees 30 minutes 0 seconds west 233.38 feet to an iron pin thence north 17 degrees 27 minutes 11 seconds east 161.04 feet to an iron pin thence north 09 degrees 10 minutes 16 seconds east 25.11 feet to an iron pin

7. (Transcribe the portion of a property description shown above, but use symbols for the directions and lengths of lines.)

8. for and in consideration of the sum of 84 thousand dollars cash in hand paid the reciept and sufficiency of which is hereby acknowledged we the undersigned have bargained and sold and do convey to the grantors the following property

9. to have and to hold the said tract or parcel of land with the appurtenances estate title and interest thereto belonging to the said grantees their heirs and assigns forever

10. for value received i promise to pay to stephen haggard the principle sum of 12 thousand dollars

RESEARCH ACTIVITIES

1. Go to the register's office in your county and make a copy of a warranty deed and deed of trust (or other mortgage instrument). Compare them to the instruments presented in this chapter.

2. Call or go to the register's office in your county to get a fee schedule for recording real estate documents.

3. Go to the office in your county where tax information can be obtained. If a computerized system is available, ask someone to show you how to access the information.

4. Try to locate a copy of a monthly payment schedule booklet in your library or local bookstore. Learn the types of information available in the booklet and write down the name of the booklet, the publisher, and publisher's address where the booklet can be ordered.

PROJECTS

Project 12-1   Transcribe a form for a warranty deed. The material dictated is taken from a form designed by Chicago Title Insurance Company, First American Center, Nashville, Tennessee, shown in Figures 12-1 and 12-2. At points where variable information is to be input, the dictator will say, "Input," and describe the type of information to be inserted.

Project 12-2   Merge the warranty deed form created in Project 12-1 with the information provided below: This is a transfer of property from Duncan Horsley and wife, Debra Horsley, to Buford Elamon and wife, Tawana Elamon. Duncan and Debra Horsley have contacted Roger D. MacKenzie, an attorney, to represent them. His address is P.O. Box 747, Springfield, MO 63841. Phone: (417) 376-8462. The closing meeting is September 24, 19—. When the document is completed, label the parts of the warranty deed in the left margin.

INPUT INFORMATION FOR PROJECT 12-2

Date: September 19—

Attorney: Roger D. MacKenzie, P.O. Box 747, Springfield, MO 63841.

New Owner and Grantee: BUFORD ELAMON et ux., 507 College Street, Springfield, MO 65641. This is the address of the new property, which is improved property, valued at $120,000.

Grantors: DUNCAN HORSLEY and wife, DEBRA HORSLEY

Send tax bills to: Federal Savings, P.O. Box 3782, Dallas, TX 75228

Map No. 51-4, Parcel No. 2

Gender: I or we (as appropriate)

Springfield, Missouri, is in Greene County.

Property description as follows:

> Land in Greene County, Missouri, beginning at a point on the center line
> of Limestone Road, one hundred fifteen (115) feet South, fifty-six (56)
> degrees, forty-five (45) seconds West one hundred fifteen (115) feet
> from the Southeast corner of the property of DAN CHRISTOPH,
> running thence with the middle of the said Limestone Road North fifty-
> six (56) degrees, forty-five (45) seconds East one hundred fifteen (115)
> feet to the Southeast corner of the property of the said DAN
> CHRISTOPH; thence with the CHRISTOPH line North thirty-four (34)
> degrees, forty-five (45) minutes West three hundred fifteen and fifteen
> one hundredths (315.15) feet to CHRISTOPH's corner; thence in a
> southwesterly direction a distance of seventy-five (75) feet to a point;
> thence in a southerly direction approximately three hundred fourteen
> (314) feet to the point of beginning. Said property consists of three-
> fourths (3/4) acre, more or less.

Derivation clause:

> Being the same property conveyed to DUNCAN HORSLEY and wife,
> DEBRA HORSLEY, by Deed from PHILHALL CORPORATION of
> record in Book 312, page 303, Register's Office for Greene County,
> Missouri.

Project 12-3   Transcribe a sales contract for the parties in Project 12-2 (see
            Chapter 10 for formatting instructions).

Project 12-4   Prepare a settlement sheet for the transactions in Projects 12-2
            and 12-3 from the information given in the dictation and from the
            warranty deed and sales contract. Assume the same rates as given
            in the text for recording the warranty deed for transfer fees.
            Property taxes for this transfer are $1,443. Suggestion: Set up a
            form similar to Figures 12-8 and 12-9, then listen to the dictation.

Project 12-5   Transcribe a deed of trust note. You are to determine and insert
            the amount of the monthly payments.

UNIT IV
PERFORMANCE ASSESSMENT

A. The following document has spelling, grammar, punctuation, and word-choice errors. Mark each error on the copy below using proofreaders' symbols. Key and print a corrected copy of the document.

This is a simple contract between Hershell E. Frierson and Robert Nash.

Contract for the Purchase of Certain Inventory

On this the 22nd day of June, current year, HERSHELL E. FRIERSON, the hereinafter called "seller", and ROBERT N. NASH, the hereinafter called "buyer", have entered into the following agreement.

The seller agrees to sale to the buyer his entire stock of Amana, General Electric, Hot Point, and Carrier refrigeraters currently located on the show room floor of Frierson's Furniture Store along with all stock located in the sellers wearhouse located at 125 Foster Avenue, West Port, Connecticut. It is further agreed that neither the seller nor Frierson's Furniture Store will carry the above named line of refrigerators for a period of three years from the date of this agreement. As an agreed upon price for the said inventory the parties agree that the merchandise shall be the amount of the invoices of the original cost on each and every item along with an additional ten per cent added for freight and expenses, and then a deduction made for any depreciation in value on account of damage ware and tare.

If the parties herein can not agree as to the valuation and deduction the same shall be determined and settled according to the appraised value by two merchents with each party to have the selection of one of the appraisers. If the referees cannot agree between themselves, they may select a third person umpire to decide any differences existing between them. The inventory, appraisal, and delivery is to take place immediately, time being of the essance.

Upon delivery, the buyer will pay down one third the agreed upon value with the remaining two thirds being represented by two separate promissory notes each representing one third of the value. The first said promissory note shall be dew and payable one year from the date of this agreement with the other being dew and payable on the second anniversary of this agreement. Each note shall carry the prevailing prime interest rate as stated in the Wall Street Journal on that date.

　　　　IN WITNESS WHEREFORE the parties hereto subscribe there name on this the _____ day of June, current year.

　　　　　　　　_____
　　　　　　　　Buyer

　　　　　　　　_____
　　　　　　　　Seller

B. Place the cassette tape for Performance Assessment IV in the transcriber. Transcribe IV-B, the Articles of Incorporation of Moore's Motor Boat & Fishing Supplies Inc. The attorney is Desmond M. Long, 2234 Clay Lick Drive, Madison, Arkansas 72359. Phone: (501) 382-8632. The incorporators are Fred L. Moore and his wife, Betsy M. Moore. The store address is Sanders Marina, 1250 East Valley Road, Madison, Arkansas 72359.

C. Listen to the recorded instructions on the cassette tape for completing Item IV-C. You will be instructed to retrieve a previously created document and will be given instructions for altering it to be used in the Moore's Motor Boat & Fishing Supplies Inc. matter.

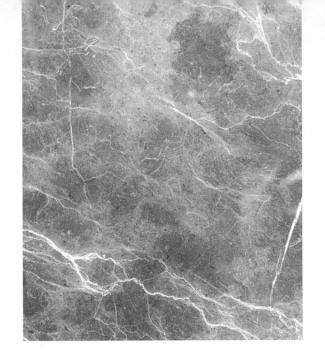

UNIT V
BANKRUPTCY

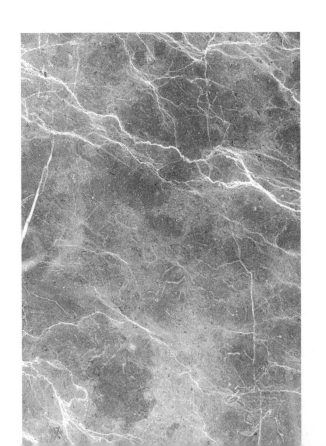

JOB DESCRIPTION
TRANSCRIPTION RESPONSIBILITIES

JOB TITLE: Legal Secretary

AREA OF PRACTICE: Bankruptcy

TRANSCRIPTION DUTIES:

1. Correctly inserts information in all forms of a bankruptcy packet.

2. Transfers totals from Schedules A through J to the Summary of Schedules.

3. Prepares an address mailing list according to the rules of the local bankruptcy court.

4. Uses word processing capabilities to alphabetize the list of creditors on the address mailing list.

CHAPTER 13

BANKRUPTCY

OBJECTIVES

When you successfully complete this chapter, you will be able to:

➤ Prepare schedules for a Chapter 7 liquidation

➤ Prepare the statement of affairs for a Chapter 7 liquidation

➤ Prepare the address matrix for a Chapter 7 liquidation

INTRODUCTION

Bankruptcy is a way to get out of debt and start over again. Some of the major causes for filing bankruptcies are divorce and separation, large medical debts, loss of a job, accidents resulting in a lawsuit, and mismanagement.

Most people who contact an attorney to discuss filing a bankruptcy are at the point where they are about to lose their homes or cars. The trustee or mortgage company may be threatening foreclosure on the home, putting it up for sale because monthly payments are not being made. The bank or lending agency may be threatening repossession of the car because payments are overdue. The situation is stressful for the client, who wants immediate help.

The process generally begins when the secretary answers the phone and either schedules an appointment for the caller or transfers the call to the attorney. At the initial meeting, the attorney evaluates the client's financial situation and explains the options available under the bankruptcy laws. If filing bankruptcy is recommended, the client is instructed to provide a list of creditors' names and addresses and the amounts owed and is interviewed to obtain information for completing the bankruptcy forms.

The accuracy of the information placed on those forms is the attorney's responsibility; however, the more a legal secretary is familiar with the content and format of those forms, the more he or she can do to aid the attorney. The purpose of this chapter is to provide background information about bankruptcy and to discuss the information placed on the forms filed in a bankruptcy matter.

A bankruptcy is filed on the behalf of one who owes debts, the **debtor**. The person or company to whom those debts are owed is the **creditor**. When a

DEBTOR
One who owes debts.

CREDITOR
One to whom money is owed.

VOLUNTARY BANKRUPTCY

A bankruptcy procedure initiated by the debtor. See involuntary bankruptcy.

INVOLUNTARY BANKRUPTCY

A bankruptcy procedure initiated by creditors against an individual or a company. See voluntary bankruptcy.

STRAIGHT BANKRUPTCY

A Chapter 7 bankruptcy; also called a liquidation.

DISCHARGE OF DEBTS

Debts are canceled or paid off entirely.

BANKRUPTCY PACKET

A packet of forms for filing a bankruptcy.

secretary is ready to enter information on the forms, it is essential to know the type of bankruptcy because each type consists of a different combination of forms. The matter can be either voluntary or involuntary. A **voluntary** bankruptcy is filed by the debtor who cannot pay his or her bills; an **involuntary** bankruptcy is filed by the creditors who are not being paid. A bankruptcy is filed in the district where the debtor has resided for the preceding six months. Well over 90 percent of the bankruptcies that are filed are voluntary cases.

Bankruptcies are federal matters and are always filed in federal bankruptcy courts. Federal laws (statutes) are printed in volumes of books known as the *United States Code*. The code is divided into "titles" and subdivided into "chapters." The bankruptcy laws are from Title 11 of the *United States Code* and specific types of bankruptcies are identified by chapter numbers; they are Chapters 7, 9, 11, 12, and 13. Our discussion will be limited to a Chapter 7 bankruptcy.

Chapter 7, also called a **straight bankruptcy or liquidation**, is a type of bankruptcy for individuals and some types of businesses where the debtor's property not exempted by law is sold to pay the creditors. A **trustee** is appointed to handle the sale of the nonexempt property and pay creditors as required by law. Any amounts owed to creditors that remain unpaid after the trustee distributes all available funds do not have to be paid by the debtor and are canceled, or **discharged**. Certain types of debts, such as alimony, child support, and income taxes from the previous three years, cannot be discharged in bankruptcy.

A **bankruptcy packet** consists of the forms to be used in filing a bankruptcy. The content and format of the official forms are also printed in Title 11 of the *United States Code*. Bankruptcy packets can be purchased from office supply stores or printing companies.

To file a voluntary Chapter 7, straight bankruptcy, prepare an original and two copies (all with original signatures) of the forms listed in the box shown on the following page, assemble them in sets in the order listed, and file them with the bankruptcy court clerk. Prepare an extra copy for the office files. To receive a copy from the clerk's office stamped "filed," send an extra copy with a return envelope and return postage.

VOLUNTARY PETITION

FILING OF PLAN

ATTORNEY'S DISCLOSURE OF COMPENSATION

**APPLICATION TO PAY FILING FEES IN INSTALLMENTS
(IF APPLICABLE)**

**AFFIDAVIT FOR PAYMENT OF FEES IN INSTALLMENTS
(IF APPLICABLE)**

SUMMARY OF SCHEDULES

SCHEDULES A THROUGH J

STATEMENT OF FINANCIAL AFFAIRS

INDIVIDUAL DEBTOR'S STATEMENT OF INTENTION

**UNSWORN DECLARATION CONCERNING
DEBTOR'S SCHEDULES**

ADDRESSES FOR MAILING LABELS

Remove the bankruptcy forms from the back of your book and read the information requested on each form, one form at a time, then read the instructions in this chapter for completing the form. Sample forms from a bankruptcy filed by Andrew Smith, the debtor, are provided in the figures to provide an example of the format for a completed form.

VOLUNTARY PETITION

A **petition,** shown in Figure 13-2, is the official form that is stamped by the clerk of the court. Once stamped, it creates what is referred to as a stay, which means that creditors cannot continue to contact the debtor to collect amounts owed.

BANKRUPTCY PETITION

The document that initiates a bankruptcy procedure.

On this form, as well as many of the other forms in the bankruptcy packet, you must provide the federal district and state in which the bankruptcy court is located. See the list of courts in Figure 13-1.

Also requested are the name (or names, if joint) of the debtor, social security or tax ID (if a business), address, county of residence, as well as other names used by the debtor. If an individual's name is Andrew Smith, other names might be Andrew R. Smith or Buddy Smith. Be sure to include any nicknames used by the debtor.

Place lowercase *x*'s in the small boxes provided on the form to indicate (1) venue, (2) type of debtor, (3) nature of debt, (4) type of business, (5) chapter of Bankruptcy Code, and (6) method of paying the filing fee. To file in the specified district, the debtor must meet the 180-day residency requirement as explained on the form.

FEDERAL BANKRUPTCY JUDICIAL DISTRICTS

States Not Listed Have Only One Bankruptcy Court

State	Section
Alabama	Northern, Middle, Southern
Arkansas	Eastern, Western
California	Northern, Eastern, Central, Southern
Florida	Northern, Middle, Southern
Georgia	Northern, Middle, Southern
Illinois	Northern, Central, Southern
Indiana	Northern, Southern
Iowa	Northern, Southern
Kentucky	Eastern, Western
Louisiana	Eastern, Middle, Western
Michigan	Eastern, Western
Mississippi	Northern, Southern
Missouri	Eastern, Western
New York	Northern, Southern, Eastern, Western
North Carolina	Eastern, Middle, Western
Ohio	Northern, Southern
Oklahoma	Northern, Eastern, Western
Pennsylvania	Eastern, Middle, Western
Tennessee	Eastern, Middle, Western
Texas	Northern, Eastern, Southern, Western
Virginia	Eastern, Western
Washington	Eastern, Western
West Virginia	Northern, Southern
Wisconsin	Eastern, Western

FIGURE 13-1. List of Federal Bankruptcy Districts

UNITED STATE BANKRUPTCY COURT MIDDLE DISTRICT OF TENNESSEE	VOLUNTARY PETITION

IN RE (Name of debtor—If individual, enter Last, First, Middle) SMITH, ANDREW	NAME OF JOINT DEBTOR (Spouse) (Last, First, Middle)

ALL OTHER NAMES used by the debtor in the last 6 years (Include married, maiden and trade names.) Smith, Andrew R. Smith, Buddy	ALL OTHER NAMES used by the joint debtor in the last 6 years (Include married, maiden, and trade names.)

SEC. SEC./TAX I.D. NO. (If more than one, state all.) 312-55-5555	SEC. SEC./TAX I.D. NO. (If more than one, state all.)

STREET ADDRESS OF DEBTOR (No. and street, city, state, and zip code) 200 Bell Road Nashville, TN 37217	STREET ADDRESS OF JOINT DEBTOR (No. and street, city, state, and zip code)

COUNTY OF RESIDENCE OR PRINCIPAL PLACE OF BUSINESS	COUNTY OF RESIDENCE OR PRINCIPAL PLACE OF BUSINESS

MAILING ADDRESS OF DEBTOR (If different from street address)	MAILING ADDRESS OF JOINT DEBTOR (If different from street address)

LOCATION OF PRINCIPAL ASSETS OF BUSINESS DEBTOR (If different from addresses listed above)	VENUE (Check one box) ☒ Debtor has been domiciled or has had a residence, principal place of business, or principal assets in this District for 180 days immediately preceding the date of this petition or for a longer part of such 180 days than in any other District. ☐ There is a bankruptcy case concerning debtor's affiliate general partner, or partnership pending in this District.

INFORMATION REGARDING DEBTOR (Check applicable boxes)

TYPE OF DEBTOR
☒ Individual   ☐ Corporation Publicly Held
☐ Joint (Husband & Wife)   ☐ Corporation Not Publicly Held
☐ Partnership   ☐ Municipality
☐ Other:

CHAPTER OR SECTION OF BANKRUPTCY CODE UNDER WHICH THE PETITION IS FILED (Check one box)
☒ Chapter 7   ☐ Chapter 11   ☐ Chapter 13
☐ Chapter 9   ☐ Chapter 12   ☐ Section 304-Case Ancillary to Foreign Proceeding

NATURE OF DEBT
☒ Non-Business/Consumer   ☐ Business-Complete A & B below

FILING FEE (Check one box)
☒ Filing fee attached
☐ Filing fee to be paid in installments (Applicable to individuals only) Must attach signed application for the court's consideration certifying that the debtor is unable to pay fee except installments. Rule 1006(b). See Official Form No. 3

A. TYPE OF BUSINESS (Check one box)
☐ Farming   ☐ Transportation   ☐ Commodity Broker
☐ Professional   ☐ Manufacturing/   ☐ Construction
☐ Retail/Wholesale   Mining   ☐ Real Estate
☐ Railroad   ☐ Stockbroker   ☐ Other Business

NAME AND ADDRESS OF LAW FIRM OR ATTORNEY

Telephone No.

B. BRIEFLY DESCRIBE NATURE OF BUSINESS

NAME(S) OF ATTORNEY(S) DESIGNATED TO REPRESENT THE DEBTOR (Print or Type Names)

☐ Debtor is not represented by an attorney

STATISTICAL ADMINISTRATIVE INFORMATION (28 U.S.C. § 604)
(Estimates only) (Check applicable boxes)

THIS SPACE FOR COURT USE ONLY

☐ Debtor estimates that funds will be available for distribution to unsecured creditors.

☒ Debtor estimates that after any exempt property is excluded and administrative expenses paid. There will be no funds available for distribution to unsecured creditors.

ESTIMATED NUMBER OF CREDITORS

1-15	16-49	50-99	100-199	200-999	1000-over
☐	☒	☐	☐	☐	☐

ESTIMATED ASSETS (In thousands of dollars)

Under 50	50-99	100-499	500-999	1000-9999	10,000-99,000	100,000-over
☐	☐	☒	☐	☐	☐	

ESTIMATED LIABILITIES (In thousands of dollars)

Under 50	50-99	100-499	500-999	1000-9999	10,000-99,000	100,000-over
☐	☐	☒	☐	☐	☐	

ESTIMATED NO. OF EMPLOYEES - CHAPTER 11 & 12 ONLY

0	1-19	20-99	100-499	500-over
☐	☐	☐	☐	☐

ESTIMATED NO. OF SECURITY HOLDERS - CHAPTER 11 & 12 ONLY

0	1-19	20-99	100-499	500-over
☐	☐	☐	☐	☐

FIGURE 13-2. Voluntary Petition

Statistical information is requested at the bottom of the petition. Estimates are acceptable; however, if the schedules are prepared at the same time as the petition, exact information can be obtained from the schedules. In the statistical information section, boxes are provided to indicate whether funds will be available to distribute to unsecured creditors (creditors who have to lien against property to ensure that the debt is paid). To determine if funds will be available, total the real and personal property from Schedules A and B; subtract the total from Schedule C, exempt property; subtract the total from Schedules D and E, secured and priority creditors, and subtract an estimated amount for administrative expenses (trustee's fee, auctioneer, etc.). Any excess amount is used to pay unsecured creditors. Note that on the form the estimated assets and liabilities are stated (in thousands of dollars).

At the bottom of the form, supply the name, telephone number, and address of the attorney and/or firm.

FILING OF PLAN

This form contains a statement signed by the debtor that he or she is aware of the kinds of relief provided by Chapters 7, 11, 12, or 13 and in this case chooses to proceed under Chapter 7. It also includes Exhibit "B" to be signed by the attorney stating that he or she has explained the relief available under each of the chapters.

DISCLOSURE OF COMPENSATION

Following the "In re" notation, insert the name of the debtor; also indicate all names used by the debtor within the last six years. For example: Andrew Smith a/k/a (also known as) Andrew R. Smith, Buddy Smith. The case number is assigned when the petition is filed and cannot be inserted until assigned.

If the attorney's fee is, for example, $750 and has been paid in full, the form shows $750 paid, and $0 to be paid. Indicate the source of the compensation paid or to be paid, such as debtor's wages, bank account, or any other source from which the money was obtained to pay the filing fees.

If the attorney has not been paid, the form shows $0 paid and $750 to be paid.

APPLICATION AND ORDER TO PAY FILING FEES IN INSTALLMENTS

When the attorney's fees have not been paid, the debtor has an option of submitting a signed application to pay filing fees in installments and an affidavit for payment of filing fees; and if it is so ordered by the court, filing fees can be paid in installments. Blanks are provided to enter any amount paid when the petition is filed, and the amounts and dates of installment payments. The form is to be dated and signed by the applicant (debtor) and his/her address provided. An order is provided at the bottom of the form for the United States bankruptcy judge to sign.

AFFIDAVIT FOR PAYMENT OF FEES IN INSTALLMENTS

(The form is not included in this text.) The affidavit must accompany the application to pay fees in installments. The affidavit is signed and sworn to by the debtor, states that he or she is filing a bankruptcy and cannot pay except in installments, and outlines the schedule of payments.

SUMMARY OF SCHEDULES

See Figure 13-3. Following the "In re" line, it is adequate to provide the full name of the debtor with no reference to other names. The summary is a listing of Schedules A through J, with blanks to indicate with "Yes" or "No" whether the schedules are attached, the number of sheets for each schedule, and the total amount from each of the schedules. A grand total for the number of sheets, the assets, and the liabilities is to be calculated.

SCHEDULE A — REAL PROPERTY

See Figure 13-4. On this schedule list all real estate in which the debtor has an interest. Under "Description and Location of the Property," be specific in the description by indicating whether the real estate is a house and lot, an undeveloped lot, or whatever. Also provide the address.

Indicate the type of interest the debtor has in the real estate under "Nature of Debtor's Interest in Property." As you learned in Chapter 12, real estate can be owned in fee simple, as tenancy in common, as a life estate, or as tenancy by the entireties. Some states have community property laws, which means that half of the property belongs to each spouse. To determine if your state has community property, look in your state statutes. Most public libraries have copies of the state codes, which are identified with the state name — *Tennessee Code Annotated*, *North Carolina Code*, and so on.

United States Bankruptcy Court

MIDDLE _____ DISTRICT OF _____ TENNESSEE _____

In re _____ Andrew Smith _____ , Case No. _____

Debtor   (If known)

SUMMARY OF SCHEDULES

Indicate as to each schedule whether that schedule is attached and state the number of pages in each. Report the totals from Schedules A, B, D, E, F, I, and J in the boxes provided. Add the amounts from Schedules A and B to determine the total amount of the debtor's assets. Add the amounts from Schedules D, E, and F to determine the total amount of the debtor's liabilities.

NAME OF SCHEDULE	ATTACHED (YES/NO)	NO. OF SHEETS	AMOUNTS SCHEDULED		
			ASSETS	LIABILITIES	OTHER
A - Real Property	Yes	1	$ 70,000.00		
B - Personal Property	Yes	3	$ 35,920.00		
C - Property Claimed as Exempt	Yes	1			
D - Creditors Holding Secured Claims	Yes	1		$ 101,000.00	
E - Creditors Holding Unsecured Priority Claims	Yes	2		$ 275.00	
F - Creditors Holding Unsecured Non Priority Claims	Yes	2		$ 8,588.83	
G - Executory Contracts and Unexpired Leases	Yes	1			
H - Codebtors	Yes	1			
I - Current Income of Individual Debtor(s)	Yes	1			$ 2,064.00
J - Current Expenditures of Individual Debtor(s)	Yes	1			$ 2,191.00
Total Number of Sheets of ALL Schedules ➤		14			
Total Assets ➤			$ 105,920.00		
Total Liabilities ➤				$ 109,863.83	

FIGURE 13-3. Summary of Schedules

United States Bankruptcy Court

__MIDDLE__   DISTRICT OF___TENNESSEE___

In re___Andrew Smith_____,   Case No._____
                    Debtor   **(If known)**

SCHEDULE A — REAL PROPERTY

Except as directed below, list all real property in which the debtor has any legal, equitable, or future interest, including all property owned as a co-tenant, community property, or in which the debtor has a life estate. Include any property in which the debtor holds rights and powers exercisable for the debtor's own benefit. If the debtor is married, state whether husband, wife, or both own the property by placing an "H," "W," "J," or "C" in the column labeled "Husband, Wife, Joint, or Community." If the debtor holds no interest in real property, write "None" under "Description and Location of Property."

Do not include interest in executory contracts and unexpired leases on this schedule. List them in Schedule G—Executory Contracts and Unexpired Leases.

If an entity claims to have a lien or hold a secured interest in any property, state the amount of the secured claim. See Schedule D. If no entity claims to hold a secured interest in the property, write "None" in the column labeled "Amount of Secured Claim."

If the debtor is an individual or if a joint petition is filed, state the amount of any exemption claimed in the property only in Schedule C—Property Claimed as Exempt.

DESCRIPTION AND LOCATION OF PROPERTY	NATURE OF DEBTOR'S INTEREST IN PROPERTY	H W J or C	CURRENT MARKET VALUE OF DEBTOR'S INTEREST IN PROPERTY WITHOUT DEDUCTING ANY SECURED CLAIM OR EXEMPTION	AMOUNT OF SECURED CLAIM
House and lot at: 300 Ashgrove Drive Nashville, TN 37217 1st Mortgage: L and L Mortgages	Owner—Fee Simple		$70,000.00	$67,000.00
		Total ➤	$ $70,000.00	

(Report also on Summary of Schedules.)

FIGURE 13-4. Schedule A — Real Property

**JOINT PETITION AND
JOINT SCHEDULES**

*One petition and one set of
schedules prepared for the
husband and wife in a
bankruptcy proceeding.*

**CURRENT MARKET
VALUE**

*Current value of a piece of
property; amount the
property could be sold for
today.*

SECURED CLAIM

*A claim in which property
has been pledged to secure
the debt.*

If the debtor is unmarried, the column labeled H, W, J, or C is left blank. In cases in which the debtor is married, husband and wife usually file a **joint petition and joint schedules**. This means that one petition and one set of schedules are completed for the husband and wife. In such cases, the owner (H) for husband, (W) for wife, (J) for joint, or (C) for community property should be indicated.

The **current market value** of the debtor's portion of the property should be provided. This is the value of the property if it were sold today. A real estate appraiser, whose telephone number can be found in the yellow pages of a phone book, can be hired to determine the value. The value assigned by the tax assessor for property tax purposes could be used.

A **secured** claim is one in which property has been pledged to secure the debt so that if the debt is not paid, the property can be sold to cover the indebtedness. Mortgages or deeds of trust are evidence of secured claims. If there are first and second mortgages, the amount of each should be listed separately. The last step in completing the schedule is to total the current market value column.

SCHEDULE B — PERSONAL PROPERTY

Schedule B, shown in Figure 13-5, consists of a three-page listing of various types of personal property, such as cash, checking accounts, wearing apparel, automobiles, animals, etc. Each item of personal property owned by the debtor is to be included on the list; and for any item on the list that the debtor does not own, a lowercase *x* should be placed in the "NONE" column. Any item to be included on Schedule C, Property Claimed as Exempt, is also included on Schedule B.

A *complete* description as well as location of the personal property is to be given. For a car, include the year, make, and model. If the personal property is a bank account, the name and address of the bank is the location. For items in the home, a street address is adequate for the location. The location of security deposits with utility companies, such as electricity and telephone, can be identified by listing the name of the company.

Sometimes there is not adequate space on the form to list all of the items in a category. For example, there may not be space available to list all of the household goods and furnishings (No. 4 on the list). If that is the case, key in "See attached list" in the "Description and Location of Property" column. On a separate sheet of paper, prepare a heading with the case name, case number, and number and name of the category. List each household item, provide the estimated current market value, and total the amount column (as shown on the next page). In this case, the total is included on Schedule B, Item 4, Household Goods and Furnishings.

United States Bankruptcy Court

_____ MIDDLE _____ DISTRICT OF _____ TENNESSEE _____

In re _____ Andrew Smith _____, Case No._____
                       Debtor   **(If known)**

SCHEDULE B — PERSONAL PROPERTY

    Except as directed below, list all personal property of the debtor of whatever kind. If the debtor has no property in one or more of the categories, place an "X" in the appropriate position in the column labeled "None." If additional space is needed in any category, attach a separate sheet properly identified with the case name, case number, and the number of the category. If the debtor is married, state whether husband, wife, or both own the property by placing an "H," "W," "J," or C in the column labeled "Husband, Wife, Joint, or Community." If the debtor is an individual or a joint petition is filed, state the amount of any exemptions claimed only in Schedule C—Property Claimed as Exempt.

    Do not list interests in executory contracts and unexpired leases on this schedule. List them in Schedule G—Executory Contracts and Unexpired Leases.

    If the property is being held for the debtor by someone else, state that person's name and address under "Description and Location of Property."

TYPE OF PROPERTY	N O N E	DESCRIPTION AND LOCATION OF PROPERTY	H W J or C	CURRENT MARKET VALUE OF DEBTOR'S INTEREST IN PROPERTY, WITHOUT DEDUCTING ANY SECURED CLAIM OR EXEMPTION
1. Cash on hand.	x			
2. Checking, savings or other financial accounts, certificates of deposit, or shares in banks, savings and loan, thrift, building and loan, and homestead associations, or credit unions, brokerage houses, or cooperatives.		Fifth National Bank, 224 Broad Street, Nashville, TN 37217 Checking Account No. 8-242-4		$ 100.00
3. Security deposits with public utilities, telephone companies, landlords, and others.	x			
4. Household goods and furnishings, including audio, video, and computer equipment.		300 Ashgrove Road See attached list		2,020.00
5. Books, pictures and other art objects, antiques, stamp, coin record, tape, compact disc, and other collections or collectibles.	x			
6. Wearing apparel.	x			
7. Furs and jewelry.	x			
8. Firearms and sports, photographic, and other hobby equipment.	x			
9. Interests in insurance policies. Name insurance company of each policy and itemize surrender or refund value of each.	x			
10. Annuities, itemize and name each issuer.	x			

FIGURE 13-5. Schedule B — Pesonal Property

Item 4, Household Goods and Furnishings, Including Audio, Video, and Computer Equipment

Andrew Smith, Debtor
Case No. (Include the number here if known)

Item	Amount
Couches, 2	$ 400.00
Chairs	50.00
End tables	35.00
Refrigerator	75.00
Beds, 2	75.00
Dresser	35.00
Stereo	200.00
Television	200.00
Antique table	150.00
Piano	200.00
TOTAL	$2,020.00

If the debtor is married, complete the H, W, J, or C column.

Determine the current market value of the debtor's interest in property and list it in the column provided with no deductions for claims of creditors. If there are any secured claims against the property, they are also to be listed on Schedule D. Make sure the value listed on Schedule B is the same as the value shown on Schedule D. The values can be estimated at or near garage sale or auction prices.

On the third page of Schedule B, indicate the number of continuation sheets (there are two continuation sheets — do not count attached lists in this number). Total the current market value from all "B" property.

SCHEDULE C — PROPERTY CLAIMED AS EXEMPT BY AN INDIVIDUAL DEBTOR

A debtor is allowed to keep certain property as outlined by the state or federal statutes. A Chapter 7 trustee can sell anything not on the exemption list. Title 11 of the United States Code Section 522(d) allows a debtor to keep the following property:

- $7,500 for the homestead — The debtor must live on the property at the time of filing the exemption in order to claim it as a homestead exemption

- Motor vehicle valued at $1,200 or less

- Each item of household and personal goods up to $200, not to exceed a total of $4,000

- Jewelry up to $500

- Professional books and tools of the trade up to $750

- Life insurance contract in any amount

- Items of property worth no more than $400 and totaling up to $3,750 of the unused homestead exemption

- Health aids in any amount

- Future benefits, including social security, unemployment benefits, veterans benefits, alimony, and child support

- Awards for lawsuits, including wrongful death benefits and insurance proceeds and compensation for bodily injury up to $7,500

Many states have passed statutes listing the types of property that are exempt. **If the state has exemptions, the state list should be used**; otherwise, the federal exemptions can be claimed.

Shown below is a partial Schedule C. It lists all property from Schedules A and B that qualifies for exemption. Specify the law that provides for the exemption, such as 11 U.S.C. 522(d), which means Title 11, Section 522(d) of the *United States Code*. If a state law is referenced, look in your state code for the correct abbreviation. The value of the claimed exemption and the current market value as shown on Schedule A or B are provided. Note that only the total of household furnishings is listed. This is acceptable if a complete itemized list is provided on Schedule B.

DESCRIPTION OF PROPERTY	SPECIFY LAW PROVIDING EACH EXEMPTION	VALUE OF CLAIMED EXEMPTION	CURRENT MARKET VALUE OF PROPERTY WITHOUT DEDUCTING EXEMPTION
House, 300 Ashgrove Drive	11 U.S.C. 522(d)	$3,000.00	$70,000.00
Household furnishings			
(listed in Schedule B herein)	11 U.S.C. 522(d)	2,020.00	2,020.00
Bank accounts	11 U.S.C. 522(d)	100.00	100.00
		$5,120.00	$72,120.00
TOTAL			

SCHEDULE D — CREDITORS HOLDING SECURED CLAIMS

See Figure 13-6 for a schedule of creditors holding secured claims. Secured creditors hold various types of liens against property. A lien is a right to repossess the property if payments are not made. Any creditor to be listed on Schedule D must hold a **security instrument**, an instrument showing a claim against real or personal property of the debtor.

To have a secured interest in personal property, to hold a lien against personal property, three documents are usually necessary:

- Contract
- Security agreement
- Financing statement

SALES CONTRACT

An agreement between the purchaser (debtor) and seller (creditor), with the purchaser agreeing to pay a stated amount for the property purchased.

SECURITY AGREEMENT

The document that grants the security interest in personal property pledged as collateral.

FINANCING STATEMENT

When filed with the appropriate office, is used to determine the creditor's right to claim the collateral pledged for a loan; U.C.C.1 form.

PERFECTION

A creditor's priority on claiming the collateral to satisfy a claim.

JUDGMENT LIEN

A lien on property as the result of a lawsuit.

GARNISHMENT

A legal claim against a portion of a person's earnings.

A **contract** is an agreement between the purchaser (debtor) and seller (creditor), with the purchaser agreeing to pay a stated amount for the personal property. The **security agreement** is a document that grants the security interest in personal property. This is usually a note at the bottom of the contract. Security interest means that the item that has been named as collateral for a loan can be repossessed by the creditor and sold, with the proceeds being used to pay the indebtedness. There is no security interest without a security agreement. The document for determining who has the first claim on the collateral when more than one creditor is holding a contract and security agreement in the same collateral is the financing statement. A **financing statement** for personal property, Form U.C.C. 1, is signed by both the debtor and creditor and filed with the secretary of state's or register's office, depending on the type of merchandise. The office with which it is filed may vary from state to state. The financing statement is the document that **perfects**, or gives priority on claiming the collateral to satisfy a claim. Generally, the creditor who first files the U.C.C.1 form has the first right to repossess and sell the collateral to satisfy the claim.

When consumer goods are sold on time and the goods serve as collateral, there is an automatic perfection, meaning the financing statement is not needed to repossess the collateral to satisfy the debt. The interest in the goods is known as a purchase money security interest (PMSI). For example, if a consumer purchases a refrigerator from an appliance store and makes payments, a PMSI is created, and only the contract and security agreement are signed. If the consumer does not make payments as agreed, the company that sold the appliance can repossess it.

A lien against a vehicle is recorded on the certificate of title.

A mortgage or deed of trust is the instrument that establishes rights of creditors in real estate.

Judgment liens, garnishments, and statutory liens can be secured claims against property. A **judgment lien** is the result of a lawsuit in which property of the debtor is subject to a lien granted by the court. A **garnishment** is a legal proceeding in which a person's money or wages are subject to being withheld and applied toward payment of a debt. A **statutory lien** is one placed on property of the debtor authorized by state statute, such as a tax lien for not paying taxes.

Schedule D is used to list the first four secured creditors and Schedule D continuation sheets are used to list additional secured creditors. If there are four or fewer secured creditors, do not include the continuation sheet in the final packet.

United States Bankruptcy Court

_____MIDDLE_____ DISTRICT OF _____TENNESSEE_____

In re_____Andrew Smith_____,   Case No._____
                    Debtor   (If known)

SCHEDULE D — CREDITORS HOLDING SECURED CLAIMS

State the name, mailing address, including zip code, and account number, if any, of all entities holding claims secured by property of the debtor as of the date of filing of the petition. List creditors holding all types of secured interests such as judgment liens, garnishments, statutory liens, mortgages, deeds of trust, and other security interests. List creditors in alphabetical order to the extent practicable. If all secured creditors will not fit on this page, use the continuation sheet provided.

If any entity other than a spouse in a joint case may be jointly liable on a claim, place an "X" in the column labeled "Codebtor," include the entity on the appropriate schedule of creditors, and complete Schedule H—Codebtors. If a joint petition is filed, state whether husband, wife, both of them, or the marital community may be liable on each claim by placing an "H," "W," "J," or "C" in the column labeled "Husband, Wife, Joint, or Community."

If the claim is contingent, place an "X" in the column labeled "Contingent." If the claim is unliquidated, place an "X" in the column labeled "Unliquidated." If the claim is disputed, place an "X" in the column labeled "Disputed." (You may need to place an "X" in more than one of these three columns.)

Report the total of all claims listed on this schedule in the box labeled "Total" on the last sheet of the completed schedule. Report this total also on the Summary of Schedules.

☐ Check this box if debtor has no creditors holding secured claims to report on this Schedule D.

CREDITOR NAME AND MAILING ADDRESS INCLUDING ZIP CODE	CODEBTOR	H W J or C	DATE CLAIM WAS INCURRED NATURE OF LIEN, AND DESCRIPTION AND MARKET VALUE OF PROPERTY SUBJECT TO LIEN	CONTINGENT	UNLIQUIDATED	DISPUTED	AMOUNT OF CLAIM WITHOUT DEDUCTING VALUE OF COLLATERAL	UNSECURED PORTION, IF ANY
ACCOUNT NO. 34-6-8753 BANK OF NASHVILLE 2838 MAIN ST NASHVILLE TN 37217-2002			1990, lien on the title Boat VALUE $ $15,000.00				$16,000.00	$1,000.00
ACCOUNT NO. 20649 GMAC BOX 8888 NASHVILLE TN 37212-3888			1993 Ford Ranger lien on title VALUE $ $11,500.00				12,000.00	500.00
ACCOUNT NO. 27091 GMAC BOX 8888 NASHVILLE TN 37212-3888			1990 Camaro lien on title VALUE $ $5,400.00				6,000.00	
ACCOUNT NO. 36-386654 L AND L MORTGAGE 3333 PARK HILL DR NASHVILLE TN 37201			1985 Deed of Trust House and Lot 300 Ashgrove Drive Nashville, Tennessee VALUE $ $70,000.00				67,000.00	

_____ continuation sheets attached

Subtotal ➤ (Total of this page) $ 101,000.00

Total (Use only on last page ➤ $ 101,000.00

(Report total also on Summary of Schedules.)

FIGURE 13-6. Schedule D — Creditors Holding Secured Claims

STATUTORY LIEN

A lien on property of the debtor imposed by law, such as a lien for not paying taxes.

Creditors are listed alphabetically. The name, mailing address including ZIP code, and account number, if any, are to be provided for each creditor. See Figure 13-6 and the instructions in the section entitled "Formatting Instructions for Mailing Labels" at the end of this chapter for formatting addresses. If anyone else is also responsible for the debt, such as a partner, check the codebtor column. Be as specific as possible with the date the claim was incurred; this might be a year, a month and year, or a specific date. The nature of the lien could be a mortgage, deed of trust, judgment lien, garnishment, or lien on the title of a vehicle or boat. Give a specific description of the collateral, such as 1993 Ford Ranger; House and Lot at 300 Ashgrove Drive, Nashville, Tennessee. The market value should be listed. The market value is not necessarily the same amount as the amount of lien. The fair market value should agree with the values listed on Schedules A and B.

CONTINGENT

A debt is contingent if it is dependent on some future event that may or may not happen.

Columns are provided for indicating whether the debt is contingent, unliquidated, or disputed. A **contingent** debt is one that has not accrued and that is dependent on some future event that may or may not happen. An **unliquidated** debt is one for which the amount owed has not been determined; and a **disputed** debt is one for which there is a difference of opinion as to whether the amount is correct or whether the debt is owed at all. A column is provided for reporting the amount of the claim by the creditor without deducting the amount of the collateral. The last column, unsecured portion, is determined by subtracting the market value of the property from the amount of the claim.

UNLIQUIDATED

A debt for which the amount owed has not been determined.

Subtotal each page of Schedule D until you get to the last page, and subtotal and total the last page. Also place that total on the Summary of Schedules page. If there are no secured creditors, place an *x* in the box provided on Schedule D for indicating that no creditors are holding secured claims, and include it in the bankruptcy packet.

DISPUTED

A debt for which there is a difference of opinion as to whether the amount is correct or whether the debt is owed at all.

SCHEDULE E — CREDITORS HOLDING UNSECURED PRIORITY CLAIMS

UNSECURED PRIORITY CREDITORS

Certain creditors are given a special status by statute; these are creditors whose claims are paid before other unsecured creditors and who have no property as collateral.

There are six categories of creditors who have **priority** claims, which means they are paid before unsecured priority creditors. Priority claims, as shown on the form, include extensions of credit in an involuntary case, payments to employees, contributions to employee benefit plans, claims of certain farmers and fisherman, deposits by individuals, and taxes and certain other debts owed to governmental units. The most common priority claims fall under taxes and certain other debts owed to governmental units and are for taxes owed to state or federal governments and for payments to child support creditors.

On the first page of Schedule E, place a check mark for each type of claim, indicate the number of continuation pages, or check the box provided if there are no such claims.

A separate Schedule E Continuation Sheet should be used for each type of priority claim checked on the first page of Schedule E. At the top of the continuation sheet above the words "Type of Priority," key in one of the six types of priority, such as "Taxes and Certain Other Debts Owed to Governmental Units," and list the creditors alphabetically per page. If there are two or more continuation pages, arrange them in the order they are listed on Schedule E. If three pages are attached, the first one is page 1 of 3; the second, page 2 of 3; and the third, page 3 of 3. The same types of information are provided for priority creditors as for secured creditors. (See Schedule D instructions.) On Schedule E, the consideration for claim is to be provided. The consideration might be taxes, wages, or employer benefit plans.

As with Schedule D, subtotal each page until the last, and subtotal and total the last page.

SCHEDULE F — CREDITORS HOLDING UNSECURED NONPRIORITY CLAIMS

Schedule F creditors include all those who do not have security and do not have priority. This is generally the largest group of creditors. Secured creditors are paid first, unsecured priority creditors are paid next, and any money left after collection and sale of assets is distributed proportionately to the unsecured nonpriority creditors. Any creditor who has already foreclosed on property assigned as collateral and to whom money is still owed, because the collateral sold for less than the amount of the claim, should also be listed on Schedule F. The amount still owed after the amount received from the sale of the property has been deducted, known as a deficiency, is an unsecured indebted-ness. If the full amount of attorney's fees have not been paid, the balance should be listed as an unsecured claim.

List the creditors alphabetically using the same format as for Schedules D and E. If there are more than four creditors, use continuation pages, and indicate at the bottom of Schedule E the number of pages attached. If there is no account number, it is suggested that you type "None" in the blank provided. If the Court has granted a judgment against the debtor, that should be indicated in the Date/Consideration column. The court and judgment number should be provided. It is possible that the consideration may not be stated if it is obvious from the type of creditor. For example, if a creditor is a doctor, it is likely that the consideration would be medical services. **Setoff** is a reduction of the amount owed because of a right to claim an asset. For example, if a person owes a bank $500 but has $100 in savings and the bank seizes the $100, then the $100 must be reduced (setoff) from the total debt. The amount owed would be $400, and it should be reported on Schedule F.

Subtotal and total as on previous schedules. Check the box provided if there are no unsecured nonpriority creditors, and include Schedule F with the bankruptcy packet.

SETOFF

A reduction of the amount owed because of an entity's right to an asset. For example, if a person owes a bank $500 but has $100 in savings and the bank seizes the $100, then the $100 is a reduction (setoff) from the total amount owed on the debt.

SCHEDULE G — EXECUTORY CONTRACTS AND UNEXPIRED LEASES

Executory contracts are those for which some future act has to take place to complete the provisions of the contract. For example, a debtor has signed a contract to buy a house, but the transaction has not been finalized. Agreements to rent property for a period of time in the future are unexpired leases. Apartment leases and vehicle leases fall in this category.

If an amount is still owed on the lease, the creditor is also listed on the appropriate schedule of creditors, Schedule D, E, or F.

SCHEDULE H — CODEBTORS

If anyone else, other than a spouse in a joint bankruptcy, is also liable for any debt shown on the schedules of creditors, the name and address of the codebtor should be provided on Schedule H.

In preparing this schedule, check the Codebtor column of Schedules D, E, or F. If a check mark is placed in the column, the creditor should be listed on Schedule H along with the name and address of the codebtor.

SCHEDULE I — CURRENT INCOME OF INDIVIDUAL DEBTOR(S)

Information about the debtor's marital status, dependents, and employment is to be provided on this form. Both debtors' income is to be provided in a case where husband and wife are filing jointly. The purpose of the form is to supply data about the debtors' income and to show the disposable monthly income (see Figure 13-7).

SCHEDULE J — CURRENT EXPENDITURES OF INDIVIDUAL DEBTOR(S)

The debtor is asked to determine and list monthly expenses for rent, food, clothing, and the like. If any debts are to be reaffirmed, as indicated on the individual debtor's statement of intention (discussed on page 372), include the monthly payments for those debts on Schedule J. The expenses are then totaled.

STATEMENT OF FINANCIAL AFFAIRS

This statement consists of nine pages of 20 questions, some with subparts. Every debtor is to answer Questions 1 through 15; debtors who have been in business should also answer Questions 16 through 20. Include all nine pages of questions in the packet, even if only 15 questions were answered. Answer each question or place an *x* in the box labeled "None." If additional pages are needed for answers, use plain paper and attach the additional pages so they can be easily located. The debtor(s) must sign the last page of the statement of financial affairs under penalty of perjury, stating that the answers are true and correct to the best of his or her knowledge, information, and belief.

United States Bankruptcy Court

_____MIDDLE_____ DISTRICT OF_____TENNESSEE_____

In re_____Andrew Smith_____, Case No._____
                    Debtor   **(If known)**

SCHEDULE I — CURRENT INCOME OF INDIVIDUAL DEBTOR(S)

The column labeled "Spouse" must be completed in all cases filed by joint debtors and by a married debtor in a chapter 12 or 13 case whether or not a joint petition is filed, unless the spouses are separated and a joint petition is not filed.

Debtor's Marital Status:	DEPENDENTS OF DEBTOR AND SPOUSE		
Divorced	NAMES Pamela Smith Sue Ellen Smith	AGE 10 6	RELATIONSHIP Daughter Daughter
Employment:	**DEBTOR**	**SPOUSE**	
Occupation	Salesman		
Name of employer	Smith Car Sales		
How long employed	15 years		
Address of employer 5333 Hickory Park Road, Nashville, TN 37217			

Income: (Estimate of average monthly income)	DEBTOR	SPOUSE
Current monthly gross wages, salary, and commissions		
(prorate if not paid monthly.)	$ 2,500.00	$_____
Estimated monthly overtime	$_____	$_____
SUBTOTAL	$ 2,500.00	$_____
LESS PAYROLL DEDUCTIONS		
a. Payroll taxes and social security	$ 436.00	$_____
b. Insurance	$ 0	$_____
c. Union dues	$ 0	$_____
s. Other (Specify:_____)	$ 0	$_____
SUBTOTAL OF PAYROLL DEDUCTIONS	$ 436.00	$_____
TOTAL NET MONTHLY TAKE HOME PAY	$ 2,064.00	$_____
Regular income from operation of profession or farm	$ 0	$_____
(attached detailed statement)		
Income from real property	$ 0	$_____
Interest and dividends	$ 0	$_____
Alimony, maintenance or support payments payable to the debtor		
for the debtor's use or that of dependents listed above.	$ 0	$_____
Social security or other government assistance		
(Specify)_____	$ 0	$_____
Pension or retirement income	$ 0	$_____
Other monthly income	$ 0	$_____
(Specify)_____	$ 0	$_____
_____	$ 0	$_____
TOTAL MONTHLY INCOME	$ 2,064.00	$_____

TOTAL COMBINED MONTHLY INCOME $_____   (Report also on Summary of Schedules)

Describe any increase or decrease of more than 10% in any of the above categories anticipated to occur within the year following the filing of this document.

FIGURE 13-7. Schedule I — Current Income of Individual Debtor(s)

On the last page of the statement, a blank is provided for inserting the number of continuation pages — "_____ continuation sheets attached." The original nine pages are not counted as they are not labeled "continuation." Include in this count only additional pages inserted to provide complete answers to the questions.

CHAPTER 7 INDIVIDUAL DEBTOR'S STATEMENT OF INTENTION

In a Chapter 7 proceeding, the debtor must state his or her intentions for surrendering or retaining each asset of the estate listed on Schedule D, Creditors Holding Secured Claims. The action to surrender or retain must be taken within 45 days of filing the statement with the court.

The property is described and the creditor's name provided. If the debtor wishes to keep or retain the property, an *x* should be placed in the column provided to indicate whether the indebtedness will be a reaffirmation, redemption, or lien avoidance. Reaffirmation means that, with court approval and an agreement signed by the debtor and creditor, the debtor can keep the property and continue making payments. Redemption allows the debtor to pay a secured creditor the current value of the property regardless of the amount owed on it and keep the property. This is a statutory right and can be done any time prior to the disposition of the collateral. Lien avoidance means the lien on the property can be avoided and the property will be claimed as exempt. Place an x in the column indicating the debtor's choice. The statement is to be dated and signed by the debtor.

UNSWORN DECLARATION CONCERNING DEBTOR'S SCHEDULES

This is a short statement signed by the debtor(s) declaring under penalty of perjury that the information in the summary and schedules is true. A blank space is provided in the declaration for inserting the number of sheets in the schedules. This refers to Schedules A through J. The number should correspond to the total sheets shown on the summary of schedules.

ADDRESSES FOR MAILING LABELS

Mailing labels are needed with names, addresses, and ZIP codes for the debtor, debtor's attorney, and all creditors who need to be notified that the petitioner is filing for bankruptcy. **You should get a copy of your local rules** for preparing the list. The list is used for duplicating mailing labels.

The most recent change in bankruptcy procedure is to automate the preparation of the mailing list. Local rules as provided by the United States Bankruptcy Court for the Middle District of Tennessee are presented here. That office has just recently automated mailing as imposed under the Bankruptcy Code and Rules.

United States Bankruptcy Court

_____ **MIDDLE** _____ **DISTRICT OF** _____ **TENNESSEE** _____

In re _____ **Andrew Smith** _____ , **Case No.** _____
                    Debtor   **(If known)**

SCHEDULE J – CURRENT EXPENDITURES OF INDIVIDUAL DEBTOR(S)

Complete this schedule by estimating the average monthly expenses of the debtor and the debtor's family. Prorate any payments made bi-weekly, quarterly, semi-annually, or annually to show monthly rate.

■ Check this box if a joint petition is filed and debtor's spouse maintains a separate household. Complete a separate schedule of expenditures labeled "Spouse."

Rent or home mortgage payment (include lot rented for mobile home)	$ 300.00
Are real estate taxes included? Yes __X__ No _____	
Is property insurance included? Yes __X__ No _____	
Utilities Electricity and Heating fuel	$ 100.00
Water and sewer	$ 35.00
Telephone	$ 30.00
Other _____	$
Home maintenance (repairs and upkeep)	$ 100.00
Food	$ 200.00
Clothing	$
Laundry and dry cleaning	$ 35.00
Medical and dental expenses	$ 50.00
Transportation (not including car payment)	$ 50.00
Recreation, clubs and entertainment, newspapers, magazines, etc.	$
Charitable contributions	$
Insurance (not deducted from wages or included in home mortgage payments)	
Homeowner's or renter's	$ 50.00
Life	$ 91.00
Health	$ 150.00
Auto	$ 50.00
Other _____	$
Taxes (not deducted from wages or included in home mortgage payments)	
(Specify) _____	$
Installment payments: (in chapter 12 or 13 cases, do not list payments to be included in the plan)	
Auto - 1993 Ranger	$ 300.00
Other _1990 Camaro___	$ 150.00
Other _1990 boat___	$ 200.00
Alimony, maintenance, and support paid to others	$ 300.00
Payments for support of additional dependents not living at your home	$
Regular expenses from operation of business, profession, or farm (attach detailed statement)	$
Other _____	$
TOTAL MONTHLY EXPENSES (Report also on Summary of Schedules)	$ 2,191.00

[FOR CHAPTER 12 AND 13 DEBTORS ONLY]
Provide the information requested below, including whether plan payments are to be made bi-weekly, annually, or at some other regular interval.

A. Total projected monthly income	$
B. Total projected monthly expenses	$
C. Excess income (A minus B)	$
D. Total amount to be paid into plan each _____	$
(interval)	

FIGURE 13-8. Schedule J — Current Expenditures of Individual Debtor(s)

Formatting Instructions for Mailing Labels

- The addresses are to be printed on 8½ x 11-inch sheets of paper, but arranged so they can be duplicated on one-column, 3½ x 1-inch mailing labels. The longest line in any address is 40 characters. Arrange the addresses as shown in Figure 13-8. (The lines shown on the form should not be printed; they are included in the illustration to mark the area within which the addresses must be printed.)

- The names and addresses from top to bottom are as follows: (1) debtor's name and address, (2) attorney's name and address, (3 and following), creditors in alphabetical order, combining all names from Schedules D, E, and F in one alphabetical listing. If a creditor appears two times on the schedules, list the creditor two times on the address matrix.

- Addresses are keyed in all capital letters. Leave one space between city, state, and ZIP code. Punctuate *only* when putting an individual's last name first. Linda Hayes would be HAYNES, LINDA.

- Insert a code at the end of each name identifying the type of creditor. (D) for debtor; (S) for secured creditor; (U) for unsecured creditor, (DA) for debtor's attorney; (A) for all other parties; (P) for priority creditor; (E) for equity security holder.

- The addressee's name is the first line of the address. No address should have more than four lines.

- If an attention or reference line is used, it is the first line. ATTN: or RE: precedes the name.

- A doctor's name is transposed with DR or MD appearing after the surname; for example, Dr. Sara Overton is OVERTON, DR SARA; or Sara Overton, M.D. is OVERTON MD, SARA.

- Add ESQ to an attorney's name. Mr. Wayne Pulliam, Attorney at Law is PULLIAM ESQ, WAYNE.

- When listing a business name, delete "The" from the beginning of business name; do not change the order of the business name if it

  includes an individual's name. The Farmers' Market is FARMERS MARKET; Robert B. Jones Company is ROBERT B JONES CO.

- Use the following abbreviations: SVC for service, HOSP for hospital, STA for station, UNLTD for unlimited, PKY for parkway, ASSOC for association, ST for street, BLVD for boulevard, AVE for avenue.

- When street names and post office box numbers are part of an address, use only the post office box numbers.

- Use the zero "0" and the number "1" for expressing numbers; do not use the alphabetic letters.

- Room and suite numbers are on the same line and after the street address.

- Titles of buildings are not used in addresses on bankruptcy mailing lists.

SMITH, ANDREW (D)
100 CHARLOTTE AVE
NASHVILLE TN 37217

LAWYER ESQ. LARRY (DA)
200 BELL RD
NASHVILLE TN 37217

BANK OF NASHVILLE (S)
2939 MAIN ST
NASHVILLE TN 37217-2002

DILL DEPT STORE (U)
5252 HICKORY PKY
NASHVILLE TN 37217

GMAC (S)
BOX 8888
NASHVILLE TN 37212-3888

GMAC (S)
BOX 8888
NASHVILLE TN 37212-3888

GREGG ELECT STORE (U)
333 THOMPSON LN
NASHVILLE TN 37207

GRISWOLD, DR JAMES (U)
MIDDLE MEDICAL CTR
8888 MEDICAL BLVD
NASHVILLE TN 37210

INTERNAL REVENUE SVC (P)
MEMPHIS TN 37501

FIGURE 13-9. Addresses for Mailing Labels

- Use numbers for streets such as 1st, 2nd, 3rd, 4th, etc.
- Use directional abbreviations recommended by the United States Postal Service: N for North, S for South, E for East, W for West, SW for Southwest, etc.
- Use two-letter state abbreviations.
- United States is abbreviated as US with no spaces or periods.

If a name was omitted from a schedule and then was added after the schedules were completed, put it at the bottom of the schedule and at the bottom of the list for mailing labels.

SUMMARY

- A Chapter 7 bankruptcy can be either voluntary or involuntary. A voluntary petition is filed by the debtor; an involuntary petition is filed by the creditors.

- Chapters 7, 9, 11, 12, and 13 are types of bankruptcy proceedings.

- A petition is the official form that is stamped by the clerk of the court. Once stamped, it creates what is referred to as a stay, which means that creditors cannot continue to contact the debtor to collect amounts owed.

- An original and two signed copies of the bankruptcy forms should be prepared, assembled, and submitted to the bankruptcy clerk. For a Chapter 7 case, include the petition, filing of plan, attorney's disclosure, application and affidavit to pay filing fees in installments (if the debtor is unable to pay the fees), Schedules A - J, summary of schedules, statement of financial affairs, debtor's statement of intention, declaration concerning debtor's schedules, and addresses for mailing labels.

- Schedule C is for property claimed as exempt by the debtor. If a state has passed laws enumerating those exemptions, use the state list; otherwise, use the federal exemptions.

- Creditors are either secured or unsecured. Secured creditors will hold documents as evidence of the security.

- Secured creditors are paid first; unsecured priority creditors are paid next; and unsecured nonpriority creditors are paid proportionately with any remaining money.

- Every bankruptcy packet contains a statement of financial affairs consisting of 20 questions. All debtors answer the first 15 questions, and those in business also answer the last five.

- The debtor must choose whether to surrender or keep each asset listed on Schedule D, Creditors Holding Secured Claims. That choice is indicated by including the asset on the Debtor's Statement of Intention and placing an x in the appropriate column.

- Addresses for mailing labels are arranged vertically with the debtor's address first; debtor's attorney second; and all creditors in alphabetical order. Format the labels according to local rules from the bankruptcy courts.

REVIEW EXERCISES

T   F   1.   Most bankruptcies are involuntary cases.

T   F   2.   In a Chapter 7 bankruptcy, the debtor does not have to give up everything that he or she owns.

T   F   3.   Laws governing bankruptcy can be found in Title 11 of the *United States Code*.

T   F   4.   The secretary should prepare an original copy of the bankruptcy forms, get them signed, and run two copies of the originals to file with the clerk of the court.

T   F   5.   An application and affidavit for paying filing fees in installments can be submitted by a debtor if he or she has already paid the attorney's fee.

T   F   6.   The summary of schedules provides boxes for inserting the amount of total assets and total liabilities of the debtor.

T   F   7.   On Schedule A, Real Property, the purchase price of a piece of real estate bought 10 years ago can be used as the current market value.

T   F   8.   Personal property includes things such as cash, checking accounts, wearing apparel, and animals.

T   F   9.   If there is inadequate space for listing personal property on Schedule B, the secretary must squeeze the information between the lines on the form.

T   F   10.   Since bankruptcies are filed in federal courts, always use federal exemptions for property claimed as exempt on Schedule C.

T   F   11.   A creditor holding a contract has a secured claim against the debtor.

T   F   12.   A U.C.C. 1 form is called a financing statement and should be filed with the appropriate office to establish the first right to repossess collateral.

T   F   13.   An unliquidated debt is one that is dependent on some future event that may or may not happen.

T   F   14.   Unsecured nonpriority creditors are in the least desirable position and are less likely to be paid than any of the other types of creditors.

T   F   15.   The list prepared for duplicating mailing labels includes only the names and addresses of creditors.

T   F   16.   Prepare five sets of bankruptcy forms.

T   F   17.   In alphabetizing names of creditors on Schedules D, E, and F, always alphabetize by a person's first name.

T   F   18.   When alphabetizing names for the address labels, combine creditor's names on all schedules as one alphabetical listing.

T   F   19.   If a name was omitted from a schedule and then was added later, it should be inserted at the end of the schedule and alphabetically in the address list for mailing labels.

TRANSCRIPTION RULES

NUMBER EXPRESSION

Aligning Amounts in Columns

Place a dollar sign by the first amount in a column and by the total. The dollar signs should align vertically. Numbers in columns are right aligned. If any amount in the column has cents, use two zeros by all even dollar amounts in the column.

```
$1,000.00
    52.80
   104.20
---------
$1,157.00
=========
```

If an amount has four or more digits, separate each group of three digits (thousands, hundreds of thousands, millions, hundred of millions, etc.) with commas. (See the illustration above — $1,000.00 and $1,157.00)

CAPITALIZATION

The name of the district and state at the top of each bankruptcy form is inserted in full caps because it is part of the title.

MIDDLE   DISTRICT OF   **TENNESSEE**

TRANSCRIPTION EXERCISES

1. Using the federal exemption list provided in this chapter for Schedule C, prepare a list of exempt items for a husband and wife filing a joint bankruptcy.

   Checking Account $100
   Household Furnishings
      Couch $230
      Chair $100
      Two tables $350 each
      Refrigerator $450
      Television $300
      Bedroom suite $300
      Washer $125
      Dryer $125
   1993 Ford Ranger $11,500
   1990 Camaro $7,000
   Boat $16,000
   Lawn mower $300
   Home worth $80,000; $75,000 still owed on the home

2. Key the following names and addresses in the proper style for an address list for mailing labels. Alphabetize the list. Use your city, state, and ZIP.

   Dr. James Griswold
   Middle Medical Center
   888 Medical Boulevard
   Unsecured

   Pediatrics Unlimited
   3888 West End Avenue
   Unsecured

   Gregg Electronic Store
   333 Thompson Lane
   Unsecured

   Andrew Smith (the debtor)
   200 Bell Road

   Lomas and Littleton
   3333 Park Hill Drive
   Secured

   Bank of (Your City)
   2838 Main Street
   Secured

   Wilkerson's Service Station
   2300 Anderson Avenue
   Unsecured

   Larry Lawyer
   Attorney for the Debtor
   100 Charlotte Avenue

RESEARCH ACTIVITIES

1. Consult your state statutes to determine whether you should use state or federal exemptions on Schedule C.

2. Obtain a copy of the local rules for preparing the address list.

PROJECTS

The information for this unit is a recorded interview between a debtor and her attorney. Forms for the unit can be found at the back of the text. If typewriters are not available, the instructor may want you to listen to the recorded interview and prepare a handwritten copy. The debtor is Marguerita Mayo Forkum; the attorney is Mr. Satya Shea, 208 Fourth Avenue North. The forms are to be signed on November 15, current year. Use your state, city, and the zip code for your area on all addresses. Refer to Figure 13-1 to determine the district in which to file the bankruptcy.

Project 13-1   Prepare the Voluntary Petition and Filing of Plan. Information is provided in the recorded interview.

Project 13-2   Prepare Schedules A and B by listening to the recorded interview.

Project 13-3   Prepare Schedule C. Refer to the federal exemption list provided in the chapter or obtain a list of state exemptions from your state statutes. You will prepare Schedule C by referring to Schedules A and B.

Project 13-4   Prepare Schedules D, E, F, G, and H. Listen to the recorded interview for the list of creditors.

Project 13-5   Prepare Schedules I and J. Listen to the recorded interview for information about the debtor's income and expenditures.

Project 13-6   Prepare Chapter 7 Individual Debtor's Statement of Intention. Information is provided on the recording.

Project 13-7   Complete the Declaration Concerning Debtor's Schedules. No recorded information is needed.

Project 13-8   Prepare the Statement of Financial Affairs. Listen to the recorded information.

Project 13-9   Prepare the Summary of Schedules. No recorded information is needed.

Project 13-10 Prepare the address list using the information from Schedules D, E, and F.

Project 13-11 Prepare the Disclosure of Compensation. Attorney's fees are $800. All have been paid from the debtor's earnings.

UNIT V
PERFORMANCE ASSESSMENT

A. Schedule F for Jerry and Rose Marie Petzer, who are filing a Chapter 7 joint bankruptcy in the Northern District of Iowa, is shown on the following page. Mark each error showing the correction. Remove Schedule F from the back of your book and prepare a corrected copy. There are additional Schedule F creditors, which would be on an additional page you do not have.

B. Listen to the recorded instructions on the cassette tape for completing Item V-B. Remove the Summary of Schedules form from the back of your book. Instructions will be given for completing the form.

C. Place the cassette tape for Performance Assessment V-C in the transcriber. Remove the blank form for the Voluntary Petition from the back of your book. Instructions will be provided for completing the form for Jerry and Rose Petzer.

United States Bankruptcy Court

_____North_____ DISTRICT OF_____Iowa_____

In re_____Jerry Petzer and Rose Marie Petzer_____, Case No._____

Debtor   (If known)

SCHEDULE F — CREDITORS HOLDING UNSECURED NONPRIORITY CLAIMS

State the name, mailing address, including zip code, and account number, if any, of all entities holding unsecured claims without priority against the debtor or the property of the debtor, as of the date of filing of the petition. Do not include claims listed in Schedules D and E. If all creditors will not fit on this page, use the continuation sheet provided.

If any entity other than a spouse in a joint case may be jointly liable on a claim, place an "X" in the column labeled "Codebtor," include the entity on the appropriate schedule of creditors, and complete Schedule H—Codebtors. If a joint petition is filed, state whether husband, wife, both of them, or the marital community may be liable on each claim by placing an "H," "W," "J," or "C" in the column labeled "Husband, Wife, Joint, or Community."

If the claim is contingent, place an "X" in the column labeled "Contingent." If the claim is unliquidated, place an "X" in the column labeled "Unliquidated." If the claim is disputed, place an "X" in the column labeled "Disputed." (You may need to place an "X" in more than one of these three columns.)

Report the total of all claims listed on this schedule in the box labeled "Total" on the last sheet of the completed schedule. Report this total also on the Summary of Schedules.

☐ Check this box if debtor has no creditors holding secured claims to report on this Schedule F.

CREDITORS NAME AND MAILING ADDRESS INCLUDING ZIP CODE	CODEBTOR	HWJ or C	DATE CLAIM WAS INCURRED AND CONSIDERATION FOR CLAIM. IF CLAIM IS SUBJECT TO SETOFF, SO STATE.	CONTINGENT	UNLIQUIDATED	DISPUTED	AMOUNT OF CLAIM
ACCOUNT NO. 46-542							
Baptist Hospital 2000 Church Street Waterloo, Iowa 50706		J	1993, Medical Services				5,437.85
ACCOUNT NO. PE-263							
Dr. Ralph Dyer 308 Cambridge Street Waterloo, Iowa 50711		J	1993, Medical Services				427.50
ACCOUNT NO. 2-348111							
Emergency Doctors Service P.O. Box 1034 Waterloo, Iowa 50704		J	December 1993, Emergency Medical Services				3,245.00
ACCOUNT NO. 38-252799							
First National Bank P.O. Box 1111 Waterloo, Iowa 50711		J	Loans, 1992 and 1993				3,075.00

___2___ continuation sheets attached

Subtotal ➤ (Total of this page) $

Total ➤ (Use only on last page of the completed Schedule F) $ 12,158.35

(Report total also on Summary of Schedules)

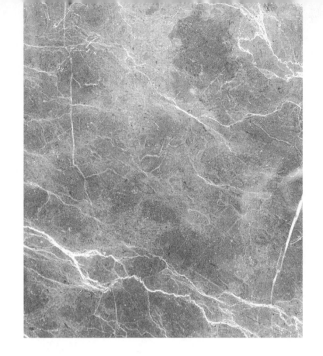

UNIT VI
APPELLATE PROCEDURE

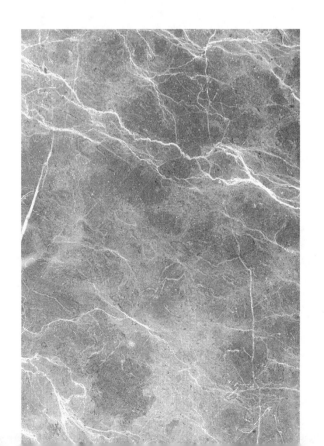

JOB DESCRIPTION
TRANSCRIPTION RESPONSIBILITIES

JOB TITLE: Legal Secretary

AREA OF PRACTICE: Appellate

TRANSCRIPTION DUTIES:

1. Correctly transcribes legal citations to state and federal constitutions, statutes, and cases.

2. Correctly transcribes citations to legal periodicals and books.

3. Correctly transcribes quotations from legal opinions, including correct citation to the source.

4. Knows the format, style, and paper size requirements for preparing appellate briefs.

5. Uses word processing software to generate a table of contents and table of authorities.

6. Prepares an adequate number of copies, sees that the copies are assembled properly, and selects the correct color of cover for the title page of an appellate brief.

CHAPTER 14

TYPING CITATIONS

OBJECTIVES

After successfully completing this chapter, you will be able to:

➤ Correctly transcribe citations to state and federal constitutions

➤ Correctly transcribe citations to state statutes

➤ Correctly transcribe citations for cases from state, regional, and federal reporters

➤ Correctly transcribe citations for periodicals

➤ Correctly transcribe quotations from legal material

INTRODUCTION

The purpose of this chapter is to provide an explanation of references to legal material so when you hear a citation dictated, you can follow an example and comprehend what you are transcribing. You will be using this material as a reference as you complete the projects for Chapter 15. At the end of this chapter, you will format the following types of quoted material:

LONG QUOTATIONS (50 WORDS OR MORE)
SHORT QUOTATIONS
QUOTES WITHIN QUOTES
QUOTES WITH ADDITIONS, OMISSIONS, AND ALTERATIONS

Legal citations, or references to legal material, are an integral part of many law office documents, such as legal memoranda and legal appellate briefs. The authority for citation and style used in this chapter is *The Bluebook, A Uniform System of Citation* (15th ed. 1991), referred to in this chapter as U.S.O.C., produced by the Columbia Law Review Association, the Harvard Law Review Association, the University of Pennsylvania Law Review, and the Yale Law Journal. Another widely acclaimed source for legal citation is the *United States*

LEGAL CITATIONS
References to legal materials, specifying where they can be found in a law library.

Government Printing Office Style Manual, which is available from the U.S. Government Printing Office in Washington, D.C.

CITING PRIMARY MATERIAL

PRIMARY MATERIAL

The law; constitutions, statutes, and cases.

Legal material is categorized into two groups: primary and secondary. **Primary material** is that which is the law and comes from the framers of our constitutions and the legislative, judicial, and executive branches of government; namely, constitutions, statutes, opinions or case law, and rules and regulations of administrative agencies. From each of these bodies of government, we have both federal and state materials.

CONSTITUTIONS

The United States Constitution is organized into articles, sections, and clauses. Following the articles are amendments, the first ten of which are called the Bill of Rights.

In the first citation to the constitution of the United States shown below, **U.S. Const**. is the abbreviation for United States Constitution; **art. III** refers to Article III; **§ 2** refers to Section 2; and **cl. 3** is the third clause in Section 2. The second citation is to Amendment 25, Section 4 of the United States Constitution. U.S.O.C. Rule 11.

U.S. CONSTITUTION

> U.S. Const. art. III, § 2, cl. 3
> or
> U.S. Const. amend. XXV, § 4

For state constitutions, follow the same format as for the U.S. Constitution, using the standard abbreviation (see Appendix C) for the name of the state. For the state of Georgia, cite as:

STATE CONSTITUTION

> Ga. Const. art. I, § 15, cl. 4

Always follow the spacing exactly as shown in the examples. In most word processing programs, a section symbol can be made by holding down the Alt key and keying 21 on the ten-key pad. The symbol is printer dependent; therefore, it may appear on the screen and not print; if so, consult your printer manual for further instructions.

STATUTES

After a bill is passed by Congress and is signed by the President, it is enacted into law and usually becomes effective when it leaves the President's desk. At that point it is a **statute**. The laws are published immediately in chronological order in a form known as "slip laws." At the end of the year, all federal laws are put in a hardbound volume entitled *Statutes at Large*. The laws are later arranged by subject matter, assigned a number, and published in a form called a code, *United States Code*.

STATUTE

A law enacted and passed by a legislative body.

If a law has been printed in the *United States Code* or its supplement, always cite to the Code. The Code is divided into 50 major subject categories called titles, and each title is divided in sections. As the new codes are added, the volumes are updated with a pocket part that fits in the back of the volume and is known as a supplement. The official publication for the United States codified statutes, *United States Code* (U.S.C.), is published by the federal government. The two unofficial publications are *United States Code Annotated* (U.S.C.A.), published by West Publishing Company, and *United States Code Service* (U.S.C.S.), published by Lawyer's Co-operative Publishing Company. The text of the law is identical in all three versions, but the publishers of unofficial versions have added annotations and analysis to their publications, as well as references to related legal materials.

Cite to the United States Code by including the following information: U.S.O.C. Rule 12.3-.3.2.

- Title number

- Abbreviation for the code — U.S.C., U.S.C.A., or U.S.C.S.

- Section number

- Year in parentheses

In the citations shown in the box below, **28** is the title number, **U.S.C., U.S.C.A., and U.S.C.S.** are abbreviations for the names of the publications; **§ 243** is the section number of the statute; **1992**, the year, is shown in parentheses. In the second and third citations to unofficial volumes, the publisher is identified in parentheses next to the year. The last reference is to material taken from pocket part (supplement) in the back of U.S.C.

U.S. STATUTE

28 U.S.C. § 243 (1992).
28 U.S.C.A. § 243 (West 1992).
28 U.S.C.S. § 243 (Law. Co-op. 1992)
28 U.S.C. § 35 (Supp. V 1988).

For citations to state statutes, include the abbreviation for the name of the state statutes, section symbol, section number, and year in parentheses. U.S.O.C. Rule 12.3-12.3.2. References to subsections, as shown in the second citation, are indicated in parentheses.

STATE STATUTE

> Miss. Code Ann. § 25-4-505 (1982).
> Tenn. Code Ann. § 36-2-103(a)(1) (1992).

CASES

Case law comes about as a result of court cases. At the federal level, a trial is initially heard in one of 93 district courts throughout the United States. Either party, the plaintiff or the defendant, has a right to appeal the decision if it can be determined that the trial court erred. The appeals are made to one of 13 circuit courts of appeal. If further appeal is desired, the applicant applies for permission to appeal, known as certiorari, to the U.S. Supreme Court. The U.S. Supreme Court chooses the cases it wishes to hear.

OPINION

A report written by the judge, stating the facts of the case, the issues to be answered, the reason for the decision, and the ruling of the court.

Much of the federal law that is cited comes from decisions made in the intermediate level courts (Circuit Courts of Appeal). Upon the conclusion of a case at the district level, the judge or justice writes an **opinion** stating the facts of the case, the issues to be answered, the reason for the decision, and the ruling of the court. If the case is appealed, the appellate level judges, a panel usually composed of three, review the case by reading briefs prepared by both sides of the case and sometimes by listening to a short oral argument by request of the attorneys. When two judges agree on a decision, the opinion at the appellate level is written. Selected opinions from district, appellate, and U.S. Supreme Court cases are published in volumes known as **reporters**.

REPORTERS

Volumes of books containing opinions.

Opinions from the United States Supreme Court are published in the official publication, *United States Reports* (U.S.), published by the federal government; and in two unofficial publications, the *Supreme Court Reporter* (S. Ct.), published by West Publishing Company, and *United States Supreme Court Reports, Lawyers' Edition* (L. Ed.), published by Lawyers Co-operative Publishing Company.

Reported opinions from the Circuit Courts of Appeal are published in the *Federal Reporter* (F. or F.2d). After the first series of volumes of the reporter reached 300 in 1924, the publisher introduced a larger, two-column series, *Federal Reporter, Second Series* (F.2d). Opinions from the U.S. District Courts appear in the *Federal Supplement* (F. Supp.).

A case citation includes the following information: U.S.O.C. Rule 10.1-7.

• Style of the case

- Volume number, abbreviation, and page number of the reporter where the case can be found

- Court that made the decision (if not previously identified)

- Year decided

Additional information that may be a part of a case citation:

- A "specific page cite"

- Parenthetical information

- History

- Signals

Style of the Case. Generally, use the name of the case as shown at the top of the page in the reporter where the opinion is published.

Not all case names involve two parties. For an adoption of Albert Strong where there is no opposing party, the name of the case would be <u>In re Adoption of Albert Strong</u>.

A case name may include the expression <u>ex rel.</u>, meaning on behalf of. If Smith is the party for whom the state of Missouri institutes an action against Jones, the defendant, the case name would be <u>State ex rel. Smith v. Jones</u>.

Volume Number, Abbreviation, and Page Number of the Reporter. List the reporter by volume number, abbreviation for the reporter, and page number where the citation begins.

There are two types of reporters within which decisions from state courts may be found: state and regional. Each state reporter contains decisions for one state only. When identifying state reporters, the highest court in the state is usually identified with the standard abbreviation for that state. For example, Penn., Ala., Mich. Abbreviations for lower courts for each state can be determined by consulting Table I of *The Bluebook, A Uniform System of Citation.* A case reported in volume 384 from the supreme court of Michigan beginning on page 589 would be

STATE REPORTER REFERENCE

384 Mich. 589

The table on page 394 provides the names of the regional reporters, abbreviations for the reporter names, and states included in each region. There are two series of volumes for each regional reporter; the older cases are in the first series and the later cases are in the second series. The second series is identified by adding 2d to the abbreviation.

Name	Abbrev.	States
Atlantic	A. and A.2d	Conn., Del., Maine, Md., N.H., N.J., Penn., R.I., Vt., Washington, D.C.
North Eastern	N.E. and N.E.2d	N.Y. (Ct. of Appeals only), Ill., Ind., Mass., Ohio
North Western	N.W. and N.W.2d	Iowa, Mich., Minn., Nebr., N. Dak., S. Dak., Wis.
Pacific	P. and P.2d	Alaska, Ariz., Calif., Colo., Hawaii, Idaho, Kans., Mont., Nev., N. Mex., Okla., Oreg., Utah, Wash., Wyo.
South Eastern	S.E. and S.E.2d	Ga., N.C., S.C., Va., W. Va.
South Western	S.W. and S.W.2d	Ark., Ky., Mo., Tenn., Tex.
Southern	So. and So. 2d	Ala., Fla., La., Miss.

Reference to a regional reporter for a case reported on page 1000 of volume 38 in North Western, Second Series, would be

REGIONAL REPORTER REFERENCE

> 38 N.W.2d 1000

Some states do not have individual state reporters; they report cases in the regional reporter only. In states that do have state reporters, the same cases are reported in both the state reporter and regional reporter. A **parallel citation** is one that shows where the same opinion can be found in both the state and regional reporter. If the citation is used in a document submitted to a state's own courts, parallel citations should be provided. In documents submitted to a federal court or any other court outside one's own state, only the regional reporter reference is needed. U.S.O.C. Table 1. In the parallel references shown below, the first part of the citation refers to page 589, Volume 384 of the Michigan State Reporter. A comma separates the state reporter reference from the regional reporter reference. The second part of the reference is to page 1000 of Volume 38 of the North Western Reporter, Second Series.

PARALLEL CITATION

A citation to the same opinion recorded in different reporters.

PARALLEL REFERENCE TO STATE AND REGIONAL REPORTER

> 384 Mich. 589, 38 N.W.2d 1000

Court That Made the Decision. Use an abbreviation for the name of the court that made the decision if not previously identified. If the name of the reporter fully identifies the court because only reports from that court are transcribed in that reporter, the court name is omitted from the citation.

When the court name must be identified, its abbreviation is placed in parentheses along with the year. For example, if the Illinois Appeals Court made the decision in 1982, the material in parentheses would be (Ill. App. 1982). Standard abbreviations are used for the state name, and App. is the abbreviation for appeals. If the decision is made by the highest state court, usually the supreme court, the state name and year are placed in parentheses. For example, if the Wisconsin Supreme Court made the decision in 1974, the material in parentheses would be (Wisc. 1974).

Year Decided. Place the year in parentheses with the abbreviation of the court name, or if the court does not need to be identified (as explained above), place the year in parentheses by itself.

Examples of Complete State Citations. Listed below are examples of complete citations for state cases. The first citation is a parallel citation and is the form used if the document is submitted to the Michigan state courts. The second citation is the style used if the document is submitted to a federal court or to a court outside the state of Michigan.

STATE COURT CASE CITATIONS

Casey v. Brod, 384 Mich. 589, 38 N.W.2d 100 (1990).
Casey v. Brod, 38 N.W.2d 100 (Mich. 1990)

Examples of Complete Federal Citations. The first citation shows the style of the case, **Kandari v. Garn**, underlined, followed by a comma; **350** is the volume number, **U.S.** identifies the reporter and also the court since only U.S. Supreme Court cases are reported therein; **33** is the page number; and **1975** the year, which is shown in parentheses without a court. The second example is a citation to a U.S. Circuit Court of Appeals case. Note that the court is identified in parentheses. **F.2d** shows the level of court (U.S. Circuit) but does not identify which circuit; therefore, **5th Cir**. is included parenthetically with the year to fully identify the court. In the third example, **F. Supp**. identifies a Federal District Court, but additional information in parentheses - **M.D. Tenn.** for Middle District of Tennessee - identifies the district and state where the court is located.

FEDERAL COURT CASE CITATIONS — U.S. SUPREME COURT, CIRCUIT COURT OF APPEALS, AND U.S. DISTRICT COURT, RESPECTIVELY

Kandari v. Garn, 350 U.S. 33 (1975).

Kandari v. Garn, 212 F.2d 45 (5th Cir. 1970).

Kandari v. Garn, 333 F. Supp 788 (M.D. Tenn. 1980).

Specific page. A specific page cite is used when citing quoted material within the opinion. Include the page number where the opinion begins, a comma and space, and the page number where the quoted material is located. U.S.O.C. Rule 3.3. In the page cite below, the opinion begins on page 50 and the specific material is on page 57.

SPECIFIC PAGE CITATION

<u>Kandari v. Garn</u>, 306 F.2d 50, 57 (2d Cir. 1985).

Parenthetical. Additional, or parenthetical, information about an opinion is part of the citation and is placed within parentheses immediately after the year. The attorney makes the decision about what to include parenthetically; the secretary needs to know how and where to place the parenthetical. The purpose of parenthetical material is to make clear the holdings of the Court. U.S.O.C. Rule 10.6.

- (en banc) — the whole court made the decision.

- (2-1 decision) — two judges agreed with and one judge disagreed with the decision.

- (Smith, J., dissenting) — Judge Smith did not agree with the opinion.

- (per curiam) — the opinion was written by one judge.

- (due process affords the putative father standing to offer evidence) — explanation of the importance of the case by the person who is citing it.

PARENTHETICAL INFORMATION

<u>Poynor v. Horowitz</u>, 500 U.S. 39 (1980) (per curiam).

SUBSEQUENT HISTORY

Citation of a later higher court decision that reversed (rev'd) or affirmed (aff'd) a lower court decision.

PRIOR HISTORY

Citation of an earlier lower court decision that a higher court is affirming (aff'g) or reversing (rev'g).

History. References to history of a case are placed after parenthetical information, if any, or after the year the decision was made. After a case is decided, a higher court may affirm (agree with) a decision or may reverse (set aside) a decision.

When the main citation is to a lower court decision that has been reversed (rev'd) or affirmed (aff'd) by a higher court, the later decision is cited as **subsequent history**. When the main citation is to a higher court decision that is affirming (aff'g) or reversing (rev'g) a lower court decision, the earlier decision is cited as **prior history**. All subsequent history phrases are expressed as past participles (<u>ed</u> endings) and are preceded and followed by a comma (, aff'd,) and all prior history phrases are present participles (<u>ing</u> endings) and are preceded but not followed by a comma (, aff'g). Also note that the historical phrase is abbreviated and underlined (<u>rev'g</u>).

In the subsequent history illustration below, a decision being cited from the 5th Circuit Court of Appeals (intermediate level federal court) was reversed by the United States Supreme Court (highest level federal court). In the prior history illustration, a case being cited from the 6th Circuit Court (intermediate level federal court) is affirming a decision made by the Middle District of Tennessee, a district court (lower level federal court). U.S.O.C. Rule 10.7.

SUBSEQUENT HISTORY

<u>United States v. Corey Construction Co.</u>, 300 F.2d 300 (5th Cir. 1980), <u>rev'd</u>, 300 U.S. 789 (1982).

PRIOR HISTORY

<u>United States v. Corey Construction Co.</u>, 200 F.2d 308 (6th Cir. 1985), <u>aff'g</u> 338 F. Supp. 388 (M.D. Tenn 1984).

Signals. Signals are introductory words at the beginnings of citations to indicate why the material is being cited. It may be cited to support the point that is being discussed, to contradict a point, etc. The attorney is responsible for choosing the phrases, but the secretary should key them correctly. Signals include expressions such as e.g., accord, see, see also, cf., compare with, contra, but see, but cf., and see generally. U.S.O.C. Rule 1.2. If these expressions are at the beginning of a citation sentence, capitalize the first letter of the signal; if they follow a semicolon that connects two citations, use a lowercase letter. If two signals are used together, such as <u>See, e.g.</u>, a solid underline is used for the signals, and they are separated with a comma. Signals are underlined separately from the case name. If using e.g., a comma follows the expression; no comma follows any other single signal listed above.

SIGNALS

Introductory words at the beginnings of citations to legal material. Signals are expressions such as e.g., accord, see, see also, cf., compare with, contra, but see, but cf., and see generally.

SIGNALS

<u>See</u> <u>Fell v. Yu</u>, 38 U.S. 248 (1991); <u>cf.</u> <u>Ticcione v. Gault</u>, 755 F. Supp. 889 (S.D. Ill. 1988).

Short Form of Case Citation

After a full citation is given in the text of legal material, a short version can be used thereafter to refer to the same case. For example, a full citation is given for <u>Jackson v. Thornton</u>, 133 Tenn. 36, 38 (1915). Thereafter any of the three forms shown below may be used. The notation "at 40" refers to page 40 of the material being cited.

SHORT FORM OF CASE CITATION

Jackson v. Thornton, 133 Tenn. at 40.
Jackson, 133 Tenn. at 40.
Id. at 40. (Use this only if referring to the immediately preceding
    case and a different page number.)
Id. (Use this if referring to the immediately preceding case and the
    same page number.)

CITING SECONDARY MATERIALS

Periodicals

Secondary material is written about the law and is found in periodicals, books, and the like. There are several hundred periodicals covering legal topics. Most law schools publish their own law school journals. The following information is included in a citation: U.S.O.C. Rule 16.

- Author's first name, middle initial, and last name

- Title of the article underlined

- Volume

- Periodical abbreviation (Table 13, U.S.O.C.)*

- Page

- Year in parentheses

Some periodicals are published so they can be bound in volumes, as Volume I, Volume II, and so on. The pages of each publication (magazine) may be numbered consecutively, with the first publication beginning with 1, the second beginning with the number where the first stopped, and so on, throughout the volume. These are referred to as consecutively paginated volumes.

Citation to a consecutively paginated volume is shown on page 399. Margaret Fisher and Stanley Womack wrote an article entitled "Law Concepts," which appeared on page 24 of Volume 35 of the *Kentucky Law Journal* in 1985. Note that in listing two authors, both names are shown in full, joined by an ampersand (&). If there are three or more authors, list the first author's name followed by **et al.**, for example, Sharon Grassmere et al.

---

* Abbreviations for the names of periodicals are provided in Table 13 of *The Bluebook, A Uniform System of Citations,* ed. 15.

CONSECUTIVELY PAGINATED VOLUME

> Margaret Fisher & Stanley Womack, <u>Law Concepts</u>, 35 Ky. L.J. 24 (1985).

If there is no volume number, the year replaces the volume number and it does not appear in parentheses at the end of the citation.

CONSECUTIVELY PAGINATED — NO VOLUME NUMBER

> Cherronda Elliott, <u>Divorce Litigation</u>, 1986 Wash. Monthly 125.

When each publication is paginated separately (each publication begins with page 1), the exact date of the periodical is included followed by the word "at" and the page number.

EACH PUBLICATION SEPARATELY PAGINATED

> Joseph Delacruz, <u>Technicalities of Probate Practice</u>, Admin. L.J., Mar. 19, 1988, at 45.

If there is no author, the citation begins with the title of the article.

NO AUTHOR

> <u>Abortion Rights of the Father</u>, 15 Litig. 203 (1992).

Law students often write articles to be printed in periodicals known as university law journals. If the student's name appears at the end or in the article, it is considered signed. In order to indicate that the author is a student, the name of the student is followed by "Note," "Comment," or "Project," as designated in the periodical.

SIGNED ARTICLE WRITTEN BY A STUDENT

> Albert LaGrone, Comment, <u>Reading Habits of Criminals,</u> 50 N.C. L. Rev. 372 (1911).

For an unsigned student article, the citation is preceded by "Note," "Comment," "Case Comment," "Project," or "Case Note," as designated in the periodical.

Note, <u>The Unauthorized Practice of Law</u>, 83 Vt. L. Rev. 55 (1976).

CITING AND FORMATTING QUOTATIONS

When quoting material, the writer must make it clear to the reader which words are the exact words of the material being quoted. Quoted material is taken from the portion of a reported case written by the judge or justice, known as the "opinion."

Quotations are either long, 50 words or more, or short, fewer than 50 words. If a quotation is long, the material is single-spaced and indented from both margins, usually one-half inch, with no quotation marks. If a quotation is short, it is spaced as the body of the document (usually double-spaced) and is surrounded by quotation marks.

LONG QUOTATIONS

A long quotation, including the citation, is shown below. Note that the lead-in words, "The Court said" are followed by a colon. When the lead-in words "The Court said that" are used to introduce the quotation, no comma or colon follows the lead-in, as it is woven into the flow of the sentence. The material quoted here is indented from both margins and the first line is not further indented. When material being quoted is from within a paragraph in the original, do not further indent the first line of the quoted matter; however, when the material being quoted is the beginning of a paragraph in the original, the first line should be indented an additional half inch. The letter T at the beginning of the quote is shown in brackets to indicate that it was a lowercase t in the original text. At the end of the long quote, return to the original margins and double spacing to key the case citation. The citation ends with a period. Space twice and continue with the text of the document.

LONG QUOTATION

The Court said:

> [T]he trial judge based his decision solely on the testimony that the defendant broke out of the tavern. While indicating some doubt concerning the defendant's testimony that he walked through an open door, the court did not attempt to resolve the conflicting evidence concerning how entry was gained into the tavern. Rather, the court assumed that the defendant did not break into the tavern and chose to base its decision on the evidence that the defendant broke out of the tavern.

<u>Sample v. Maryland</u>, 365 A.2d 773, 775 (1976). The Court goes on to explain that the defendant breaking out of a tavern is quite different from

SHORT QUOTATIONS AND QUOTES WITHIN QUOTES

Short quotations fall within the text of the document, followed by the legal citation. The following example also shows a quote within a quote. The judge in <u>Sample v. Maryland</u>, in writing his opinion, quoted the phrase "the actual intention at the time of the breaking is controlling," from <u>Ridley v. State</u>. Note that quotes within quotes are enclosed in single marks. The citation must also indicate that material in single quotes is from another source. Had this been a long quotation, the quote within the quote would have been cited in the same manner, but the quote within the long quote would have been enclosed in double quotation marks.

QUOTE WITHIN A QUOTE

> It is clear from the facts of the case that the breaking was not a malicious attempt to break and enter. "It is well settled that under our storehouse breaking statute, 'the actual intention at the time of the breaking is controlling.'" <u>Sample v. Maryland</u>, 365 A.2d 773, 777 (1976) (quoting <u>Ridley v. State</u>, 228 Md. 281, 282, 179 A.2d 710, 711 (1962)). It was the defendant's belief at the time the event took place that he was within his

ADDITIONS, OMISSIONS, AND ALTERATIONS

Any added words, errors in the original, change of number (singular to plural or plural to singular), change in capitalization, added emphasis, or omissions from the quoted material must be indicated. Words or letters added to quoted text are identified by placing brackets around the additions. In the example below, the word "criminal" has been added.

ADDITIONS

> ordinary [criminal] case

Any errors in the text being quoted should be indicated by [sic] in brackets following the error. In the following example, the original text was "The statue was enacted on June 15 of last year." The correct word choice in this case is "statute."

ERRORS IN THE ORIGINAL

> "The statue [sic] was enacted on June 15 of last year."

Any change from singular to plural or plural to singular should be indicated in the quoted material with brackets. In the first example below, words "judgments" and "set" appeared in the original text, but because of subject and verb agreement in the writer's document, "judgment" is the term needed. In the second illustration, the word "defendant" appeared in the original text; but in the construction of the writer's sentence, a plural form is needed.

CHANGE OF NUMBER

> It is the "judgment[ ] of this appellate court which set[s] the precedent."
>
> In our case, like the <u>Sample</u> case, "the defendant[s] broke out of the tavern."

Any change in capitalization because of sentence structure should be indicated by enclosing the letter in brackets. In the illustration below, a lowercase i was used in the material being quoted. The original sentence was: "The decision was not based on all evidence, but it was based solely on the testimony."

CHANGE IN CAPITALIZATION

> The judge said, "[I]t was based solely on the testimony."

Emphasis can be added to words by underlining, bolding, or italicizing them. Such emphases added to the original quotation are indicated in the citation with the parenthetical notation (emphasis added). In the example below, the words "is not" were not bold in the original. The word "in" was italicized (equivalent to underlining in typed copy) in the original. Since there were two emphases shown, the emphasis not in the original is identified by the notation (first emphasis added) in the case citation.

EMPHASIS ADDED

> "Consequently, the value of the goods actually taken **is not** determinative of intent in the ordinary case where the breaking element of the statute is satisfied by a breaking <u>in</u>." <u>Sample v. Maryland</u>, 365 A.2d 773, 777 (1976) (first emphasis added).

Omissions of material in the middle of a sentence are shown by three spaced periods with a space before and after, called an ellipsis. At the end of a sentence, omitted material is shown with three spaced periods and a final closing period. An omitted paragraph is shown by four spaced indented periods on a separate line. An ellipsis should not be used at the beginning of the first paragraph in a quoted passage; however, an ellipsis may be placed at the beginning of the second, third, etc., paragraphs within the quoted passage.

In the following example, the quotation begins with the beginning of a paragraph (it is indented); a phrase was omitted after the first five words of the paragraph (shown by three spaced periods); text was omitted at the end of the first paragraph (shown by four spaced periods); paragraph two was omitted (shown by four, indented spaced periods on a separate line); and a sentence at the beginning of the third paragraph was omitted (shown by three spaced periods). Note that there is a single space between the quoted paragraphs. U.S.O.C. Rule 5.3.

OMISSIONS OF TEXT

> Although the record reflects evidence . . . that the defendant broke into the building, the trial judge based his decision solely on the testimony that the defendant broke out . . . .
>
> . . . .
>
> . . . In England, prior to 1713, there were differing views with regard to whether entering a house without a breaking and subsequently breaking the close of the house in order to escape constituted a burglary.
>
> Sample v. Maryland, 365 A.2d 773, 775-6 (1976).

Omissions of citations are indicated with a parenthetical notation (citation omitted); do not show the omission with an ellipsis. In the following example, a citation appeared in the original between the first and second sentences.

OMISSIONS OF A CITATION

> "Whether or not a court orders a pre-sentence investigation in a particular case is within the discretion of the court. There was no abuse of that discretion in this case." Sample v. Maryland, 365 A.2d 773, 778 (citation omitted).

SUMMARY

- Citations are references to legal material. The authority for the citation style used in this chapter is *The Bluebook, A Uniform System of Citation,* 15th ed.

- Legal material is categorized into two groups — primary and secondary. Primary material includes constitutions, statutes and legislative materials, case law, and administrative agency regulations. Secondary material includes periodicals, books, and other material written about the law.

- The following are citations to primary material:

  U.S. Constitution: U.S. Const. art. III, § 2, cl. 3.
  Case in U.S. Supreme Court: <u>Kandari v. Garn</u>, 350 U.S. 33 (1975).
  Case in U.S. Circuit Court: <u>Kandari v. Garn</u>, 212 F.2d 45 (5th Cir. 1970).
  Case in U.S. District Court: <u>Kandari v. Garn</u>, 333 F. Supp. 788 (M.D. Tenn. 1980).

- The following is a citation to a periodical:

  Margaret Fisher & Stanley Womack, <u>Law Concepts</u>, 35 Ky. L.J. 24 (1985).

- The United States statutes are published in *United States Code, United States Code Annotated,* and *United States Code Service.*

- Quoted material of 50 words or more should be indented from both the left and right margins and single-spaced. Quotation marks are omitted because the indention identifies the material as being quoted. Quotes within an indented quote are surrounded by double quotation marks (").

- Quoted material of fewer than 50 words is double-spaced and surrounded by quotations marks; quotes within quotes are surrounded by single quotation marks.

- Three spaced periods, an ellipsis, is used to indicate material omitted from a quotation. If the omission is at the end of a sentence, a fourth period is added to represent the period at the end of a sentence. An omitted paragraph is indicated by four indented, spaced periods on a separate line.

- When "The Court said" is used as a lead-in to quoted material, a colon follows the word "said"; when "The Court said that" is used as a lead-in, no punctuation follows.

- Brackets are used to surround substituted words or letters and change in capitalization; empty brackets indicate the omission of letters. Errors in the original are indicated by [sic] in brackets.

REVIEW EXERCISES

T   F   1. The legal transcriptionist needs to know how to type legal citations for primary and secondary materials.

T   F   2. 21 U.S.C. § 108 refers to Section 108, Title 21, of the *United States Code*.

T   F   3. Citation to state constitutions includes the name of the case, volume, and page number.

T   F   4. Cases from the United States Courts of Appeal are published in the *United States Reports*.

T   F   5. An example of a signal is (per curium).

T   F   6. An example of parenthetical information in a citation is (2-1 decision).

T   F   7. (S.D. Ark. 1980) refers to a case heard in 1980 in the Southern District Court in Arkansas.

T   F   8. (3d Cir. 1992) refers to a case heard in the U.S. Supreme Court.

T   F   9. When referring to the second series of the *Southern Reporter,* the abbreviation is So. 2d.

T   F   10. Cases heard in the U.S. District Court in Michigan are reported in the North Eastern Reporter.

TRANSCRIPTION RULES

ABBREVIATIONS

Abbreviations for Federal Reporter Citations:

United States Reports	U.S.
Supreme Court Reporter	S. Ct.
United States Supreme Court Reports, Lawyers' Edition	L. Ed.
Federal Reporter	F. or F.2d
Federal Supplement	F. Supp.
Circuit	Cir.
Middle District	M.D.
Southern District	S.D.

Abbreviations for Regional Reporters

The following abbreviations have been assigned to West's regional reporters:

Pacific	P. or P.2d
North Western	N.W. or N.W.2d
South Western	S.W. or S.W.2d
North Eastern	N.E. or N.E.2d
Atlantic	A. or A.2d
South Eastern	S.E. or S.E.2d
Southern	So. or So. 2d

Punctuation with Abbreviations

(1) Place a period after abbreviations. (2) Do not use a period if the last letter of the word is part of the abbreviation and is set off with an apostrophe from the rest of the word. (3) Do not include periods in organizations known by their initials.

(1) Bldg.   Jan.   Wed.
(2) Ass'n
(3) NAACP

CITATIONS

Initials

In text, space once between initials in personal names; however, in citations, do not space. U.S.O.C. Rule 6.1

In text: L. C. Johansen
In citations: L.C. Johansen

Multiple and Parallel Citations

A parallel citation is a reference to one case that is printed in two or more publications; a multiple citation consists of references to two or more different cases. Parallel citations are separated by commas; multiple citations by semicolons. The first example below is a parallel citation; the second, a multiple citation:

Smith v. Jones, 14 Tenn. 234, 385 S.W.2d 143 (1970).
Parsons v. Pedigo, 989 P.2d 899 (1990); Baker v. Cook, 389 N.E. 389 (1989).

Page Number References in Citations

Never use "p." or "pp." for "page" or "pages" in citations. In citing consecutively numbered pages, separate the range of pages with a hyphen. When referring to a range of pages, nonidentical digits in a series are repeated; however, always repeat at least the last two digits. For scattered pages, separate the specific page numbers with commas.

500 to 525	500-25 (two digits are different)
1585 to 1643	1585-643 (three digits are different)
1450 and 1460	1450, 1460 (scattered pages)

Section and Paragraph References in Citations

Spell word "Section" or the word "paragraph" when it appears in text; use the symbols (§ and ¶) in citations. Space once before and once after the symbol. Use two symbols to indicate multiple sections.

In text:		In citations:	
	Section 14(b)		§ 14(b)
	Sections 14 to 16		§§ 14-16
	paragraph 25		¶ 25
	paragraphs 15 to 20		¶¶ 15-20

Multiple Section References in Citations

When referring to a range of section numbers, retain all digits except when there are identical digits or letters preceding a punctuation mark. U.S.O.C. Rule 3.4. Subsection designations should be enclosed in parentheses even if printed in the source without parentheses.

Section 245	245 (one section)
Sections 1114 to 1133	§§ 1114-1133 (a range of sections)
Section 1330, subsections a and 3	§1330(a), (3) (one section and two subsections)

Sections 3.25-46, 3.25-52,
    and 3.25-59   §§ 3.25-46, -52, -59 (The identical
                                           digits preceding a punctuation
                                           mark are 3.25, and they do not
                                           have to be repeated each time.)

Some authors use <u>et seq.</u> when referring to multiple sections of statutes. "Et seq." means *and following*. A reference to multiple sections of the Missouri Revised Statutes could be expressed as Mo. Rev. Stat. §§ 12-5-543 <u>et seq.</u>

Spacing in Reporter Abbreviations

Do not space between single-letter abbreviations in names of reporters. If the abbreviation of the name of a reporter is more than one letter, space once before and once after the abbreviation. Note that when the abbreviation for a word consists of two letters or more, the first letter is capitalized and the other letters are lowercase. Use full caps for single-letter abbreviations. Treat the reference to a series of volumes (2d or 3d) of a reporter as a single-letter abbreviation.

> S.W.
> S.W.2d
> So. 2d
> Cal. App. 2d

Underlining

The following items are underlined in citations: U.S.O.C. Rules 2 and 7. Italicizing is an alternative to underlining.

> Case names, including <u>v.</u>
> Book titles
> Article titles
> Committee hearings
> Terms indicating prior and subsequent history, <u>rev'd</u>, <u>aff'g</u>
> Capital letters representing names: <u>A</u> sued <u>B</u>
> The letter "l" when it represents a subsection, § 32(<u>l</u>)
> Foreign words or phrases not a part of common English usage
> Emphasized material
> Related authority, <u>reprinted in</u>
> Introductory signals, <u>See</u>, <u>Cf.</u>, etc.

(a) Underline the title of a publication when referring to it in the text of a document. (b) Publications titles are always abbreviated in citations.

(a) The information can be found in the <u>Pacific Reporter</u>.

(a) <u>Tennessee Code Annotated</u> provides for blood testing.

(b) In <u>Smith v. Norton</u>, 35 P.2d 385 (1993), guidelines are provided for blood testing.

QUOTATIONS

Punctuation With Quotation Marks

Periods and commas are always placed before a closing double or single quotation mark. Colons and semicolons are always placed after a closing double or single quotation mark. Question marks and exclamation points are typed before a quotation mark if the question or exclamation is part of the quoted matter.

"I have only five minutes," she said, "to finish this exercise."

When the attorney announced that we needed two more documents, my question was "Why?"; the other secretary asked "When?"

In <u>Rogers v. Lambert</u> the judge asked, "How can we determine guilt or innocence without evidence to support the allegations?"

TRANSCRIPTION EXERCISES

Using the material presented in this chapter, key and print answers to the following exercises:

1. Quote the following material omitting the words "trial" and "solely": The trial judge based his decision solely on the testimony of the defendant.

2. Quote the following sentence: There is no evidence to convict the accused. Introduce the quote with The judge said that.

3. Write a citation to a case heard in the Missouri Supreme Court in 1980 styled Vinson v. Casper, reported in South Western Reporter at page 40 in Volume 84.

4. Show how to cite Section 955 to Section 975.

5. Show how to cite page 955 to page 975.

6. Show the proper format for referring to the South Western Reporter in text material. Show the abbreviation for writing a citation to the South Western Reporter.

7. The author is quoting Article 4, Section 3, and Clause 4 of the United States Constitution. Write the citation.

You hear the following statement on the tape as you are transcribing. Show how you would transcribe.

8. but a state cannot preclude him from establishing a relationship with his child id

9. see e g in re lisa r 532 pacific second 123 california 1975

10. compare cunningham 652 south western second at 912

RESEARCH ACTIVITIES

1. Consult *The Bluebook, A Uniform System of Citation.* Turn to Table 1, find the abbreviations for your state materials, and make a list. Turn to Table 13 and copy the abbreviations for periodicals.

2. To familiarize yourself with *The Bluebook,* refer to the table of contents and make a list of the major divisions of the book.

PROJECTS

Project 14-1   The project for this chapter is shown below. There is not a
cassette tape to transcribe for this unit. You will need to know the
content of this unit in order to transcribe the appellate brief
presented in Chapter 15.

QUOTING EXERCISES

A copy of an opinion styled <u>Rogers v. Rogers</u> appears in your text following this exercise.
Quote each of the following passages. To help you in locating the material, the passages are
marked on the opinion. Use one-inch margins and double spacing except for long quotations.
Left justify the text. In each exercise, include the proper citation following the quotation.
Place the number of each exercise on a line by itself.

1. Page 81

    Quote the material beginning **By this will** to the end of the sentence.

2. Page 81

    Quote the material beginning with **their 1968** through **Ann** in the same sentence. Use the
    word "Consequently," as a lead-in for the quote. Add the word "joint" before the word "will."

3. Pages 81, 82

    Quote the marked section of the paragraph that begins with **Sadie Warden**; skip the
    following paragraph; quote the marked material from the next paragraph that begins with **In
    accordance** through **upkeep**.

4. Page 82

    Quote and indicate the error in the material beginning **The Chancellor entered** through the
    end of the sentence.

5. Page 82

    Quote the paragraph from column 2 beginning with **A joint will**. Use the lead-in "The Judge
    said that."

6. Page 83

    Quote the marked portion of the paragraph beginning with **The most persistent** through **of
    the first testator.** Use the lead-in "The Court said."

7. Page 84

    Quote the material from column 2 beginning with **this observation has** through the end of the
    sentence. Boldface the word **no**. Use the lead-in "The Court said."

8. Page 84

    Quote the marked material from column 1 beginning with **Therefore** through the end of the
    sentence, skipping the phrase **to dispose of an estate in a particular manner or not to alter**.

9. Page 85

    Quote the material marked on page 85 beginning with **no court in this State** through the end
    of the paragraph. Omit the citation in the middle of the paragraph. Use the lead-in "The
    Judge said."

10. Page 85

    Quote the material on page 85 beginning with **The Tennessee Supreme Court** through
    executing it.

ROGERS v. RUSSELL   Tenn. 79
Cite as 733 S.W.2d 79 (Tenn. App. 1986)

**J. Michael ROGERS,
as guardian for
Tracee Rogers and Keely Rogers,
Plaintiffs/Appellees,**

v.

**Ann RUSSELL, Kenneth Russell,
and Sundee Russell,
Defendants/Appellants,**

Steven Russell, Defendant

Court of Appeals of Tennessee,
Middle Section, at Nashville.

Sept. 25, 1986.

Opinion Taxing Costs on Appeal
Feb. 6, 1987.

Published pursuant to
Tenn.Ct.App.R. 11.

Petition was brought to probate testatrix' will in solemn form. Testatrix' daughter and others contested will on grounds of lack of testamentary capacity, undue influence and irrevocability of prior joint will. Contestants moved for directed verdict based on irrevocability. The Circuit Court, Houston County, Leonard W. Martin, J., denied motion, entered judgment on jury verdict finding substituted instrument to be testatrix' will and denied contestants' posttrial motions. Contestants appealed. The Court of Appeals, Koch, J., held that: (1) trial court lacked jurisdiction as to enforceability of alleged contract to dispose of estate in accordance with joint will; (2) question of validity of substituted will was for jury; (3) execution of joint will was not by itself conclusive proof of existence of contract; and (4) proponents of will were entitled to taxing of costs on appeal against contestants for preparation of transcript.

Affirmed and remanded.

1. Wills ⟜ 100
    A "joint will" is nothing more than the separate wills of more than one person contained in the same instrument.
    See publication Words and Phrases for other judicial constructions and definitions.

2. Wills ⟜ 222
    A will contest proceeding in circuit court is an in rem proceeding analogous to the probate of a will in solemn form and is governed by statute. T.C.A. § 32-4-101 et seq.

3. Wills ⟜ 222
    The purpose of a will contest proceeding in circuit court is to determine whether the instrument offered for probate is the will of the deceased, and is intended to test the external validity of the will. T.C.A. § 32-4-101.

4. Wills ⟜ 310
    Circuit court lacked jurisdiction to consider enforceability of alleged contract to dispose of testatrix' property according to terms of prior joint will in statutory will contest proceeding considering validity of testatrix' substituted will. T.C.A. § 32-4-101 et seq.

5. Wills ⟜ 324(2,3)
    Proof concerning testatrix' testamentary capacity and freedom from undue influence presented jury question in will contest, and contestants' assertions of irrevocability of prior joint will based on contractual agreement did not warrant removing validity issue from consideration of jury. T.C.A. § 32-4-101 et seq.

6. Wills ⟜ 58(2)
    Proof of execution of joint will was insufficient to sustain claim that contract existed between husband and wife to dispose of their estates in accordance with its terms, in contest as to validity of substituted will, absent evidence of proof of existence of a testamentary contract. T.C.A. § 32-4-101 et seq.

7. Wills ⟜ 64, 188
    Joint will did not become "irrevo-

cable" upon death of first testator, since will, by its very nature, remained revocable until death of surviving testator and only contract to dispose of property in accordance with terms of will could have been deemed "irrevocable" upon death of first testator. T.C.A. § 32-4-101 et seq.

8. Wills ⇐ 329(1)

Trial court's instructions in will contest adequately submitted to jury claim that substituted will should not be admitted to probate because prior joint will became irrevocable upon death of first testator, in view of totality of original instructions, supplemental instructions and special interrogatories. T.C.A. § 32-4-101 et seq.

9. Wills ⇐ 400

Trial court's remarks concerning likelihood of an appeal of will contest did not affect judgment rendered or prejudice judicial process. Rules App.Proc., Rule 36(b); T.C.A. § 32-4-101 et seq.

10. Costs ⇐ 264

Trial courts do not have the authority to tax costs incurred on appeal and taxation of such costs is within jurisdiction of the appellate courts.

11. Costs ⇐ 264

A party seeking to raise an issue concerning taxation of costs on appeal may do so in the appellate court by proper motion and it is not necessary that such issue be presented to or preserved in the trial court. Rules App.Proc., Rules 3(e), 13(a, b).

12. Wills ⇐ 410

Will contestants failed to carry their burden of demonstrating that less than a complete transcript of trial court record conveyed fair, accurate and complete account of what transpired with respect to issues they sought to raise on appeal, and were therefore subject to taxing of costs of preparation of entire transcript of trial court proceedings since, contrary to contestants' claim, Court of Appeals was required to review entire transcript in

order to resolve issues raised.

––––––––

George R. Fleming, Sr., Fleming, Fleming & Ross, Clarksville, for defendants/appellants.

William L. Harbison, Kenneth R. Jones, O'Hare, Sherrard & Roe, Nashville, for plaintiffs/appellees.

––––––– OPINION –––––––

KOCH, Judge.

This appeal involves the probate of the will Sadie M. Warden executed on August 18, 1977. Her great grandchildren filed this will for probate following Mrs. Warden's death in 1981. Mrs. Warden's daughter and the daughter's children of her second marriage contested this will in part on the grounds of lack of testamentary capacity, undue influence, and the alleged "irrevocability" of the joint will Mrs. Warden had executed with her husband on April 1, 1968. These issues were certified to the Circuit Court for Houston County for a jury trial pursuant to Tenn.Code Ann. § 32-4-101 *et seq.* The jury found in favor of the 1977 will after a five day trial.

Mrs. Warden's daughter and her children have perfected this appeal. They do not take issue with the jury's decision concerning the validity of the manner in which Mrs. Warden's 1977 will was prepared and executed. They assert that they were entitled to a directed verdict on their claim that Mrs. Warden's 1977 will was invalid because the joint will she executed with her husband in 1968 became irrevocable upon her husband's death. They also challenge the trial court's jury instructions concerning this theory. We hold that Tenn.Code Ann. § 32-4-101 *et seq.* did not give the trial court the subject matter jurisdiction to consider the claim that Mrs. Warden's 1977 will was invalid because its execution allegedly violated her contract with her late husband to dispose of her estate in accordance with the terms of

ROGERS v. RUSSELL   Tenn. **81**

Cite as 733 S.W.2d 79 (Tenn. App. 1986)

their joint will executed in 1968. Thus, we affirm the judgment certifying to the Chancery Court for Houston County that the 1977 will is Mrs. Warden's valid last will and testament.

I.

Sadie M. Warden and her husband, Wiley C. Warden resided in Houston County for many years. Mr. Warden ran a saw mill and later operated a store on Highway 49 and Yellow Creek Road. Mr. and Mrs. Warden owned a home on Yellow Creek Road across from their store as well as a farm known as the Cooksey farm. They were a frugal couple who managed their affairs carefully.

The Wardens' daughter, Ann, was born in 1920. She was their second and only surviving child. Ann married Harry Wells. Her first child, Randee, was born in 1944. Ann divorced her first husband a year after Randee was born and married her second husband, Kenneth Russell, in 1946. She had four children with her second husband.[1] Ann had a progressively severe alcohol problem from 1962 through 1969 brought on by the retardation of her oldest son and problems with the oldest daughter of her second marriage. Her condition caused her parents a great deal of concern. She was able to bring her alcoholism under control in 1969.

Ann Warden Russell's first daughter, Randee, married Michael Rogers and gave birth to two children.[2] These children were Sadie Warden's only great grandchildren. Randee divorced her husband in 1976 and died in a freak accident in 1980.

Sadie and Wiley Warden executed a joint will on April 1, 1968. At that time, they owned some property as tenants by the entirety and other property in their individual name. **By this will, both Sadie and Wiley left their entire estate** to their survivor **"in fee simple and absolutely."** The will also provided for the creation of a trust in the event the survivor was adjudged legally incompetent. The trustee was specifically authorized to invade the corpus of this trust to care for the survivor.

The Wardens were also concerned about Ann's alcohol and health problems. Thus, **their 1968 will also provided for the creation of a spendthrift trust for Ann** upon the death or incompetency of the survivor. Upon Ann's death, the will provided that the residue of the Wardens' estate should be distributed to their grandchildren in equal shares when the youngest grandchild became of legal age. The bequest to any child deemed to be incompetent was limited to a $250 trust.

Wiley Warden died on August 6, 1968. The joint will he and his wife had executed four months earlier was duly probated on August 10, 1968. **Sadie Warden was appointed executrix. She continued to operate the store on Yellow Creek Road until she sold it in 1970. She also remained in the home across the street from the store.** She was able to live on her own and to take care of herself. She expected her daughter, grandchildren and great grandchildren to visit her, and they often did. Mrs. Warden enjoyed these visits and continued to take an active interest in her family and her church.

Mrs. Warden first thought about executing a new will as early as 1973. She finally executed a new will on August 18, 1977. The prospect of Mrs. Warden executing a new will caused great dissension among her daughter and grandchildren. Ann Russell and Rena Russell Trent thought that Randee Rogers would try to obtain the house on Yellow Creek Road that Mrs. Warden had promised to give to Rena. These fears ultimately proved to be unfounded.

---

1. These children are (1) Kenneth Russell who was born with severe mental retardation in 1948; (2) Rena Russell Trent who was born in 1950; (3) Steven Russell who was born in 1956; and (4) Sundee Russell who was born in 1961.

2. These children are: (1) Tracee Rogers who was born in 1966 and (2) Keely Rogers who was born in 1970.

82   Tenn.   733 SOUTH WESTERN REPORTER, 2d SERIES

However, it is this dispute that ultimately caused Ann Russell and her children to contest Mrs. Warden's 1977 will.

3. Mrs. Warden's 1977 will specifically revoked all earlier wills and was significantly different from the joint will she and her husband had executed in 1968. **In accordance with her promise, she left her house on Yellow Creek Road to Rena Russell Trent together with a $3,000 trust for its maintenance and upkeep.** She also created a $13,200 trust to pay Ann Russell's medical expenses and a $2,000 trust for the maintenance and support of her retarded grandson, Kenneth Russell. She directed that the Cooksey farm be sold and that the proceeds be divided in six equal shares to be distributed among her daughter, her three granddaughters, and her two great granddaughters. The will's residuary clause directed that the remainder of her estate be divided equally among her three granddaughters and her two great granddaughters.

Ann Russell petitioned the Chancery Court to appoint her as the administrator of her mother's estate as if she had died intestate. However, the father of Mrs. Warden's two great grandchildren had already filed a petition to probate her August 18, 1977 will in solemn form. Ann Russell and the children of her second marriage decided to contest the 1977 will and to offer the 1968 joint will for probate. **The Chancellor entered a order pursuant to Tenn.Code Ann. § 32-4-101** *et seq.* **certifying this matter to the Circuit Court for a trial to determine whether the August 18, 1977 document was Mrs. Warden's will. The** jury determined that it was, and this appeal ensued.[3]

II.

The Jurisdiction of the Circuit Court in a Tenn.Code Ann. § 32-4-101 Proceeding

We must first consider whether the circuit court in a Tenn.Code Ann. § 32-4-101 proceeding to contest a will can hear and decide a contestant's claim based upon an alleged testamentary contract by the testator. Mrs. Warden's great grandchildren, as proponents of the 1977 will, challenged the ability of Ann Russell and her children to do so in their motion in limine filed prior to trial. However, the trial court overruled this motion and allowed this question to go to the jury.

The proponents of the 1977 will prevailed at trial and thus, understandably, have not directly raised this issue on appeal. The question is jurisdictional, however, and thus Tenn.R.App.P. 13(b) permits this Court to raise and decide this issue on our own motion. *Dalton v. Dean,* 22 Tenn.App. 56, 57, 117 S.W.2d 973, 974 (1938).

This case appears to be the first time a Tennessee court has addressed the question of whether contestant in a Tenn.Code Ann. § 32-4-101 *et seq.* proceeding should be permitted to assert its rights under an alleged contract not to dispose of one's property contrary to the terms of a joint will.[4] We have determined that a will contest proceeding is not the proper forum to assert these contractual rights. Our decision is based upon a recognition of the purpose of a will contest proceeding as well as a recognition of the difference between the testamentary and contractual aspects of a joint will.

[1] A joint will is nothing more than the separate wills of more than one person contained in the same instrument. *Richmond v. Richmond,* 195

---

3. Steven Russell does not join his mother or her and sisters in this appeal. He received under the terms of his grandmother's will.

4. This practice appears to have been followed in *First Christian Church of Guthrie, Kentucky v. Moneypenny,* 59 Tenn.App. 229, 237, 439 S.W.2d 620, 623 (1968). However, this court was not called upon to review the correctness of this procedure and thus did not approve it.

ROGERS v. RUSSELL   Tenn. 83
Cite as 733 S.W.2d 79 (Tenn. App. 1986)

Tenn. 704, 709-10, 227 S.W.2d 4, 6 (1950). While joint wills have been recognized as valid in Tennessee, *Popejoy v. Peters,* 173 Tenn. 484, 487, 121 S.W.2d 538, 539 (1938) and *Epperson v. White,* 156 Tenn. 155, 160, 299 S.W. 812, 813 (1927), their use has been discouraged because of the very problems made obvious by this case. See 1 H. Phillips & J. Robinson, *Pritchard on the Law of Wills and Administration of Estates* § 23, at 30 (4th ed. 1983) [hereinafter cited as "Pritchard"]; McMurray, *Joint and Mutual Wills in Tennessee: Validity, Contractual Limitations, and Effect on the Estate Tax Marital Deduction,* 42 Tenn.L.Rev. 305, 322 (1975); and 1 W. Bowe & D. Parker, *Page on the Law of Wills* § 11.1 at 553 (rev. 1960) [hereinafter cited as "Page"].

The most persistent problems stemming from the execution of a joint will relate to the contractual implications of the joint will itself. It has often been asserted that the mere execution of a joint will is tantamount to a contract between the testators to dispose of their estates only in accordance with the terms of the joint will and thus that the joint will becomes irrevocable upon the death of the first testator. It is also asserted that the execution of a joint will amounts to a contract by the testators not to revoke the will after the death of the last testator. [6.]

The Tennessee Supreme Court has stated that these propositions are legally erroneous because they ignore the difference between the will and the accompanying contract. *Ashley v. Volz,* 218 Tenn. 420, 425, 404 S.W.2d 239, 241 (1966) and *Church of Christ Home for Aged v. Nashville Trust Co.,* 184 Tenn. 629, 637, 202 S.W.2d 178, 181 (1947). These holdings are in accord with the majority rule. One treatise points out:

> Frequently joint or mutual wills are made in pursuance of an agreement or compact not to revoke them. Here it is important to distinguish between the concept of

wills and that of contracts. Our law has no separate concept of "will made in pursuance of contract;" we must treat the will part as a will and the contract part as a contract. Viewed in the aspect of a will, such instruments do not differ from other wills. In order to be effective, they must be admitted to probate and they are revocable although there has been an agreement not to revoke. The matter of the contractual aspect does not properly arise upon probate, but only when the agreement is sought to be established as a claim against the estate, or in a proceeding against the successors of the decedent. T. Atkinson, *Handbook on the Law of Wills* § 49, at 224 (2d ed. 1953).

See also Page § 11.9, at 569.

While the Tennessee Supreme Court, in an opinion involving an independent action for specific performance of a contract not to revoke a mutual will, stated that the will/contract distinction was immaterial, *Church of Christ Home for Aged v. Nashville Trust Co.,* 184 Tenn. 629, 637, 202 S.W.2d 178, 181 (1947), **this observation has no application to the jurisdictional issue presently before this Court.** [7.] This issue was not before the Tennessee Supreme Court at the time, and the statement is, at most, dictum to its main holding. We find that this distinction is quite material in this case.

[2] A will contest proceeding in circuit court pursuant to Tenn.Code Ann. § 32-4-101 is governed by statute. *Petty v. Call,* 599 S.W.2d 791, 793 (Tenn.1980). It is an *in rem* proceeding analogous to the probate of a will in solemn form. *Bearman v. Camatsos,* 215 Tenn. 231, 238, 385 S.W.2d 91, 94-95 (1964) and *Durell v. Martin,* 172 Tenn. 97, 104, 110 S.W.2d 316, 318 (1937).

[3] The purpose of the proceeding is to determine whether the instrument offered for probate is the will of the deceased. *Carver v. Anthony,* 35

Tenn.App. 306, 312-313, 245 S.W.2d 422, 425 (1951). It is intended to test the external validity of the will. Professor Atkinson has noted that

> a will may be contested upon the ground that it was not duly executed, which objection may include failure to observe the statutory formalities of execution, alterations or additions after execution, or forgery of the instrument. The contest may also be based upon the grounds that the testator lacked testamentary capacity, that undue influence or fraud were practiced upon him, or that he was laboring under a mistake of the sort which invalidates the instrument. A will may be contested upon the ground that it has been revoked. The objection that the instrument was not intended as a will and did not possess testamentary character can likewise be ground of contest. T. Atkinson, *Handbook on the Law of Wills* § 98, at 517 (2d ed. 1953).

See also *Clark v. Hefley,* 34 Tenn.App. 389, 397, 238 S.W.2d 513, 516 (1950) (lack of testamentary capacity and undue influence).

Recognizing the purpose of a will contest proceeding, most courts addressing the question have held that a will contest does not involve a decedent's right to devise and bequeath property. **Therefore, the trial court does not have jurisdiction to entertain a claim based upon an alleged contract** to dispose of an estate in a particular manner or not to alter **or revoke a will.** *Kozyra v. Jackman,* 60 Mich.App. 7, 230 N.W.2d 284, 287-88 (1975); *Huston v. Cole,* 139 Tex. 150, 162 S.W.2d 404, 406 (1942); *Pullen v. Russ,* 209 S.W.2d 630, 634 (Tex.Civ.App. 1948); *Ellsworth v. Aldrich,* 295 S.W. 206, 209 (Tex.Civ.App. 1927); and *Chitwood v. Collins,* 122 W.Va. 267, 8 S.E.2d 830, 831-32 (1940). See also 80 Am.Jur.2d *Wills* § 860 (1975); 3 W. Bowe & D.

8.

Parker, *Page on the Law of Wills* § 26.82, at 172 (rev. 1961); 95 C.J.S. *Wills* § 328b. (1957); and T. Atkinson, *Handbook on the Law of Wills* § 49, at 224 (2d ed. 1953).

[4] The Tennessee Supreme Court has stressed that courts should decline to adopt procedures that have the effect of lengthening the time needed to probate a will. *Lillard v. Tolliver,* 154 Tenn. 304, 315, 285 S.W. 576, 579 (1926). We recognize and concur in this policy. However, it is not our prerogative to expand a court's statutory jurisdiction in the name of expediency. The issues in a will contest proceeding pursuant to Tenn.Code Ann. § 32-4-101 *et seq.* should not be obscured by issues that are not within the court's jurisdiction to decide. In accordance with the majority rule, a revoked will, even if it is a joint will, should be denied probate even though its revocation was a breach of contract, and the substituted will should be admitted to probate if it is otherwise proper.[5] Then the persons claiming that the decedent's execution of a subsequent will breached a contract may seek relief by filing a claim against the decedent's estate.

III.

The Contestants' Motion for a Directed Verdict

Ann Russell and her children insist that they were entitled to a directed verdict on the invalidity of Mrs. Warden's 1977 will. Our review of the trial court's denial of their motion is based upon the same standards applied to Tenn.R.Civ.P. 50 motions in other civil cases. *Curry v. Bridges,* 45 Tenn.App. 395, 406, 325 S.W.2d 87, 91 (1959) and *Scott v. Atkins,* 44 Tenn.App. 353, 371, 314 S.W.2d 52, 60 (1957). After reviewing the evidence in a light most favorable to the motion's opponent, the trial court should grant a directed verdict only when one conclusion can be drawn from the evidence. *Arp v. Wolfe,* 49 Tenn.App.

5. See Page § 11.9 n. 9 and T. Atkinson, Handbook on the Law of Wills § 48, at 217 (2d ed. 1953).

ROGERS v. RUSSELL   Tenn. **85**

Cite as 733 S.W.2d 79 (Tenn. App. 1986)

294, xxx, 354 S.W.2d 799, 801-02 (1956) and *Cude v. Culberson,* 30 Tenn.App. 628, 637, 209 S.W.2d 506, 513 (1947). A directed verdict should not be granted if there is any substantial dispute concerning the material evidence or if there is any doubt concerning the ultimate conclusion of the case. *Curry v. Bridges,* 45 Tenn.App. 395, 406, 325 S.W.2d 87, 91 (1959).

[5] The trial court's decision to deny Ann Russell's motion for directed verdict was proper for two reasons. First, the proof concerning Mrs. Warden's testamentary capacity and her freedom from undue influence presented a jury question. Second, Ann Russell's theory that the 1968 joint will was irrevocable is based upon two erroneous legal assumptions—that the existence of a joint will is, by itself, conclusive evidence of a contract and that a joint will becomes "irrevocable" when the first testator dies.

9. [6] Contrary to Mrs. Russell's assertion, **no court in this State has held that the execution of a joint will is, by itself, conclusive proof of the existence of a contract. While the courts have recognized that a joint will or mutual wills may satisfy the statute of frauds,** *Harris v. Morgan,* 157 Tenn. 140, 154, 7 S.W.2d 53, 57 (1928), **they have never adopted the** *per se* **rule relied upon by the contestants in this case. Instead, the courts have made clear that the existence of a testamentary contract is proved by reference to the nature of the contract, its terms, the circumstances antecedent to the will, and the circumstances existing when the parties joined in the will's execution.**

The Tennessee Supreme Court has stated that in the case of joint wills:

10. **the courts generally, though not uniformly, held that the understanding to make a joint reciprocal will may be conclusively inferred from the fact of its**

10. **execution, together with the provisions of the will and the circumstances existing when the parties joined in executing it.** *Seat v. Seat,* 172 Tenn. 618, 624, 113 S.W.2d 751, 754 (1938).

See also *Church of Christ Home for Aged v. Nashville Trust Co.,* 184 Tenn. 629, 636, 202 S.W.2d 178, 180-81 (1947).

By requiring more proof of the existence of a contract other than the execution of a joint will, our courts have followed the majority view recognizing that

The fact that joint wills and mutual wills are usually executed as a result of a common intention does not in any way mean that they are always executed pursuant to a contract between the parties respecting the making of such wills ... It is more logical to expect that in many settings, particularly that of husband and wife, the reciprocity or similarity in the dispositive provisions of the two wills results from similar tastes and affections that have resulted from years of living together, and the making of identical or similar wills was spontaneous thing unaccompanied by even so much as a thought on the part of either the husband or wife that they should enter into a contract with each other. Page § 11.1, at 554.

Thus, our courts have always required more than the proof of the execution of a joint will to sustain a claim that a contract existed between the two parties to dispose of their estates in accordance with the terms of the will. *Harris v. Morgan,* 12 Tenn.App. 445, 448 (1930).

[7] Ann Russell's second erroneous assertion is that a joint will becomes "irrevocable" upon the death of the first testator. This fails to recognize the distinction between the contractual and the testamentary character of the instrument. Wills, by their very nature, must remain revocable until the testator's death. Pritchard §§ 27 & 243 and Page §

86 Tenn.   733 SOUTH WESTERN REPORTER, 2d SERIES

5.17. It is the contract to dispose of property in accordance with the terms of the will that becomes irrevocable at the death of the first testator. *Church of Christ Home for Aged v. Nashville Trust Co.,* 184 Tenn. 629, 637, 202 S.W.2d 178, 181 (1947).

IV.

The Trial Court's Instructions

[8] The parties contesting the validity of Mrs. Warden's 1977 will also take issue with the trial court's instructions to the jury concerning their claim that the 1977 will should not be admitted to probate because the 1968 will became irrevocable when Mrs. Warden's husband died. This issue is without merit in light of our determination that the enforceability of Mrs. Warden's alleged contract with her husband to dispose of her estate in the manner provided in the 1968 will was not a proper matter to consider on the probate of the 1977 will. Even if it were, we find the issue was adequately submitted to the jury when the trial court's original instructions, its supplemental instructions and the special interrogatories submitted to the jury are considered.

[9] The trial court's remarks concerning the likelihood of an appeal in this case did not affect the judgment or prejudice the judicial process. Thus, in accordance with Tenn.R.App.P. 36(b), we find this issue to be without merit.

IV.

The decision of the trial court is affirmed, and the case is remanded for further appropriate proceedings. The costs of this appeal are taxed against the appellants and their surety for which execution, if necessary, may issue.

LEWIS and CANTRELL, JJ., concur.

OPINION TAXING COSTS ON APPEAL

KOCH, Judge.

This Court affirmed the judgment of the trial court in an opinion filed on September 25, 1986. This opinion taxed the costs of the appeal against the appellants and their surety. On October 29, 1986, the appellees requested that the Clerk of this Court treat as costs to be taxed on appeal the costs they incurred in preparing portions of the transcript of proceedings which the appellants had not designated originally as part

CHAPTER 15

PREPARING AN APPELLATE BRIEF

OBJECTIVES

When you successfully complete this chapter, you will be able to:

➤ Transcribe an appellate brief

➤ Prepare a title page

➤ Prepare a table of contents

➤ Prepare a table of authorities

INTRODUCTION

This chapter discusses the documents prepared when a party is dissatisfied with the decision made by the judge of the court where a trial took place, known as a trial-level court. The decision can be appealed to the next level of court, where a panel of judges or justices review the case but there is no testimony of the parties or witnesses. In the appellate process, a panel (usually three) of appellate judges review the documents, review a transcript of the testimony from the trial court, read the written arguments (appellate briefs) presented by attorneys for both sides of the case, and sometimes listen to oral argument by the attorneys. The appellate judges may uphold the decision of the lower court, reverse the decision, or send the case back to the lower court for further action.

The party appealing the decision of a trial court is the **appellant**; the party opposing the appeal is the **appellee**. If the defendant appeals, he or she is the defendant-appellant; the opposing party is the plaintiff-appellee. If the plaintiff appeals, he or she is the plaintiff-appellant; the opposing party is the defendant-appellee.

The attorney for the party who wishes to appeal must either state it in court at the end of the trial or file a notice of appeal with the clerk of the trial-level court and serve a copy on the opposing party within 30 days after the final judgment of the trial judge.

APPELLANT

The party appealing a decision from a lower court.

APPELLEE

The party opposing the appeal.

Upon receiving the notice of appeal, the clerk of the trial-level court sends the documents and transcripts filed in case, known as the **record**, to the appropriate appellate court. Volume 1 of the record contains copies of documents filed in the trial court, such as pleadings, exhibits, and orders. Volume 2 of the record is the word-for-word transcript of the trial-level proceedings. Only essential parts of the record are forwarded to the appellate court, as the judges need to decide only on the matter being reviewed. The larger the record, the more it costs.

The next step is for the attorneys for both parties to prepare appellate briefs. The attorney for the appellant argues that the lower court erred in arriving at its decision; the attorney for the appellee argues that the court acted correctly. The first briefs filed by each side are principal briefs; responses to the principal briefs are known as reply briefs. Principal briefs are usually limited to 50 pages; reply briefs, 25 pages.

The attorney composes the text of the brief, but the legal secretary or transcriptionist is usually responsible for preparing tables and indexes. The first step in adequately preparing to format a brief is to study the court rules.

RULES OF APPELLATE PROCEDURE

The rules for filing an appeal are found in the state appellate rules of court or, at the federal level, in the *Federal Rules of Appellate Procedure*.

Rules for filing briefs vary from one jurisdiction to another. Usually **appellate briefs** filed in state courts and in United States Courts of Appeal can be typed or prepared on a word processor, using the formatting instructions outlined in the rules of appellate procedure.

The following guidelines for formatting an appellate brief are found in Rule 32(a) of the *Federal Rules of Appellate Procedure*.

- Use opaque, unglazed white paper.
- Use any method to get a clear black image.
- Use 8½- by 11-inch paper, if typewritten.
- Double-space except for quoted matter, which may be single-spaced.
- Use a type size not smaller than standard elite, or print with at least an 11-point font.
- The typing on the page should not exceed 6½ by 9½ inches.
- If the brief is printed, the copy on the page should not exceed 4⅛ by 7⅛ inches, printed on paper 6⅛ by 9¼ inches.
- Pages are to be numbered at the bottom.
- Pages are to be fastened on the left.

PARTS OF A BRIEF

The sections of the brief described in this chapter will provide a framework for understanding the format and organization of an appellate brief. A brief has the following sections: Fed. R. Civ. P. 28.

TITLE PAGE
TABLE OF CONTENTS
TABLE OF AUTHORITIES
ISSUES PRESENTED
STATEMENT OF THE CASE AND STATEMENT OF THE FACTS
ARGUMENTS
CONCLUSION
CERTIFICATE OF SERVICE
APPENDIX

The illustrations for this discussion are excerpts from an appellate brief filed on behalf of Michael Craig Saunders, the plaintiff-appellant. This is a case where a decedent died and had no children. Everyone else in the family who might inherit his estate was deceased except a child of the decedent's brother (a nephew) and children of the half-brothers and half-sisters (half-nieces and half-nephews). At the trial level the judge ruled that the estate should go to all nieces and nephews. The nephew of the only whole-blooded brother was dissatisfied and his attorney filed an appellate brief.

Title Page

Rule 32(a) of the *Federal Rules of Appellate Procedure* specifies that the following information be displayed on the front cover. See Figure 15-1, a sample title page.

- The number of the case in the appellate court and the name of the court

- The title of the case as it appeared in the trial court, except the status of each party in the appellate court is indicated

- The nature of the proceeding in the appellate court (such as appeal or petition for review) and the name of the court, agency, or board below

- The title of the document

- The name and address of counsel

The attorney may wish to present an oral argument before the appellate court. If so, on the cover of the brief ORAL ARGUMENT REQUESTED should be centered at the bottom of the cover page. Thirty minutes is allowed for an oral argument unless additional time is requested and granted.

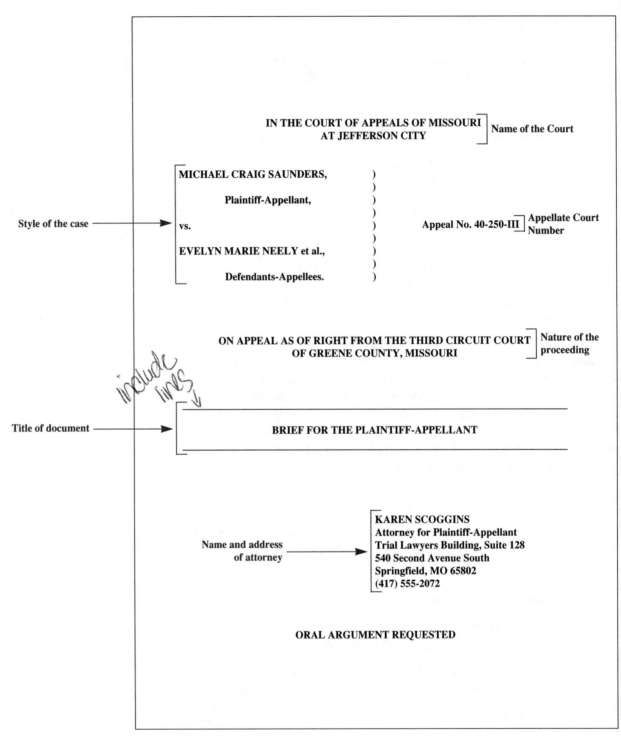

FIGURE 15-1. Title Page of an Appellate Brief

The rules also specify that the cover of the brief for the appellant be blue; the brief for the appellee be red; and the reply briefs by both parties be gray.

Table of Contents

The **table of contents** is an outline of the sections of the brief, indicating page numbers where each section begins. It is prepared after the body of the brief is completed. Refer to Figure 15-2 for an appropriate style.

Center the title, TABLE OF CONTENTS, in full caps two inches from the top of the page. Triple-space after the title and double-space between entries. Use either open leaders (periods with a space between each one) or closed leaders (periods with no space between them) from the section name to the page numbers. Align page numbers at the right. The first page should be numbered with the roman number -i- centered at the bottom of the page. If the table continues to the second page, it would be numbered -ii-.

Arguments are enumerated with roman numerals and indented one-half inch from the left margin. Align the roman numerals at the right. Additional subdivisions, labeled A, B, C, and 1, 2, 3, may be needed. Align each subdivision with an additional indention as shown below. Also note the capitalization for each subdivision — full caps on level-one entries (I, II, III), initial caps on all words with second-level entries (A, B, C), and initial caps on the first word with third-level entries (1, 2, 3).

   I. THE TRIAL COURT ERRED . . . .

  II. THE TRIAL COURT ERRED . . . .

      A. Consistent With the Due Process and Equal Protection . . . .

      B. <u>Cunningham v. Golden</u> Represents a Departure From . . . .

        1. The state has provided . . . .

        2. Equal protection is defined . . . .

Table of Authorities (Citations)

The **table of authorities** is an alphabetical list of each and every citation included in the appellate brief, with references to the pages in the brief where they are cited. The authorities are separated into at least two categories: (1) cases and (2) other authorities. Some writers create additional groupings; namely, constitutions, statutes, cases, and other authorities. Alphabetize the cases by the first word in the case name; alphabetize other authorities by the first number or word in the citation. The citation form presented in Chapter 14 should be used as a guide for preparing the table of authorities.

Every page on which a citation appears should be listed as shown in Figure 15-3. Single-space the entries with a double space between each entry.

TABLE OF CONTENTS

An outline of the sections of a brief, indicating page numbers where each section begins.

TABLE OF AUTHORITIES

An alphabetical listing of each and every citation included in an appellate brief, with references to the pages in the brief where they are cited.

TABLE OF CONTENTS

- i -

FIGURE 15-2. Table of Contents

Use leaders from each citation to the page numbers where it can be found. Use a roman numeral at the bottom of the page. It is a continuation number from the table of contents; therefore, if the last page of the table of contents was -i-, the first page of the table of authorities would be -ii-.

Issues Presented for Review

The **issues** are legal questions to be answered. One or several issues to be reviewed by the court may be presented. These are claimed errors of law made by the trial court. The appellate court judges consider and decide the issues. The issues, which are usually presented as an enumerated list, are presented in question form or in a phrase beginning with the word *whether*. These are the same matters addressed in the argument portion of the brief. This section may be titled Questions Presented, Points in Error, Issues Presented or Issues Presented for Review.

ISSUES

Legal questions.

This, as well as each of the following sections of the brief, begins on a new page. Format the issues as shown in Figure 15-4. Center the title in full caps two inches from the top of the page. Arabic page numbering begins with the first page of Issues Presented and continues to the end of the document. The rules do not indicate that any page numbers are to be omitted; therefore, it is suggested that all pages be numbered.

Statement of the Case and Statement of Facts

The **statement of the case** provides a description and history of the case and indicates the outcome of lower court proceedings. The **statement of facts** is a detailed description of the facts surrounding the case. Only information relevant to the appeal is included.

STATEMENT OF THE CASE

A description and history of the case, including the outcome of lower court proceedings.

In describing the facts of the case, references to the record can be indicated in the text of the brief by inserting (R.) and the page and volume number. See Figure 15-5. Each volume of the record is numbered, beginning with the roman numeral I. Another method of indicating references to the record is to use (R.) for record and the page number for the **documents** filed at the trial level and (T.) or (TR.) and the page number to refer to the **transcript** of testimony at trial. The method of referring to the record is often mentioned in an introductory statement, such as "References to the record will be noted as follows: Documents at trial, by page number (R. ____) and transcript by page number (TR., ____)." If there are two volumes of the transcript, an abbreviation such as (TR. I, 25) could be used. Two consecutive references could be expressed as (TR. I, 42; R. 24). Several consecutive references may be expressed as (TR I, 45; II, 27; II; 80; II, 101) All of these are references to the transcript. The abbreviation Ex. is often used to refer to Exhibits made at trial. (Ex. 4).

STATEMENT OF FACTS

A detailed description of the facts surrounding a case.

If the reference is at the end of a sentence, place it in parentheses followed by a period. For example: (R. 92). If it is in the middle of a sentence, place parentheses around the reference and punctuate according to the sentence structure. For example: A Memorandum Opinion was recently rendered (R. 5-6), and in September the Court issued an Order.

TABLE OF AUTHORITIES

- ii -

FIGURE 15-3. Table of Authorities

ISSUES PRESENTED FOR REVIEW

I.   WHETHER THE TRIAL COURT ERRED IN HOLDING THAT PERSONALTY OF A DECEDENT WITHOUT ISSUE IS DIVIDED EQUALLY AMONG HALF BROTHERS AND SISTERS AND WHOLE BROTHERS AND SISTERS.

II.   WHETHER THE TRIAL COURT ERRED IN HOLDING THAT MISSOURI HAS CHANGED THE DISTRIBUTION OF PERSONALTY SET OUT IN THE STATUTES OF 1850.

- 1 -

FIGURE 15-4. Issues Presented for Review

Some writers prepare this portion of the brief as one section; others prepare one section for the statement of the case and another section for the statement of the facts.

Arguments

ARGUMENT

A discussion of the law as applied to the legal question; the attorney's support for his or her side of the case.

Each **argument** clearly discusses the law as applied to the legal question being presented; it is the attorney's argument for his or her side of the case. Each argument is numbered with a roman numeral. This section of the brief contains numerous citations to legal authority.

Begin each argument on a separate page. Note in Figure 15-6 that ARGUMENT I is centered. The three-line title of the argument is displayed in full caps, single-spaced.

Conclusion

CONCLUSION

A statement resulting from the argument, including the relief sought from the appellate court.

The **conclusion** is a statement resulting from the argument and should state the relief sought.

Following the conclusion, double space and at center point key "Respectfully submitted," and prepare a signature block for the attorney as shown below:

Respectfully submitted,

KAREN SCOGGINS (No. 38783)
Attorney for Plaintiff-Appellant
Trial Lawyers Building, Suite 128
540 Second Avenue South
Springfield, MO 65802
(417) 555-2072

Certificate of Service

A certificate of service for the attorney's signature, as in litigation documents, is prepared, stating that a copy of the brief has been mailed to the opposing attorney. If space is available, the certificate can be placed on the page with the conclusion. It may be single- or double-spaced.

Appendices to the Brief

APPENDIX

An additional section at the back of an appellate brief containing material to support the brief; it can be a separately bound volume with a title page.

An **appendix** is an additional section at the back of the appellate brief, containing material to support the brief. Not all briefs have an appendix or appendices. When there is one, it can be included at the back of the brief or can be a separately bound volume. A separately bound volume should have a white cover with the same information as is on the title page of the appellate brief.

A table of contents for the appendix, listing the contents of the materials it contains in the order they are arranged, is inserted after the cover page of the appendix page. The appendix may contain copies of any unpublished opinions

STATEMENT OF THE CASE

The case was filed by the administrator of the estate desiring instructions as to the proper distribution of the estate, which consisted of realty and personalty. The decedent died, having never been married and having been predeceased by his mother and father, his brother and sister, and two half brothers and three half sisters. (R. I, 22). In an action between the administrator and the half brothers and sisters, the administrator contended that distribution should be made solely to the child of the decedent's only brother.

The Court held that proper construction of the statutes of distribution requires that the property be distributed among all nieces and nephews, including those who take by representation as children of half brothers and half sisters.

- 2 -

FIGURE 15-5. Statement of the Case

Don't tab in

All caps — not hanging

ARGUMENT I

THE TRIAL COURT ERRED IN HOLDING THAT PERSONALTY OF A DECEDENT WITHOUT ISSUE IS DIVIDED EQUALLY AMONG HALF BROTHERS AND SISTERS AND WHOLE BROTHERS AND SISTERS.

The law in this state as to the transfer of ownership of property upon death is found in the Missouri Revised Statutes which provides that distribution of real property should be to "brother[s] and sisters of the whole and half blood . . . to be divided among them equally." Mo. Rev. Stat. § 36-2-103(a) (1989). The legislature carefully provided for the descent and distribution of personalty by providing that it be inherited by "brothers and sisters, or the children of brothers and sisters representing them, equally." Mo. Rev. Stat. § 36-2-103(a)(1) (1989).

The trial court judge erred in holding that when a decedent dies without issue, spouse, father, or mother, the personalty be divided among half brothers and half sisters as well as among brothers and sisters of the whole blood. Id.

Under the Missouri statutes of 1850, in the absence of surviving parents or descendants, a decedent's personalty was inherited equally by brothers and sisters and half brothers and half sisters because they were of equal degree of kinship to the decedent.[1] Under the provisions of the statute, such personalty should be distributed "to the next of kindred, in equal degree, of, or unto the intestate, and their legal representatives as aforesaid, and in no other manner whatsoever." Kyle v. Moore, 24 Mo. 183, 13 S.W. 238 (1872).

By the enactment of the Missouri Revised Statutes, the law as to distribution of a decedent's personalty was changed. When a decedent dies without descendants, widow, father or mother, his personalty should go "exclusively to the brothers and sisters, or their children representing them." Mo. Rev. Stat. § 22-6-75 (1989). This re-enactment of a statute which omits portions of a prior statute constitutes a repeal of the omitted portions. Barham v. Holland, 67 Mo. 104, 100 S.W. 184 (1877).

---

[1] Missouri's Statutes of Descent and Distribution have their origin in the common law and the early statutes of the state of Missouri. See, e.g., Mo. Ann. Stat. § 20-301 (Vernon 1943); Mo. Rev. Stat. § 25-2-410 (1989).

e.g.

- 12 -

FIGURE 15-6. Argument I

(written opinions by judges obtained from the clerk of the court but not printed in reporters) cited in a brief, relevant portions of the record, relevant parts of constitutional provisions or statutes cited but not quoted in the body of the brief, or any other authorities to aid the court in reviewing the case.

Formatting Instructions for an Appellate Brief

- Check the local rules of appellate procedure to determine the proper number of copies to make for the appellate court. In addition, make a copy to be served on the opposing attorney and an office copy.

- Set margins according to the *Federal Rules of Appellate Procedure* listed on page 422. Make the left margin wider than the right to allow additional blank space for binding at the left.

- Proofread and assemble the completed brief in the order presented on page 423. Bind or staple the brief about one-quarter inch from the left edge. Three equally spaced staples are adequate.

- Once a case has been cited, the author of an appellate brief may, in a general discussion of the case, refer to it by name without further citation; for example, <u>Drinkard v. State</u> may be referred to later in the document as <u>Drinkard</u>. Underline the shortened form.

- The author of an appellate brief may use standard footnotes as a means of adding a comment or source reference. A superscripted footnote number appears at the end of the referenced word or phrase in the text, and the footnotes are placed at the bottom of the page, single-spaced, and separated from the text with a dividing line.

SUMMARY

- After a case is heard at the trial level, it can be appealed to an appellate court provided an error occurred at the trial level. At the appellate level, judges or justices review cases but do not hear testimony.

- The party appealing a decision of a lower court is the appellant; the opposing party is the appellee. An appellate brief is prepared by the attorney for the appellant and the attorney for the appellee.

- Unless an oral notice to appeal is made in court, a written notice of appeal is filed with the clerk of the court within 30 days after the final judgment and is served on the opposing party.

- A record is sent up from the trial-level court to the appellate court when a case is appealed. The record consists of copies of documents filed with the clerk of the trial-level court and a transcript of the testimony given at trial.

- The appellate brief is to be typewritten or printed. Sections of the brief are the title page, table of contents, table of authorities, issues presented, statement of the case and statement of facts, arguments, conclusion, certificate of service, and sometimes an appendix.

- The title page identifies the court, style and number of the case, the parties, and counsel, and includes a request for oral argument, if desired.

- The table of contents outlines all sections of the appellate brief and indicates the page number where each section begins.

- The table of authorities lists all legal references used in the paper and includes **all** page numbers where the authorities are cited.

- Issues presented are the legal questions to be answered.

- The statement of the case provides a description and history of the case and indicates the outcome of the lower court proceeding. The statement of facts is a detailed description of the facts surrounding the case. This part of the brief includes references to the record and transcript.

- The argument is the attorney's justification for his or her side of the case. This section of the brief has numerous citations to legal authority.

- Every brief should have a conclusion. The certificate of service can be placed on the page with the conclusion if space permits.

- An appendix contains such things as copies of unpublished opinions, a portion of the record, and portions of the constitution or statutes cited but not quoted in the text of the brief. Not all appellate briefs have an appendix.

REVIEW EXERCISES

T F   1. A notice of appeal is always prepared when a party wishes to appeal to a higher court.

T F   2. The record is always compiled into one volume and is referred to as (R. I).

T F   3. The appellant is the party opposing the appeal and can always be identified as the defendant-appellant.

T F   4. An appellate brief is prepared by attorneys on each side of the case.

T F   5. The first brief filed by the appellant's attorney is a principal brief, and the first brief filed by the appellee's attorney is a reply brief.

T F   6. Rules of appellate courts provide information for formatting an appellate brief.

T F   7. An appendix is always inserted at the end of an appellate brief.

T F   8. If the attorney wishes to have 30 minutes to present an oral argument before the judge, ORAL ARGUMENT REQUESTED should be printed on the title page.

T F   9. Page numbers for sections of the table of contents should be aligned at the left.

T F   10. The title of each section of a brief should be keyed in full caps two inches from the top of the page.

T F   11. There may be one or several arguments presented in a brief.

T F   12. In the table of authorities, list the page number where the first citation to a case or legal authority appears, but do not show additional pages where the case is cited.

T F   13. The table of citations and table of authorities are numbered at the bottom with arabic numerals 1 and 2.

T F   14. Following the conclusion is a signature block for the attorney, which includes the name, address, attorney's number, and telephone number.

T F   15. The left and right margins of a typewritten brief should be equal.

T F   16. If a standard footnote is used in a brief, a superscript number appears at the end of the reference word or phrase in the text.

TRANSCRIPTION EXERCISES

Transcribe the following material, which consists of excerpts from the appellate brief of Joseph Frazier, II. The appellees are Betty Lou Harvey and Phillip Robert Harvey. Correct the spelling and capitalization, and use the correct style.

1. the court refused to admit into evidence the results of the hla blood test and otherwise limited plaintiffs proof at trial transcript two page 189 transcript 1 page 50

2. he bought cynthia clothes on several occasions transcript page one hundred thirty-five.

3. the tests concluded the liklihood of mr. fraziers being the natural father of cynthia

4. the case was assigned to the second circuit court

5. the court heard the defendants motion to dismiss (There are two defendants.)

6. defendants application for permission to appeal was denied by the court of appeals for failure to conform to the tennessee rules of civil procedure (There are two defendants.)

7. he often picked her up at her parents home

8. see tenn code ann section 36-2-103 a 1 queen v jolly 219 tenn 427 410 south western second 416 1966

Use a reference manual to help you in making the correct word choices:

9. The Petition did not specifically (site, sight, cite) the statutory basis for the suit.

10. The Court having read the brief of (counsel, council) and upon stipulation that Joseph Frazier, (2d, II) is the true biological father finds that no policy exists to prevent him from claiming his rights.

11. Tennessee has provided a legitimation (preceeding, proceeding) so a father can establish his paternity.

12. (Never the less, Nevertheless,) he believed that Ms. Harvey loved him.

13. On one (occasion, occassion) Mr. Frazier kept Cynthia for nearly a week.

14. The trial court removed custody from Ms. Harvey (altogether, all together) and placed custody with her mother.

15. The court established the modern (principal, principle) that the presumption of legitimacy may be rebutted.

16. The best interest of the child is the (sole, soul) determining factor.

RESEARCH ACTIVITIES

1. Read one or more opinions from a state or regional reporter to learn how legal citations are incorporated into legal writing.

2. Consult the local rules of appellate procedure for your state and make a copy of the guidelines for preparing briefs.

PROJECTS

The projects for this chapter are parts of an appellate brief.[1] This is a case where Joseph P. Frazier II is the plaintiff-appellant. Betty Lou Harvey and Phillip Robert Harvey are the defendants. The appeal is to the Court of Appeals in Nashville, Tennessee. The case is being appealed from the Second Circuit Court of Davidson County, Tennessee. You will be transcribing portions of the brief of the appellant. The attorney for the appellant is Ms. Florence Bittner of SCOTT, BITTNER & CALLIS, 204 Central Towers Building, 2000 Music Row, Nashville, TN 37203-3798. No. 29762. Phone: (615) 555-8777.

Use initial caps on names of parties and names of documents. Type "plaintiff," "defendant," and "appellant" with lowercase letters.

Project 15-1   Based on the information given above, prepare a title page for the brief of the appellant. The attorney wishes to request oral argument.

Project 15-2   Transcribe Argument I. Follow the format shown in Figure 15-6.

Project 15-3   Using the table of contents feature of your software, generate a table of contents to be formatted as shown in Figure 15-2.

Project 15-4   Using the table of authorities feature of your software, generate a table of authorities. Format it as shown in Figure 15-3.

---

[1]Brief written by Barbara Holmes, third year law student under the direction of Andrew J. Shookhoff, Vanderbilt Law School, Nashville, Tennessee. The names of all parties and attorneys have been changed.

UNIT VI
PERFORMANCE ASSESSMENT

A. The following document has spelling, grammar, punctuation, and word-choice errors. Mark each error on the copy below using proofreaders' symbols. Key and print a corrected copy of the document.

The statement of facts is a portion of the appellate brief for Joseph Frazier, a continuation of the projects for Chapter 15.

STATEMENT OF THE FACTS

Plaintiff Joseph Frazier is the unwedd natural father of Cynthia Ann Harvey, a child conceived and born shortly before the divorce of defendants Betty Lou Harvey an Phillip Robert Harvey. (Tr. ii, 37).

In 1979, Joseph Frazier and Betty Lou Harvey went to high school together and dated casually during that time. (Tr. I, 18). They then lost contact with each other until 1984, when Ms. Harvey started contacting Mr. Frazier by phone and they begin to see each other again socially. (TR. I, 19). Mr. Frazier fell in love with Ms. Harvey and eventually this relationship became sexually intimate. (TR. I, 21).

When the relationship began Mr. Frazier believed Ms. Harvey was unmarried. (TR I, 21). He believed she lived with her parents, since he often picked her up at her parents home. (TR.I, 20). Only after he had fallen in love and became intimately involved with Ms. Harvey did Mr. Frazier learn that Ms. Harvey was, in fact, married to Philip Harvey. (TR. I, 21; I, 22). Never the less he believed that Ms. Harvey loved him and Ms. Harvey fostered that belief. (TR. I, 24, II, 54, I, 55). Mr. Frazier even gave Ms. Harvey money on two different occassions so that she could pay for a lawyer to help her obtain a divorce from Phillip Harvey. (TR. I, 42; I, 43).

On August 26, 1985, Ms. Harvey gave birth to a daughter Cynthia Ann Harvey. (TR. I, 27). Ms. Harvey implied to Mr. Frazier that he was Cynthia's father that she had planned the pregnancy and that she was not, at the time of Cynthia's conception, having sexual relations with Phillip Harvey. (Tr. I, 26; I, 27; I, 81).

Betty Lou and Phillip Harvey were divorced in 1987. (TR. I, 83). Upon the granting of that divorce, the court ordered that Ms. Harvey retain custody of the children, but only so long as she continued to live with her children in her parent's home. (R. 90).

Following Cynthias birth, Mr. Frazier did many things evidencing his concern for and feelings toward her. He bought Cynthia clothes on several occassions. (TR. I, 35). He saw Cynthia often and kept her at his home often when she was toddler age. (TR. I, 28; I, 34). On one occasion, in 1987, Mr. Frasier kept Cynthia for nearly a week when Ms. Harvey left her with him. (TR. I, 28). Mr. Frazier's family also bought clothes for Cynthia, (TR, I, 29), and cared for her. (Ex. 2). A family photo album reflects some of these early times together. (Ex. 4).

B. Place the cassette tape for Performance Assessment VI in the transcriber. Transcribe VI-B. The attorney has completed another portion of the appellate brief, Argument III, prepared on behalf of Joseph P. Frazier, II. Number the first page of Argument III as page 22.

C. Retrieve the Table of Contents, Project 15-3, and update it by adding the Statement of Facts, PAVI-A, and Argument III.

IN-BASKET EXERCISES

Your attorney is Andrew M. Reed, 233 12th Avenue North, St. Louis, MO 35233. His Court Number is 22222. Phone: (314) 555-4242. The date is January 6, (current year). Your attorney will be out of town until Monday. After you left the office Wednesday afternoon, he talked with a client and has left you in-structions to prepare rough draft copies of the documents needed for the new client for his approval on Monday. If any information is missing, highlight the area where it should be inserted with a yellow marker. If you have any questions, insert them in the document, and highlight them for his attention.

DETAILS OF THE DISCUSSION WITH THE CLIENT

Candace Helen Parsons of 607 Division Street, St. Louis, Missouri 35237, came by to see me concerning a divorce. She believes her husband, Alan Stephen Parsons, will sign a marital dissolution agreement if everything is divided down the middle. There are several things she wants though. He has been charging on their Sears credit card, and she wants this stopped. We will need to prepare a motion to handle this matter for her. The parties also have one son who is one year old, born December 20, (2 years ago). Alan has agreed to allow her to have custody and pay $200 child support directly to her every other week. He has already moved out of their house on Division Street, and he says he will sign over any interest he has in the house to her. We will need to prepare a quitclaim deed to make that transfer. She wants the marital dissolution agreement to include a simple statement saying that all the personal property currently in the house is hers and that everything he took with him is his. She also wants her maiden name of Neal back.

Candace has an elderly aunt who is about to die and leave her a fairly large sum of money. Just in case the divorce is not completed before the aunt dies, we need to prepare a last will and testament for Candace.

In any divorce where the opposing party may agree to sign a marital dissolution agreement, we make a practice of preparing the complaint, the marital dissolution agreement, and a letter informing the defendant-husband that his wife is seeking a divorce.

You can use previously transcribed documents to aid you in preparing the documents for Candace Parsons.

1. Use Projects 8-1 and 8-2 to prepare a complaint for divorce to be filed in the Family Court of St. Louis County, Missouri. The divorce is to be based on grounds of irreconcilable differences, and in the complaint ask that the marital dissolution agreement be approved. Also include in the prayer that Candace receive her maiden name of Neal.

    a. Statistics obtained for the divorce are basically stated in the "facts" situation above. We are relying on Section 32-33-763 of the <u>Missouri</u>

<u>Revised Statutes</u> for the divorce. The parties are all Caucasian. The husband now lives with a friend at 432 River Road, St. Louis, MO 35230. He still works at Cummings Delivery Services as a truck driver. He was born on March 4, (23 years ago), but we are not sure where.

b.   Neither party has ever been married previously.

c.   Candace Helen Parson was born November 27, 21 years ago, in East St. Louis, Illinois, but has lived in St. Louis, Missouri most of her life. She currently works at Waylon Road Baptist Church located at 1700 Waylon Road, St. Louis, MO 35233, as a secretary.

d.   The parties were married at Waylon Road Baptist Church on February 10, (2 years ago).

e.   The husband moved out on November 30, current year.

f.   Use Project 8-2 to prepare the body of the complaint and use irreconcilable differences as grounds.

g.   There will be no show cause order or fiat.

h.   The parties do not own a car.

2.   Use Project 8-4 to prepare the marital dissolution agreement. Leave blanks for the date since we do not know when it will be signed. All paragraphs up until you begin numbering them are standard paragraphs and should be included. From the facts given above, construct in rough draft form the numbered paragraphs within the body of the marital dissolution agreement. Paragraphs 1-7 will need to be altered or deleted. Highlight those about which you have a question. Beginning with paragraph No. 8 of Project 8-4, the remaining paragraphs and the oath are standard form paragraphs and should be included. Change all references to names, dates, state, and county.

Use Figures 12-14 and 12-15 in your textbook to prepare a quitclaim deed transferring all interest Alan Stephen Parsons has in the house at 607 Divis Street, St. Louis, Missouri, to Candace Helen (Parsons) Neal. At the top of document, both parties will transfer it to Andrew M. Reed as Trustee, and the bottom, Andrew Reed transfers it back to Candace. Tax bills are to be s to the Security Mortgage Company, 573 24th Avenue North, St. Louis, Missouri 35230. No money (consideration) will be used on the transfer; instead, you will use the terms "love and affection" even though the partie getting a divorce.

The property description is as follows:

Land in St. Louis County, Missouri, being Lot No. 45 on the Plan of Emerald Hills, a planned unit development, the plat of which is recorded in Book 9600, pages 926-929, Register's Office for St. Louis County, Missouri, to which reference is hereby made for a more accurate and complete description.

Being the same property conveyed to Alan Stephen Parsons and wife, Candace Helen Parsons, by Warranty Deed from William Grady of record in Book 5989, page 868, Register's Office for St. Louis County, Missouri.

4. Use Project 5-3B and paragraph M of the standardized paragraphs in Project 5-3A to compose a last will and testament for Candace. You will need to include all paragraphs taken from Project 5-3B, but you will need to change paragraph "Specific Bequests" to state that Candace gives everything she owns at death to her son, David Lewis Parsons. The residuary clause will end with "to my son, David Lewis Parsons." The personal representative will be her mother, Cynthia C. Neal. Add one additional paragraph appointing a guardian for the minor child, who will also be Mrs. Cynthia Neal (see Project 5-3A). The remainder will be quite similar to Project 5-3B except for the name changes and data changes.

5. Use Project 2-2 to compose a "Motion to Restrain Defendant's Use of Credit Cards." The body of the motion will be one paragraph asking (moving) the court to restrain the defendant-husband from charging any more on the parties' credit card. The certificate will state it was mailed directly to the defendant.

6. Draft a letter to the defendant as if it were from me. Explain in the letter that his wife, Candace H. Parsons, has contacted me concerning obtaining a divorce on irreconcilable differences, which is a type of "no-fault" divorce. Tell him that if he, too, wants a divorce, as Candace has told us, and wants to settle it without an expensive court fight, all he needs to do is sign the marital dissolution agreement in front of a Notary Public and get the original of the agreement back to us. He should read both documents carefully. Tell him not to sign it unless he agrees to every provision and that he is welcome to take it to any attorney for legal advice. However, state specifically in the letter, "I recommend you talk with an attorney of your choosing, but I will not be able to talk with you nor advise you since I have been hired by your wife in this matter." Inform him that his wife has agreed to pay my fee so long as he does not contest the divorce and that she will sign the marital dissolution agreement.

In this letter will be the original of the marital dissolution agreement plus one copy for the defendant to keep and a copy of the complaint for divorce for him to keep. He is to keep all the copies of the documents enclosed in this letter except the original of the marital dissolution agreement.

APPENDIX A
TRANSCRIPTION RULES

ABBREVIATIONS

ABBREVIATIONS FOR FEDERAL REPORTERS

United States Reports	U.S.
Supreme Court Reporter	S. Ct.
United States Supreme Court Reports, Lawyers' Eduction	L. Ed.
Federal Reporter	F. or F.2d
Federal Supplement	F. Supp.
Circuit	Cir.
Middle District	M.D.
Southern District	S.D.

ABBREVIATIONS FOR REGIONAL REPORTERS

The following abbreviations have been assigned to West's regional reporters:

Pacific	P. or P.2d
North Western	N.W. or N.W.2d
South Western	S.W. or S.W.2d
North Eastern	N.E. or N.E.2d
Atlantic	A. or A.2d
South Eastern	S.E. or S.E.2d
Southern	So. or So. 2d

PUNCTUATION WITH ABBREVIATIONS

(1) Place a period after abbreviations. (2) Do not use a period if the last letter of the word is part of the abbreviation and is set off with an apostrophe from the rest of the word. (3) Do not include periods in organizations known by their initials.

(1) Bldg.   Jan.   Wed.
(2) Ass'n
(3) NAACP

CAPITALIZATION

Attorneys and law offices sometimes have their own capitalization rules. If yours does not, use the following. In either case, always be consistent.

ATTORNEY

Capitalize Attorney for Plaintiff and Attorney for Defendant when it is part of an address. The term *attorney* is not capitalized if used alone as a common noun.

I have sent a copy of the documents to Mr. ROBERT W. MITCHELL, *Attorney for the Plaintiff,* 804 Stahlman Building, Nashville, TN 37201.

COMES NOW the Plaintiff, JOHN J. McGOWAN, through his *attorney* and presents the following allegations:

COURT

Capitalize the word "Court" when it refers to the Judge. Also capitalize Court when used with the official name of a tribunal.

It is ordered by the *Court* that the Plaintiff recover compensatory damages.

The Honorable BETTY C. TRAUBER is Judge of the *Circuit Court* of Davidson County.

DOCUMENT TITLES — CENTERED

Titles of documents are centered in full caps. The name of the district and state at the top of each bankruptcy form is inserted in full caps because it is part of the centered title of the document.

<u>MIDDLE</u> DISTRICT OF <u>TENNESSEE</u>

DOCUMENT TITLES WITHIN THE BODY OF A DOCUMENT

When a document title is used within the body of the document, capitalize the first letter of each word that has four or more letters except short prepositions, conjunctions, or articles (a, an, the). Some firms choose to use lowercase letters. Consistently use one method or the other.

The Plaintiff's attorney filed a *Complaint for Damages* on January 1, 1995.

or

The Plaintiff's attorney filed a *complaint for damages* on January 1, 1995.

Below is a partial list of document titles:

Affidavit to Prove Will	Order to Appoint a Guardian
Answer to Complaint	Petition
Complaint	Petition for Change of Name
Codicil	Petition for Appointment of a Conservator
Last Will and Testament	Petition for Appointment of a Guardian
Letters of Administration	Petition for Letters of Administration
Letters Testamentary	Petition to Probate a Will
Living Will	Power of Attorney
Motion for Default Judgment	Request for Production of Documents
Notice of Hearing	Will
Order to Appoint a Conservator	

GEOGRAPHIC TERMS

Capitalize the words City, County, State, and similar terms when they appear before the name of the geographic location. In routine correspondence, these terms are not capitalized. Capitalize City, County when they appear after geographic name of the location. Always capitalize the name of the county and state.

He is a resident of the *City of Nashville, County of Davidson, State of Tennessee.* (legal document)

He is a resident of the *city of Nashville, county of Davidson, state of Tennessee.* (routine correspondence)

He is a resident of *Davidson County, Tennessee.*

IN LETTERS AND OTHER CORRESPONDENCE

Names used in legal correspondence (letters, memoranda, etc.) are generally keyed with initial caps. More often than not, the terms "plaintiff" and "defendant" are keyed in lowercase letters. Names of documents, such as complaint, answer, and motion to dismiss, may be typed with lowercase letters or with initial caps. Consistently follow the capitalization pattern preferred by the attorney.

After going to *Central Hospital*, he was referred to you.

The *plaintiff* was injured on December 15, 1994.

Enclosed is a copy of the *Summons* and *Complaint.*
or
Enclosed is a copy of the *summons* and *complaint*.

NAMES OF PARTIES

Many legal firms use full caps on names of parties, attorneys, and judges in legal documents; others use initial caps. Always check the preference of your firm by looking at documents in the files. Consistently use one method or the other.

Plaintiff, *WILLIAM F. OLDHAM*, is a resident of the County of Davidson, State of Tennessee.

or

Plaintiff, *William F. Oldham*, is a resident of the County of Davidson, State of Tennessee.

PARTY DESIGNATIONS

Capitalize the first letter of the party designation (Plaintiff or Defendant) in legal documents. Some firms choose to use lowercase letters. Consistently use one method or the other.

On June 27, 1993, the *Defendant* EXPRESS DELIVERY SERVICES, INC., was the registered owner of a Ford truck.

or

On June 27, 1993, the *defendant* EXPRESS DELIVERY SERVICES, INC., was the registered owner of a Ford truck.

Below is a partial list of party designations:

Administrator	Partner
Agent	Party of the First Part
Attorney in Fact	Party of the Second Part
Clerk	Personal Representative
Conservator	Petitioner
Court (meaning Judge)	Plaintiff
Declarant	Principal
Defendant	Respondent
Executor	Second Party
Executrix	Tenant
First Party	Testator
Guardian	Testatrix
Guardian Ad Litem	Trustee
Husband	Wife
Judge	Ward
Landlord	
Lessee	
Lessor	

PHRASES IN FULL CAPS

Key the following and similar phrases in full caps. Note the punctuation following some of the phrases.

COMES
COMES NOW
ENTERED
IN WITNESS WHEREOF,
IT IS FURTHER AGREED
IT IS THEREFORE ORDERED, ADJUDGED, AND DECREED
KNOW ALL MEN BY THESE PRESENTS:
NOW, THEREFORE,
PREMISES CONSIDERED, PETITIONER PRAYS:
THIS AGREEMENT
THIS CONTRACT
THIS INDENTURE

TO HAVE AND TO HOLD
WHEREAS,
WHEREFORE,
WITNESS
WITNESSETH:

Word/Number Sequences

Capitalize word/number sequences, except numbers used with the terms *page* and *paragraph*.

Book 3368 (refers to the book number where deeds are recorded)
Interrogatory No. 5
Interrogatory 7
Allegation IV
Allegation 4
Room 24
Question 6
page 504
paragraph I
paragraph 1

CITATIONS

Initials

In text, space once between initials in personal names; however, in citations, do not space. U.S.O.C. Rule 6.1

In text: L. C. Johansen

In citations: L.C. Johansen

Multiple and Parallel Citations

A parallel citation is a reference to one case that is printed in two or more publications; a multiple citation consists of references to two or more different cases. Multiple citations are separated by semicolons; parallel citations, by commas. The first example below is a parallel citation; the second, a multiple citation:

Smith v. Jones, 14 Tenn. 234, 385 S.W.2d 143 (1970).

Parsons v. Pedigo, 989 P.2d 899 (1990); Baker v. Cook, 389 N.E. 389 (1989).

Page Number References in Citations

Never use "p." or "pp." for "page" or "pages" in citations. In citing consecutively numbered pages, separate the range of pages with a hyphen. When referring to a range of pages, nonidentical digits in a series are repeated; however, always repeat at least the last two digits. For scattered pages, separate the specific page numbers with a comma.

500 to 525	500-25 (two digits are different)
1585 to 1643	1585-643 (three digits are different)
1450 and 1460	1450, 1460 (scattered pages)

SECTION AND PARAGRAPH REFERENCES IN CITATIONS

Spell word "Section" or the word "paragraph" when it appears in text; use the symbols (§ and ¶) in citations. Space once before and once after the symbol. Use two symbols to indicate multiple sections.

In text: Section 14(b)
Sections 14 to 16
paragraph 25
paragraphs 15 to 20

In citations: § 14(b)
§§ 14-16
¶ 25
¶¶ 15-20

MULTIPLE SECTION REFERENCES IN CITATIONS

When referring to a range of section numbers, retain all digits except when there are identical digits or letters preceding a punctuation mark. U.S.O.C. Rule 3.4. Subsection desig-nations should be enclosed in parentheses even if printed in the source without parentheses.

Section 245	§ 245 (one section)
Sections 1114 to 1133	§§ 1114-1133 (a range of sections)
Section 1330, subsections a and 3	§ 1330(a), (3) (one section and two subsections)
Sections 3.25-46, 3.25-52, and 3.25-59	§§ 3.25-46, -52, -59 (The identical digits preceding a punctuation mark are 3.25, and they do not have to be repeated each time.)

Some authors use et seq. when referring to multiple sections of statutes. "Et. seq." means *and following*. A reference to multiple sections of the Missouri Revised Statutes could be expressed as Mo. Rev. Stat. §§ 12-5-543 et seq.

SPACING IN REPORTER ABBREVIATIONS

Do not space between single-letter abbreviations in names of reporters. If the abbreviation of the name of a reporter is more than one letter, space once before and once after the abbreviation. Note that when the abbreviation for *a word* consists of two letters or more, the first letter is capitalized and the other letters are lowercase. Use full caps for single-letter abbreviations. Treat the reference to a series of volumes (2d or 3d) of a reporter as a single-letter abbreviation.

S.W.
S.W.2d
So. 2d
Cal. App. 2d

UNDERLINING

The following items are underlined in citations: U.S.O.C. Rules 2 and 7.
Italicizing is an alternative to underlining.

Case names, including <u>v.</u>
Book titles
Article titles
Committee hearings
Terms indicating prior and subsequent history, <u>rev'd</u>, <u>aff'g</u>
Capital letters representing names: <u>A</u> sued <u>B</u>
The letter "l" when it represents a subsection, § 32(<u>l</u>)
Foreign words or phrases not a part of common English usage
Emphasized material
Related authority, <u>reprinted in</u>
Introductory signals, <u>See</u>, <u>Cf.</u>, etc.

Underline the title of a publication when referring to it in the text of a
document. Publications titles are always abbreviated in citations.

The information can be found in the <u>Pacific Reporter</u>.

<u>Tennessee Code Annotated</u> provides for blood testing.

In <u>Smith v. Norton</u>, 35 P.2d 385 (1993), guidelines are provided for blood
testing.

COLON

FORMAL LIST

Use a colon to introduce a formal list; however, do not use a colon after a verb or
preposition if the items are to continue on the same line.

The assets that have come into the hands of the Executor *are:*

Cash on Hand $ 350.50
Stocks and Bonds   1,000.00

The assets that have come into the hands of the Executor *are* cash on hand
and stock and bonds.

HOURS AND MINUTES

Place a colon between hours and minutes when expressing time. Use figures with
a.m. and p.m. Also use figures with o'clock, except in formal correspondence.
Do not use a.m. or p.m. and o'clock together. With even hours, omit the zeros.

8 a.m. (not 8:00 a.m.)
8:25 a.m. (not 8:25 a.m. o'clock or 8:25 o'clock a.m.)
6 o'clock (not 6:00 o'clock)

INTRODUCTORY STATEMENT

Use a colon after introductory words such as "following" or "as follows."

I have received into the estate for this reporting period the *following:* two (2) automobiles, one (1) boat, and money on deposit.

COMES NOW your Petitioner, ARTHUR P. DUDLEY, and would respectfully show unto the Court the *following:*

1. The decedent died on June 27, 1993.
2. The decedent is survived by three (3) heirs.

COMMA

ADDRESSES

Set off the elements of an address with commas if used within a sentence. The two letter state code may be used if a ZIP code is included.

The law firm is located at *2800 Wallace Road, Nashville, Tennessee.*
The law firm is located at *2800 Wallace Road, Nashville, TN 37000.*

"AND" OMITTED BETWEEN TWO ADJECTIVES

Use a comma between two or more consecutive adjectives not joined by "and" that modify the same noun. If the first adjective modifies the combined thought of the second adjective and noun, do not separate the adjectives with a comma. TEST: If inserting the word "and" between the adjectives makes sense, the comma is placed between the adjectives.

The Wife charges that the Husband has been guilty of cruel, inhuman treatment. (Comma needed — cruel and inhuman clearly describes the treatment.)

The Petitioner prays that the Court approve the property settlement and make it a part of a final divorce decree. (No comma needed between "final" and "divorce" — it is not a final and a divorce decree; it is a divorce decree that is final.)

APPOSITION

An appositive explains the noun or pronoun that precedes it. Use commas to set off (place a comma before and after) a word or words in apposition that are nonessential; do not place commas around the word or words which are essential. In legal documents, a name often appears after the designation "Plaintiff" or "Defendant." If there is only one plaintiff or one defendant in a case, the name is nonessential because the party is fully identified by the word "plaintiff" or "defendant"; however, if there are multiple defendants or plaintiffs, the name is essential to identify which plaintiff or defendant. If the word "the" does not precede the word "Plaintiff" or "Defendant," treat it as a title and do not set it off with commas. In some cases, the writer may be the only one to know whether an appositive is essential.

In a case in which William F. Oldham is the plaintiff and James A. Pizzini and Express Delivery Services, Inc., are the defendants, reference to the parties would be as follows:

The Plaintiff, *WILLIAM F. OLDHAM,* sustained serious and permanent injuries. (Nonessential, there is only one plaintiff.)

Plaintiff WILLIAM F. OLDHAM sustained serious and permanent injuries. ("Plaintiff" is used as a title.)

Plaintiff OLDHAM sustained serious and permanent injuries. ("Plaintiff" is used as a title.)

The Defendant *JAMES A. PIZZINI* carelessly and negligently drove his vehicle at a high rate of speed. (Essential — there are two defendants so the name is necessary to identify which one.)

The Plaintiff, WILLIAM F. OLDHAM, demands judgment against the Defendants, *JAMES A. PIZZINI and EXPRESS DELIVERY SERVICES, INC.* (Nonessential — there are only two defendants, so the names are not necessary to identify the defendants.)

CONTRASTING EXPRESSIONS

A contrasting expression provides a thought different from the original statement and usually begins with "but" or "not." Separate a contrasting expression from the rest of the sentence with a comma or commas.

The Petition for Adoption, *not the Order of Reference,* consists of three pages.

He was willing to pay child support, *but only on his own terms*.

DATES

Set off the year with commas when used with a month and day. If the day precedes the month, add d, th, or st to the day. No commas are needed when referring to a month and year with no day.

On *June 27, (current year)* the Defendant was the registered owner of a Ford truck.

On the *27th day of June, (current year)* the Defendant was the registered owner of a Ford truck.

It was in *June* — that the accident occurred.

DEPENDENT CLAUSES — ESSENTIAL

Do not place commas around dependent clauses that appear within or at the end of a sentence if they are essential to the meaning of the sentence. If an essential clause is omitted, it changes the meaning of the sentence.

The Defendant stated to the Plaintiff that he would be responsible for the future rent of the student *who was residing on the Plaintiff's rental property.* (Without the "who" clause, this could mean any student, not just the one who was riding on the rental property.)

DEPENDENT CLAUSES — INTRODUCTORY

A dependent clause has a subject and verb but cannot stand alone as a sentence because it does not express a complete thought. Dependent clauses often begin with words such as the following: *if, when, after, as, although, before, since,* and *unless.* Place a comma after an introductory dependent clause.

Although EXPRESS DELIVERY SERVICES, INC., lists an address in the Nashville telephone directory, it maintains no employees or equipment in Tennessee. (Dependent clause beginning with "although.")

Since the Cross-Defendant was an independent contractor at the time and place of the accident, the Cross-Complainant had no control over any of his negligent acts. (Dependent clause beginning with "since.")

DEPENDENT CLAUSES — NONESSENTIAL

Place commas around dependent clauses that appear within or at the end of a sentence that are not essential to the meaning of the sentence. A nonessential clause can be omitted from the sentence and not change the meaning of the sentence; it simply provides additional information.

We will need a copy of your bill to forward to the insurance company, *even though the statement may be sent to Mr. Oldham's personal insurer through his work.*

The Defendant stated to the Plaintiff that he would be responsible for the future rent of Joseph Hill, *who was residing at the Plaintiff's rental property.* (This could be only Joseph Hill; the other information does not change the meaning of the sentence if omitted.)

ELLIPTICAL EXPRESSIONS

Elliptical expressions have key words (usually subject and verb) omitted. The expression "If possible," is interpreted to mean "if it is possible"; and the expression "If so," is interpreted to mean "if it is so." If the elliptical expression precedes an independent clause, place a comma after the elliptical expressions, treating it as an introductory dependent clause.

If so, what is the nature of his physical condition?

State whether a prognosis has been made by anyone; and *if so,* state the prognosis, when made, and by whom made. (The elliptical expression precedes the second independent clause.)

Be careful to determine whether the expression is nonessential or introductory clause. If the elliptical expression (clause) is nonessential, set it off from the rest of the sentence with two commas.

Describe the final status of the suit and, *if concluded,* the final result of the suit. (Nonessential clause — you could not say "If it is concluded, the final result of the suit.")

Et al.

"Et al." is often used in a case name. "Et" means and; "al." means others. Punctuate the expression as you would any other items joined by "and." If you have only one item followed by "et al.," no comma is required. If you have two or more items in a series followed by "et al.," a comma is needed. See the following examples:

Baldwin's Furniture v. Appleton Shopping Center et al. (No comma is needed — two items joined by "and" do not require a comma. It can be read as Appleton Shopping Center Inc. and others.)

Baldwin's Furniture v. Albert Jones, Trucking Company, et al. (Comma is needed because there are three items in a series — Albert Jones, Trucking Company, and others.)

Geographic Locations

Separate geographic locations with commas. Set off the name of the state when used with the city.

He is a resident of the *City of Nashville, County of Davidson, State of Tennessee.*

The principal places of business are Nashville, *Tennessee,* and Paducah, *Kentucky*.

Inc.

If a company uses a comma before Inc. in its name, place a comma after Inc. if the name appears anywhere except the end of a sentence. If a company does not use a comma before Inc. in its name, the comma after Inc. is omitted.

JAMES A. PIZZINI was an employee of EXPRESS DELIVERY SERVICE, *INC.,* and was operating the said vehicle in the course of employment.

JAMES A. PIZZINI was an employee of EXPRESS DELIVERY SERVICE *INC.* and was operating the said vehicle in the course of employment. (The company does not use a comma before Inc. in its name.)

JR. AND SR.

If a person prefers a comma before Jr. or Sr. in his name, also place a comma after Jr. unless it is the end of a sentence. If a person does not use a comma before Jr. or Sr., the comma after Jr. or Sr. is omitted.

Send the Answers to Interrogatories to J. B. Merry, *Jr.* (Individual writes his name with a comma before Jr.)

Send the Answers to Interrogatories to J. B. Merry *Jr.* (Individual writes his name without a comma before Jr.)

Ask J. B. Merry, *Jr.,* to review the documents before they are placed in the mail. (individual writes his name with a comma — the sentence continues so a comma is placed after Jr.)

OMITTED WORD OR WORDS

If a repetitive word or words are omitted in a compound sentence, use a comma where the word or words are omitted.

Mitchell and Mitchell had a reputation for representing its clients competently; Ernst & Jordon, for questionable competence. (The repetitive words omitted are *had a reputation.*)

PARENTHETICAL EXPRESSIONS

Parenthetical terms are explanatory words added by the writer. Such expressions that are introductory or interrupt the flow of the sentence are set off with commas. Examples are *in addition, in my opinion, of course, consequently, however, further, furthermore, nevertheless, besides,* and *however.* Voice inflection can be used to determine whether or not the element is essential. If the voice drops the expression is nonessential and should be set off with commas. If the voice rises, the expression is essential and should not be set off.

You, *I believe,* are a licensed physician.

Further, it is agreed that all formalities as to reading and signing of the deposition are waived.

Will you tell us, *please,* the purpose of the blood test?

PHRASES — INTERRUPTING

Set off phrases that interrupt the flow of the sentence. An interrupting phrase may be essential or nonessential information that interrupts the flow of the sentence from the subject to the verb or from the verb to the object. With the phrase omitted, the remaining sentence should express a complete thought.

The Corporation may dispose of all property, *real and personal,* as is deemed necessary.

The undersigned persons, *having capacity to contract,* adopt the following Charter.

The meeting shall be at such time and place, *either within or without this state,* as may be designated by the directors.

PHRASES — INTRODUCTORY

A phrase is a group of two or more words with no subject. Place a comma after an introductory phrase if it has five or more words, if it contains a verb, or if it is an independent comment. If the phrase is short and does not contain a verb form and is not an independent comment, the comma may be omitted. Some writers prefer to place commas after all introductory phrases.

After hearing the decision of the Court, the Plaintiff was devastated. (contains a verb form)

For an answer to paragraph I of the Complaint, Defendant admits that the accident occurred on May 21, 1993, about 5 p.m. (long phrase)

Of course, the Defendant would show to the Court that the Plaintiff was a licensee. (short phrase; used as an independent comment; comma not omitted)

In 1991 the Defendant purchased a riding lawn mower. (short phrase, comma omitted)

PHRASES WITHIN A SENTENCE — NONESSENTIAL

Set off phrases that are nonessential to the meaning of the sentence.

He still has some thickening, *some residual thickening,* of the tissue on the great toe. (nonessential)

SERIES

Set off three or more items in a series with commas.

In attendance were *the Plaintiffs, the Defendant, their attorneys,* and *a jury of good and lawful citizens*. (four items in a series)

SERIES JOINED BY CONJUNCTIONS

If the items in a series are joined by conjunctions, do not separate them with commas.

I have signed and declared and published with to be my Last Will and Testament.

Two Independent Clauses Joined by a Conjunction — No Other Commas

An independent clause has a subject and verb and expresses a complete thought. Place a comma between two independent clauses joined by a conjunction such as *and, but, or,* or *nor.* If the clauses are short and closely related, no comma is needed. If commas appear within either independent clause, a semicolon is placed between the two clauses (see semicolon rule below).

The mower is not an attractive nuisance, and the Defendant did not breach any duty of care owed to the Plaintiff. (two independent clauses joined by a conjunction)

The Defendant had written a contract and it is sufficient proof. (short, closely related clauses)

HYPHENATION

Attorney at Law

It is common practice not to hyphenate Attorney at Law; however, some authorities show it hyphenated.

Mail a copy to Robert W. Mitchell, ***Attorney at Law***, 804 Stahlman Building, Nashville, TN 37201.

Fractions

In letters, spell out and hyphenate fractions. Use numbers if the spelled-out form is long and awkward.

One-half
Two-thirds
42/100

Modifiers Before a Noun

When two or more words function together as one to modify a noun, use a hyphen to connect them. If the modifiers do not appear before a noun, generally do not insert the hyphens. Do not insert the hyphen if one of the words is an adverb (usually ending in ly).

Refer to the ***above-referenced*** case. The case is referenced above.
Use a ***six-inch*** line. The line is six inches.
He is a ***highly paid*** attorney. (ends in ly)
He purchased ***over-the-counter drugs***. The drugs are sold over the counter.

NUMBER EXPRESSION

AGES

In legal documents, ages are expressed in words and then in numerals; however, if the ages are shown in a table, use figures only.

LUCY PEREZ died at the age of seventy (70).

The name, age, and relationship of my beneficiaries are:

Name	Relationship	Age
MATTHEW PEREZ	Husband	75
SIMON PEREZ	Son	45

ALIGNING AMOUNTS IN COLUMNS

Place a dollar sign by the first amount in a column and by the total. The dollar signs should align vertically. Numbers in columns are right aligned. If any amount has cents, use two zeros by all even dollar amounts.

```
$1,000.00
    52.80
   104.20
$1,157.00
```

DAYS PRECEDING THE MONTH

Days that precede the month can be expressed in ordinals (first, second, third, or 1st, 2d, 3d). Avoid the spelled-out version if it is more than one word.

The *first* day of December, 1995
The *1st* day of December, 1995
The *21st* day of December, 1995

DOLLAR AMOUNTS

In legal documents, dollar amounts are written in words and figures. The first letter of each word is capitalized. The second term in a hyphenated number is keyed in lowercase letters. Place parentheses around the numeric figures that express exactly what is written in words. Note the use of "and" between dollars and cents.

One Hundred Thousand Dollars ($100,000)—do not include .00 because cents is not referred to in the spelled-out version.
One Hundred Thousand and no/100 Dollars ($100,000.00)
Twenty-one Thousand and 00/100 (21,000.00) Dollars—do not include the $ in parentheses because the words before the parentheses do not refer to dollars.
Twenty-five and 25/100 Dollars ($25.25)
Twenty-five dollars and Twenty-five Cents ($25.25)

FRACTIONS IN LEGAL DOCUMENTS

In legal documents, express fractions in written and numeric form.

Not less than *one-tenth (1/10th)* of the directors must vote.

NUMBERS IN LEGAL CORRESPONDENCE

In legal correspondence, numbers ten and under are spelled out; numbers over ten are written in figures. Amounts of money are shown in numeric form only. Some attorneys may prefer to follow the method used in legal documents.

The facts should be admitted within *30* days after service.
My client is willing to agree to a settlement of *$20,000.*

NUMBERS IN LEGAL DOCUMENTS

In legal documents, numbers other than dollar amounts are written in words and figures. The written amount is keyed in lowercase letters.

Plaintiff requests that the facts be admitted within **thirty (30)** days.

PERIODS

ENUMERATED PARAGRAPHS BEGINNING WITH "THAT"

Use a period after paragraphs beginning with the word "That" when they occur after an introductory statement that serves as the subject. If the last paragraph is preceded by the word "and," a semicolon is used after each one except the last paragraph, which ends with a period (see semicolon rule and example below).

The Plaintiff would show:

1. That on June 17, 1993, the Defendant was the registered owner of a Ford truck bearing Tennessee License No. CEW-549.

2. That on June 17, 1993, the Plaintiff, WILLIAM F. OLDHAM, was driving his Dodge automobile in a northwardly direction.

3. That Defendant PIZZINI struck the Plaintiff's vehicle.

RUN-IN HEADING

Place a period after a run-in heading, which is a heading on the same line as the paragraph it describes. The heading should be either boldfaced or underlined. The preferred style for word processing is boldface. Leave two spaces after the period.

Court Jurisdiction. The minor in this cause of action is a resident of Fairfax County, Virginia, living at 1243 Braddock Place, Alexandria, VA 22314.

POSSESSION

PLURAL POSSESSION

Show possession of a plural noun not ending in *s* by adding an apostrophe and s. Show possession of a plural noun ending in *s* by adding an apostrophe.

The ***men's*** claims that they are joint owners of the property are totally incorrect.

My ***clients'*** documents were filed before the deadline.

SINGULAR POSSESSION

Show singular possession of a noun not ending in s by adding an apostrophe and s. Show possession of a singular noun ending with an s, sh, z, ch, or zh by adding an apostrophe and s. If the word is hard to pronounce when adding an apostrophe and s, add an apostrophe only.

The defendant felt her ***boss's*** actions were the proximate cause of the accident.

The defendant felt that Mr. ***Smith's*** response to the request for settlement was not satisfactory.

Mr. Robins' testimony convinced the jury that the defendant was guilty.

QUOTATIONS

PUNCTUATION WITH QUOTATION MARKS

Periods and commas are always typed before a closing double or single quotation mark. Colons and semicolons are always typed after a closing double or single quotation mark. Question marks and exclamation points are typed before a quotation mark if the question or exclamation is part of the quoted matter and after the quotation mark when the question or exclamation applies to the entire sentence.

"I have only five minutes," she said, "to finish this exercise."

When the attorney announced that we needed two more documents, my question was "Why?"; the other secretary asked "When?"

In <u>Rogers v. Lambert</u> the judge asked, "How can we determine guilt or innocence without evidence to support the allegations?"

Was it last week that you said, "I do not want to be the judge for this highly publicized case"?

SEMICOLONS

ENUMERATED LISTS

In legal writing, semicolons are often used after consecutive paragraphs or items in a list. Place a semicolon after each item in the list except the last item, which ends with a period. If the word "and" appears before the last item in the list, it is a signal to use semicolons rather than periods. See also the rule for periods after enumerated paragraphs beginning with "That."

The following statutes will be read at the trial in their entirety:

Tenn. Code Ann. § 55-8-103, "Required Obedience to Traffic Laws";
Tenn. Code Ann. § 55-8-115, "Driving on the Right Side of Roadway"; and
Tenn. Code Ann. § 55-8-120, "Limitations on Driving to Left of Center."

INDEPENDENT CLAUSES — NO CONJUNCTION

Use a semicolon between two closely related independent clauses not joined by a conjunction. Each clause should be a separate sentence if the clauses are not closely related.

The Complainant would show that the Husband has kicked over furniture; he has broken the chain lock off the front door. (These clauses both relate to the husband's behavior.)

The parties shall have joint custody of the minor children. Each party shall pay his or her own attorney. (These clauses are addressing separate, unrelated matters.)

INDEPENDENT CLAUSES WITH COMMAS JOINED BY A CONJUNCTION

Place a semicolon between two independent clauses joined by a conjunction if either clause contains commas.

Defendant, HERMAN SHULMAN, denies the allegations in paragraphs 1, 2, 3, and 4; and he demands that the Complaint be dismissed with costs adjudged against the Plaintiff.

SERIES CONTAINING COMMAS

Set off items in a series containing commas with a semicolon.

The nature of the business is to construct and distribute cabinets; to lease, purchase, or sell all such property; and to engage in any lawful act for which a corporation is organized.

SERIES OF LONG, PARALLEL DEPENDENT CLAUSES

Use semicolons to separate three or more long, parallel dependent clauses in a series.

After testimony in open court, the Judge determined that said paper writing was written and signed by the decedent; that said instrument was executed by the deceased as his Last Will and Testament; and that the deceased was at the time of sound mind.

IT IS FURTHER ORDERED that the fee of the attorney for the Petitioner be set at Five Hundred Dollars ($500); that the fee of the Guardian Ad Litem be set at Three Hundred Dollars ($300); and that these fees and costs be paid from the estate of the Ward.

IT IS FURTHER ORDERED that the fee of the attorney for the Petitioner be set at Five Hundred Dollars ($500) and that the fee be paid from the estate of the Ward. (There are not three clauses, so no semicolon is needed.)

TO WIT

"To wit" is a term meaning *namely* or *that is.* Place a colon before and a comma after *to wit* if the emphasis is on the material that follows the expression. Place a comma before and a comma after *to wit* if the emphasis is on what precedes.

As Executor you have four (4) responsibilities: *to wit,* notifying heirs, pay paying debts, taking inventory, and preparing an accounting. (Emphasis is on what follows *to wit* rather than on the introductory statement.)

The Executor notified all of the beneficiaries, *to wit,* the three children and wife of the deceased. (Emphasis is on the fact that the beneficiaries were notified.)

TWO INDEPENDENT CLAUSES JOINED BY A CONJUNCTIVE ADVERB

A conjunctive adverb is an adverb that connects two independent clauses. Some conjunctive adverbs are the following: *however, so, also, nevertheless, consequently, hence, otherwise, furthermore, therefore,* and *accordingly.* When two independent clauses are joined by these terms, place a semicolon before the conjunctive adverb and a comma after it.

Mr. Baldwin has waived all of his rights to a trial; *however,* we may be able to work out a settlement.

Barbara Harding did not retain counsel due to her financial condition; *therefore,* we request that the default judgment be dismissed.

WHEREAS

When WHEREAS is used to introduce a series of paragraphs, place a comma after WHEREAS and a semicolon at the end of each paragraph. The last paragraph will normally begin with NOW, THEREFORE. Place a comma before and after THEREFORE.

WHEREAS, ...;
WHEREAS, ...;
WHEREAS, ...; and
NOW, THEREFORE, ... : (Use a colon here if the paragraph contains terms such as "follows" or "the following.")

TRANSCRIPTION HINTS

REQUIRED SPACE

When using a word processing program with justification turned on, leave requires spaces, sometimes called fixed spaces, after numbered paragraphs. Tab in one inch from the left margin, key the number and period, then insert required spaces. Some programs use code space to create a fixed space. This keeps an equal amount of space locked in following each number.

When referring to section numbers being cited, such as Tenn. Code Ann. § 2-35-7889, the section symbol can be created in most software programs by holding down the Alt key and entering 21 from the ten key pad. Space once before and after the symbol.

UNDERLINE OR ITALICIZE

COMPLETE PUBLISHED WORKS

The titles of books and magazines or any complete published legal materials are underlined or italicized.

This document is construed as a Durable Power of Attorney for Health Care according to the **General Statutes of North Carolina**.

VERSUS

Both "v." and "vs." can be used for "versus" in a case name. Jones v. Smith or Jones vs. Smith.

WORD DIVISION

Keep the following elements together at the end of a line:

June 29
DALE M. or D.M. (first and middle name or initial; two initials)
7 p.m.
paragraph III
Book 3368
page 504
22d Floor
201 Finch (street number and name)
AL 55201 (two-letter state code and ZIP code)

APPENDIX B
COURT CAPTIONS

The arrangement of the data in court captions varies significantly from one jurisdiction to another. The rules for preparing captions and court documents appear in each state's rules of court, which can be found in the state statutes. In addition to the content and arrangement of captions, the size of paper to be used is also specified.

In this appendix are shown several styles of captions used by courts within the United States. Following the samples are two tables: one showing the size of paper and another showing the general arrangement of data in the caption used by the court of general jurisdiction in a major city of most states. This will guide you in determining the arrangement of data in the caption for your state. You should, however, obtain a copy of the court rules for your county and state and also check with a secretary or the clerk of the court in your area to get a sample caption for the local courts.

SAMPLE CAPTIONS

STYLE 1 — Venue at left; court identification at right, Case No. and title at right.

```
STATE OF (STATE)          )                 In the District Court
                          ) ss.             First Judicial District
COUNTY OF (COUNTY)  )                 Civil Action No. _____


WILLIAM OLDHAM,                 )
                                )
          Plaintiff,            )
                                )
          vs.                   )         COMPLAINT
                                )
JAMES PIZZINI,                  )
                                )
          Defendant.            )
```

STYLE 2 — Attorney's address and phone number at left, title centered, Case No. and title at right.

Robert W. Mitchell
Attorney for the Plaintiff
804 Stahlman Building
CITY, ST 555-5555
(555) 555-5555

IN THE (TYPE OF COURT) COURT FOR (COUNTY), (STATE)

WILLIAM OLDHAM,	)	
	)	
Plaintiff,	)	
	)	Case No. _____
vs.	)	
	)	COMPLAINT
JAMES PIZZINI,	)	
	)	
Defendant.	)	

STYLE 3 — Court identification centered, Case No. at right, title centered.

IN THE (TYPE OF COURT) COURT FOR (COUNTY), (STATE)

WILLIAM OLDHAM,	)	
	)	
Plaintiff,	)	
	)	
vs.	)	No. _____
	)	
JAMES PIZZINI,	)	
	)	
Defendant.	)	

COMPLAINT

STYLE 4 — Cause No. centered at top, court identification at right.

Cause No. _____

WILLIAM OLDHAM	In the District Courts of (County) County, State
Plaintiff	
	_____ Judicial District
v.	
JAMES PIZZINI	
Defendant	

STYLE 5 — Parties' names at left, court identification at right.

WILLIAM F. OLDHAM

versus

JAMES PIZZINI

NUMBER: _____ DIV. ____
19th Judicial District Court
Parish of East Baton Rouge
State of LOUISIANA

STYLE 6 — Court identification centered, parties' names at left, the words "plaintiff" and "defendant" at right, Case No. at right, title centered.

IN THE (TYPE OF COURT) COURT FOR (COUNTY), (STATE)

WILLIAM F. OLDHAM

vs.

JAMES PIZZINI

PLAINTIFF

CASE NO. _____

DEFENDANT

COMPLAINT

STYLE 7 — Case No. at left, court identification at right, title centered.

NO. _____

WILLIAM F. OLDHAM

v.

JAMES PIZZINI

:   SUPERIOR COURT
:
:   JUDICIAL DISTRICT OF
:   HARTFORD/NEW BRITAIN
:
:   AT HARTFORD
:
:   May 21, 1993

COMPLAINT

STYLE 8 — State identifification centered, county and style of the case at left, court identification and title at right.

COMMONWEALTH OF MASSACHUSETTS

SUFFOLK, ss.

SUPERIOR COURT DEPARTMENT
CIVIL ACTION
NO. _____

WILLIAM F. OLDHAM, PLAINTIFF

v.   COMPLAINT

JAMES PIZZINI, DEFENDANT

SIZE AND TYPE OF PAPER FOR LEGAL PLEADINGS

State, City	11-inch ruled	11-inch plain	14-inch ruled	14-inch plain
Alabama, Montgomery		x		
Alaska, Juneau		x	x	
Arizona, Phoenix	x (N)	x		
Arkansas, Little Rock		x		
Colorado, Denver		x		
Connecticut, Hartford		x		
Delaware, Wilmington		x		
Florida, Tallahassee		x		
Georgia, Atlanta		x		
Hawaii, Honolulu		x		
Idaho, Boise		x		
Illinois, Springfield		x		
Indiana, Indianapolis		x		
Iowa, Des Moines		x		
Kentucky, Lexington		x		
Louisiana, Baton Rouge				x
Maine, Portland		x		
Maryland, Baltimore		x		
Massachusetts, Boston		x		
Michigan, Lansing		x		
Minnesota, St. Paul		x		
Mississippi, Jackson		x		
Missouri, Columbia		x		
Montana, Helena		x		
Nebraska, Lincoln		x		
New Hampshire, Manchester		x		
New Mexico, Albuquerque		x		
North Dakota, Bismarck		x		
Ohio, Columbus		x		
Oklahoma, Oklahoma City		x		x
Oregon, Salem	x (N)			
Pennsylvania, Harrisburg		x		
South Carolina, Columbia		x		
South Dakota, Pierre		x		
Tennessee, Nashville				x
Texas, Austin		x		
Utah, Salt Lake City		x		
Virginia, Richmond		x		
Washington, Olympia	x (N)			
West Virginia, Charleston		x		
Wyoming, Cheyenne				x

(N) Numbered lines

ARRANGEMENT OF DATA IN CAPTIONS FOR COURTS WITHIN THE UNITED STATES

State, City[1]	Style of Case at Left	Atty's Address at Top/Left Margin	Court and Venue Centered	Court and Venue at Right Margin	Case No./Document Title at Right	Case No. at Right/Center Title Below	Venue Before Style at Left Margin
Alabama, Montgomery	x		x			x	
Alaska, Juneau	x		x			x	
Arizona, Phoenix	x*		x			x	
Arkansas, Little Rock	x		x			x	
Colorado, Denver	x*		x			x**	
Connecticut, Hartford	x*			x		x	
Delaware, Wilmington	x		x			x	
Florida, Tallahassee	x			x		x	
Georgia, Atlanta	x		x			x	
Hawaii, Honolulu	x		x		x		
Iowa, Des Moines	x		x			x	
Idaho, Boise	x	x	x			x	
Illinois, Springfield	x		x			x	
Indiana, Indianapolis	x*			x		x***	x
Kentucky, Lexington	x*					x	
Louisiana, Baton Rouge	x			x			x at Right Omit ss:
Maine, Portland	x			x		x	
Maryland, Baltimore	x					x	x
Massachusetts, Boston	x		x	x	x		County:ss
Michigan, Lansing	x		x			x	

State, City[1]	Style of Case at Left	Atty's Address at Top/Left Margin	Court and Venue Centered	Court and Venue at Right Margin	Case No./Document Title at Right	Case No. at Right/Center Title Below	Venue Before Style at Left Margin
Minnesota, St. Paul	x			x	x		x
Mississippi, Jackson	x*		x			x	
Missouri, Columbia	x		x			x	
Montana, Helena	x	x	x Line 8		x		
Nebraska, Lincoln	x	x	x			x	
New Hampshire, Manchester	x			x	x		x
New Mexico, Albuquerque	x			x	x		x No ss:
North Dakota, Bismarck	x			x	x		x
Ohio, Columbus	x		x			x	
Oklahoma, Oklahoma City	x		x			x	
Oregon, Salem	x		x			x	
Pennsylvania, Harrisburg	x		x			x	
South Dakota, Pierre	x		x	x	x		x
South Carolina, Columbia	x	x	x		x		
Tennessee, Nashville	x		x			x	
Texas, Austin	x				x****		
Utah, Salt Lake City	x				x + Judge's Name		
Virginia, Richmond	x					x	
Washington, Olympia	x		x		x		
West Virginia, Charleston	x		x			x	
Wyoming, Cheyenne	x		x	x			x

*Include only the names of the parties, not the words "Plaintiff" and "Defendant." Delaware does not place the terms "plaintiff" or "defendant" in the caption.

**The title is centered; the number is in the upper lefthand corner.

***The terms "plaintiff" and "defendant" are on the right side of the page.

****The court title is centered at the right; the cause # is centered above everything else.

[1]Information presented in this table was obtained from a questionnaire sent to court clerks in each state and was summarized from the responses.

APPENDIX C
STATE ABBREVIATIONS

State	Two-Letter Code	Standard Abbreviation
Alabama	AL	Ala.
Alaska	AK	
Arizona	AZ	Ariz.
Arkansas	AR	Ark.
California	CA	Calif.
Colorado	CO	Colo.
Connecticut	CT	Conn.
Delaware	DE	Del.
District of Columbia	DC	D.C.
Florida	FL	Fla.
Georgia	GA	Ga.
Hawaii	HI	
Idaho	ID	
Illinois	IL	Ill.
Indiana	IN	Ind.
Iowa	IA	
Kansas	KS	Kans.
Kentucky	KY	Ky.
Louisiana	LA	La.
Maine	ME	
Maryland	MD	Md.
Massachusetts	MA	Mass.
Michigan	MI	Mich.
Minnesota	MN	Minn.
Mississippi	MS	Miss.
Missouri	MO	Mo.
Montana	MT	Mont.
Nebraska	NE	Nebr.
Nevada	NV	Nev.
New Hampshire	NH	N.H.
New Jersey	NJ	N.J.
New Mexico	NM	N.Mex.
New York	NY	N.Y.
North Carolina	NC	N.C.
North Dakota	ND	N.Dak.
Ohio	OH	
Oklahoma	OK	Okla.
Oregon	OR	Oreg.
Pennsylvania	PA	Pa.
Rhode Island	RI	R.I.

State	Two-Letter Code	Standard Abbreviation
South Carolina	SC	S.C.
South Dakota	SD	S.Dak.
Tennessee	TN	Tenn.
Texas	TX	Tex.
Utah	UT	
Vermont	VT	Vt.
Virginia	VA	Va.
Washington	WA	Wash.
West Virginia	WV	W.Va.
Wisconsin	WI	Wis.
Wyoming	WY	Wyo.

GLOSSARY

Abandon
> To willfully desert, leave, or forsake a child or an adult.

Acceptance
> A required element of an enforceable contract; to accept the offer.

Accounting
> A report of the income and expenses of an estate.

Acknowledgment
> A statement by the person who signs a document that it was done as his or her free act and deed.

Administrator
> A male appointed to administer the estate of a decedent who left no will.

Administratrix
> A female appointed to administer the estate of a decedent who left no will.

Adoptee
> One who is adopted.

Affiant
> The person who signs an affidavit.

Affidavit
> A statement under oath by the person who signs it.

Affidavit of consent
> A sworn document by a natural parent giving consent to adoption.

Affidavit of value
> An affidavit stating the value of the property or amount paid, whichever is greater.

Affirmative defense
> A legal defense when the defendant has allegations that are made against the plaintiff.

Age of majority
> When a minor reaches the legal age of an adult, usually 18 years of age.

Agent for service of process
> A person named to accept service of document if a corporation is sued.

Alias summons

The second summons delivered to a defendant.

Alien corporation

One organized out of the country and doing business within the United States.

Alimony

Payments to support spouse or ex-spouse; also called spousal support, spousal maintenance.

Allegations

Statements the accusing party expects to prove.

Alleged father

One who is charged with being the biological father of a child.

Answer

An document in which the defendant responds to the allegations in the complaint and defends against those charges.

Answer and consent

A verified document answering a petition and consenting to the adoption of one's birth child, thus giving up parental rights.

Appellant

The party appealing a decision from a lower court.

Appellate brief

Written argument presented by each side of a case, either supporting or opposing the decision of the lower court.

Appellee

The party opposing the appeal.

Appendix

An additional section at the back of an appellate brief containing material to support the brief; it can be a separately bound volume with a title page.

Argument

A discussion of the law as applied to the legal question; the attorney's support for his or her side of the case.

Articles of incorporation

Also known as a charter.

Assign

To give a legal right to another party, such as to sublease real property.

Attachment

A method and also a document used to "attach the body" or property of a defendant.

Attorney in fact

One who is appointed to act in the place of another.

Averments

Allegations.

Bankruptcy packet

A packet of forms for filing a bankruptcy.

Bankruptcy petition

The document that initiates a bankruptcy procedure.

Birth parent

Parent to whom a child is born; also known as biological or natural parent.

Block letter

All letter parts begin at the left margin.

Blood grouping tests

Tests to determine the father of a child born out of wedlock.

Board of directors

Elected representatives of a corporation who are given authority to establish policy for the corporation.

Bond

An insurance policy issued by a bonding company to ensure that duties are faithfully and honestly performed.

Bylaws

The basic rules and regulations adopted by the board of directors for running a corporation.

Calculating time

Using the rules of court to determine when a document should be filed or served.

Caption

The introductory part of a court document. It includes the name and location of the court, style of the case, docket number, and title of the document.

Cause of action

The wrong or injury that occurred to cause a party to sue another.

Certificate of service

A certificate stating that the document has been mailed to the opposing attorney or opposing party if there is no attorney.

Certified copy

A copy of a document upon which the clerk of the court has stamped or embossed the clerk's seal.

Charter

A document filed with the secretary of state to organize a corporation; also a charter.

Child custody

The primary care and maintenance of a child.

Child support

The money paid by one party to the other for the support of the minor child no longer in that party's custody.

Claims

A document filed by a creditor to whom money is owed, to which is attached an itemized statement.

Clerk of the Court

An official of the court whose job includes filing documents, officially issuing summonses, and keeping records of court proceedings.

Codicil

An addition or amendment to a will.

Common stock

A type of stock whose owners are paid last in case a corporation dissolves; represents ownership in a corporation.

Competence

Being of legal age and having the mental ability to enter into a contract.

Complaint

The first document filed in a lawsuit.

Conclusion

A statement resulting from the argument, including the relief sought from the appellate court.

Conforming

Adding notations of signatures to a copy of a document to indicate that the parties have signed the original; for example, "/s/ Casandra Baker" on a signature line means she signed the original document.

Conservator

One appointed by the court to oversee and manage the affairs of a disabled or incompetent adult. In some states, synonymous with guardian.

Consideration

Whatever one demands from another as the price for entering a contract. It is usually an amount of money or something of value.

Contingent

A debt is contingent if it is dependent on some future event that may or may not happen.

Corporate minute kits or outfits

A binder, minute paper, corporate seal, dividers, stock certificates, and other legal documents of the corporation.

Corporate seal

A seal used by a corporation, which imprints stock certificates and other legal documents of the corporation.

Corporation

A legal entity separate and apart from the persons who own and control it.

Cost bond

A statement signed by the plaintiff and attorney, stating that they will guarantee the payment of court costs not to exceed a stated amount.

Count

Each separate cause of action.

Counterclaim

An allegation made by the defendant against the plaintiff in the same action.

Creditor

One to whom money is owed.

Cross-complaint

Allegations made by one defendant against another defendant.

Current market value

Current value of a piece of property; amount the property could be sold for today.

Debtor

One who owes debts.

Decedent

A deceased person.

Declarant

Sometimes used as a party designation in living wills in which the person who signs makes declarations about life-support devices being used or not used.

Declaration

A statement similar to a verification. The statement is not made before a notary public. Some states call complaints declarations.

Deed

A written instrument by which title to real estate is conveyed from one person to another.

Deed of trust

An instrument conveying ownership of property to a trustee to secure a debt; a mortgage.

Deed of trust note

A promissory note; a document in which the maker promises to pay to the lender a stated sum of money.

Defendant

The party who is being sued.

Defense

A reason why the plaintiff should not win or recover damages from the defendant.

Deposition

Question and answer testimony taken under oath out of court and usually recorded by a court reporter.

Derivation clause

Provides the name of the previous owners of real property and the filing location in the office of public records.

Discharge of debts

Debts that are canceled or paid off entirely.

Disputed

A debt for which there is a difference of opinion as to whether the amount is correct or whether the debt is owed at all.

Dissolution

A process for terminating a marriage, usually on a no-fault basis.

Divorce

A process for terminating a marriage, usually based on legal grounds as defined in the state statutes.

Domestic corporation

One operating in the state where it was organized or incorporated.

Domicile

A person's true, permanent home, to which he or she plans to return though residing elsewhere.

Durable power of attorney for health care

A written instrument in which the maker appoints someone other than the physician to make health care decisions for the maker.

Earnest money

An amount of money given by the buyer to someone else, such as a real estate agent or escrow agent, to ensure a good-faith intent to buy.

Escrow agent

One who holds funds and distributes them according to the contract.

Exception

A document filed by a personal representative of an estate, objecting to the claim of a creditor.

Execution

All the formalities of signing and completing a document or contract.

Executor

A male named to administer a will.

Executrix

A female named to administer a will.

Extraordinary relief

A plaintiff's request for relief from the defendant before there is a hearing, such as requiring the defendant to support the children, stop harassing, etc.

Federal estate tax

A federal tax imposed on the privilege of transmitting property at death.

Federal Rules of Appellate Procedure

The procedural rules for the appellate procedure in federal cases.

Federal Rules of Civil Procedure

The procedural rules for federal civil cases.

Federal tax number

A number required by the Internal Revenue Service for businesses.

Fiat

A court order within a document, such as a complaint for divorce.

Fiduciary

One who manages money or property for another. In probate matters, this is the personal representative.

File number or docket number

A number assigned to a case by the clerk of the court when the completed summons and complaint are filed.

File with the clerk

To have signed, stamped, and dated by the clerk of the court.

Financing statement

When filed with the appropriate office, is used to determine the creditor's right to claim the collateral pledged for a loan; U.C.C.1 form.

Foreign corporation

A corporation is foreign to all states except the state in which it was organized and officially incorporated.

For-profit corporation

Corporation organized for the purpose of making a profit.

Foster home

A home where a child lives and is cared for before being adopted.

Garnishment

A legal claim against a portion of a person's earnings.

General partners

Partners who are personally liable for all debts owed by a partnership, share in the profits, and have equal voice in making partnership decisions.

Grace period

The period of time within which a debt, such as a lease, will not be terminated for late payments.

Grantee

One who purchases, buys, or is the receiver of a transfer of property.

Granting clause

A statement that property was conveyed or transferred to another.

Grantor

One who grants, sells, or transfers property to another.

Grounds

The state-approved legal reasons a divorce or annulment can be granted.

Guardian

One appointed by the court to oversee and manage the affairs of one incapable of managing his or her own affairs, such as a minor child or incompetent adult.

Guardian ad litem

One appointed by the court to represent the interests of a minor child or disabled or incompetent adult at a court hearing.

Habendum

A clause that defines the interest conveyed in property; generally begins with the words "To have and to hold."

Hearing on a motion

An appearance before a judge, during which the motion is either granted or denied.

Holographic will

A will written in the testator/trix's own handwriting.

Incorporators

Those who do all things necessary to form a corporation.

Installment deed

A type of deed in which the seller finances the unpaid balance owed by the buyer on a piece of property.

Interlocutory decree

A temporary order, such as the temporary assignment of the child care and custody of a child to the petitioners.

Interrogatories

Written questions about a case submitted by one side of the lawsuit to the other.

Intestate

A procedure for settling an estate for a person who died after having made a will.

Inventory

An itemized list of property, usually with estimated values for each item.

Involuntary bankruptcy

A bankruptcy procedure initiated by creditors against an individual or a company. See voluntary bankruptcy.

Irreconcilable differences

A no-fault ground for terminating a marriage; also irretrievable breakdown.

Irretrievable breakdown

A no-fault ground for terminating a marriage; also irreconcilable differences.

Issues

Legal questions.

Joint custody

Custody in which the parents have equal input into decisions about the welfare and care of a child. See also split and sole custody.

Joint petition and joint schedules

One petition and one set of schedules prepared for the husband and wife in a bankruptcy proceeding.

Judgment lien

A lien on property as the result of a lawsuit.

Jurat

The following statement: "Sworn to and subscribed before me this the _____ day of _____, 1994."

Jurisdiction

The authority of a court to hear a case.

Jury

A group of citizens selected to hear a case, who are sworn to arrive at the truth of a matter and make a decision for or against the defendant.

L.S.

An abbreviation for locus sigilli, meaning in the place of a seal.

Landlord

One who rents or leases real property.

Last will and testament

An instrument in which a person states how his or her property is to be distributed after his or her death.

Lawful purpose

A required element of an enforceable contract; cannot be to commit a crime, to defraud someone, or to do harm to someone.

Laws of succession

(also known as laws of descent and distribution) Laws that govern the way property passes if one dies without leaving a will.

Lease

A contract between a landowner and a tenant; also called an indenture, contract, or agreement.

Legal back

A sheet of paper (sometimes colored) slightly larger and heavier than the paper on which a document is printed. It is used for placing a cover on documents.

Legal cap

Paper with ruled vertical lines at the left and right margins.

Legal citations

References to legal materials, specifying where they can be found in a law library.

Legally binding

Legally obligated; can be enforced in a court of law.

Lessee

One who leases property.

Lessor

One who leases property to another.

Letters of administration

An instrument or document of authority issued to the administrator or administratrix of an estate of a person who dies without leaving a will.

Letters of administration, c.t.a.

(cum testamento annexo — with will attached) An instrument of document issued to a person who was not named executor or executrix in a will, giving the person to whom it is issued authority to administer the will.

Letters of conservatorship

An instrument or document giving authority to manage the property of a disabled or incompetent adult.

Letters of guardianship

An instrument or document giving authority to manage the property of a minor child. In some states, to manage property of a disabled or incompetent adult.

Letters testamentary

An instrument or document of authority issued to the executor or executrix of an estate of a person who dies leaving a will.

Lien

A claim against property to secure a debt.

Limited partners

Partners who are personally liable for the debts of a partnership only up to the amount they invest, share in the profits, but have no voice in making partnership decisions.

Litigation

The process of carrying on a lawsuit when one party sues another party in a court of law.

Living will

Written instructions to the medical profession not to provide or to withdraw medical treatment when there is no reasonable expectation of recovery.

Map and parcel numbers

Numbers assigned to each parcel of land, which can be obtained from the trustee's office or from the register's (known as the registrar in some areas) office.

Marital dissolution agreement

An agreement between parties to a divorce about such matters as property division, alimony, child support, child custody, etc. Also referred to as a property settlement agreement.

Minor

One who has not reached the age of majority as defined by law, usually 18 years of age.

Minute book

A notebook where minutes of a corporation are filed.

Minutes

A written record of the business conducted at a meeting.

Modified block letter

All letter parts begin at the left margin except the date, complimentary closing, and typed signature, which begin at center point.

Mortgage

A lien against real estate.

Motion

An application to the court, based on a specific ground or reason, requesting that the court make an order (rule) in favor of the applicant.

Motion to dismiss

A request to the judge to dismiss a case.

Natural parent

A biological, or birth, parent.

No par stock

Stock that does not state a value on the face of the stock certificate.

Noncustodial parent

The parent who does not have custody of a child.

Not-for-profit corporation

Religious, social, or charitable corporation that is set up for benevolent purpose and not to make a profit.

Notary public

A public officer who administers oaths and takes acknowledgments.

Notice of taking a deposition

A document notifying parties of the time, date, and place of taking a deposition.

Offer

A required element of an enforceable contract; to present something for acceptance.

Officers

Elected individuals whose function is to carry out policy of a corporation. Example, president and secretary.

Opinion

A report written by the judge, stating the facts of the case, the issues to be answered, the reason for the decision, and the ruling of the court.

Oral will

A will spoken by the testator before witnesses during the last days of illness or injury and afterwards reduced to writing.

Order

A command. A document signed by the judge giving directions of the court in writing.

Order of abandonment

An order of the court stating that a child has been abandoned.

Order of reference

The document that orders an investigation of a proposed adoptive home by the welfare department of the state.

Par value

Stock that shows a value per share on the stock certificate.

Parallel citation

A citation to the same opinion recorded in different reporters.

Partnership

An arrangement where two or more persons, as co-owners, agree to carry on a business for profit.

Paternity

A procedure to establish fatherhood.

Pauper's oath

A statement under oath that the party is unable to pay court costs.

Per capita

Grandchildren cannot inherit their parent's share if the parent dies before the grandparent. Property is divided among the living children.

Per stirpes

Grandchildren can inherit their parent's share if the parent dies before the grandparent.

Perfection

Priority on claiming the collateral to satisfy a claim.

Personal representative

Anyone who administers a will or estate of a decedent.

Petition

Also known as a complaint or declaration. A method of legally asking for something.

Petition to probate a will

A document asking that a will be admitted to probate court.

Plaintiff

The party who is suing.

Pluries summons

The third and subsequent summonses delivered to a defendant.

Prayer clause

The last paragraph or paragraphs of each count or the last paragraph of the complaint or petition, in which the plaintiff demands judgment against the defendants. Also the last paragraph in a counter-claim or cross-claim. Often referred to as the "WHEREFORE" clause.

Preferred stock

A type of stock whose owners are paid first in case a corporation dissolves or goes out of business.

Premises

The portion of a deed that includes the names of parties, consideration, granting clause, property description, and derivation clause.

Primary material

The law; constitutions, statutes, and cases.

Prior history

Citation of an earlier lower court decision that a higher court is affirming (aff'g) or reversing (rev'g).

Probate

The term probate means "to prove"; thus, probating a will is proving a will to be valid.

Probate estate

All property to be distributed by will or by descent and distribution after death.

Probate master

An officer of the probate court who can conduct hearings on probate matters.

Professional corporation

Licensed individuals, such as doctors and certified public accountants, who incorporate themselves as a business.

Property description

A description of property giving boundaries, angles, and lengths and property lines around a piece of property.

Public charge

One who is supported at public expense.

Public corporation

Cities, town, or government-owned corporations.

Quitclaim deed

A deed that transfers only the ownership that one has in property with no further warranties.

Real estate closing

A meeting where all parties sign the documents and transfer money as outlined in the settlement sheets.

Real estate

Land and anything attached to it.

Record

Copies of documents filed in the trial court and the transcript prepared by a court reporter of the trial-level proceedings.

Register or registrar

One responsible for filing public records.

Reporter

Volumes of books containing opinions.

Request for admissions

A document requesting the party on the opposing side of a case to admit or deny certain listed statements.

Request for production

A document requesting the opposing side of the case to produce documents or things relevant to the case for inspection, copying, etc.

Resolution

A formal written statement of an opinion or intention adopted by a group.

Respondent

The minor child or disabled or incompetent adult in guardianship and conservatorship matters. One who is a party to a legal action; thus, petitioner and respondent.

Responsive pleadings

The documents filed in response to a complaint, counterclaim, or cross-claim.

Right to survivorship

A type of joint ownership in property in which the property goes to the survivor upon the death of one of the owners.

Sales agreement

A contract between the buyer and seller, specifying the terms of the sale.

Sales contract

An agreement between the purchaser (debtor) and seller (creditor), with the purchaser agreeing to pay a stated amount for the property purchased.

Secondary material

Material written about the law; found in legal periodicals, books, encyclopedias, etc. See primary material.

Secretary of state

A government official (one of the duties of that office is to license corporations).

Secured claim

A claim in which property has been pledged to secure the debt.

Security agreement

The document that grants the security interest in personal property put up as collateral.

Security deposit

> An amount of money paid to the landlord to cover any damages caused by the tenant or to cover loss of rent if the tenant does not pay.

Self-proving affidavit

> A sworn statement before a notary by the witnesses to a will.

Setoff

> A reduction of the amount owed because of an entity's right to an asset. For example, if a person owes a bank $500 but has $100 in savings and the bank seizes the $100, then the $100 is a reduction (setoff) from the total amount owed on the debt.

Settlement sheet

> A statement showing all costs involved in a real estate transaction.

Shareholders

> People who own shares of stock of a corporation; also stockholders.

Signals

> Introductory words at the beginnings of citations to legal material. Signals are expressions such as e.g., accord, see, see also, cf., compare with, contra, but see, but cf., and see generally.

Sole custody

> Custody in which one parent has the total responsibility of caring for the child. See also split and joint custody.

Split custody

> Custody in which the child is awarded to one parent for a portion of the time and to the other parent for the remaining time, with the custodial parent making all decisions. See also joint and sole custody.

State inheritance taxes

> Taxes on the amounts received by beneficiaries.

Statement of facts

> A detailed description of the facts surrounding a case.

Statement of the case

> A description and history of the case, including the outcome of lower court proceedings.

Statute

> A law enacted and passed by a legislative body.

Statutory lien

A lien on property of the debtor imposed by law, such as a lien for not paying taxes.

Stock certificate

A certificate issued to a stockholder, providing written evidence of ownership in a corporation.

Stock ledger

A form used for keeping a record of the names and addresses of shareholders and of the issuance and transfer of stock certificates.

Stockholders

People who own shares of stock of a corporation; also shareholders.

Straight bankruptcy

A Chapter 7 bankruptcy; also called a liquidation.

Style of the case

The names of the plaintiffs and defendants in a case. For example, Cynthia Whitson, Plaintiff vs. George Kelly, Defendant.

Subchapter S

A type of small business organization that is incorporated and allows the owners to be taxed individually rather than as a corporation.

Sublease

To transfer the right to use property to a third party.

Sublessee

One who subleases property from another.

Sublessor

One who subleases property to another.

Subpoena

A command to appear at a certain time and certain place to give testimony.

Subscription agreement

A contract for the purchase of securities or of stock in a corporation.

Subsequent history

Citation of a later higher court decision that reversed (rev'd) or affirmed (aff'd) a lower court decision.

Summons

A document notifying the defendant that a lawsuit is being filed against him or her.

Sworn petition

A petition that contains a statement sworn to before a notary public by the petitioner that the contents of the document are true.

Table of authorities

An alphabetical listing of each and every citation included in an appellate brief, with references to the pages in the brief where they are cited.

Table of contents

An outline of the sections of a brief, indicating page numbers where each section begins.

Tenant

One who rents or leases real property.

Testamentary instrument

Any documents, such as a will or codicil, to take effect after the death of the maker.

Testamentary trust

A trust to take effect upon the death of the maker.

Testate

A procedure for settling an estate for a person who died not having made a will.

Testator

A male who makes a will.

Testatrix

A female who makes a will.

Testimonium

A clause that begins with "IN WITNESS WHEREOF," or "IN TESTIMONY WHEREOF," and includes the grantor's signature and an acknowledgment.

Third-party complaint

A complaint filed by the defendant against a person or business not in the original lawsuit.

Third-party defendant

A party brought into a lawsuit who was not in the original action.

Third-party plaintiff

The defendant in the original action who files a third-party complaint.

Title of the document

A name given to a document, indicating its purpose, such as complaint, complaint for damages, or motion to dismiss.

Transfer tax

The charge for transferring property from one owner to another.

Trust

Property or money held by one party for the benefit of another.

Trustee

The party who is holding the property named in the trust.

Trustor

The person whose property is being held in trust and the one who creates the trust.

Typewritten or formal will

A will that has been prepared following all the formalities of law.

Unliquidated

A debt for which the amount owed has not been determined.

Unsecured priority creditors

Certain creditors that given a special status by statute; creditors whose claims are paid before other unsecured creditors and who have no property as collateral.

Venue

The geographic location of a court.

Verification

A statement made under oath as to the correctness and truth of a matter. The statement is made before a notary public.

Verification of consent

A sworn statement by a birth parent giving consent to adoption. A verification is a statement at the end of a document.

Voluntary bankruptcy

A bankruptcy procedure initiated by the debtor. See involuntary bankruptcy.

Ward

One who is placed under the care of a guardian or conservator.

Warranties

Promises or guarantees made by a grantor.

Warranty deed

A deed that contains general warranties.

Witness

One who observes the signing of a document and adds his or her name on a line prepared for the witness.

INDEX

FORMS FOR COMPLETING PERFORMANCE REVIEWS

Project 1-2, Circuit Court Summons

Project 3-5, Subpoena

Project 11-6, Stock Certificates

Project 13-1, Voluntary Bankruptcy Petition and Filing of Plan
Project 13-2, Schedules A and B
Project 13-3, Schedule C
Project 13-4, Schedules D, E, F, G, and H
Project 13-5, Schedules I and J
Project 13-6, Individual Debtor's Statement of Intention
Project 13-7, Declaration Concerning Debtor's Schedules
Project 13-8, Statement of Financial Affairs
Project 13-9, Summary of Schedules
Project 13-10, Mailing List Matrix
Project 13-11, Disclosure of Compensation

STATE OF TENNESSEE
20th JUDICIAL DISTRICT   **FILE NO.**_____

_____

_____

_____
                                                    Plaintiff

VS.

_____

_____

_____

_____
                                                    Defendant

To the above named Defendant:

    You are summoned to appear and defend a civil action filed against you in Circuit Court, Davidson County, Tennessee, and your defense must be made within thirty (30) days from the date this summons is served upon you. You are further directed to file your defense with the Clerk of the Court and send a copy to the Plaintiff's attorney at the address listed below.

    In case of your failure to defend this action by the above date, judgement by default will be rendered against you for the relief demanded in the complaint.

ISSUED:_____, 19_____.   **GEORGE L. ROOKER**
                                                                          Circuit Court Clerk
                                                                    Davidson County, Tennessee

                                                          By_____
                                                                          Deputy Clerk

ATTORNEY FOR PLAINTIFF   _____

        or   _____
                                            Address

PLAINTIFF'S ADDRESS   _____

TO THE SHERIFF:
    Please execute this summons and make your return hereon as provided by law.

                                                          GEORGE L. ROOKER
                                                            Circuit Court Clerk

Received this summons for service this the _____ **day of** _____, 19_____.

                                                    _____
                                                          SHERIFF

RETURN ON PERSONAL SERVICE OF SUMMONS

I hereby certify and return, that on the _____ day of _____, 19____ I served this summons together with the complaint herein as follows:

_____

_____

_____

_____

_____

SHERIFF

BY: _____

RETURN ON SERVICE OF SUMMONS BY MAIL

I hereby certify and return, that on the _____ day of _____, 19___ I sent, postage prepaid, by registered return receipt mail or certified return receipt mail, a certified copy of the summons and a copy of the complaint in Case No. _____ to the defendant, _____. On the _____ day of _____, 19___ I received the return receipt for said registered or certified mail, which had been signed by _____ on the _____ day of _____, 19___. Said return receipt is attached to this original summons and both documents are being sent herewith to the Circuit Court Clerk for filing.

SWORN TO AND SUBSCRIBED BEFORE ME THIS THE _____ DAY OF _____, 19___.

PLAINTIFF, PLAINTIFF'S ATTORNEY, OR OTHER PERSON AUTHORIZED BY STATUTE TO SERVE PROCESS

_____

_____ NOTARY PUBLIC or _____ DEPUTY CLERK
MY COMMISSION EXPIRES: _____
_____

NOTICE

TO THE DEFENDANT(S):

Tennessee law provides a four thousand dollar ($4,000.00) debtor's equity interest personal property exemption from execution or seizure to satisfy a judgement. If a judgement should be entered against you in this action and you wish to claim property as exempt, you must file a written list, under oath, of the items you wish to claim as exempt with the clerk of the court. This list may be filed at any time and may be changed by you thereafter as necessary; however, unless it is filed before the judgement becomes final, it will not be effective as to any execution or garnishment issued prior to the filing of the list. Certain items are automatically exempt by law and do not need to be listed; these include items of necessary wearing apparel (clothing) for yourself and your family and trunks or other receptacles necessary to contain such apparel, family portraits, the family Bible, and school books. Should any of these items be seized you would have the right to recover them. If you do not understand your exemption right or how to exercise it, you may wish to seek the counsel of a lawyer.

ATTACH
RETURN
RECEIPT
HERE
(IF APPLICABLE)

STATE OF TENNESSEE

COUNTY OF DAVIDSON

(To be completed only if copy certification required).

I, George L. Rooker, Clerk of the Circuit Court in the State and County aforesaid, do hereby certify this to be a true and correct copy of the original summons issued on this case.
GEORGE L. ROOKER, CLERK

By: _____ D.C.

STATE OF TENNESSEE DAVIDSON COUNTY Circuit Court	**SUBPOENA** (ORDER TO APPEAR)	CASE FILE NUMBER

PLAINTIFF	**DEFENDANT**
	VS.

TO: (Name, Address, & Telephone Number of Witness)

You are hereby commanded to appear at the time, date and place specified for the purpose of giving testimony. In addition, if indicated, you are to bring the items listed. Failure to appear may result in punishment by fine and/or imprisonment as provided by law.

TIME	**DATE**	**ITEMS TO BRING:**
PLACE Circuit Court, Division_____ Metropolitan Courthouse Nashville, Tennessee (OR)		

This subpoena is being issued on behalf of
☐ **plaintiff** ☐ **defendant.**
Attorney: (Name, Address & Telephone Number)

☐ **Additional List Attached**

DATE ISSUED

**ATTORNEY'S
SIGNATURE:**

**GEORGE L. ROOKER, CIRCUIT COURT CLERK
BY:**

DESIGNEE:

**DESIGNEE'S
SIGNATURE:**

Deputy Clerk

RETURN ON SERVICE

Check one: (1 or 2 are for the return of an authorized officer or attorney; an attorney's return must be sworn to; 3. is for the witness who will acknowledge service and requires the witness's signature.)

1. ☐ I certify that on the date indicated below I served a copy of this subpoena on the witness stated above by

_____

2. ☐ I failed to serve a copy of this subpoena on the witness because

_____

3. ☐ I acknowledge being served with this subpoena on the date indicated below.

Sworn to and subscribed before me this the ____ day of _____. Signature of Notary Public or Deputy Clerk My Commission Expires:	**DATE OF SERVICE** **SIGNATURE OF WTINESS, OFFICER, ATTORNEY OR ATTORNEY'S DESIGNEE**

FORM NO. GR-107   Submit Original, Witness Copy & File Copy.

FIGURE 3-5. Subpoena

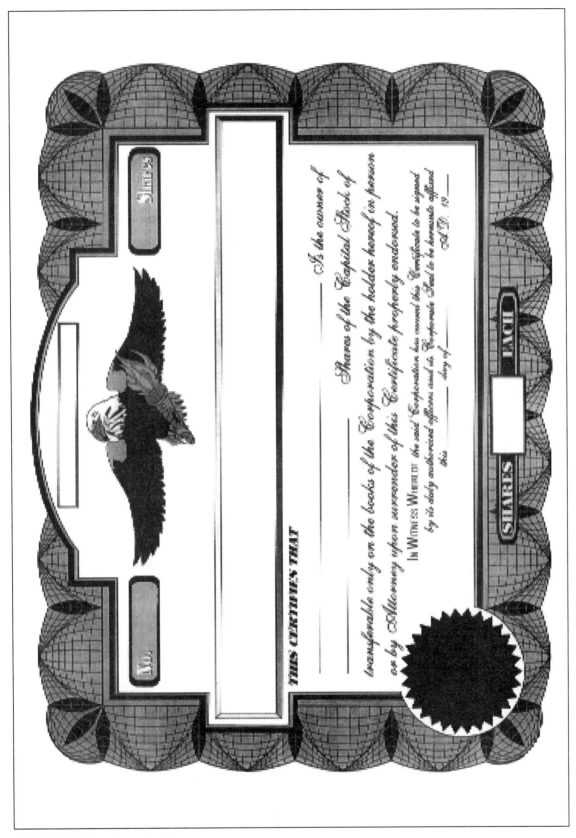

PROJECT 11-6, Stock Certificate

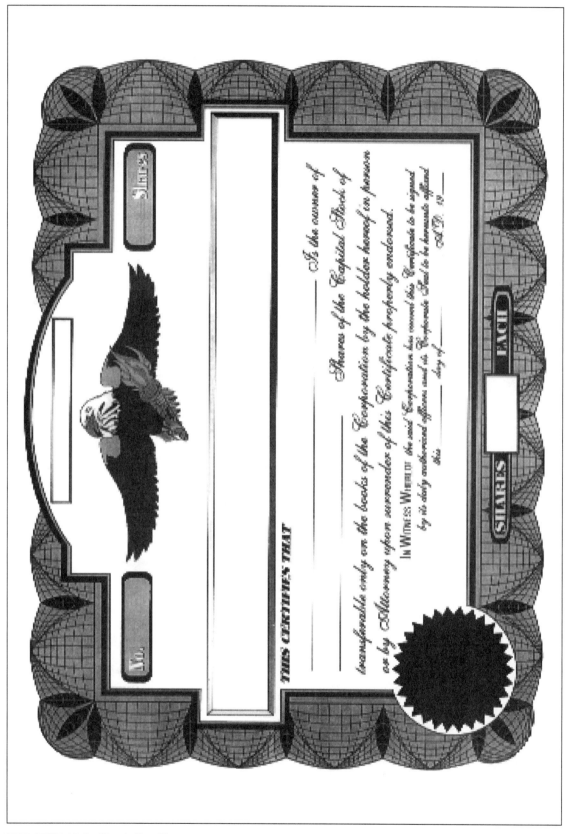

PROJECT 11-6, Stock Certificate

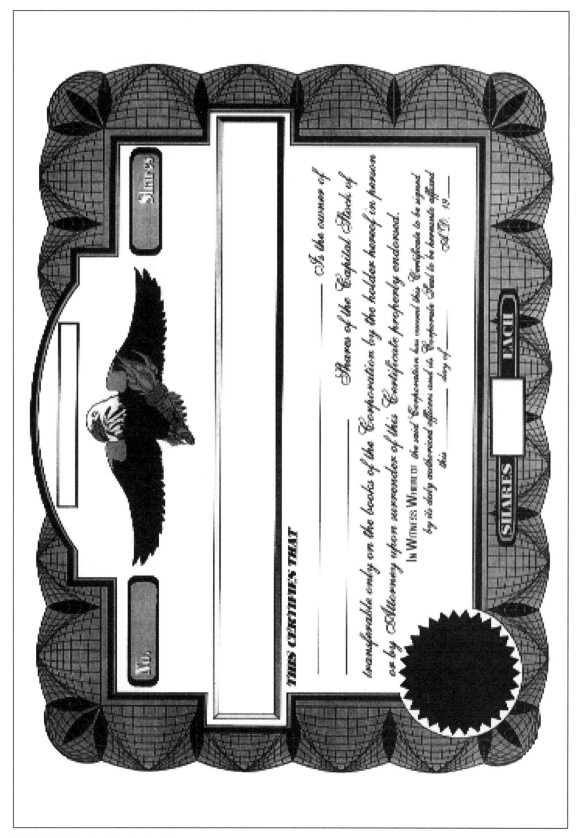

PROJECT 11-6, Stock Certificate

UNITED STATE BANKRUPTCY COURT _____DISTRICT OF_____	VOLUNTARY PETITION

IN RE (Name of debtor—If individual, enter Last, First, Middle)	NAME OF JOINT DEBTOR (Spouse) (Last, First, Middle)

ALL OTHER NAMES used by the debtor in the last 6 years (Include married, maiden and trade names.)	ALL OTHER NAMES used by the joint debtor in the last 6 years (Include married, maiden, and trade names.)

SEC. SEC./TAX I.D. NO. (If more than one, state all.)	SEC. SEC./TAX I.D. NO. (If more than one, state all.)

STREET ADDRESS OF DEBTOR (No. and street, city, state, and zip code)	STREET ADDRESS OF JOINT DEBTOR (No. and street, city, state, and zip code)
COUNTY OF RESIDENCE OR PRINCIPAL PLACE OF BUSINESS	COUNTY OF RESIDENCE OR PRINCIPAL PLACE OF BUSINESS

MAILING ADDRESS OF DEBTOR (If different from street address)	MAILING ADDRESS OF JOINT DEBTOR (If different from street address)

LOCATION OF PRINCIPAL ASSETS OF BUSINESS DEBTOR (If different from addresses listed above)	VENUE (Check one box) ☐ Debtor has been domiciled or has had a residence, principal place of business, or principal assets in this District for 180 days immediately preceding the date of this petition or for a longer part of such 180 days than in any other District. ☐ There is a bankruptcy case concerning debtor's affiliate general partner, or partnership pending in this District.

INFORMATION REGARDING DEBTOR (Check applicable boxes)

TYPE OF DEBTOR ☐ Individual ☐ Corporation Publicly Held ☐ Joint (Husband & Wife) ☐ Corporation Not Publicly Held ☐ Partnership ☐ Municipality ☐ Other:	"CHAPTER OR SECTION OF BANKRUPTCY CODE UNDER WHICH THE PETITION IS FILED (Check one box) ☐ Chapter 7 ☐ Chapter 11 ☐ Chapter 13 ☐ Chapter 9 ☐ Chapter 12 ☐ Section 304-Case Ancillary to Foreign Proceeding
NATURE OF DEBT ☐ Non-Business/Consumer ☐ Business-Complete A & B below	FILING FEE (Check one box) ☐ Filing fee attached ☐ Filing fee to be paid in installments (Applicable to individuals only) Must attach signed application for the court's consideration certifying that the debtor is unable to pay fee except installments. Rule 1006(b). See Official Form No. 3
A. TYPE OF BUSINESS (Check one box) ☐ Farming ☐ Transportation ☐ Commodity Broker ☐ Professional ☐ Manufacturing/ ☐ Construction ☐ Retail/Wholesale Mining ☐ Real Estate ☐ Railroad ☐ Stockbroker ☐ Other Business	NAME AND ADDRESS OF LAW FIRM OR ATTORNEY Telephone No.
B. BRIEFLY DESCRIBE NATURE OF BUSINESS	NAME(S) OF ATTORNEY(S) DESIGNATED TO REPRESENT THE DEBTOR (Print or Type Names) ☐ Debtor is not represented by an attorney

STATISTICAL ADMINISTRATIVE INFORMATION (28 U.S.C. § 604) (Estimates only) (Check applicable boxes)	THIS SPACE FOR COURT USE ONLY

☐ Debtor estimates that funds will be available for distribution to unsecured creditors.

☐ Debtor estimates that after any exempt property is excluded and administrative expense s paid. There will be no funds available for distribution to unsecured creditors.

ESTIMATED NUMBER OF CREDITORS

1-15	16-49	50-99	100-199	200-999	1000-over
☐	☐	☐	☐	☐	☐

ESTIMATED ASSETS (In thousands of dollars)

Under 50	50-99	100-499	500-999	1000-9999	10,000-99,000	100,000-over
☐	☐	☐	☐	☐	☐	☐

ESTIMATED LIABILITIES (In thousands of dollars)

Under 50	50-99	100-499	500-999	1000-9999	10,000-99,000	100,000-over
☐	☐	☐	☐	☐	☐	☐

ESTIMATED NO. OF EMPLOYEES - CHAPTER 11 & 12 ONLY

0	1-19	20-99	100-499	500-over
☐	☐	☐	☐	☐

ESTIMATED NO. OF SECURITY HOLDERS - CHAPTER 11 & 12 ONLY

0	1-19	20-99	100-499	500-over
☐	☐	☐	☐	☐

PROJECT 13-1, Voluntary Bankruptcy Petition

Name of Debtor _____

Case No. _____

FILING OF PLAN

For Chapter 9, 11, 12 and 13 cases only. Check appropriate box.

☐ A copy of debtor's proposed plan dated _____ is attached.

☐ Debtor intends to file a plan within the time allowed by statute, rule, or order of the court.

PRIOR BANKRUPTCY CASE FILED WITHIN LAST 6 YEARS
(If more than one, attach additional sheet)

Location Where Filed	Case Number	Date Filed

PENDING BANKRUPTCY CASE FILED BY ANY SPOUSE, PARTNER, OR AFFILIATE OF THIS DEBTOR
(If more than one, attach additional sheet)

Name of Debtor	Case Number	Date
Relationship	District	Judge

REQUEST FOR RELIEF

Debtor requests relief in accordance with the chapter of title 11, United States Code, specified in this petition.

SIGNATURES

ATTORNEY

X_____   _____
Signature   Date

INDIVIDUAL/JOINT DEBTOR(S)	**CORPORATE OR PARTNERSHIP DEBTOR**
I declare under penalty of perjury that the information provided in this petition is true and correct.	I declare under penalty of perjury that the information provided in this petition is true and correct, and that the filing of the petition on behalf of the debtor has been authorized.
X_____ Signature of Debtor	X_____ Signature of Authorized Individual
_____ Date	_____ Print or Type Name of Authorized Individual
X_____ Signature of Joint Debtor	_____ Title of Individual Authorized by Debtor to File this Petition
_____ Date	_____ Date

EXHIBIT "A" (To be completed if debtor is a corporation requesting relief under chapter 11.)

☐ Exhibit "A" is attached and made a part of this petition.

TO BE COMPLETED BY INDIVIDUAL CHAPTER 7 DEBTOR WITH PRIMARILY CONSUMER DEBTS
(See P.L. 99-353 § 322)

I am aware that I may proceed under chapter 7, 11, or 12, or 13 of title 11, United States Code, understand the relief available under each such chapter, and choose to proceed under chapter 7 of such title.

If I am represented by an attorney, Exhibit B has been completed.

X_____   _____
Signature of Debtor   Date

X_____   _____
Signature of Joint Debtor   Date

EXHIBIT "B" (To be completed by attorney for individual chapter 7 debtor(s) with primarily consumer debts.)

I, the attorney for the debtor(s) named in the foregoing petition, declare that I have informed the debtor(s) that (he, she, or they) may proceed under chapter 7, 11, 12, or 13 of title 11, United States Code, and have explained the relief available under each such chapter.

X_____   _____
Signature of Attorney   Date

PROJECT 13-1, Filing of Plan

United States Bankruptcy Court

_____DISTRICT OF_____

In re_____,   Case No._____
　　　　　　　Debtor　　　　　　　　　　　　　　　(If known)

SCHEDULE A — REAL PROPERTY

　　　　Except as directed below, list all real property in which the debtor has any legal, equitable, or future interest, including all property owned as a co-tenant, community property, or in which the debtor has a life estate. Include any property in which the debtor holds rights and powers exercisable for the debtor's own benefit. If the debtor is married, state whether husband, wife, or both own the property by placing an "H," "W," "J," or "C" in the column labeled "Husband, Wife, Joint, or Community." If the debtor holds no interest in real property, write "None" under "Description and Location of Property."

　　　　Do not include interest in executory contracts and unexpired leases on this schedule. List them in Schedule G—Executory Contracts and Unexpired Leases.

　　　　If an entity claims to have a lien or hold a secured interest in any property, state the amount of the secured claim. See Schedule D. If no entity claims to hold a secured interest in the property, write "None" in the column labeled "Amount of Secured Claim."

　　　　If the debtor is an individual or if a joint petition is filed, state the amount of any exemption claimed in the property only in Schedule C—Property Claimed as Exempt.

DESCRIPTION AND LOCATION OF PROPERTY	NATURE OF DEBTOR'S INTEREST IN PROPERTY	H W J or C	CURRENT MARKET VALUE OF DEBTOR'S INTEREST IN PROPERTY WITHOUT DEDUCTING ANY SECURED CLAIM OR EXEMPTION	AMOUNT OF SECURED CLAIM
		Total ➤	$	

(Report also on Summary of Schedules.)

PROJECT 13-2, Schedule A

United States Bankruptcy Court

_____DISTRICT OF_____

In re_____,   Case No._____
         Debtor   **(If known)**

SCHEDULE B — PERSONAL PROPERTY

Except as directed below, list all personal property of the debtor of whatever kind. If the debtor has no property in one or more of the categories, place an "X" in the appropriate position in the column labeled "None." If additional space is needed in any category, attach a separate sheet properly identified with the case name, case number, and the number of the category. If the debtor is married, state whether husband, wife, or both own the property by placing an "H," "W," "J," or C in the column labeled "Husband, Wife, Joint, or Community." If the debtor is an individual or a joint petition is filed, state the amount of any exemptions claimed only in Schedule C—Property Claimed as Exempt.

Do not list interests in executory contracts and unexpired leases on this schedule. List them in Schedule G—Executory Contracts and Unexpired Leases.

If the property is being held for the debtor by someone else, state that person's name and address under "Description and Location of Property."

TYPE OF PROPERTY	N O N E	DESCRIPTION AND LOCATION OF PROPERTY	H W J or C	CURRENT MARKET VALUE OF DEBTOR'S INTEREST IN PROPERTY, WITHOUT DEDUCTING ANY SECURED CLAIM OR EXEMPTION
1. Cash on hand.				
2. Checking, savings or other financial accounts, certificates of deposit, or shares in banks, savings and loan, thrift, building and loan, and homestead associations, or credit unions, brokerage houses, or cooperatives.				
3. Security deposits with public utilities, telephone companies, landlords, and others.				
4. Household goods and furnishings, including audio, video, and computer equipment.				
5. Books, pictures and other art objects, antiques, stamp, coin record, tape, compact disc, and other collections or collectibles.				
6. Wearing apparel.				
7. Furs and jewelry.				
8. Firearms and sports, photographic, and other hobby equipment.				
9. Interests in insurance policies. Name insurance company of each policy and itemize surrender or refund value of each.				
10. Annuities, itemize and name each issuer.				

PROJECT 13-2, Schedule B

Official Bankr.Form B6B, 11 U.S.C.A.

United States Bankruptcy Court

_____DISTRICT OF_____

In re_____, Case No._____
                    Debtor   **(If known)**

SCHEDULE B — PERSONAL PROPERTY
(Continuation Sheet)

TYPE OF PROPERTY	N O N E	DESCRIPTION AND LOCATION OF PROPERTY	H W J or C	CURRENT MARKET VALUE OF DEBTOR'S INTEREST IN PROPERTY, WITHOUT DEDUCTING ANY SECURED CLAIM OR EXEMPTION
11. Interests in IRA, ERISA, Keogh or other pension or profit sharing Plans. Itemized.				
12. Stock and interests in incorporated and unincorporated businesses. Itemized.				
13. Interests in partnerships or joint ventures. Itemized.				
14. Government and corporate bonds and other negotiable and nonnegotiable instruments.				
15. Accounts Receivable.				
16. Alimony, maintenance, support, and property settlements to which the debtor is or may be entitled. Give particulars.				
17. Other liquidated debts owing debtor including tax refunds. Give particulars.				
18. Equitable or future interests, life estates, and rights or powers exercisable for the benefit of the debtor other than those listed in Schedule of Real Property.				
19. Contingent and non-contingent interests in estate of a decedent, death benefit plan, life insurance policy, or trust.				
20. Other contingent and unliquidated claims of every nature, including tax refunds, counterclaims of the debtor, and rights to setoff claims. Give estimated value of each.				
21. Patents, copyrights, and other intellectual property. Give particulars.				
22. Licenses, franchises, and other general intangibles. Give particulars.				

PROJECT 13-2, Schedule B (Continuation Sheet)

United States Bankruptcy Court

_____DISTRICT OF_____

In re_____,   Case No._____
                    Debtor   **(If known)**

SCHEDULE B — PERSONAL PROPERTY
(Continuation Sheet)

TYPE OF PROPERTY	N O N E	DESCRIPTION AND LOCATION OF PROPERTY	H W J or C	CURRENT MARKET VALUE OF DEBTOR'S INTEREST IN PROPERTY, WITHOUT DEDUCTING ANY SECURED CLAIM OR EXEMPTION
23. Automobiles, trucks, trailers, and other vehicles and accessories.				
24. Boats, motorws, and accessories.				
25. Aircraft and accessories.				
26. Office equipment, furnishings, and supplies.				
27. Machinery, fixtures, equipment, and supplies used in business.				
28. Inventory.				
29. Animals.				
30. Crops—growing or harvested. Give particulars.				
31. Farming equipment and implements.				
32. Farm supplies, chemicals, and feed.				
33. Other personal property of any kind not already listed. Itemized.				

_____ continuation sheets attached   Total ➤ $

(Include amounts from any continuation sheets attached. Report total also on Summary of Schedules.)

PROJECT 13-2, Schedule B (Continuation Sheet)

United States Bankruptcy Court

_____DISTRICT OF_____

In re_____,   Case No._____
    Debtor   **(If known)**

SCHEDULE C — PROPERTY CLAIMED AS EXEMPT

Debtor elects the exemption to which debtor is entitled under.
(Check one box)
☐ 11 U.S.C. § 522(b)(1)   Exemptions provided in 11 U.S.C. § 522(d). Note: These exemptions are available only in certain states.
☐ 11 U.S.C. § 522(b)(2)   Exemptions available under applicable nonbankruptcy federal laws, state or local law where the debtor's domicile has been located for the 180 days immediately preceding the filing of the petition, or for a longer portion of the 180-day period than in any other place, and the debtor's interest as a tenant by the entirety or joint tenant to the extent the interest is exempt from process under applicable nonbankruptcy law.

DESCRIPTION OF PROPERTY	SPECIFY LAW PROVIDING EACH EXEMPTION	VALUE OF CLAIMED EXEMPTION	CURRENT MARKET VALUE OF PROPERTY WITHOUT DEDUCTING EXEMPTION

PROJECT 13-3, Schedule C

United States Bankruptcy Court

_____DISTRICT OF_____

In re_____,   Case No._____

               Debtor   **(If known)**

SCHEDULE D — CREDITORS HOLDING SECURED CLAIMS

State the name, mailing address, including zip code, and account number, if any, of all entities holding claims secured by property of the debtor as of the date of filing of the petition. List creditors holding all types of secured interests such as judgment liens, garnishments, statutory liens, mortgages, deeds of trust, and other security interests. List creditors in alphabetical order to the extent practicable. If all secured creditors will not fit on this page, use the continuation sheet provided.

If any entity other than a spouse in a joint case may be jointly liable on a claim, place an "X" in the column labeled "Codebtor," include the entity on the appropriate schedule of creditors, and complete Schedule H—Codebtors. If a joint petition is filed, state whether husband, wife, both of them, or the marital community may be liable on each claim by placing an "H," "W," "J," or "C" in the column labeled "Husband, Wife, Joint, or Community."

If the claim is contingent, place an "X" in the column labeled "Contingent." If the claim is unliquidated, place an "X" in the column labeled "Unliquidated." If the claim is disputed, place an "X" in the column labeled "Disputed." (You may need to place an "X" in more than one of these three columns.)

Report the total of all claims listed on this schedule in the box labeled "Total" on the last sheet of the completed schedule. Report this total also on the Summary of Schedules.

☐ Check this box if debtor has no creditors holding secured claims to report on this Schedule D.

CREDITOR NAME AND MAILING ADDRESS INCLUDING ZIP CODE	CODEBTOR	HWJ or C	DATE CLAIM WAS INCURRED NATURE OF LIEN, AND DESCRIPTION AND MARKET VALUE OF PROPERTY SUBJECT TO LIEN	CONTINGENT	UNLIQUIDATED	DISPUTED	AMOUNT OF CLAIM WITHOUT DEDUCTING VALUE OF COLLATERAL	UNSECURED PORTION, IF ANY
ACCOUNT NO.								
			VALUE $					
ACCOUNT NO.								
			VALUE $					
ACCOUNT NO.								
			VALUE $					
ACCOUNT NO.								
			VALUE $					

_____ continuation sheets attached

Subtotal ➤ $ _____
(Total of this page)

Total
(Use only on last page ➤) $ _____

(Report total also on Summary of Schedules.)

PROJECT 13-4, Schedule D

United States Bankruptcy Court

_____DISTRICT OF_____

In re_____, Case No._____
                      Debtor   **(If known)**

SCHEDULE D — CREDITORS HOLDING SECURED CLAIMS
(Continuation Sheet)

CREDITOR NAME AND MAILING ADDRESS INCLUDING ZIP CODE	C O D E B T O R	H W J or C	DATE CLAIM WAS INCURRED NATURE OF LIEN, AND DESCRIPTION AND MARKET VALUE OF PROPERTY SUBJECT TO LIEN	C O N T I N G E N T	U N L I Q U I D A T E D	D I S P U T E D	AMOUNT OF CLAIM WITHOUT DEDUCTING VALUE OF COLLATERAL	UNSECURED PORTION, IF ANY
ACCOUNT NO.								
			VALUE $					
ACCOUNT NO.								
			VALUE $					
ACCOUNT NO.								
			VALUE $					
ACCOUNT NO.								
			VALUE $					
ACCOUNT NO.								
			VALUE $					

Sheet no. _____ of _____ continuation
sheets attached to Schedule of Creditors
Holding Secured Claims.

Subtotal ➤ $
(Total of this page)

Total
(Use only on last page) ➤ $

(Report total also on Summary of Schedules.)

PROJECT 13-4, Schedule D (Continuation Sheet)

United States Bankruptcy Court

_____DISTRICT OF_____

In re_____,   Case No._____
              Debtor   **(If known)**

SCHEDULE E — CREDITORS HOLDING UNSECURED PRIORITY CLAIMS

A complete list of claims entitled to priority, listed separately by type of priority, is to be set forth on the sheets provided. Only holders of unsecured claims entitled to priority should be listed in this schedule. In the boxes provided on the attached sheets, state the name and mailing address, including zip code, and account number, if any, of all entities holding priority claims against the debtor of the property of the debtor, as of the date of the filing of this petition.

If any entity other than a spouse in a joint case may be jointly liable on a claim, place an "X" in the column labeled "Codebtor," include the entity on the appropriate schedule of creditors, and complete Schedule H—Codebtors. If a joint petition is filed, state whether husband, wife, both of them, or the marital community may be liable on each claim by placing an "H," "W," "J," or "C" in the column labeled "Husband, Wife, Joint, or Community."

If the claim is contingent, place "X" in the column labeled "Contingent".If the claim is unliquidated, place an "X" in the column labeled "unliquidated." If the claim is disputed, place an "X" in the column labeled "Disputed." (You may need to place an "X" in more than one of these three columns).

Report the total of claims listed on each sheet in the box labeled "Subtotal" on each sheet. Report the total of all claims listed on this Schedule E in the box labeled "Total" on the last sheet of the completed schedule. Repeat this total also on the Summary of Schedules.

☐   Check this box if debtor has no creditors holding unsecured priority claims to report on this Schedule E.

TYPES OF PRIORITY CLAIMS (Check the appropriate box(es) below if claims in that category are listed on the attached sheets)

☐   **Extensions of credit in an involuntary case**

Claims arising in the ordinary course of the debtor's business or financial affairs after the commencement of the case but before the earlier of the appointment of a trustee or the order for relief. 11 U.S.C. § 507(a)(2)

☐   **Wages, salaries, and commissions**

Wages, salaries, and commissions, including vacation, severance, and sick leave pay owing to employees, up to a maximum of $2,000 per employee, earned within 90 days immediately preceding the filing of the original petition, or the cessation of business whichever occurred first, to the extent provided in 11 U.S.C. § 507(a)(3).

☐   **Contributions to employee benefit plans**

Money owed to employee benefit plans for services rendered with 180 days immediately preceding the filing of the original petition, or the cessation of business, whichever occurred first, to the extent provided in 11 U.S.C. § 507(a)(4).

☐   **Certain farmers and fishermen**

Claims of certain farmers and fishermen, up to a maximum of $2,000 per farmer or fisherman, against the debtor, as provided in 11 U.S.C. § 507(a)(5).

☐   **Deposits by individuals**

Claims of individuals up to a maximum of $900 for deposits for the purchase, lease, or rental of property or services for personal, family, or household use, that were not delivered or provided. 11 U.S.C. § 507(a)(6).

☐   **Taxes and Certain Other Debts Owed to Governmental Units**

Taxes, customs duties, and penalties owing to federal, state, and local governmental units as set forth in 11 U.S.C. § 507(a)(7).

_____ continuation sheets attached

PROJECT 13-4, Schedule E

United States Bankruptcy Court

_____DISTRICT OF_____

In re_____,   Case No._____
                          Debtor   (If known)

SCHEDULE E — CREDITORS HOLDING UNSECURED PRIORITY CLAIMS
(Continuation Sheet)

_____
TYPE OF PRIORITY

CREDITOR NAME AND MAILING ADDRESS INCLUDING ZIP CODE	C O D E B T O R	H W J or C	DATE CLAIM WAS INCURRED AND CONSIDERATION	C O N T I N G E N T	U N L I Q U I D A T E D	D I S P U T E D	AMOUNT OF CLAIM	AMOUNT ENTITLED TO PRIORITY

Sheet no. _____ of _____ sheets attached
to Schedule of Creditors Holding
Unsecured Priority Claims

Subtotal ➤
(Total of this page) $

Total ➤ $
(Use only on last page of the completed Schedule E.)

(Report total also on Summary of Schedules.)

PROJECT 13-4, Schedule E (Continuation Sheet)

United States Bankruptcy Court

_____DISTRICT OF_____

In re_____,   Case No._____
       Debtor   **(If known)**

SCHEDULE F — CREDITORS HOLDING UNSECURED NONPRIORITY CLAIMS

State the name, mailing address, including zip code, and account number, if any, of all entities holding unsecured claims without priority against the debtor or the property of the debtor, as of the date of filing of the petition. Do not include claims listed in Schedules D and E. If all creditors will not fit on this page, use the continuation sheet provided.

If any entity other than a spouse in a joint case may be jointly liable on a claim, place an "X" in the column labeled "Codebtor," include the entity on the appropriate schedule of creditors, and complete Schedule H—Codebtors. If a joint petition is filed, state whether husband, wife, both of them, or the marital community may be liable on each claim by placing an :H", :W", "J", or "C" in the column labeled "Husband, Wife, Joint, or Community."

If the claim is contingent, place an "X" in the column labeled "Contingent." If the claim is unliquidated, place an "X" in the column labeled "Unliquidated." If the claim is disputed, place an "X" in the column labeled "Disputed." (You may need to place an "X" in more than one of these three columns.)

Report the total of all claims listed on this schedule in the box labeled "Total" on the last sheet of the completed schedule. Report this total also on the Summary of Schedules.

☐ Check this box if debtor has no creditors holding secured claims to report on this Schedule F.

	CODEBTOR	HWJ or C	DATE CLAIM WAS INCURRED AND CONSIDERATION FOR CLAIM. IF CLAIM IS SUBJECT TO SETOFF, SO STATE	CONTINGENT	UNLIQUIDATED	DISPUTED	AMOUNT OF CLAIM
ACCOUNT NO.							
ACCOUNT NO.							
ACCOUNT NO.							
ACCOUNT NO.							

_____ continuation sheets attached   Subtotal ➤ $_____
                                     (Total of this page)
                                          Total ➤ $_____
(Use only on last page of the completed Schedule F

(Report total also on Summary of Schedules.)

PROJECT 13-4, Schedule F

United States Bankruptcy Court

_____DISTRICT OF_____

In re_____, Case No._____
               Debtor   **(If known)**

SCHEDULE F — CREDITORS HOLDING UNSECURED NONPRIORITY CLAIMS
(Continuation Sheet)

CREDITOR NAME AND MAILING ADDRESS INCLUDING ZIP CODE	CODEBTOR	HWJ or C	DATE CLAIM WAS INCURRED AND CONSIDERATION FOR CLAIM. IF CLAIM IS SUBJECT TO SETOFF, SO STATE.	CONTINGENT	UNLIQUIDATED	DISPUTED	AMOUNT OF CLAIM
ACCOUNT NO.							
ACCOUNT NO.							
ACCOUNT NO.							
ACCOUNT NO.							
ACCOUNT NO.							

Sheet no. _____ of _____ sheets attached
to Schedule of Creditors Holding
Unsecured Nonpriority Claims

Subtotal ➤ | $
(Total of this page)

Total ➤ | $
(Use only on last page of the completed Schedule F.)

(Report total also on Summary of Schedules.)

PROJECT 13-4, Schedule F (Continuation Sheet)

United States Bankruptcy Court

_____DISTRICT OF_____

In re_____,   Case No._____
                   Debtor   **(If known)**

SCHEDULE G — EXECUTORY CONTRACTS AND UNEXPIRED LEASES

Describe all executory contracts of any nature and all unexpired leases of real or personal property. Include any timeshare interests.
State nature of debtor's interest in contract, i.e., "Purchaser," "Agent," etc. State whether debtor is the lessor or lessee of a lease.
Provide the names and complete mailing addresses of all other parties to each lease or contract described.
    NOTE: A party listed on this schedule will not receive notice of the filing of this case unless the party is also scheduled in the
appropriate schedule of creditors.

☐ Check this box if debtor has no executory contracts or unexpired leases.

NAME AND MAILING ADDRESS, INCLUDING ZIP CODE, OF OTHER PARTIES TO LEASE OR CONTRACT.	DESCRIPTION OF CONTRACT OR LEASE AND NATURE OF DEBTOR'S INTEREST. STATE WHETHER LEASE IS FOR NONRESIDENTIAL REAL PROPERTY. STATE CONTRACT NUMBER OF ANY GOVERNMENT CONTRACT.

PROJECT 13-4, Schedule G

Official Bankr.Form B6H, 11 U.S.C.A.

United States Bankruptcy Court

_____DISTRICT OF_____

In re_____,   Case No._____
                          Debtor   **(If known)**

SCHEDULE H — CODEBTORS

   Provide the information requested concerning any person or entity, other than a spouse in a joint case, that is also liable on any debts listed by debtor in the schedules of creditors. Include all guarantors and co-signers. In community property states, a married debtor not filing a joint case should report the name and address of the nondebtor spouse on this schedule. Include all names used by the nondebtor spouse during the six years immediately preceding the commencement of this case.

☐ **Check this box if debtor has no codebtors.**

NAME AND ADDRESS OF CODEBTOR	NAME AND ADDRESS OF CREDITOR

PROJECT 13-4, Schedule H

United States Bankruptcy Court

_____DISTRICT OF_____

In re_____, Case No._____
              Debtor   **(If known)**

SCHEDULE I — CURRENT INCOME OF INDIVIDUAL DEBTOR(S)

The column labeled "Spouse" must be completed in all cases filed by joint debtors and by a married debtor in a chapter 12 or 13 case whether or not a joint petition is filed, unless the spouses are separated and a joint petition is not filed.

Debtor's Marital Status:	DEPENDENTS OF DEBTOR AND SPOUSE		
	NAMES	**AGE**	**RELATIONSHIP**

Employment:	**DEBTOR**	**SPOUSE**
Occupation		
Name of employer		
How long employed		
Address of employer		

Income: (Estimate of average monthly income)	**DEBTOR**	**SPOUSE**
Current monthly gross wages, salary, and commissions (prorate if not paid monthly.)	$_____	$_____
Estimated monthly overtime	$_____	$_____
SUBTOTAL	$_____	$_____
LESS PAYROLL DEDUCTIONS		
a. Payroll taxes and social security	$_____	$_____
b. Insurance	$_____	$_____
c. Union dues	$_____	$_____
s. Other (Specify:_____)	$_____	$_____
SUBTOTAL OF PAYROLL DEDUCTIONS	$_____	$_____
TOTAL NET MONTHLY TAKE HOME PAY	$_____	$_____
Regular income from operation of profession or farm (attached detailed statement)	$_____	$_____
Income from real property	$_____	$_____
Interest and dividends	$_____	$_____
Alimony, maintenance or support payments payable to the debtor for the debtor's use or that of dependents listed above.	$_____	$_____
Social security or other government assistance (Specify)_____	$_____	$_____
Pension or retirement income	$_____	$_____
Other monthly income	$_____	$_____
(Specify)_____	$_____	$_____
_____	$_____	$_____
TOTAL MONTHLY INCOME	$_____	$_____

TOTAL COMBINED MONTHLY INCOME $_____   (Report also on Summary of Schedules)

Describe any increase or decrease of more than 10% in any of the above categories anticipated to occur within the year following the filing of this document.

PROJECT 13-5, Schedule I

United States Bankruptcy Court

_____DISTRICT OF_____

In re_____,   Case No._____
　　　　　　　Debtor　　　　　　　　　　　　　　**(If known)**

SCHEDULE J — CURRENT EXPENDITURES OF INDIVIDUAL DEBTOR(S)

Complete this schedule by estimating the average monthly expenses of the debtor and the debtor's family. Prorate any payments made bi-weekly, quarterly, semi-annually, or annually to show monthly rate.

☐ Check this box if a joint petition is filed and debtor's spouse maintains a separate household. Complete a separate schedule of expenditures labeled "Spouse."

Rent or home mortgage payment (include lot rented for mobile home)	$_____
Are real estate taxes included?　Yes_____　No_____	
Is property insurance included?　Yes_____　No_____	
Utilities　　Electricity and Heating fuel	$_____
Water and sewer	$_____
Telephone	$_____
Other_____	$_____
Home maintenance (repairs and upkeep)	$_____
Food	$_____
Clothing	$_____
Laundry and dry cleaning	$_____
Medical and dental expenses	$_____
Transportation (not including car payment)	$_____
Recreation, clubs and entertainment, newspapers, magazines, etc.	$_____
Charitable contributions	$_____
Insurance (not deducted from wages or included in home mortgage payments)	
Homeowner's or renter's	$_____
Life	$_____
Health	$_____
Auto	$_____
Other_____	$_____
Taxes (not deducted from wages or included in home mortgage payments)	
(Specify)_____	$_____
Installment payments: (in chapter 12 or 13 cases, do not list payments to be included in the plan)	
Auto	$_____
Other_____	$_____
Other_____	$_____
Alimony, maintenance, and support paid to others	$_____
Payments for support of additional dependents not living at your home	$_____
Regular expenses from operation of business, profession, or farm (attached detailed statement)	$_____
Other_____	$_____

TOTAL MONTHLY EXPENSES (Report also on Summary of Schedules)　　$_____

[FOR CHAPTER 12 AND 13 DEBTORS ONLY]

Provide the information requested below, including whether plan payments are to be made bi-weekly, annually, or at some other regular interval.

A.　Total projected monthly income	$_____
B.　Total projected monthly expenses	$_____
C.　Excess income (A minus B)	$_____
D.　Total amount to paid into plan each _____	$_____
(interval)	

PROJECT 13-5,　Schedule J

United States Bankruptcy Court

_____DISTRICT OF_____

In re_____,   Case No._____

                 Debtor   **(If known)**

CHAPTER 7 INDIVIDUAL DEBTOR'S
STATEMENT OF INTENTION

1. I, the debtor, have filed a schedule of assets and liabilities which includes consumer debts secured by property of the estate.

2. My intention with respect to the property of the estate which secures those consumer debts is as follows:

     a. *Property to Be Surrendered.*

         Description of Property   **Creditor's Name**

1._____   _____

2._____   _____

3._____   _____

     b. *Property to be Retained. [Check applicable statement of debtor's intention concerning reaffirmation, redemption, or lien avoidance.]*

Description of Property	Creditor's Name	Debt will be reaffirmed pursuant to § 524(c)	Property is claimed as exempt and will be redeemed pursuant to § 722	Lien will be avoided pursuant to § 522(f) and property will be claimed as exempt
1._____	_____	_____	_____	_____
2._____	_____	_____	_____	_____
3._____	_____	_____	_____	_____
4._____	_____	_____	_____	_____
5._____	_____	_____	_____	_____

3. I understand that § 521(2)(B) of the Bankruptcy Code requires that I perform the above stated intention within 45 days of the filing of this statement with the court, or within such additional time as the court, for cause, within such 45-day periods fixes.

Date:_____

                          Signature of Debtor_____

PROJECT 13-6, Individual Debtor's Statement of Intention

Official Bankr. Form B6, 11 U.S.C.A.

United States Bankruptcy Court

_____DISTRICT OF_____

In re_____,   Case No._____

Debtor   (If known)

DECLARATION CONCERNING DEBTOR'S SCHEDULES

DECLARATION UNDER PENALTY OF PERJURY BY INDIVIDUAL DEBTOR

I declare under penalty of perjury that I have read the foregoing summary and schedules, consisting of _____
sheets, and that they are true and correct to the best of my knowledge, information and belief.   (Total shown on summary page plus 1.)

Date_____   Signature_____

Debtor

Date_____   Signature_____

(Joint Debtor, if any)

(If joint case, both spouses must sign.)

- -

DECLARATION UNDER PENALTY OF PERJURY ON BEHALF OF CORPORATION OR PARTNERSHIP

I, the _____ [the president or other officer or an authorized agent of the corporation
or a member or an authorized agent of the partnership] of the _____ [corporation
or partnership] named as debtor in this case, declare under penalty of perjury that I have read the foregoing summary and schedules,
consisting of _____ sheets, and that they are true and correct to the best of my knowledge,

(Total shown on summary page plus 1.)

information and belief.

Date_____   Signature_____

_____

[Print or type name of individual signing on behalf of debtor.]

[An individual signing on behalf of a partnership or corporation must indicate position or relationship to debtor.]

- -

Penalty for making a false statement or concealing property: Fine of up to $500,000 or imprisonment for up to 5 years or both.
18 U.S.C. §§ 152 and 3571.

PROJECT 13-7, Declaration Concerning Debtor's Schedules

United States Bankruptcy Court

_____DISTRICT OF_____

In re_____, Case No._____

(Name)   Debtor   (If known)

STATEMENT OF FINANCIAL AFFAIRS

This statement is to be completed by every debtor. Spouses filing a joint petition may file a single statement on which the information for both spouses is combined. If the case if filed under Chapter 12 or Chapter 13, a married debtor must furnish information for both spouses whether or not a joint petition is filed, unless the spouses are separated and a joint petition is not filed. An individual debtor engaged in business as a sole proprietor, partner, family farmer, or self-employed professional, should provide the information requested on this statement concerning all such activities as well as the individual's personal affairs.

Questions 1-15 are to be completed by all debtors. Debtors that are or have been in business, as defined below, also must complete Questions 16-21. EACH QUESTION MUST BE ANSWERED. IF THE ANSWER TO ANY QUESTION IS "NONE," OR THE QUESTION IS NOT APPLICABLE, MARK THE BOX LABELED "NONE." If additional space is needed for the answer to any questions, use and attach a separate sheet properly identified with the case name, case number (if known), and the number of the question.

DEFINITIONS

"In business." A debtor is "in business" for the purpose of this form if the debtor is a corporation or partnership. An individual debtor is "in business" for the purpose of this form if the debtor is or has been, within the two years immediately preceding the filing of this bankruptcy case, any of the following: an officer, director, managing executive, or person in control of a corporation; a partner, other than a limited partner, or a partnership; a sole proprietor or self-employed.

"Insider." The term "insider" includes but is not limited to: relatives of the debtor; general partners of the debtor and their relatives; corporation of which the debtor is an officer, director, or person in control; officers, directors, and any person in control of a corporate debtor and their relatives; affiliates of the debtor and insiders of such affiliates; any managing agent of the debtor. 11 U.S.C. § 101(30).

---

1. INCOME FROM EMPLOYMENT OR OPERATION OF BUSINESS

None ☐ State the gross amount of income the debtor has received from employment, trade, or profession or from operation of the debtor's business form the beginning of this calendar year to the date this case was commenced. State also the gross amounts received during the TWO YEARS immediately preceding this calendar year. (A debtor that maintains, or has maintained, financial records on the basis of a fiscal rather than a calendar year may report fiscal year income. Identify the beginning and ending dates of the debtor's fiscal year.) If a joint petition is filed, state income for each spouse separately. (Married debtors filing under Chapter 12 or Chapter 13 must state income of both spouses whether or not a joint petition is filed, unless the spouses are separated and a joint petition is not filed.)

        AMOUNT   SOURCE (if more than one)

PROJECT 13-8, Statement of Financial Affairs, Page 1

2. INCOME OTHER THAN FROM EMPLOYMENT OR OPERATION OF BUSINESS

None ☐

State the amount of income received by the debtor other than from employment, trade, profession, or operation of the debtor's business during the TWO YEARS immediately preceding the commencement of this case. Give particulars. If a joint petition is filed, state income for each spouse separately. (Married debtors filing under Chapter 12 or Chapter 13 must state income for each spouse whether or not a joint petition is filed, unless the spouses are separated and a joint petition is not filed.)

AMOUNT	SOURCE

3. PAYMENTS TO CREDITORS

None ☐

a. List all payments on loans, installment purchases of goods or services, and other debts, aggregating more than $600 to any creditor, made within 90 DAYS immediately preceding the commencement of this case. (Married debtors filing under Chapter 12 or Chapter 13 must include payments by either or both spouses whether or not a joint petition is filed, unless the spouses are separated and a joint petition is not filed.)

NAME AND ADDRESS OF CREDITOR	DATES OF PAYMENTS	AMOUNT PAID	AMOUNT STILL OWING

None ☐

b. List all payments made within ONE YEAR immediately preceding the commencement of this case to or for the benefit of creditors who are or were insiders. (Married debtors filing under Chapter 12 or Chapter 13 must include payments by either or both spouses whether or not a joint petition is filed, unless the spouses are separated and a joint petition is not filed.)

NAMED AND ADDRESS OF CREDITOR AND RELATIONSHIP TO DEBTOR	DATE OF PAYMENT	AMOUNT PAID	AMOUNT STILL OWING

4. SUITS, EXECUTIONS, GARNISHMENTS AND ATTACHMENTS

None ☐

a. List all suits to which the debtor is or was a party within ONE YEAR immediately preceding the filing of this bankruptcy case. (Married debtors filing under Chapter 12 or Chapter 13 must include information concerning either or both spouses whether or not a joint petition is filed, unless the spouses are separated and a joint petition is not filed.)

CAPTION OF SUIT AND CASE NUMBER	NATURE OF PROCEEDING	COURT AND LOCATION	STATUS OR DISPOSITION

PROJECT 13-8, Statement of Financial Affairs, Page 2

None b. Describe all property that has been attached, garnished or seized under any legal or equitable process
☐ within ONE YEAR immediately preceding the commencement of this case. (Married debtors filing under
Chapter 12 or Chapter 13 must include information concerning property of either or both spouses
whether or not a joint petition is filed, unless the spouses are separated and a joint petition is not filed.)

NAME AND ADDRESS OF PERSON FOR WHOSE BENEFIT PROPERTY WAS SEIZED	DATE OF SEIZURE	DESCRIPTION AND VALUE OF PROPERTY

---

5. REPOSSESSIONS, FORECLOSURES AND RETURNS

None List all property that has been repossessed by a creditor, sold at a foreclosure or returned to the seller,
☐ within ONE YEAR immediately preceding the commencement of this case. (Married debtors filing under
Chapter 12 or Chapter 13 must include payments by either or both spouses whether or not a joint
petition is filed, unless the spouses are separated and a joint petition is not filed.)

NAME AND ADDRESS OF CREDITOR OR SELLER	DATE OF REPOSSESSION, FORECLOSURE SALE, TRANSFER OR RETURN	DESCRIPTION AND VALUE OF PROPERTY

---

6. ASSIGNMENTS AND RECEIVERSHIPS

None a. Describe any assignment of property for the benefit of creditors made within 120 DAYS immediately
☐ preceding the commencement of this case. (Married debtors filing under Chapter 12 or Chapter 13 must
include payments by either or both spouses whether or not a joint petition is filed, unless the spouses are
separated and a joint petition is not filed.)

NAME AND ADDRESS OF ASSIGNEE	DATE OF ASSIGNMENT	TERMS OF ASSIGNMENT OR SETTLEMENT

None b. List all property which has been in the hands of a custodian, receiver, or court-appointed official
☐ within ONE YEAR immediately preceding the commencement of this case. (Married debtors filing under
Chapter 12 or Chapter 13 must include information concerning either or both spouses whether or not a
joint petition is filed, unless the spouses are separated and a joint petition is not filed.)

NAME AND ADDRESS OF CUSTODIAN	NAME AND LOCATION OF COURT CASE TITLE & NUMBER	DATE OF ORDER	DESCRIPTION AND VALUE OF PROPERTY

PROJECT 13-8, Statement of Financial Affairs, Page 3

7. GIFTS

None ☐ List all gifts or charitable contributions made within ONE YEAR immediately preceding the commencement of this case except ordinary and usual gifts to family members aggregating less than $200 in value per individual family member and charitable contributions aggregating less than $100 per recipient. (Married debtors filing under Chapter 12 or Chapter 13 must include payments by either or both spouses whether or not a joint petition is filed, unless the spouses are separated and a joint petition is not filed.)

NAME AND ADDRESS OF PERSON OR ORGANIZATION	RELATIONSHIP TO DEBTOR, IF ANY	DATE OF GIFT	DESCRIPTION AND VALUE OF GIFT

8. LOSSES

None ☐ a. List all losses from fire, theft, other casualty or gambling within ONE YEAR immediately preceding the commencement of this case OR SINCE THE COMMENCEMENT OF THIS CASE. (Married debtors filing under Chapter 12 or Chapter 13 must include payments by either or both spouses whether or not a joint petition is filed, unless the spouses are separated and a joint petition is not filed.)

DESCRIPTION AND VALUE OF PROPERTY	DESCRIPTION OF CIRCUMSTANCES AND, IF LOSS WAS COVERED IN WHOLE OR IN PART BY INSURANCE, GIVE PARTICULARS	DATE OF LOSS

9. PAYMENTS RELATED TO DEBT COUNSELING OR BANKRUPTCY

None ☐ List all payments made or property transferred by or on behalf of the debtor to any persons, including attorneys, for consultation concerning debt consolidation, relief under the bankruptcy law or preparation of a petition in bankruptcy within ONE YEAR immediately preceding the commencement of this case.

NAME AND ADDRESS OF PAYEE	DATE OF PAYMENT, NAME OF PAYOR IF OTHER THAN DEBTOR	AMOUNT OF MONEY OR DESCRIPTION AND VALUE OF PROPERTY

10. OTHER TRANSFERS

None ☐ a. List all other property other than property transferred in the ordinary course of the business or financial affairs of the debtor, transferred either absolutely or as security within ONE YEAR immediately preceding the commencement of this case. (Married debtors filing under Chapter 12 or Chapter 13 must include payments by either or both spouses whether or not a joint petition is filed, unless the spouses are separated and a joint petition is not filed.)

NAME AND ADDRESS OF TRANSFEREE, RELATIONSHIP TO DEBTOR	DATE	DESCRIBE PROPERTY TRANSFERRED AND VALUE RECEIVED

PROJECT 13-8, Statement of Financial Affairs, Page 4

11. CLOSED FINANCIAL ACCOUNTS

None   List all financial accounts and instruments held in the name of the debtor or for the benefit of the
☐   debtor which we closed, sold, or otherwise transferred within ONE YEAR immediately preceding the
         commencement of this case. Include checking, savings, or other financial accounts, certificates of deposit,
         or other instruments; shares and share accounts held in banks, credit unions, pension funds,
         cooperatives, associations brokerage houses and other financial institutions. (Married debtors filing
         under Chapter 12 or Chapter 13 must include payments by either or both spouses whether or not a joint
         petition is filed, unless the spouses are separated and a joint petition is not filed.)

NAME AND ADDRESS OF INSTITUTION	TYPE AND NUMBER OF ACCOUNT AND AMOUNT OF FINAL BALANCE	AMOUNT AND DATE OF SALE OR CLOSING

12. SAFE DEPOSIT BOXES

None   List each safe deposit or other box or depository in which the debtor has or had securities, cash, or
☐   other valuables within ONE YEAR immediately preceding the commencement of this case. (Married
         debtors filing under Chapter 12 or Chapter 13 must include payments by either or both spouses whether
         or not a joint petition is filed, unless the spouses are separated and a joint petition is not filed.)

NAME AND ADDRESS OF BANK OR OTHER DEPOSITORY	NAMES AND ADDRESSES OF THOSE WITH ACCESS TO BOX OR DEPOSITORY	DESCRIPTION OF CONTENTS	DATE OF TRANSFER OR SURRENDER, IF ANY

13. SETOFFS

None   List all setoffs made by any creditor, including a bank, against a debt or a deposit of the debtor within
☐   90 DAYS preceding the commencement of this case. (Married debtors filing under Chapter 12 or Chapter
         13 must include payments by either or both spouses whether or not a joint petition is filed, unless the
         spouses are separated and a joint petition is not filed.)

NAME AND ADDRESS OF CREDITOR	DATE OF SETOFF	AMOUNT OF SETOFF

14. PROPERTY HELD FOR ANOTHER PERSON

None   List all property owned by another person that the debtor holds or controls.
☐

NAME AND ADDRESS OF OWNER	DESCRIPTION AND VALUE OF PROPERTY	LOCATION OF PROPERTY

15. PRIOR ADDRESS OF DEBTOR

None   If the debtor has moved within TWO YEARS immediately preceding the commencement of this case, list
☐   all premises which the debtor occupied during that period and vacated prior to the commencement of
this case. If a joint petition is filed, report also any separate address of either spouse.

ADDRESS	NAME USED	DATES OF OCCUPANCY

The following questions are to be completed by every debtor that is a corporation or partnership and by any individual debtor who is or has been, within the TWO YEARS immediately preceding the commencement of this case, any of the following: an officer, director, managing executive, or owner of more than 5 percent of the voting securities of a corporation; a partner, other than a limited partner, of a partnership; a sole proprietor or otherwise self-employed.

(An individual or joint debtor should complete this portion of the statement ONLY if the debtor is or has been in business, as defined above, within the TWO YEARS immediately preceding the commencement of this case.)

16. NATURE, LOCATION AND NAME OF BUSINESS

None   a. If the debtor is an individual, list the names and addresses of all businesses in which the debtor was an
☐   officer, director, partner, or managing executive of a corporation, partnership, sole proprietorship, or
was a self-employed professional with the TWO YEARS immediately preceding the commencement of this
case, or in which the debtor owned 5 percent of more than the voting or equity securities within the TWO
YEARS immediately preceding the commencement of this case.

b. If the debtor is a partnership, list the names and addresses of all businesses in which the debtor was a
partner or owned 5 percent of more of the voting securities, within the TWO YEARS immediately preceding
the commencement of this case.

c. If the debtor is a corporation, list the names and addresses of all businesses in which the debtor was a
partner or owned 5 percent of more of the voting securities within TWO YEARS immediately preceding the
commencement of this case.

NAME	ADDRESS	NATURE OF BUSINESS	BEGINNING AND ENDING DATES OF OPERATION

17. BOOKS, RECORDS AND FINANCIAL STATEMENTS

None   a. List all bookkeepers and accountants who within the SIX YEARS immediately preceding the filing of this
☐   bankruptcy case kept or supervised the keeping of books of account and records of the debtor.

NAME AND ADDRESS	DATES SERVICES RENDERED

PROJECT 13-8, Statement of Financial Affairs, Page 6

None ☐ b. List all firms or individuals who within the TWO YEARS immediately preceding the filing of this bankruptcy case have audited the books of account and records, or prepared a financial statement of the debtor.

NAME	ADDRESS	DATES SERVICES RENDERED

None ☐ c. List all firms or individuals who at the time of the commencement of this case were in possession of the books of account and records of the debtor. If any of the books of account and records are not available, explain.

NAME	ADDRESS

None ☐ d. List all financial institutions, creditors and other parties, including mercantile and trade agencies, to whom a financial statement was issued within the TWO YEARS immediately preceding the commencement of this case by the debtor.

NAME AND ADDRESS	DATE ISSUED

18. INVENTORIES

None ☐ a. List the dates of the LAST TWO inventories taken of your property, the name of the person who supervised the taking of each inventory, and the dollar amount and basis of each inventory.

DATE OF INVENTORY	INVENTORY SUPERVISOR	DOLLAR AMOUNT OF INVENTORY (Specify cost, market or other basis)

None ☐ b. List the name and address of the person having possession of the records of each of the two inventories reported in a., above.

DATE OF INVENTORY	NAME AND ADDRESSES OF CUSTODIAN OF INVENTORY RECORDS

19. CURRENT PARTNER, OFFICERS, DIRECTORS AND SHAREHOLDERS

None ☐ a. If the debtor is a partnership, list the nature and percentage of partnership interest of each member of the partnership.

NAME AND ADDRESS	NATURE OF INTEREST	PERCENTAGE OF INTEREST

PROJECT 13-8, Statement of Financial Affairs, Page 7

None ☐ **b.** If the debtor is a corporation, list all officers and directors of the corporation, and each stockholder who directly or indirectly owns, controls, or holds 5 percent or more of the voting securities of the corporation.

NAME AND ADDRESS	TITLE	NATURE AND PERCENTAGE OF STOCK OWNERSHIP

20. Former partners, officers, directors and shareholders

None ☐ **a.** If the debtor is a partnership, list each member who withdrew from the partnership within ONE YEAR immediately preceding the commencement of this case.

NAME	ADDRESS	DATE OF WITHDRAWAL

None ☐ **b.** If the debtor is a corporation, list all officers, or directors whose relationship with the corporation terminated within ONE YEAR immediately preceding the commencement of this case.

NAME AND ADDRESS	TITLE	DATE OF TERMINATION

21. Withdrawals from a partnership or distributions by a corporation

None ☐ If the debtor is a partnership or corporation, list all withdrawals or distributions credited or given to an insider, including compensation in any form, bonuses, loans, stock redemptions, options exercised and any other perquisite during ONE YEAR immediately preceding the commencement of this case.

NAME AND ADDRESS OF RECIPIENT, RELATIONSHIP TO DEBTOR	DATE AND PURPOSE OF WITHDRAWAL	AMOUNT OF MONEY OR DESCRIPTION AND VALUE OF PROPERTY

[If completed by an individual or individual and spouse]

I declare under penalty of perjury that I have read the answers contained in the foregoing statement of financial affairs and any attachments thereto and that they are true and correct.

Date_____   Signature _____
                                          of Debtor

Date_____   Signature _____
                                          of Joint Debtor
                                          (if any)

- -

[If completed on behalf of a partnership or corporation]

I declare under penalty of perjury that I have read the answers contained in the foregoing statement of financial affairs and any attachments thereto and that they are true and correct to the best of my knowledge, information and belief.

Date_____   Signature_____

                                          _____

                                          Print Name and Title

[An individual signing on behalf of a partnership or corporation must indicate position or relationship to debtor.]

_____ continuation sheets attached

Penalty for making a false statement: Fine of up to $500,000 or imprisonment for up to 5 years, or both. U.S.C. §§ 152 and 3571.

United States Bankruptcy Court

_____DISTRICT OF_____

In re_____,   Case No._____

Debtor   (If known)

SUMMARY OF SCHEDULES

Indicate as to each schedule whether that schedule is attached and state the number of pages in each. Report the totals from Schedules A, B, D, E, F, I, and J in the boxes provided. Add the amounts from Schedules A and B to determine the total amount of the debtor's assets. Add the amounts from Schedules D, E, and F to determine the total amount of the debtor's liabilities.

NAME OF SCHEDULE	ATTACHED (YES/NO)	NO. OF SHEETS	AMOUNTS SCHEDULED		
			ASSETS	LIABILITIES	OTHER
A - Real Property			$		
B - Personal Property			$		
C - Property Claimed as Exempt					
D - Creditors Holding Secured Claims				$	
E - Creditors Holding Unsecured Priority Claims				$	
F - Creditors Holding Unsecured Non Priority Claims				$	
G - Executory Contracts and Unexpired Leases					
H - Codebtors					
I - Current Income of Individual Debtor(s)					$
J - Current Expenditures of Individual Debtor(s)					$
Total Number of Sheets of ALL Schedules ➤					
Total Assets ➤			$		
Total Liabilities ➤				$	

PROJECT 13-9, Summary of Schedules

PROJECT 13-10, Mailing List Matrix

United States Bankruptcy Court

_____DISTRICT OF_____

In re

Case No._____

Debtor *

DISCLOSURE OF COMPENSATION UNDER 11 U.S.C. § 329

      I certify that I am the attorney for the above-named debtor and that the compensation paid or agreed to be paid to me for services rendered or to be rendered in behalf of the debtor in or in connection with a case under title 11 of the United States Code, such payment or agreement having been made after one year before the date of the filing of the petition, is as follows:

    $ paid,

    $ to be paid,

that the source of the compensation paid was

and that the source of the compensation agreed to be paid is

Dated:_____

_____
Attorney for the Debtor

Include here all names used by Debtor within last 6 years.

PROJECT 13-11, Disclosure of Compensation